Introductory Accounting

Dedication

To my wife Elaine, and my children Kevin and Beth — a special thank you for your patience and understanding during the writing of this book.

Acknowledgements

I acknowledge with thanks the help of the following reviewers:

Stan Dunster, Centennial School

Guy Drolet, Ottawa Board of Education

Dwight Gibson, Confederation High School

Paul Herbert, London Board of Education

I am also very grateful to David Crittenden of College Avenue Secondary School for his advice and his help in testing this material in the classroom.

INTRODUCTORY ACCOUNTING

Ron Cougler, B.A., C.M.A.

Business Director
College Avenue Secondary School

WILEY

John Wiley & Sons

Toronto New York Chichester Brisbane Singapore

The Office of the Comptroller General of Canada has issued (79-04-09) a Circular stating that it is the policy of the Government of Canada to continue to use the period as the decimal marker and the comma to separate triads of numbers on payment instruments and financial documents within the government. It has noted that this policy is consistent with that accepted by the Canadian Bankers' Association.

Canadian Cataloguing in Publication Data

Cougler, Ronald A.
Introductory accounting

For use in high schools.
Includes index.
ISBN 0-471-79691-3

1. Accounting. I. Title.

HF5635.C68 1988 657 C87-095088-6

Cover photo: Jeremy Jones; inserts courtesy of Gabe Palmer/ Masterfile, Janeart Ltd./ The Image Bank, Walter Bibikow/ The Image Bank, Ben Mitchell/ The Image Bank, Lars Ternblad/ The Image Bank, IBM, Imperial Oil.

Design: Blair Kerrigan/Glyphics

Illustrations: Heather Collins/Glyphics

Technical art: Melissa Nelson/Glyphics

Typesetting: Jay Tee Graphics

Printed and bound in Canada by The Bryant Press
10 9 8 7 6 5 4 3 2 1

Table of Contents

To The Student

Welcome to the world of accounting! Businesses, big or small, depend on people with accounting skills to keep their finances in order. This book will introduce you to the concepts and skills that are necessary to keep businesses functioning.

The aim of this book is to make learning these skills and concepts as enjoyable as possible. You will be introduced to accounting skills in practical ways through examples and exercises and through interesting case studies. You will find out about the role computers play in accounting and about some of the careers that are open to people with the knowledge you will gain.

I hope that you enjoy using this book, and that it opens up to you many exciting possibilities for the future.

The Author

Features of *Introductory Accounting*

- *Introductory Accounting* begins by dealing with the accounting cycle, cash and banking, and payroll. From there it progresses to the more complex subject areas of adjusting entries, merchandise accounting, and subsidiary ledgers.

- **Computerized accounting** is given a whole chapter in the text, and it is also dealt with at first hand in an *Accounting at Work* profile taken from life.

- **Accounting at Work** appears at the end of every Unit, to introduce an individual at work in the accounting field. Questions which follow each of these profiles involve the student with the day-to-day challenges and opportunities in the field.

- **Careers in accounting** are also given an entire chapter in which the variety of levels and specialties in accounting are discussed, and paths to higher achievement and recognition are presented.

- **New material is integrated** in each chapter through several review techniques — exercises, review questions, challenge questions, a review case, a challenge case, and a ''Quick re-cap'' which guides the student back through a new procedure.

- **The supportive style of the text** anticipates students' questions with plentiful examples, graphically presented. Essential definitions and descriptions of stages in the accounting cycle are boxed in the text for easy reference. All new vocabulary is **bold-faced** and defined when it is first used. A dictionary of terms is placed at the end of each chapter, and a glossary at the end of the book. ''Take-a-break'' activities at the end of chapters make learning about the world of accounting fun.

- A ***Student Workbook*** and comprehensive ***Teacher's Guide*** complete the ***Introductory Accounting*** program.

1

THE NEW
ROGET'S
THESAURUS
IN
DICTIONARY FORM
REVISED, GREATLY EXPANDED

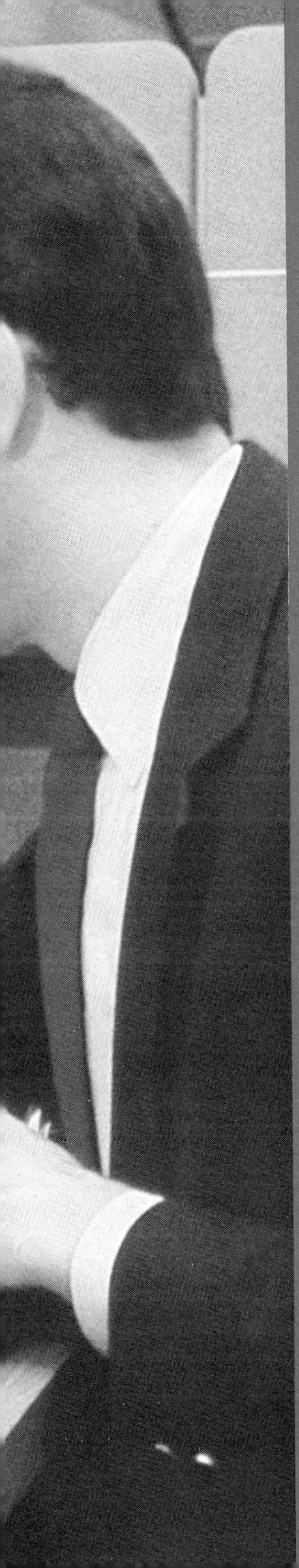

Beginning the Cycle

Chapter 1
The Balance Sheet

Chapter 2
Changes to the Balance Sheet

Chapter 1 The Balance Sheet

Objectives

At the end of this chapter, you will be able to

1. recognize the fundamental accounting equation;
2. prepare a balance sheet in good form;
3. demonstrate a knowledge of the basic rules of accounting practice;
4. show an understanding of the order of assets on a balance sheet; and
5. show a basic knowledge of accounting careers.

1.1 Assets

Allan Trent has just graduated from a community college. He is now a qualified electronics technician and is considering starting his own business. He wants to repair televisions, radios, and video cassette recorders, and he thinks there is a strong demand for his services. His financial condition is fairly good since most of his college education was paid for from part-time jobs, bursaries, and some help from his parents. Allan knows he will have to buy some expensive equipment for his business. To do this, he will have to borrow some money from a bank or trust company to get started properly. So Allan makes an appointment to see the manager of a trust company, Ms. Medeiros.

Figure 1-1
A local trust company

"I took accounting at college and I've made a list of all of the items I own at the present time. Some of these, the calculator and the computer, will be helpful in my new business," says Allan. He passes Ms. Medeiros the list he has made up, to show her what a good financial position he is in.

Things I Own	
Bank Balance	$ 200
Car	2 000
Calculator	100
Computer	1 700
	$ 4000

Ms. Medeiros is very helpful and anxious to set Allan off on the right path to financial success. "You are in a good position to start your own business," says Ms. Medeiros. "The car will be useful if you make service calls and you may be able to do some of your own accounting work on the computer. Let's rewrite your list with the proper accounting terms as an accountant would do."

Assets

Bank Balance	$ 200
Car	2 000
Calculator	100
Computer	1 700
Total	$4 000

Things that a person or business owns are called "assets." The assets a business has depend on the nature of the business. If you think about a restaurant business, the assets will include tables, chairs, ovens, cutlery, refrigeration equipment, etc. If you are a carpenter, your assets might include a truck, and some tools and equipment, such as a drill press or a band saw. A dentist's assets include furniture, dental equipment, and dental supplies. A photographer's assets include cameras and equipment for developing film. Some assets are the same from one business to the next, but some are special and only useful in certain businesses. For example, you will not find an asset such as an oven in a car dealership, but you will find it in a restaurant business.

Assets refers to anything that a person or business owns.

1.2 Liabilities and Owner's Equity

"The next step in looking at your financial picture is to determine if you have any outstanding debts," continues Ms. Medeiros. "Do you owe money to anyone?" Allan tells her that his parents helped him buy his computer and that he still owes them $1 500 for this purchase. Apart from this Allan owns everything else, that is, all his other assets are fully paid for.

Debts that one person owes to another are called "liabilities." They are listed under the heading **Liabilities**, like this:

Liabilities

Owing to Parents $1 500

Liabilities are any debts owing to other people or businesses.

Once we know a person's assets and liabilities, we can subtract these two figures. The difference is called "owner's equity." Allan's owner's equity is $2 500, and when we write it down on paper, it looks like this:

Owner's Equity
Allan Trent, Capital $2 500

Owner's equity is the difference between assets and liabilities.

The three terms that you have now learned are the parts of a fundamental accounting equation. This is an important equation that you must know to master accounting.

Assets = Liabilities + Owner's Equity

If we apply the fundamental accounting equation to Allan's finances and put in the figures, his equation would be:

Assets	=	**Liabilities**	+	**Owner's Equity**
$4 000	=	$1 500	+	$2 500

1.3 The Balance Sheet

Once we know Allan's assets and liabilities, we can calculate his owner's equity very easily by using the accounting equation. "Once we have all three parts, that is, assets, liabilities and owner's equity, we can prepare a document called a balance sheet," says Ms. Medeiros. "Whenever we grant a loan to a customer, it is common practice to prepare a balance sheet so that we can see what kind of financial shape your business is in. I prepared a balance sheet for you while we were talking."

Before we see the balance sheet, here is a short definition to describe what it is.

A balance sheet is a statement showing the financial condition of a business or person on a specific date.

Given the information for Allan Trent that we have seen so far, here is the balance sheet prepared for him by Ms. Medeiros (top of page 6).

Note that in the balance sheet the totals appear on the same line. This is good accounting practice and makes the balance sheet easy to read. Note also the dollar signs. When a balance sheet is typed, dollar signs are inserted at the top of each money column and beside all totals. We will expand on this later.

Allan Trent
Balance Sheet
as at June 30, 19___

Assets		**Liabilities**	
Bank Balance	$ 200	Owing to Parents	$1 500
Car	2 000		
Calculator	100	**Owner's Equity**	
Computer	1 700	Allan Trent, Capital	2 500
Total	$4 000	Total	$4 000

In Allan's case, thanks to the assistance of Ms. Medeiros, we can see his financial condition as of June 30th. Preparing a balance sheet is like taking a picture of a person's financial position on a certain date. It would be possible to prepare a balance sheet for Allan's business at the end of each month, but this would be very time-consuming and not that helpful. All businesses will prepare a balance sheet at the end of a year and many will prepare them on a quarterly or monthly basis, especially if they use computers to do some of their accounting.

"I am very impressed," says Ms. Medeiros. "You have a sound looking balance sheet and I am prepared to talk about lending you some money for your new business."

Now let's look at the balance sheet that Ms. Medeiros drew up for Allan and study some of the main characteristics.

1.4 The Heading

Allan Trent	answers the question *who?*
Balance Sheet	answers the question *what?*
as at June 30, 19___	answers the question *when?*

The **heading** is always written in the same order, that is, the name of the person or business, the words "Balance Sheet" (they do not have to be capitalized), and the date on which it is prepared. In addition, the heading is centered at the top of the balance sheet.

The first line of the heading contains the name of the person or business, in this case, Allan Trent. If Allan had a business name such as "Trent Electronics" or "Munro Jewellery," then the business name would go on the first line of the heading. Other balance sheets can also have a personal name. Doctors who have their own practice would use personal names on their balance sheets, for example, "L. Applebaum, M.D." Dentists would also use personal names on their balance sheets, for example, "D. O. Yank, D.D.S."

The second line of the heading always says "Balance Sheet." This merely identifies this formal accounting document so that readers will know it is an important financial statement.

The third line of the heading shows the date of the balance sheet. Balance sheets are drawn up as of one particular day. Many businesses select December 31st for the end of their business year. But it is a modern trend to see balance sheets dated at other month ends such as June 30th or September 30th. It is also possible to see a balance sheet dated on another day such as the middle of the month but this is rare and you will not see this in any of the problems in this text. The term "fiscal year" is used to cover the time period of one business year. Here are four examples of balance sheet headings that show you different business names and different dates.

D. O. Yank, D.D.S.
Balance Sheet
as at December 31, 19 ____

Harrison's Video
Balance Sheet
as at April 30, 19 ____

James P. Snell, C.A.
Balance Sheet
as at September 30, 19 ____

Munro Jewellery
Balance Sheet
as at February 28, 19 ____

Fiscal year is the time period over which a business keeps track of its operations.

1.5 Sub-Headings

The term "sub-headings" refers to the three groups of figures on a balance sheet, namely, the assets, liabilities, and owner's equity. The sub-headings on the balance sheet usually appear centered over each side of the balance sheet. See the placing of the sub-headings in the following example. You do not have to capitalize the heading or sub-headings. Thus, you may write either "ASSETS" or "Assets." Both are correct. Likewise, the sub-headings do not have to be underlined.

Allan Trent
Balance Sheet
as at June 30, 19 ____

Assets		**Liabilities**	
Bank Balance	$ 200	Owing to Parents	$1 500
Car	2 000		
Calculator	100	**Owner's Equity**	
Computer	1 700	Allan Trent, Capital	2 500
Total	$4 000	Total	$4 000

Note: The year in all the examples is never filled in. When you do problems, put in the year that has gone by. Therefore, if you are working in September and you see a June date, you may put the current year on your balance sheet.

1.6 Accounting Practices

Ruled Lines

A single line is used to indicate that you are adding or subtracting a column of figures. Add up your figures, draw a single line, and write in the answer.

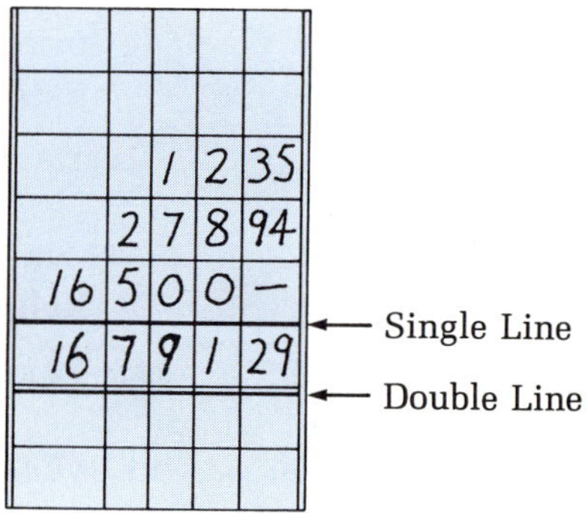

A double line indicates a final total. Therefore when you calculate the total of the asset column, use a double line.

Note: Use a ruler to draw all lines neatly.

Columnar Paper

Accountants and bookkeepers will usually use paper that has ruled lines on it. This type of paper is called *columnar paper* and it is what you will use for most of your exercises. Notice how the money amounts are placed in the example below.

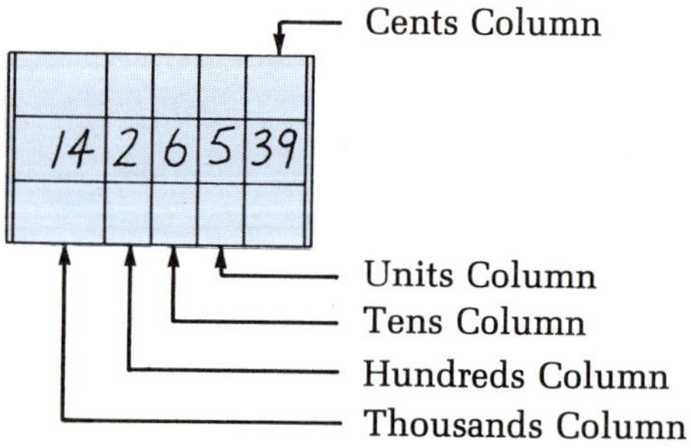

When using columnar paper, no periods, dollar signs, or commas are used. The cents column and the thousands column are usually wider because they contain two or more digits.

Zeroes and Dashes

It is acceptable to place either two zeroes or a dash in the cents column when using columnar paper. Use either zeroes or dashes but be consistent If you are preparing a formal statement such as a balance sheet, use zeroes instead of dashes.

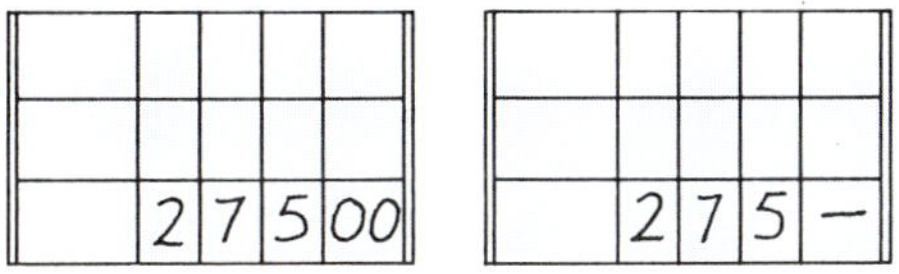

Abbreviations

Avoid using abbreviations when preparing a formal accounting document such as a balance sheet. Some abbreviations are acceptable, for example, Ltd. (Limited) or Co. (Company). In this text, however, all businesses are **proprietorships** (one owner), and these abbreviations will not be necessary. Write proprietorship names in full, for example, "Andy's Video Station."

Neatness

It is important that accounting work be done as neatly as possible. Use pencil for your work so that you can make corrections easily and neatly. Formal accounting statements are either typed or produced on computers.

1.7 Accounts Receivable and Accounts Payable

The Balance Sheet below shows Allan Trent's business, one year later. If you look carefully, you will see two new items on the balance sheet, ''Accounts Receivable' on the left and ''Accounts Payable'' on the right. Accounts receivable is a new asset; accounts payable a new liability. These new terms will be explained once you have looked over the new balance sheet. For the moment, note that Allan Trent's capital has increased from last year. In other words, the amount that Allan is worth has gone up from $2 500 to $7 000.

Allan Trent
Balance Sheet
as at June 30, 19 ____

Assets		**Liabilities**	
Bank Balance	$ 200	Bank of Montreal	$1 500
Accounts Receivable	700	Accounts Payable	500
Car	2 000	Total Liabilities	$2 000
Electronic Equipment	3 500		
Shop Tools	800	**Owner's Equity**	
Office Equipment	1 800	Allan Trent, Capital	7 000
Total	$9 000	Total	$9 000

Just a couple of points about this balance sheet. The word ''Total'' at the bottom of the balance sheet is really not necessary. Modern balance sheets do not show this and you should start leaving it off your balance sheets at this point! Secondly, notice the dollar signs on the balance sheet. They are put there because this is not columnar paper. Dollar signs go at the top of money columns and beside totals.

When Allan Trent performs repair services for a customer and the customer does not pay immediately, then the amount owing to Allan becomes an account receivable. The customer who owes Allan money is a ''debtor'' of the business. The accounts receivable of any business are assets of the business.

Accounts Receivable are the total amounts owing to a business by all of its customers for the sale of goods and services.

A debtor is a customer who owes money to a business.

When Allan buys goods or services from another person or business, and does not pay immediately, then the amount owing becomes an account payable of the business. The person or business to whom the money is owed is referred to as a ''creditor'' and the amount owing appears as an account payable under the heading liabilities on the balance sheet.

Accounts Payable are the total amounts owing to other people or businesses for the purchase of goods and services.

A creditor is a firm or person to whom we owe money.

1.8 Owner's Equity

The section on Owner's Equity could be defined as the owner's claim against the assets of the business. The creditors of the business have first claim against the assets if the business goes bankrupt. Then the owner's claim comes next. To find out what this idea means we can return to Allan Trent's last balance sheet. He had Assets of $9 000, Liabilities of $2 000, and Owner's Equity of $7 000. If he had sold his assets, he might not have received $9 000 for them, if people are not willing to pay $9 000. Therefore, had Allan sold his business, he might not have $7 000 left over for himself. His *claim* would have been reduced. This is why we cannot say that the owner's equity represents the true worth of the business. The Owner's Equity section of the balance sheet may be called ''net worth'' or it may be called ''proprietorship,'' but the term ''Owner's Equity'' represents modern accounting practice and will be used in this text.

1.9 Order of Assets

When professional accountants prepare balance sheets, they always list assets in order of their ''liquidity.'' The word **liquidity** means the ability of a business to convert assets into cash quickly and easily. Allan has $700 in Accounts Receivable and a car that cost him $2 000. Accounts receivable are more liquid because it will be easier to collect accounts receivable than to sell a car. Accounts receivable are the more liquid asset. Cash is already in liquid form and therefore it appears first when the assets are listed on the balance sheet. Here is a list of assets from another balance sheet, to illustrate this idea further.

Look at the assets below.

Assets	
Cash on Hand	$ 100
Accounts Receivable	8 000
Equipment	900
Furniture	11 000
	$20 000

The list is in the order of the most liquid asset first. There is no asset more liquid than cash and Cash on Hand will always appear first when you prepare a balance sheet. The next asset will usually be the Accounts Receivable because the cash for these can be collected if needed. The next two assets, Equipment and Furniture, are not very liquid. They are not usually sold and therefore cannot be easily converted into cash. Because of this factor, they rank down the list. Any other assets that cannot be sold quickly, such as a building or land, would also be near the bottom of the list.

1.10 Service Businesses

The main focus of this text will be on **service businesses.** These are businesses where the skill of the owner, or other staff, is sold to the customer. Examples are service stations (Figure 1-2), photographers, accountants, plumbers, doctors, and computer analysts. The other main type of business is a **merchandise business**. A merchandise business sells goods, not services. Some examples are clothing stores, grocery stores, hardware stores, and jewellery stores.

Figure 1-2
A service station is an example of a service industry.

1.11 Accounting in the Job Market

The study of accounting leads to a variety of jobs in business which rely on a knowledge of accounting principles. Students who graduate from high school, community college, or university may find it possible to obtain jobs which are accounting related. The more education you have, of course, the more opportunities there are available to you, and the more challenging the work. There are three professional accounting designations in Canada, C.A. (Chartered Accountant), C.M.A. (Certified Management Accountant), and a C.G.A. (Certified General Accountant). Students who aspire to be a C.A. must go on to university. It is possible to study to be a C.M.A. or a C.G.A. without having gone to university. More will be said on this later in Chapter 17 on accounting careers, but for now, here are some ads for accounting jobs (see page 14).

The newspaper clippings that follow will help illustrate the demand for employees who have a working knowledge of accounting principles. Note that some of the jobs which require the study of accounting are advertised as bookkeepers, clerks, and accountants. The term ''bookkeepers'' usually refers to someone, such as a high school graduate, who has taken basic training in bookkeeping and accounting. Those students who go on to community colleges can expect to work in more challenging accounting positions than high school graduates. Look over the ads — and, in class, answer the following questions:

- Which jobs are for people starting a new career and which are for experienced workers? How can you tell?
- Which jobs involve the supervision of others?
- Which jobs combine accounting skills with other skills?
- Which jobs involve working in service businesses (Figure 1-3) and which in merchandise businesses?
- Does it surprise you how many jobs call for computer experience? (This aspect of accounting will be discussed in Chapter 16.)

Figure 1-3
People with accounting skills are needed in service industries.

ACCOUNTS Receivable/Order Desk Clerk incl. general office duties, some exper. required. French an asset. 536-0101

BOOKKEEPER-SECRETARY, Required for central office of National non-profit organization. Must be self-starter. Please call 468-3321 for appt.

ACCOUNTS Payable and Bookkeeper, knowledge of A/P and G.L essential. Computer Experience an asset. Must be independent. Send resume to box 661.

Accounts Payable

Downtown property management firm requires a responsible Accounts Payable supervisor. Candidates should have two yrs. experience in computerized environment. Send resume and salary expectations to Box 898.

ACCOUNTS RECEIVABLE CLERK

NEEDED for retail clothing store. To set up interview, call 765-0097.

Accounts Receivable Clerk
STRONG collection and reconciliation skills required, as well as pleasant telephone manner when dealing with customers. 341-0041

INVOICING CLERK, for expanding paper manufacturer. Duties include computerized billing, cash receipts, typing of export documents. Excellent benefits and salary. Call 221-9986.

SR. BOOKKEEPER, bilingual. Must be fully qualified. Call Ms Pacini, 331-9986.

ACCOUNTS Receivable Clerk, must be exper. in manual One-Rite system, posting to subledgers , invoicing, collections.

BOOKKEEPER, Housing Co-op requires bookkeeper 2 days per week. Computerized system. Experience in non-profit volunteer organization an asset. Non-smoking office. Apply in writing with references to Northern Housing Co-op, Box 331.

ADMINISTRATIVE ASSISTANT
$27 K to the right person

Required immediately for Property Management Co. Must have bookkeeping and possess excellent typing and communication skills. Call Mary Oldsworth, Howarth Associates

ACCOUNTS PAYABLE CLERKS

Required for contracting industry. Must be organised and communicate well. Construction experience an asset. Enrolment in 1st yr. CMA, CGA, also an asset. Salary dependent on experience. Call Don at 433-9987.

BOOKKEEPER, exper. to trial balance, typing & general office duties, property management office. 451-0031.

1.12 Summary

The study of accounting can begin in different ways. This text has chosen to start with the balance sheet, a formal accounting statement which shows you the financial condition of a business or person on a given date. By studying and preparing balance sheets, students learn some basic rules about accounting. One of the most important facts about accounting is that we are often keeping figures in balance. Balance sheets are one of many accounting documents prepared by accountants to help provide information about businesses to the owners, their bankers, creditors, and others who might be interested. Anyone who is going to lend your business money will want to know that the business is financially sound. A balance sheet will provide that information.

Now that you have completed the first chapter you should have met all the objectives outlined at the start of the chapter. Check the list again. You should now be able to

1. recognize the fundamental accounting equation;
2. prepare a balance sheet in good form;
3. demonstrate a knowledge of the basic rules of accounting practice;
4. show an understanding of the order of assets on a balance sheet; and
5. show a basic knowledge of accounting careers.

Dictionary of Terms

Assets Anything that a person or business owns.

Accounts Payable Amounts owing to other people or businesses for the purchase of goods and services.

Accounts Receivable Amounts owing to a business by its customers for the sale of goods and services.

Balance Sheet A statement showing the financial condition of a business or person on a specific date.

Creditor A firm or person to whom we owe money.

Debtor A customer who owes money to a business.

Fiscal Year The time period over which a business keeps track of its operations.

Heading The main title on a balance sheet showing the name of the person or business, the title, and the date.

Liabilities Any debts owing to other people or businesses.

Liquidity The ability of a business to convert its assets into cash quickly and easily.

Merchandise Business A business which sells goods to the customer.

Owner's Equity The difference between assets and liabilities.

Proprietorship Businesses which have only one owner.

Service Businesses Businesses where the skill of the owner or other staff is sold to the customer.

Exercises

1. A donut shop is only five blocks away from your house. One of the assets of the business is a cash register to hold the money and record sales. List five other assets that the owner needs to run a donut shop.

2. Most of us have been to the dentist, even though it is not our favourite place. Think about a dentist's office and list five assets that you would see there.

3. A student was asked to list five assets of a funeral home and was able to list only the building and the chairs. Help him complete the list by adding three more assets.

4. Dawn Lennox has just started up a photography business, and her first balance sheet is given below. What is her capital?

Dawn's Photography
Balance Sheet
as at July 31, 19___

Assets		**Liabilities**	
Cash on Hand	$ 50	Bank Loan	$4 000
Bank	2 000	**Owner's Equity**	
Photography Equipment	7 950	D. Lennox, Capital	?
	$?		$?

5. Look at the balance sheet below and answer the questions.

Al's Repair Service
Balance Sheet
as at August 31, 19___

Assets		**Liabilities**	
Cash on Hand	$ 800	Bank Loan	$3 000
Bank	9 000	Accounts Payable	5 000
Tools	5 200		
Office Equipment	6 000	Total Liabilities	$?
Delivery Truck	15 000	**Owner's Equity**	
		Al Jabinski, Capital	?
	$?		$?

(a) Calculate the missing amounts indicated by the four question marks.

(b) Who is the owner of the business?

(c) How much money does the business have altogether?

(d) Is there enough money to pay the bank loan?

(e) Complete the equation by filling in the blanks with the correct figures from the balance sheet.

Assets	=	Liabilities	+ Owner's Equity
?		?	?

6. Classify each of these items as an Asset (A), or a Liability (L).

   Truck; Cash on Hand; Equipment; Bank; Furniture; Supplies; Bank Loan; Accounts Receivable; Building; Land; Accounts Payable; and Automobile.

7. If the assets of a business are \$85 500 and the owner's equity is \$63 200, how much do the liabilities total?

8. The Copy Shoppe is a store which specializes in typing and photocopying documents for small businesses. The owner is A. King. Given the information below, prepare a balance sheet in good form as at July 31, 19 ____. (The assets are in their liquidity order for you.) You will have to calculate the owner's equity.

Assets	Cash on Hand	\$ 1 452
	Accounts Receivable	2 348
	Supplies	3 247
	Equipment	12 323
Liabilities	Bank Loan	\$ 8 235
	Accounts Payable	5 505

9. Dr. A. Hunter is a veterinarian whose business year end falls on April 30th each year. Given the following data for last year end, prepare a balance sheet in good form.

   Cash on Hand \$300; Accounts Receivable \$10 000; Supplies \$750; Equipment \$25 750; Medical Instruments \$4 000; Furniture \$5 000; Van \$20 000; Bank Loan \$16 400; and Accounts Payable \$8 600.

10. A friend of yours, Susan Belko, has operated a business for one year and has passed you the following list of her assets and liabilities in alphabetical order. She wants you to prepare a balance sheet for her, in good form, so that she can show her banker her financial condition. The fiscal year end is October 31, 19 ____. Her business name is "Belko Daycare."

Accounts Payable $345; Accounts Receivable $855; Bank Loan $615; Cash on Hand $165; Equipment $1 735; and Furniture $4 000.

11. P. Calvert, P.Eng., is a professional engineer who specializes in helping radio and television stations when they have trouble with their equipment. Given the information below, prepare a balance sheet for P. Calvert as at December 31, 19 ____. Notice that Accounts Receivable and Accounts Payable are listed separately to the right. You will have to add up each of these lists and then show only each total on the balance sheet. The total Accounts Receivable will be listed beside the description "Accounts Receivable" and the total Accounts Payable will be listed beside the description "Accounts Payable."

Cash on Hand	700
Accounts Receivable	?
Tools	8 900
Equipment	7 600
Automobile	14 000
Bank Loan	3 300
Accounts Payable	?
P. Calvert, Capital	?

Accounts Receivable	
CFCA	2 000
CKCO	1 800
CFPL	900
CKDK	300

Accounts Payable	
Merlan Inc.	600
TMW Company	1 100
National Cable	400

12. Bert Oliver runs a small business which specializes in repairs to boats. The business is known as Convert-A-Boat. Its year end is April 30th each year. The owner has provided the list below for your use and has asked you to prepare a balance sheet for him. You will want to separate the assets, liabilities, and owner's equity before you proceed. Once you have prepared the balance sheet, answer the questions that follow.

Cash on Hand	50
Bank	4 950
Accounts Receivable	7 000
Office Equipment	2 400
Shop Equipment	8 600
Bank Loan	2 000
Accounts Payable	4 000
B. Oliver, Capital	?

Questions

(a) What is the total amount of money that the business has?

(b) When you add the Cash on Hand and the Bank balance, is there enough money to pay off the bank loan?

(c) Does Burt have enough money to pay off all liabilities?

(d) Name three assets that have probably been grouped together under the one name "Office Equipment."

(e) How much equity does Bert have in his business?

Review Questions

1. When Allan Trent first went to see Ms. Medeiros what assets did he have? Were any of these assets "liquid"? Explain.
2. The list of assets for a restaurant would include tables, chairs, ovens, cutlery, and refrigeration equipment. Picture a restaurant you know and list three more assets that would be found there.
3. Explain how we arrived at Allan Trent's Owner's Equity.
4. What are the three main parts to a balance sheet?
5. Which name goes in the heading on a balance sheet — the name of the owner or the name of the business? Explain and give an example to clarify your answer.
6. Write down the names of six businesses in your town or city. Make sure three of them have personal names and three have business names.
7. What are the three sub-headings that appear on a balance sheet?
8. In adding up a column of figures, when do you use a single line and when do you use double lines?
9. A friend of yours who is not studying accounting this year has heard you mention "columnar paper." Explain to your friend about what you are talking.
10. Is it proper to prepare a balance sheet using pencil? Why or why not?
11. Look at the balance sheet for Allan Trent in Section 1.7 of the text. Does his business have enough cash to pay off the Accounts Payable?
12. A local business has filed for bankruptcy. Among the assets that will be sold are two unusual items, a 1950 jukebox and a 1952 milk shake machine. Which asset do you feel is more liquid? Why?

13. Why are the accounts receivable regarded as a liquid asset?

14. Name three personal assets you own.

Challenge Questions

1. (a) What are the three professional accounting bodies in Canada and the three designations you can earn?

   (b) Do some research and find out the educational requirements to be a professional accountant. Select one of the three professional groups to do your research.

2. Assume that you own a business and have just purchased a new car for the business which cost $15 000. You paid part of the purchase in cash but you borrowed $7 500 from the bank to help pay the balance. How would this appear on a balance sheet?

3. An accountant is retiring from practice and has Assets of $85 000, Liabilities of $18 000, and Owner's Equity of $67 000. Will the accountant get $67 000 in cash when the business is sold? Explain.

Review Case

Robert J. Leopard, a lawyer who has been practising law for only a year, has received his first balance sheet from his accountant. Look at the balance sheet and answer the questions that follow.

Robert J. Leopard, B.A., LLB.
Balance Sheet
as at July 31, 19 ___

Assets		**Liabilities**	
Bank	$ 700	Bank Loan	$11 000
Fees Receivable	3 500	Accounts Payable	2 000
Furniture	6 800	Total Liabilities	$13 000
Equipment	3 000		
Land	12 000	**Owner's Equity**	
Building	49 000	R. Leopard, Capital	62 000
	$75 000		$75 000

Questions

(a) If Robert collected all his fees receivable, how much cash would he have on hand and in the bank? Would he be able to pay off all of his liabilities?

(b) How many of the assets on Robert Leopard's balance sheet would you say are "liquid"? Name them.

Challenge Case

Speedy Electric is owned by a young man named Ken Ishizu. The latest balance sheet for the business is shown below. The object of this exercise is to look at Ken's present balance sheet, make some changes to his financial position, and then draw up a new balance sheet. Once you have done this, answer the questions about his business.

Speedy Electric
Balance Sheet
as at May 31, 19___

Assets		**Liabilities**	
Cash on Hand	$ 120	Bank Loan	$ 2 800
Bank	3 100	Accounts Payable	6 700
Accounts Receivable	7 700	Total Liabilities	9 500
Supplies	2 080		
Tools	8 000	**Owner's Equity**	
Truck	14 000	Ken Ishizu, Capital	25 500
	$35 000		$35 000

The day after the balance sheet above was drawn up, the following accounting transactions took place.

Transactions

1. A customer who owed him $2 800 paid him in cash.
2. Ken put $120 from his Cash on Hand into the business Bank account.
3. Ken paid the Bank Loan by writing a cheque on the business Bank account.

Each of the changes above will affect two of the items on the balance sheet. Think about what will change and then draw up a new balance sheet for the business which will be dated as at June 1, 19 ___.

Questions

1. Did the Owner's Equity figure change for the better or worse as a result of these transactions?
2. Ken has been thinking about borrowing $5 000 from the bank to buy a new piece of equipment for his business. As his accountant, write him a formal report to indicate why you think this is a good or bad idea. Use your old and new balance sheets to back up your arguments.

Take-a-Break

1. **What's in a Name?**

   The people listed below are all unusual because you can play anagrams with their names, that is, change the order of the letters and you have the name of an asset of a business.

   e.g. Tim Quepen = Equipment

   (a) Tom Pruce
   (b) Dan Swab
   (c) Rudy Vileckert
   (d) Priss Drell
   (e) Fern Uritu
   (f) Carl Tacoul

2. **Change for a Buck?**

   Can you change one dollar into exactly 50 coins using at least one penny, nickel, dime, and quarter?

3. **Service Business Slogans**

   The ten service businesses listed all use catchy slogans to attract the attention of their customers. Match the name of the service business with its slogan.

   (1) Moe's Air Conditioning
   (2) Northern Air
   (3) Burglar Guard
   (4) Loyd's Asphalt Service
   (5) One-Stop Auto Refinish
   (6) Andre's Barber Shop
   (7) Jensen Carpet Care
   (8) Daytun Copying
   (9) Mclintock Drilling
   (10) Fumigator Fred

   (a) "Got a pest in your house?"
   (b) "Cool down a minute!"
   (c) "We're cleaning up on you!"
   (d) "Well! Well! Well!"
   (e) "Don't be alarmed!"
   (f) "Do that again, we dare you!"
   (g) "Want to get clipped?"
   (h) "Business is soaring!"
   (i) "Paving the way to success."
   (j) "Want a new body?"

Chapter 2 Changes to the Balance Sheet

Objectives

At the end of this chapter, you will be able to

1. make changes to the balance sheet;
2. show a knowledge of the rules for recording transactions in T-accounts; and
3. prepare a trial balance of a general ledger.

2.1 Balance Sheet Changes

Chapter 1 gave you a quick look at a formal document called a balance sheet. A balance sheet is prepared as of a given day in the life of a business, that is, it is only good for one day. Think of it as a snapshot of the financial condition of a business on one day. We could take a snapshot every day of the year and have 365 balance sheets if we wanted them. But businesses don't do this because it is neither useful nor practical.

Let's take a look at a balance sheet for Judy Keaton, an architect (Figure 2-1). Then we will make some changes to her balance sheet.

Figure 2-1
An architect's office, like any business, will draw up a balance sheet every year. You can see the balance sheet for Judy Keaton below.

Judy Keaton, Architect
Balance Sheet
as at October 31, 19 ___

Assets		Liabilities	
Bank	$ 1 800	Accounts Payable	$ 2 400
Accounts Receivable	7 100		
Drafting Equipment	8 550	**Owner's Equity**	
Automobile	12 550	Judy Keaton, Capital	27 600
	$30 000		$30 000

The balance sheet for Judy Keaton, Architect, is only true for October 31st, because on the next day, November 1st, something happened that changed two of the figures on the balance sheet. Judy Keaton gave a creditor a cheque for $400. In accounting this is called a **transaction**. It affects two items on the balance sheet — Bank and Accounts Payable.

Transaction 1

The business paid $400 cash to its creditors to reduce the Accounts Payable. (This transaction will decrease the Bank balance and decrease the Accounts Payable figure as well.)

After this transaction took place, here is Judy's balance sheet.

Judy Keaton, Architect
Balance Sheet
as at November 1, 19 ___

Assets		Liabilities	
Bank	$ 1 400	Accounts Payable	$ 2 000
Accounts Receivable	7 100		
Drafting Equipment	8 550	**Owner's Equity**	
Automobile	12 550	Judy Keaton, Capital	27 600
	$29 600		$29 600

2.2 Accounts

Time for a short lesson in accounting terms. When accountants talk about individual items on a balance sheet, they refer to them as "accounts." Therefore, when they refer to the Bank balance, they are talking about the Bank "account." Similarly, they say the Automobile "account" has a balance of $12 550. Look again at the last balance sheet for Judy Keaton. How many accounts do you see on the balance sheet? If your answer is six, you are correct.

An account is the place to record the effects of business transactions.

2.3 Other Transactions

Now, here are two more changes that occur to Judy's business. Read about each of the transactions below and then note the changes that occur to the balance sheet each time. Notice, also, that the date of the balance sheet keeps changing to reflect the dates of the transactions.

Transaction 2

(November 2nd)
Customers (debtors) pay the business $700 in cash that they owe. The money was put into the Bank account. (This transaction will increase the Bank balance and decrease the Accounts Receivable balance.) Here is the balance sheet dated November 2nd, to show the effect of this transaction.

Judy Keaton, Architect
Balance Sheet
as at November 2, 19 ____

Assets		**Liabilities**	
Bank	$ 2 100	Accounts Payable	$ 2 000
Accounts Receivable	6 400		
Drafting Equipment	9 550	**Owner's Equity**	
Automobile	12 550	Judy Keaton, Capital	28 600
	$30 600		$30 600

Transaction 3

(November 3rd)
Judy paid off all the creditors, $2 000. (The effect of this transaction is to decrease the Bank balance and to eliminate the Accounts Payable balance altogether.)

Judy Keaton, Architect
Balance Sheet
as at November 3, 19 ____

Assets		**Liabilities**	
Bank	$ 100		
Accounts Receivable	6 400		
Drafting Equipment	9 550	**Owner's Equity**	
Automobile	12 550	Judy Keaton, Capital	28 600
	$28 600		$28 600

Figure 2-2
Have you ever wondered why accountants talk of "balancing the books"? Many jobs in accounting make sure that the accounts of a company are balanced, like a weigh scale.

Think of the balance sheet as a weigh scale. When you make changes to the balance sheet, you must always keep it balanced (Figure 2-2). You can make as many changes as you like as long as the balance sheet stays in balance.

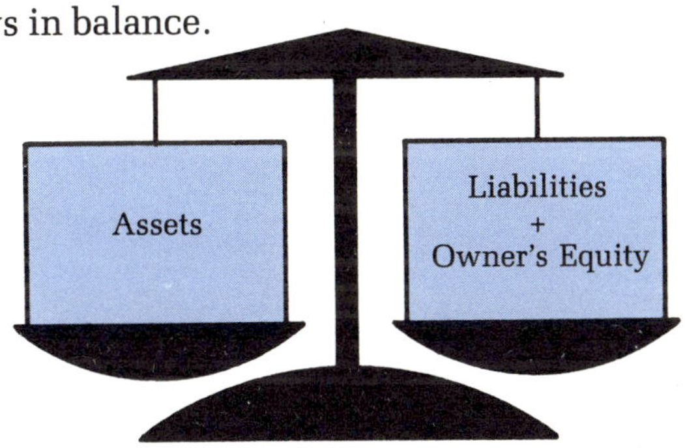

In the three transactions so far, we made these changes:

Transaction 1

Asset (Bank) –400   Liability (Accounts Payable) –400

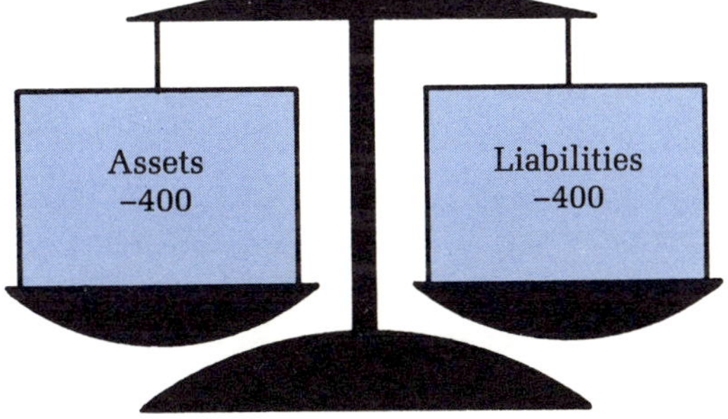

Transaction 2

Asset (Bank)	+ 700
Asset (Accounts Receivable)	− 700

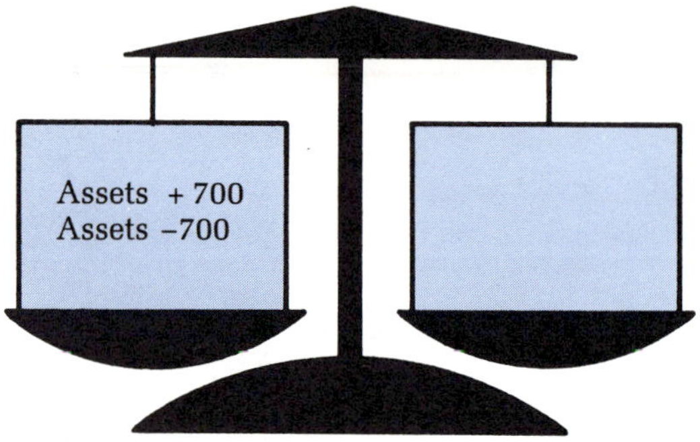

Transaction 3

Asset (Bank)	−2 000	Liability (Accounts Payable)	−2 000

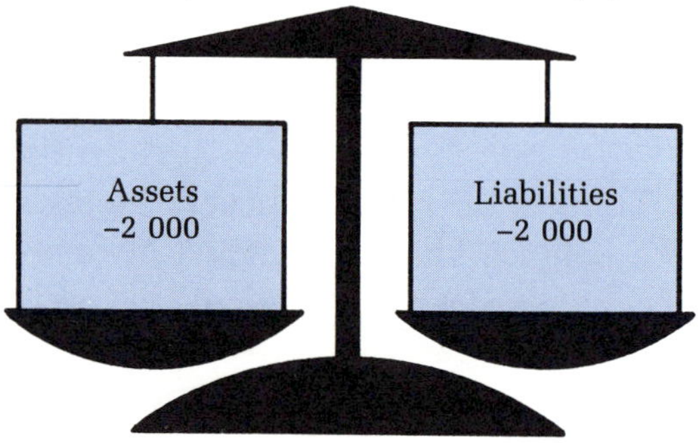

Note: The balance sheet always stays in balance.

2.4 Fundamental Accounting Equation

Here is another way of looking at these transactions using the **fundamental accounting equation.**

	Assets	=	**Liabilities**	+	**Owner's Equity**
	$31 000	=	$2 400	+	$28 600
Transaction 1	−400		−400		
	$30 600	=	$2 000	+	$28 600
Transaction 2	+ 700				
	−700				
	$30 600	=	$2 000	+	$28 600
Transaction 3	−2 000		−2 000		
	$28 600	=	$ Nil	+	$28 600

Now this is going to get very messy unless we think of a better way to record transactions. There are different ways to record changes, but let's look at a method called "T-accounts."

2.5 T-Accounts

A T-account looks like this:

Bank	

Notice it has a left side and a right side, and the name of the account appears at the top of the T. We need one T-account for every account on the balance sheet.

A T-account is an account in the shape of a "T" used to record financial changes.

Let's look at a TV repair business and see how T-accounts work. The balance sheet below has six accounts and therefore to record changes from transactions, Jones Electronics would need six T-accounts. The accounts are shown below the balance sheet.

Jones Electronics
Balance Sheet
as at May 31, 19___

Assets		**Liabilities**	
Bank	$ 500	Bank Loan	$ 4 000
Supplies	900		
Equipment	4 800	**Owner's Equity**	
Truck	9 800	R. Jones, Capital	12 000
	$16 000		$16 000

We take each item on the balance sheet and open a T-account for that item. Therefore, we have drawn up four Asset accounts, one Liability account, and one Capital account. These are also grouped together, depending on whether the account appears on the left side or the right side of the balance sheet.

Bank	
500	

Supplies	
900	

Bank Loan	
	4 000

Equipment	
4 800	

Truck	
9 800	

R. Jones Capital	
	12 000

Notice that when an account appears on the left hand side of the balance sheet, the T-account balance goes on the left. When an account appears on the right hand side of the balance sheet, the balance in the T-account appears on the right hand side.

T-accounts are a very useful way to learn the rules of accounting but they are not used in real business situations. Once we have used them to master how to record transactions, we will study the actual way that businesses record transactions in their books. This section is one of the most important in the textbook. Study it carefully and memorize it quickly and it will build a good foundation for further study.

2.6 Rules for T-accounts

account name	
Debit	Credit

When accountants talk about a T-account, they refer to the two sides as "debit" (left) and "credit" (right). So when we put an entry on the left hand side of an account, we call it a debit entry, and when we put an entry on the right hand side of the account, we call it a credit entry.

Here are the rules for increasing and decreasing any accounts which appear on the balance sheet. (There are other rules, but these will be introduced later in other chapters.)

Assets	
Increase Debit	Decrease Credit

Liabilities	
Decrease Debit	Increase Credit

Owner's Equity	
Decrease Debit	Increase Credit

Notice that when you are using an Asset account, a debit entry will increase the account, but when you are talking about a Liability account or Owner's Equity, an increase is a credit entry. In case this is confusing, go back to the start of Section 2.6 and look at the rule again.

Debit means the left side of an account and credit means the right side of an account.

Here is one more way of looking at the rules for accounts. The rules are the same as above, but are shown in a table form instead of using T-accounts. Use whichever method is easier to help you memorize.

	DEBIT	CREDIT
Assets	increase	decrease
Liabilities	decrease	increase
Owner's Equity	decrease	increase

2.7 Using the Rules

Shown below are some transactions which are also entered into T-accounts. Read over each transaction and each T-account entry to make sure you understand the rules mentioned in the last section.

Sample Transaction 1

Owner invests $5 000 cash into the business. The money is put into the Bank account immediately.

balance sheet

Bank		Capital	
5 000			5 000

Note: Bank increases (debit) and *Capital* increases (credit).

(The balance sheet outline is shown to remind you that the accounts are part of the overall balance sheet for the business.) Since Bank is an asset and appears on the left hand side of the balance sheet, its balance goes on the left hand side of the balance sheet. Since Capital is part of the Owner's Equity and appears on the right hand side of the balance sheet its balance goes on the right hand side of the account.

Sample Transaction 2

Customers paid $1 200 cash to reduce the amounts they owe the business. The money is deposited into the business bank account.

balance sheet

Bank	
1 200	

Accounts Receivable	
	1 200

Note: Bank increases (debit) and *Accounts Receivable* decreases (credit). Both of these accounts are asset accounts and appear on the left hand side of the balance sheet.

Sample Transaction 3

We bought a new car for the business. Cost was $15 000. Paid for it by cheque.

balance sheet

Bank	
	15 000

Automobile	
15 000	

Note: Automobile increases (debit) and *Bank* decreases (credit). Both accounts are assets again.

Sample Transaction 4

Bought new office furniture for $2 100. Promised to pay for it in 30 days. The creditor is Foulds Furniture.

balance sheet

Office Furniture		Accounts Payable	
2 100			2 100

Note: Furniture increases (debit) and *Accounts Payable* increases (credit).

Sample Transaction 5

Paid Foulds Furniture the balance we owed them. We wrote out a cheque.

balance sheet

Bank		Accounts Payable	
	2 100	2 100	

Note: Accounts Payable decreases (debit) and *Bank* decreases (credit).

Sample Transaction 6

Borrowed $10 000 from the bank to eventually buy new equipment for the business.

balance sheet

Bank		Bank Loan	
10 000			10 000

Note: Bank increases (debit) and *Bank Loan* increases (credit).

2.8 More Examples — Debit and Credit Entries

Let's look at more examples of transactions that change Balance Sheet accounts, and note which accounts are debited and which accounts are credited. Accounting is best learned by seeing examples and by doing as many problems as possible. The more entries you make, the more comfortable you will feel with this new subject. Here are some transactions that will change the accounts for Jones Electronics. The entries are all numbered as they are entered into the accounts so you should be able to trace them fairly easily. Make sure that you know how to apply the rules for increases and decreases by following these four examples.

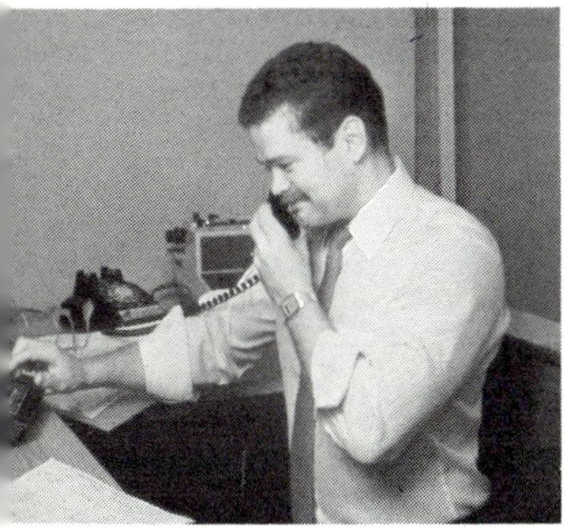

Figure 2-3
When the owner of a business orders supplies, a transaction occurs that will alter the balance sheet.

Transaction 1

Bought new equipment for $1 200. Wrote a cheque to pay the bill.

Transaction 2

The owner, R. Jones, invested $5 000 cash into the business. The money was deposited into the Bank account.

Transaction 3

The business paid off the Bank Loan $4 000. A cheque was issued to pay this.

Bank	
500	1 200 (1)
(2) 5 000	4 000 (3)

Supplies	
900	
(4) 400	

Equipment	
4 800	
(1) 1 200	

Bank Loan	
(3) 4 000	4 000

Accounts Payable	
	400 (4)

Transaction 4

We bought more supplies for the business from Carr Ltd. Cost $400 (Figure 2-3). We promised to pay in 30 days.

Truck	
9 800	

R. Jones Capital	
	12 000 5 000 (2)

2.9 The Ledger

When we have a group of accounts together such as you see above, they are referred to in accounting terminology as a ''ledger.'' The ledger for Jones Electronics above has seven accounts in it. Ledgers for real businesses usually have many more accounts but we will deal with this later on. If a transaction occurs that needs a new account, then we simply make up a new account and add it to the ledger. This happened above with the new account, ''Accounts Payable.'' It was not part of the original ledger for Jones Electronics.

A ledger is a group of accounts.

The general ledger is the main ledger with accounts used to prepare the financial statements of a business.

2.10 Account Balances

Balances for T-accounts are obtained by subtracting the total credits from the total debits, or by subtracting total debits from total credits. If the account is an Asset account, then the debit side will usually add up to more than the credit side. If the account is a Liability account or an Owner's Equity account, then usually the total credits will be greater than the total debits. This means that *Assets* normally have *debit* balances and *Liabilities* and *Owner's Equity* usually have *credit* balances. Notice in the *sample accounts* below how the balances are found, and written on the correct side of the account and circled.

The Asset account is on the left hand side of the balance sheet and therefore its balance is shown on the left hand side of a T-account. A Liability account balance is on the right hand side of a balance sheet and therefore, the T-account balance is on the right hand side. Also, the Owner's Equity account is found on the right hand side of the balance sheet and the T-account balance goes on the right side.

Asset

Cash on Hand

6 000	1 500
1 800	300
(6 000)	

Liability

Accounts Payable

600	3 000
1 400	
	(1 000)

Owner's Equity

Capital

	20 000
	10 000
	(30 000)

An account balance is the amount obtained by subtracting one side of an account from the other.

If we look at the general ledger for Jones Electronics again, we can see how the balances for each account are shown. The balances are written on the appropriate side of the account and then circled. Notice that all Asset accounts have their balance on the debit side and the Liabilitiy accounts and Owner's Equity have their balances on the credit side.

Jones Electronics
General Ledger

Bank

500	1 200
5 000	4 000
(300)	

Supplies

900	
400	
(1 300)	

Bank Loan

4 000	4 000
	(0)

Accounts Payable

	400
	(400)

Equipment

4 800	
1 200	
(6 000)	

Truck

9 800	
(9 800)	

R. Jones Capital

	12 000
	5 000
	(17 000)

If we are talking about these accounts to someone, we would say, "The Bank account has a debit balance of $300; the Accounts Payable account has a credit balance of $400, and so on."

2.11 The Trial Balance

Once the ledger balances are calculated, we should take a "trial balance" of the ledger to see if everything is balanced. If we have recorded all the transactions properly, the ledger accounts will still be in balance, or to put it in a more formal way, *Assets = Liabilities + Owner's Equity*. Does this look familiar? It's the accounting equation you saw a little earlier. It must always be in balance if you do your work properly. There are three ways to take a trial balance. All are shown below. Unless instructed otherwise, use any of the three methods.

Formal Trial Balance

Jones Electronics
Trial Balance
June 30, 19 ___

	Debit	Credit
Bank....................	$ 300	
Supplies...............	1 300	
Equipment............	6 000	
Truck....................	9 800	
Accounts Payable ...		$ 400
R. Jones, Capital		17 000
	$17 400	$17 400

Tape Trial Balance

debits = credits

O.T
300. +
1 300. +
6 000. +
9 800. +
17 400.T

400. +
17 000. +
17 400.T

zero proof

O.T
300.T
1 300. +
6 000. +
9 800. +
400. –
17 000. –
O.T

The trial balance is a listing of all balances in a ledger to see if the accounting books are balanced.

2.12 Summary

Chapter 2 has focussed on the changes that take place on a balance sheet when transactions are recorded. The most important principle discussed in this chapter is that the fundamental accounting equation must always be kept in balance. Whatever changes we make to the balance sheet must be done so that this equation remains intact. The second key idea in this chapter is the basic rules of accounting. To learn these rules, we study the use of T-accounts knowing that this is merely a quick way to learn the rules and that businesses actually use other methods to record transactions from day to day. These other methods will eventually be learned, but for the moment it is wise to learn the basic rules.

Check now and see if you have met the objectives of this chapter. You should now be able to

1. make changes to the balance sheet;
2. show a knowledge of the rules of recording transactions in T-accounts; and
3. prepare a trial balance of a general ledger.

Dictionary of Terms

Account A place to record the effects of business transactions.

Account Balance The amount obtained by subtracting one side of an account from the other.

Credit The right side of an account.

Debit The left side of an account.

Fundamental Accounting Equation Assets = Liabilities + Owner's Equity

General Ledger The main ledger with accounts used to prepare the financial statements of a business.

Ledger A book of accounts.

T-account An account in the shape of a "T" used to record financial changes.

Transaction A business event that affects two or more accounts in the ledger.

Trial Balance A listing of all balances in a ledger to see if the accounting books are balanced.

Exercises

1. Identify the following accounts as an Asset (A), a Liability (L), or Owner's Equity (OE).

(a) Bank Loan	(d) Accounts Payable	(g) Automobile
(b) Furniture	(e) Accounts Receivable	(h) Bank
(c) Land	(f) K. Fox, Capital	(i) Supplies

2. Find the new balance in the fundamental accounting equation.

	Assets	=	Liabilities	+	Owner's Equity
	$25 900	=	?	+	$18 750
Borrowed cash from bank	+ 6 000		+ 6 000		
Paid creditors in cash	−1 500		−1 500		
Owner invested cash	+ 4 000				+ 4 000
	$?	=	$?	+	?

3. Copy out the table below, and then indicate what account will debit and what account will credit for each transaction.

Example		Debit	Credit
	Owner invests $10 000 Cash into the business. The money was deposited into the bank.	Bank	Capital
(a)	Bought new office furniture and wrote a cheque, $7 500.	?	?
(b)	Bought new equipment costing $1 850. Will pay in 30 days	?	?
(c)	Customers paid us $2 325 cash for amounts owing to business.	?	?
(d)	Owner withdrew $600 cash from the business for personal use.	?	?
(e)	Reduced bank loan by paying $2 400 in cash to the bank.	?	?
(f)	Bought a new truck, $17 000. Paid by cheque.	?	?

4. Find the balance of each of these T-accounts.

Bank Loan	
300	2 700
	1 800

Bank	
9 450	250
	725
	840

Accounts Receivable	
3 675	275
	700

Capital	
1 280	8 200
2 190	

Supplies	
1 275	
375	
534	

5. In your notebook, write whether each of these accounts normally has a Debit (Dr) or a Credit (Cr) balance by identifying each account as an Asset, Liability, or Owner's Equity account.

(a) Accounts Payable (d) Supplies (g) Cash on Hand

(b) Accounts Receivable (e) Truck (h) Bank

(c) K. King, Capital (f) Bank Loan (i) Furniture

6. In your notebook, write out an appropriate name to go in each blank, using the accounts listed in Question 5.

(a) When the owner invested in the business we would have credited the account ___?___.

(b) When we credit the ___?___ account, it means that we have bought something from a creditor without paying for it.

(c) If we owned a jewellery store and bought wrapping paper, bags, and string for the business, we would debit ___?___ to record this asset purchase.

(d) We credit ___?___ to show that customers have paid part or all of their account.

(e) We credit the account ___?___ when we borrow money from the bank.

7. Open the ledger below in your workbook, and then record the transactions in the ledger. Take a trial balance to check your accuracy. (The date is September 30, 19 ___.)

Figure 2-4
A doctor's office has a general ledger. You will be working with the general ledger of a doctor in Question 7.

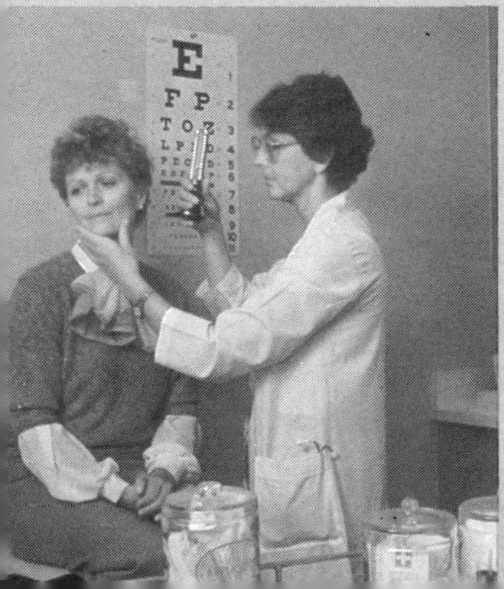

Dr. Helen Winter
General Ledger

Cash on Hand	
300	

Bank	
6 200	

Accounts Receivable	
9 100	

Supplies	
1 800	

Furniture	
4 600	

Equipment	
8 000	

Land	
15 000	

Building	
45 000	

Accounts Payable	
	3 000

Bank Loan	
	7 000

Helen Winter Capital	
	80 000

Transactions

1. Received $575 cash for Accounts Receivable.
2. Borrowed $8 100 from the bank. Deposited the money.
3. Transferred $300 from Cash on Hand to the Bank account.
4. Paid $1 840 to creditors to reduce the Accounts Payable. Wrote a cheque.
5. Dr. Winter withdrew $270 from the Bank account for her personal use.
6. Bought new furniture, $1 540. Paid $300 in cash; the rest will be paid in 30 days.

8. (a) Set up a ledger that has eleven T-accounts for Sharkey's Shoe Shop. The ledger should have the following accounts. (Make sure you put the balances on the correct side of the account.)

   Cash on Hand $700; Bank $2 500; Accounts Receivable $400; Supplies $800; Tools $2 100; Equipment $6 900; Land $12 000; Building $35 000; Accounts Payable $400; Bank Loan $1 200; and G. Sharkey, Capital $?

   (b) Record the following April transactions in T-accounts.

   (1) Customers paid Sharkey $300 cash to reduce amounts owing.

   (2) Put $650 from Cash on Hand into the Bank account.

   (3) Paid the Accounts Payable in full, $400.

   (4) Bought new tools on account from Welland Tool & Die, $520.

   (5) Wrote a cheque to Shooshoney Shoes Ltd. for shoe supplies for the business, $250.

   (6) Wrote a cheque for $200 payable to the bank to reduce the Bank Loan.

   (c) Take a trial balance of your T-account ledger.

   (d) Prepare a balance sheet as of April 30, 19 ____.

9. (a) Set up the following ledger of T-accounts for Jane Chasowy, D.V.M., who has a veterinary practice.

   Cash on Hand $42; Bank $900; Accounts Receivable $3 800; Supplies $2 700; Equipment $8 200; Bank Loan $2 500; Accounts Payable $300; and Dr. Jane Chasowy, Capital $?

   (b) Record the following June transactions in your new ledger.

   (1) Accounts Payable were paid in full. Wrote a cheque.

   (2) Bought a new x-ray machine for small animals. The cost was $5 400. The whole amount is still owing to Vet Supply Ltd.

   (3) During June Dr. Chasowy collected $2 400 in Accounts Receivable balances. Money was deposited into the bank.

   (4) Bought more veterinarian supplies, $500. Paid by cheque.

   (5) Bought a new computer for the office to handle billing of clients. Total cost was $2 500. Part of the cost was paid for by writing a cheque, $1 500. The rest is still owed to the Computer Shoppe.

   (6) A payment of $500 was made by cheque on the Bank Loan.

   (7) Dr. Chasowy invested $5 000 that she received from an inheritance into her veterinary practice. Deposited into bank.

   (c) Take a trial balance of your T-account ledger, using one of the three methods described in this chapter.

   (d) Prepare a balance sheet as of the last day of June.

Review Questions

1. (a) Why do we say that a balance sheet of a company is like a "snapshot" of the financial condition of a business?

   (b) How many balance sheets could a business have in one year?

2. Try to explain the word "account" in your own words.

3. Why is a balance sheet like a weigh scale?

4. State the fundamental accounting equation in full.

5. Indicate if these statements about the fundamental accounting equation are true or false.

   (a) The fundamental accounting equation is always in balance.

(b) The fundamental accounting equation can be stated as Assets = Liabilities + Owner's Equity.

(c) Any transaction always has to affect the left side of the equation and the right side of the equation.

(d) The fundamental accounting equation is used for the books of any service business.

6. Do businesses like Jones Electronics really use T-accounts to record day-to-day transactions? Explain.

7. What do we call the left hand side and the right hand side of a T-account?

8. Draw the following table in your notebook. Complete the table by filling in the missing entries to indicate how to increase each account with a debit or credit.

Account	**Increase**
e.g. Cash on Hand	Debit
Bank Loan	?
Equipment	?
Accounts Payable	?
Building	?

9. What does "debit" mean? What does "credit" mean?

10. How many accounts do ledgers usually have?

11. What happens if you need to record a transaction in an account and there is no such account in the ledger?

12. What is a trial balance? Explain fully.

13. What procedure do we follow when we want to record the balance in a T-account?

14. When you use T-accounts, on what side of the account will you usually find the balances for Assets, Liabilities, and Owner's Equity?

Challenge Questions

1. Assume that you have just graduated from the Glamour School of Hairdressing and you are going to open you own hair salon. Think about your new operation and list seven Asset accounts and three Liability accounts you will have.

2. Set up enough T-accounts to record the following transaction. When you are done, make sure your debit balances equal your credit balances.

Century 22 Real Estate had a car that belonged to the business and the balance in the T-account was $5 400. They decided to buy a new car for the business; cost was $16 000. The car dealer allowed them $3 000 trade for the old car. The new car was financed by paying $4 000 down payment by cheque. The balance of money owing on the new car purchase was due to be paid to Snob Motors in 30 days. Record this transaction in T-accounts. (Hint: You will need a new account called ''Loss on Sale of Automobile'' to handle this one.)

3. We recorded a transaction in this chapter by which the owner invested money into the business. What do you expect the entry will look like when the owner takes cash out of the business for her/his personal use? Explain the reasoning behind your answer.

Review Case

Look at the T-accounts below. They belong to a teenager, Andy Pine, who runs a service using his home computer to do mailing lists for clubs, churches, and organizations. Make a list of the account balances and then answer these questions.

Andy Pine
General Ledger

Account	Debit	Credit
Cash on Hand	200	
Bank	900	
A/R	1 200	
Computer	1 400	
A/P		1 300
A. Pine, Capital		2 400

1. Does Andy have enough money now to pay his Accounts Payable?
2. Andy wants to buy another disk drive for his computer. It costs $300. If Andy doesn't pay any money on the Accounts Payable at the present time, can he afford the new disk drive?
3. If all of Andy's customers paid their accounts in full, how much money would Andy have in his business?

Challenge Case

Joanna Meyer runs a sewing machine business, called Joanna's Sewing. She operates out of her parents house since she is only 17 and still going to high school. Look at her latest balance sheet below.

1. Record the transactions for January in T-accounts.

2. Take a trial balance of your T-account ledger.
3. Prepare a balance sheet for Joanna as of January 31st.
4. Answer the questions about Joanna's business.

Joanna's Sewing
Balance Sheet
as at December 31, 19 ___

Assets		**Liabilities**	
Bank	$ 250.24	Accounts Payable	$325.12
Accounts Receivable	402.31		
Sewing Supplies	126.79	**Owner's Equity**	
Sewing Machine	1 042.50	J. Meyer, Capital	?
	$?		$?

Transactions

Jan. 5: A customer paid $65.20 cash toward a balance owing. Joanna immediately put the money into the bank.

8: Joanna bought sewing supplies costing $82.32. Cheque.

18: Wrote cheque $110.00 to pay off one of her suppliers.

20: Bought an adaptor for the sewing machine that allowed her to program some stitch patterns into the sewing machine. The cost was $525.80 and it was financed half by a bank loan and the other half by buying on account from Sew Right Sewing Machines.

Questions

(a) Calculate the balance of Joanna's liquid assets. When you compare this figure to her liabilities, are the liabilities too high? Why or not? Explain.

(b) Joanna has $2 000 in a savings account that she has been thinking about putting into her business account so that the business would be on a better financial footing. The money was a legacy from her aunt. What would you advise her to do?

(c) Joanna needs more business to improve her financial condition. Where would you advise her to advertise her sewing business so that she can do more sewing and increase her cash income?

(d) Is there anything else that Joanna can do to improve her financial picture on her balance sheet?

Take-a-Break

1. **What's My Line?**

If "NOW and THIN" is the name of a reducing salon, can you match each imaginery business name below with its service or product?

(a) The Hitching Post	(1) shoe store
(b) Time Out	(2) video game store
(c) Pick of the Litter	(3) wedding chapel
(d) Sole Brothers	(4) bicycle shop
(e) Tic Tac	(5) garbage collection
(f) Coinucopia	(6) towing service
(g) This Bud's For You	(7) watch repair shop
(h) The Spokesman	(8) flower shop

2. **The Fiscal Year**

Accountants are used to measuring figures in yearly time periods. How many times does the year 1986 appear in the grid?

```
1 9 8 6 1 9 8 6
9 8 6 1 9 8 6 1
8 6 1 9 8 6 1 9
6 1 9 8 6 1 9 8
1 9 8 6 1 9 8 6
```

3. **Wacky Words**

The symbolic diagrams below can all be interpreted into accounting terms or phrases that you learned in Chapter 2. Try your luck!

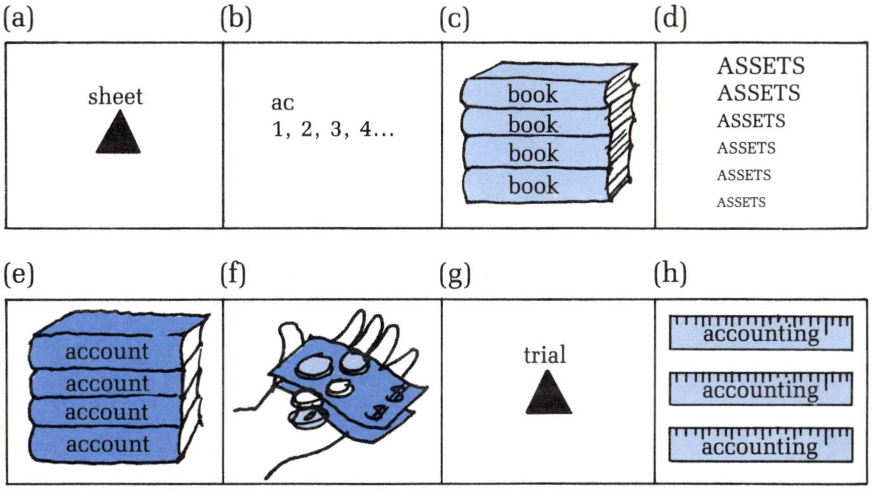

Accounting at Work

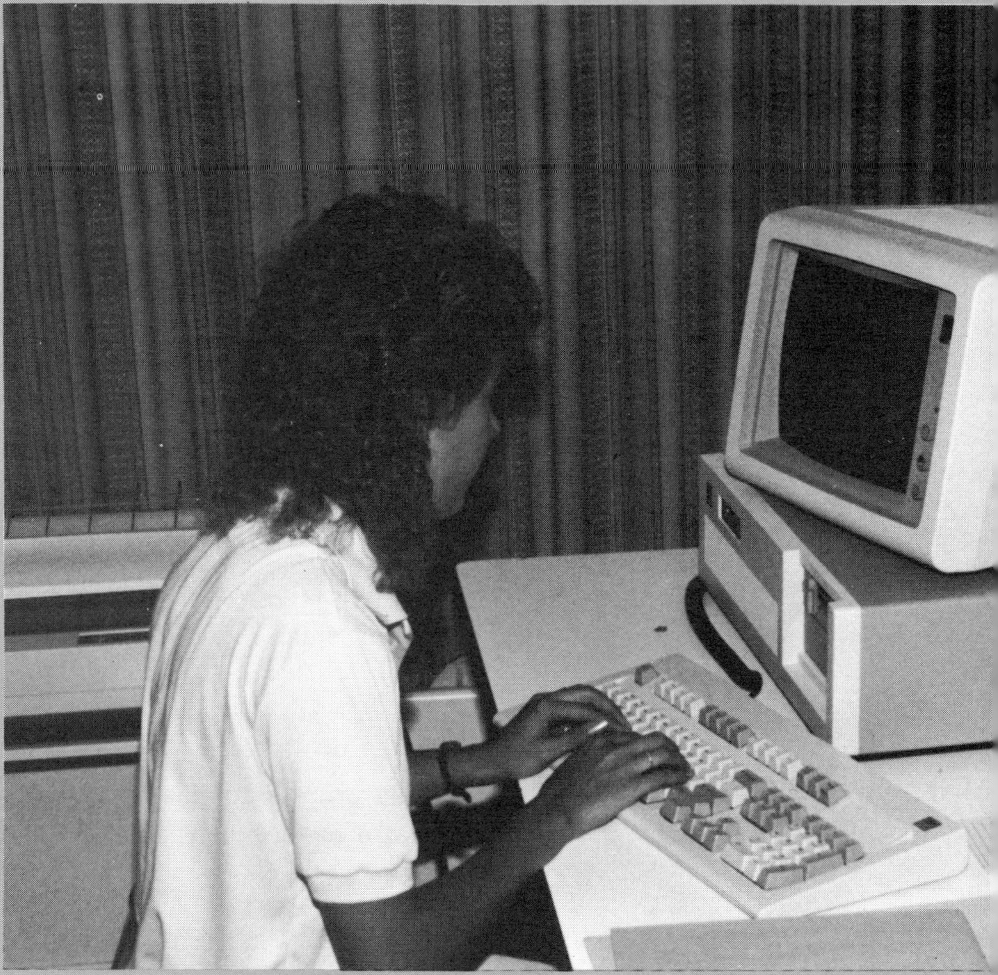

Accounts Receivable Clerk

Debbie Van Ryswick is an accounting clerk at Radio Station 102-FM. Debbie was hired two years ago as a general office worker and now is in complete charge of all accounts receivable for the radio station.

Debbie keeps track of all radio station customers and the amounts owing to 102 for advertising on the radio. To assist her with this role, Debbie uses a microcomputer system with an accounts receivable software package. She enters transactions daily into the computer, which then posts automatically to the customer's accounts. Debbie's main responsibility is to ensure that the data entered into the computer is correct, and is correctly entered. At the end of the day, Debbie requests a trial balance of the accounts receivable ledger which the computer also produces. The trial balance is turned over to her boss, the chief accountant for the radio station who can follow up any overdue accounts personally.

At the end of every month, Debbie has the computer produce customer statements for all the customers of the radio station. Each statement is a listing for the customer of the final balance owing at the end

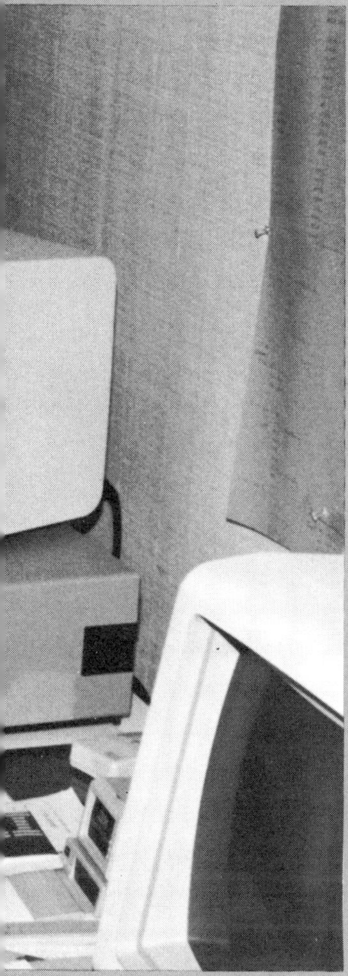

of the month to the radio station, along with a list of all transactions for the month. The transactions are the times that the customer's ad was put on the air, the length of each commercial, and any payments on account that the customer might have made during the month. If customers call up the radio station to query their statement, Debbie must be able to explain to the customer exactly what the statement items are all about.

Debbie's training consists of a high school diploma, where she majored in Business Studies courses, and accounting in particular. In the evening, Debbie has enrolled for the past two years in community college courses to try to upgrade her training and become more valuable to the radio station. She has ambition and hopes to advance to a more responsible level in the station as soon as possible.

Questions for Discussion

1. Has Debbie's high school education been important in terms of her job at the radio station? How?
2. What kinds of courses do you expect Debbie is taking in the evening at community college?
3. What role does the computer play in her job?
4. If you were Debbie's boss, how could you encourage Debbie to improve herself, and what are her chances for advancement at the radio station?

2

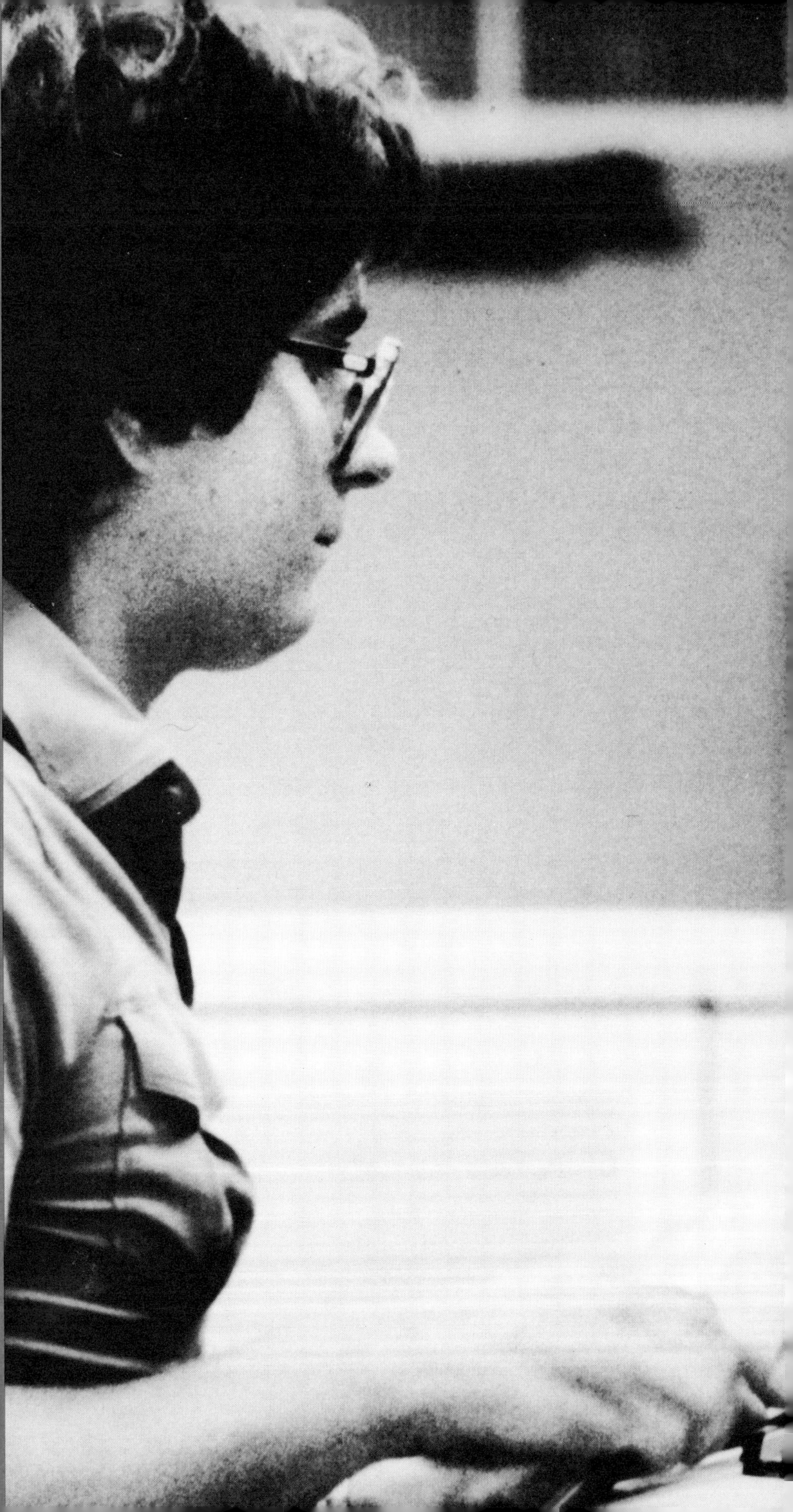

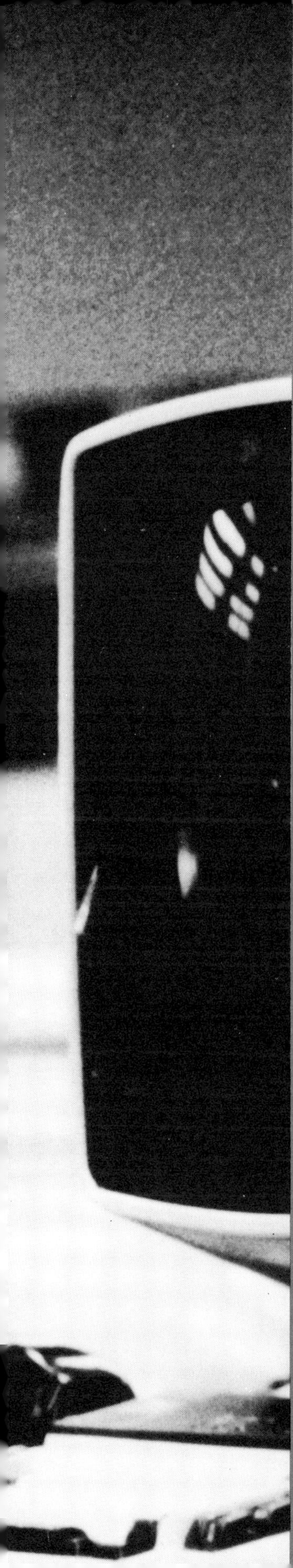

Expanding the Cycle

Chapter 3
Journalizing/Posting Transactions

Chapter 4
Revenue and Expense Transactions

Chapter 3 Journalizing/Posting Transactions

Objectives

By the end of this chapter, you will be able to

1. journalize in a general journal;
2. post to a general ledger;
3. recognize a chart of accounts; and
4. prepare a balance sheet from a trial balance.

3.1 The General Journal

In Chapter 2 you learned all about T-accounts and accounting rules. T-accounts are useful for making accounting entries quickly but a business needs something more organized for business transactions. One way of keeping transactions in an efficient order is by using a ''general journal.'' A general journal is often called a **book of original entry** because it is where accounting transactions are first recorded. The general journal provides an accounting history of the business. In the general journal, we record the date of the transaction, the debit amount, the credit amount, and an explanation for each business transaction. Here is what part of a general journal page looks like:

GENERAL JOURNAL

PAGE

DATE	PARTICULARS	PR	DEBIT	CREDIT

The general journal is the place where accounting transactions are formally recorded.

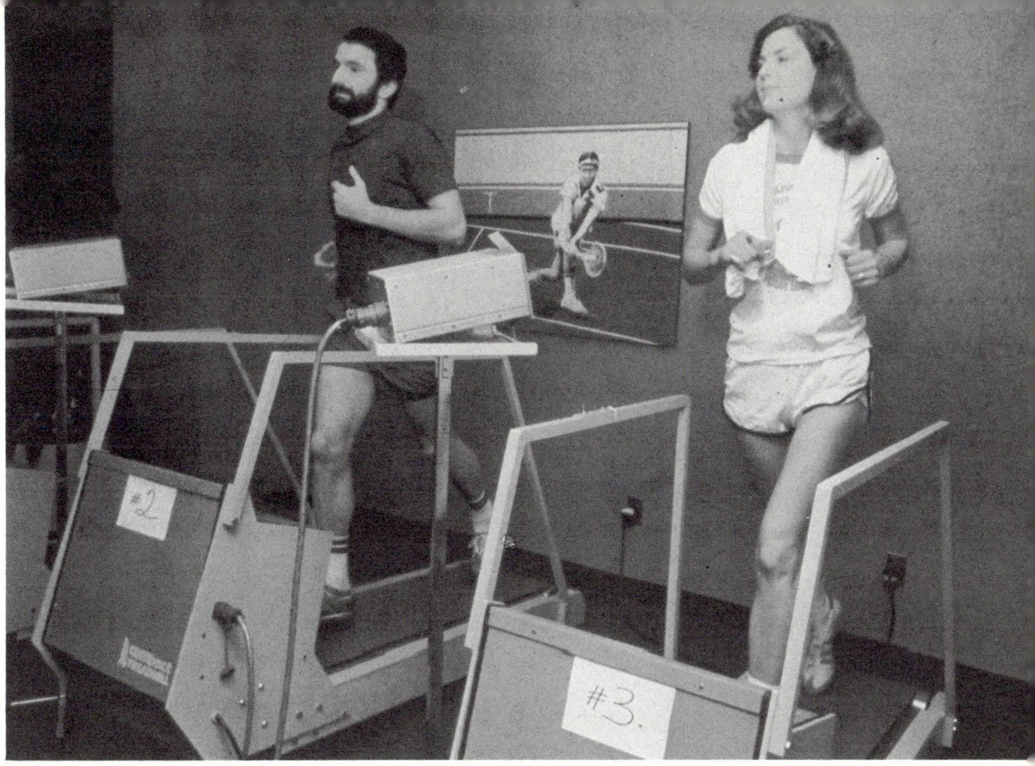

Figure 3-1
If you were opening an aerobics centre, it would be wise to open a general journal for your business.

3.2 The Opening Entry

Let's take a look at a brand new business. Janice Kirktown has just decided to open a new studio to teach aerobics classes (Figure 3-1). Her new business is called Fitness Fun, and the only asset she has at the present time is a balance of $1 800 in her business Bank account.

This is the *capital* that Janice brings to the business and it creates something called an "opening entry" for the business that must be recorded in a general journal. We do this in four steps:

Step 1 Enter the date.

Step 2 Enter the account debited and the amount.

Step 3 Enter the account credited and the amount.

Step 4 Write an explanation about the journal entry.

If this is a new page in the general journal we should start each page with the year at the top under the word "date." The page number is written in the top right hand corner of the general journal.

GENERAL JOURNAL

PAGE 1

DATE 19—		PARTICULARS	PR	DEBIT	CREDIT
May	1	Bank		1 800 —	
		J. Kirktown, Capital			1 800 —
		To record the opening entry for a			~~1 800 —~~
		new business – Fitness Fun.			

Now, let's review a few points about the general journal.

1. The year usually appears at the top of the Date column.
2. The account we are going to debit always appears first when we write it in the Particulars column.
3. The account we are going to credit always appears after the debit and is **indented** for ease of reading.
4. When we use columnar paper, there are no decimals used. The column lines separate dollars and cents.
5. The last line of the accounting entry is an **explanation** of the transaction, and is for future reference.
6. Leave one blank line after each accounting entry.

An opening entry is made when a business starts out. It is a beginning for recorded transactions, the first entry in a general journal.

3.3 Journalizing

Now that we are off to a good start, let's do some more entries in the general journal. When we write entries in the general journal we say that we are **journalizing**.

May 2: Janice borrowed $2 000 from the bank to buy office furniture so that she would have a place to do her books. The loan was to be paid back in less than a year from the business profits. Here is the general journal entry:

GENERAL JOURNAL

PAGE 1

DATE 19__		PARTICULARS	PR	DEBIT	CREDIT
May	2	Bank		2000 –	
		Bank Loan			2000 –
		Borrowed money from the bank, to			
		be repaid within a year.			

Note: The column designated PR will be discussed later in this chapter when we follow up this theory. For now you only need to know that PR stands for **posting reference.**

May 3: Janice bought office furniture she needed for the business. Total cost was $420, and she wrote a cheque to pay for it.

GENERAL JOURNAL

PAGE 1

DATE		PARTICULARS	PR	DEBIT	CREDIT
May	3	Office Furniture		420 —	
		Bank			420 —
		Bought furniture. Cheque #1			

Let's have a reminder about basic rules for debits and credits. Remember that you have to know these rules before we go on to Section 3.4.

Assets	
Increase Debit	Decrease Credit

Liabilities	
Decrease Debit	Increase Credit

Owner's Equity	
Decrease Debit	Increase Credit

3.4 On Account

When you use a credit card, such as the one shown in Figure 3-2, you do not pay for the goods you buy immediately. Many businesses, when they buy for the business, do the same thing. They do not pay for the goods immediately, but agree to pay for them within 30 days. This is referred to as buying goods or services **on account.** This means that instead of crediting the bank when we buy something, we have to credit the Accounts Payable account. We can see how this works by studying Janice's next business transaction.

Figure 3-2
When you use a credit card, you are buying goods on account.

May 4: Janice bought a new stereo system to play music for her aerobics students. She bought the stereo on account from Jones Electronics at a cost of $380.

GENERAL JOURNAL

PAGE

DATE		PARTICULARS	PR	DEBIT	CREDIT
May	4	Equipment		380 —	
		Accounts Payable - Jones Electronics			380 —
		Bought stereo system on account.			

Note: Look again at the general journal entry. Remember that the credit side of the entry is always indented and a blank line is left before each new entry to make it easier to read the general journal.

May 5: Bought new mats for the fitness studio on account from Curry Mfg. Co. The cost of the mats was $1 200.

GENERAL JOURNAL

PAGE

DATE		PARTICULARS	PR	DEBIT	CREDIT
May	5	Equipment		1 200 —	
		A/P – Curry Mfg. Co.			1 200 —
		Bought new exercise mats on account			

Note: The short form for Accounts Payable is A/P.

3.5 The Drawings Account

It's time to learn about a new account. Assume that Janice needs $50 cash to buy her brother a birthday present. This is for personal use and does not really belong to the business. If she writes herself a cheque, she is withdrawing money from the business for personal use. We say that she is "drawing" money out of the business, and this creates a new account called Drawings. Notice the entry in the journal.

GENERAL JOURNAL

PAGE

DATE		PARTICULARS	PR	DEBIT	CREDIT
May	6	J. Kirktown, Drawings		50 —	
		Bank			50 —
		Withdrew cash from the business			
		bank account for personal use.			

Drawings is an amount withdrawn by an owner from a business for personal use.

The Drawings account is really the left hand side of the Capital account. We put the debit into Drawings instead of decreasing Capital so that the business has a separate record of all the owner's drawings from the business. Think of these two accounts this way:

Drawings		Capital	
Increase Debit			Increase Credit

Note: When we show these accounts on the balance sheet, we will put them back together.

We have simply separated the Capital account into two halves. It means that we will not put any entries on the credit side of the Drawings account or on the debit side of the Capital account.

Now that we have looked at six different accounting entries, let's take a look at the whole page in the general journal. This will give you a better picture of how the journal works. Check the rules that you learned earlier in the chapter and see if they have all been followed.

1. The year appears at the top of the Date column.
2. The debit entry is written first in the Particulars column.
3. The credit entry is written after the debit and is indented a couple of spaces to make it easier to read.
4. When we use columnar paper, there are no decimals used. The column lines separate dollars and cents.
5. The explanation for each transaction goes on the last line of the entry.
6. Leave one blank line after each journal entry.

GENERAL JOURNAL

PAGE 1

DATE 19__		PARTICULARS	PR	DEBIT	CREDIT
May	1	Bank		1800 —	
		J. Kirktown, Capital			1800 —
		To record the opening entry for			
		Fitness Fun.			
	2	Bank		2000 —	
		Bank Loan			2000 —
		Borrowed money from the bank.			
	3	Office Furniture		420 —	
		Bank			420 —
		Bought furniture. Cheque #1			
	4	Equipment		380 —	
		Accounts Payable – Jones Electronics			380 —
		Bought stereo system on account.			
May	5	Equipment		1200 —	
		A/P - Curry Mfg. Co.			1200 —
		Bought new exercise mats on account			
	6	J. Kirktown, Drawings		50 —	
		Bank			50 —
		Withdrew cash from the business			
		bank account for personal use.			

3.6 Posting to the General Ledger

Remember back in Chapter 2 when you learned about the ledger? We could take the general journal transactions for Janice's business and put the entries into a T-account ledger, like this:

Bank	
1 800	420
2 000	50

Equipment	
380	
1 200	

Furniture	
420	

Bank Loan	
	2 000

Accounts Payable	
	380
	1 200

J. Kirktown, Capital	
	1 800

J. Kirktown, Drawings	
50	

In a real business they do not use T-accounts for their day-to-day transactions because this is not a formal way to do accounting. Once an entry is recorded in a general journal, it is then posted into a 3-column ledger account. Janice's first entry is posted below. Look it over and then we will explain what is happening.

GENERAL JOURNAL

PAGE 1

DATE 19—		PARTICULARS	PR	DEBIT	CREDIT
May	1	Bank	2	1 800 –	
		J. Kirktown, Capital	30		1 800 –
		To record the opening entry for a			
		new business – Fitness Fun.			

posted

GENERAL LEDGER

ACCOUNT Bank NO. 2

DATE 19—		PARTICULARS	PR	DEBIT	CREDIT	DR CR	BALANCE
May	1		GJ1	1 800 –		DR	1 800 –

Posting is transferring an entry from a journal to a ledger.

The opening entry affects two accounts and, therefore, each debit or credit is posted to its own account. When the Bank debit is posted to the Bank account, we write "GJ1" in the PR column of the 3-column ledger account to show that the entry has come from the General Journal, page 1. Then we go back to the General Journal, and in the PR column there, we write the number "2" to show that we have posted that entry to the Bank account, which is account #2, in the General Ledger. Then we post the credit side of the General Journal entry to Janice's Capital account.

Look at the Bank account in the General Ledger again. Note that the Particulars column is very seldom used. Remember that the PR column stands for Posting Reference. And finally, notice that there is a little square that appears before the Balance column DR./CR.

This is used to indicate whether the account balance is a debit (Dr) or credit (Cr) balance. In the first amount posted, we put $1 800 in debits into the account, so the account has a debit balance. You will have to use this notation when it comes time to take a trial balance of the general ledger.

The other half of the opening entry still has to be posted.

GENERAL JOURNAL

PAGE 1

DATE 19—		PARTICULARS	PR	DEBIT	CREDIT
May	1	Bank	2	1800 –	
		J. Kirktown, Capital	30		1800 –
		To record the opening entry for a			
		new business – Fitness Fun.			

GENERAL LEDGER

ACCOUNT: J. Kirktown, Capital NO. 30

DATE 19—		PARTICULARS	PR	DEBIT	CREDIT	DR. CR.	BALANCE
May	1		GJ1		1800 –	CR	1800 –

3.7 A Chart of Accounts

Just a brief word about the general ledger. The **general ledger** is the main ledger with a group of accounts. When we first had a group of accounts, they were T-accounts. Now we have accounts that are 3-column accounts.

A chart of accounts is a list of the accounts used by a business.

Every account in a general ledger needs a number so that we can refer to it when we are posting. The numbers used by businesses will be different from one business to the next. We can use this grouping for our ledger accounts.

Assets . . 1-19 **Liabilities** . . 20-29 **Owner's Equity** . . 30-39

If we use these numbers for Janice's business, her chart of accounts would look like this:

Fitness Fun
Chart of Accounts

Account	No.	Group
Cash on Hand	1	Assets
Bank	2	Assets
Accounts Receivable	3	Assets
Equipment	10	Assets
Furniture	11	Assets
Bank Loan	20	Liabilities
Accounts Payable	21	Liabilities
J. Kirktown, Capital	30	Owner's Equity
J. Kirktown, Drawings	31	Owner's Equity

Here's what Janice's General Ledger would look like when the entries made in her General Journal have all been posted. Study it for a couple of minutes and look specifically at the account numbers.

ACCOUNT: Cash on Hand NO. 1

DATE 19—		PARTICULARS	PR	DEBIT	CREDIT	DR/CR	BALANCE

ACCOUNT: Bank NO. 2

DATE 19—		PARTICULARS	PR	DEBIT	CREDIT	DR/CR	BALANCE
May	1		GJ1	1 800 —		DR	1 800 —
	2		GJ1	2 000 —		DR	3 800 —
	3		GJ1		420 —	DR	3 380 —
	6		GJ1		50 —	DR	3 330 —

ACCOUNT: Equipment NO. 10

DATE 19__		PARTICULARS	PR	DEBIT	CREDIT	DR CR	BALANCE
May	4		GJ1	380 –		DR	380 –
	5		GJ1	1 200 –		DR	1 580 –

ACCOUNT: Furniture NO. 11

DATE 19__		PARTICULARS	PR	DEBIT	CREDIT	DR CR	BALANCE
May	3		GJ1	420 –		DR	420 –

ACCOUNT: Bank Loan NO. 20

DATE 19__		PARTICULARS	PR	DEBIT	CREDIT	DR CR	BALANCE
May	2		GJ1		2 000 –	CR	2 000 –

ACCOUNT: Accounts Payable NO. 21

DATE 19__		PARTICULARS	PR	DEBIT	CREDIT	DR CR	BALANCE
May	4		GJ1		380 –	CR	380 –
	5		GJ1		1 200 –	CR	1 580 –

ACCOUNT: J. Kirktown, Capital NO. 30

DATE 19__		PARTICULARS	PR	DEBIT	CREDIT	DR CR	BALANCE
May	1		GJ1		1 800 –	CR	1 800 –

ACCOUNT: J. Kirktown, Drawings NO. 31

DATE 19__		PARTICULARS	PR	DEBIT	CREDIT	DR CR	BALANCE
May	6		GJ1	50 –		DR	50 –

Once the general ledger has been posted, the next step is to take a trial balance for Janice's business. If the trial balance balances, then we can prepare a formal balance sheet for her. You may remember from

Chapter 2 that there are three ways to take a trial balance. Two of these are shown. See if you can remember the third method without looking back.

TRIAL BALANCE

Fitness Fun
Trial Balance
May 6, 19—

NO	ACCOUNT TITLE	DEBIT	CREDIT
2	Bank	3330 –	
10	Equipment	1580 –	
11	Furniture	420 –	
20	Bank Loan		2000 –
21	Accounts Payable		1580 –
30	J. Kirktown, Capital		1800 –
31	J. Kirktown, Drawings	50 –	
		5380 –	5380 –

0.00T
3330.00 +
1580.00 +
420.00 +
50.00 +
5380.00T

2000.00 +
1580.00 +
1800.00 +
5380.00T

Note: The Cash on Hand account does not have a balance. When an account has a zero balance, you do not have to include it in the trial balance. Also, the Cash on Hand account is a new asset account and it refers to a small pool of money that is sometimes kept in an office.

3.8 Preparing a Balance Sheet from a Trial Balance

When the **trial balance** balances, we are ready to prepare the balance sheet for Fitness Fun. If we prepare a formal balance sheet for the business as of the date of the last transaction, it would look like this on columnar paper:

FITNESS FUN
Balance Sheet
as at May 6, 19—

ASSETS		LIABILITIES	
Bank	3330 –	Bank Loan	2000 –
Equipment	1580 –	Accounts Payable	1580 –
Furniture	420 –	Total Liabilities	3580 –
		OWNER'S EQUITY	
		J. Kirktown, Capital 1800–	
		J. Kirktown, Drawings (50–)	1750 –
	5330 –		5330 –

This balance sheet is different from the others you have prepared because it has the Drawings account on it. Notice how the Drawings account is subtracted from the original Capital. The net figure, or $1 750, represents the new Capital balance as of May 6th. In other words, the original capital was $1 800 but the owner took out drawings of $50 and therefore the capital balance is $1 750.

This balance sheet could also be typed or produced on a computer. If this method is used instead of doing it by hand, then dollar signs must be inserted, according to the rules you learned in Chapter 1.

1. Dollar signs at the top of a new money column.
2. Dollar signs beside sub-totals and final totals.

Fitness Fun
Balance Sheet
as at May 6, 19 ____

Assets		**Liabilities**		
Bank	$3 330.00	Bank Loan		$2 000.00
Equipment	1 580.00	Accounts Payable		1 580.00
Furniture	420.00	Total Liabilities		$3 580.00
		Owner's Equity		
		J. Kirktown, Capital	$1 800.00	
		J. Kirktown, Drawings	(50.00)	1 750.00
	$5 330.00			$5 330.00

3.9 Summary

This chapter has taught you four basic steps in accounting and you have learned a great deal about the basic accounting cycle. This is what you have covered, if we put it in symbol form:

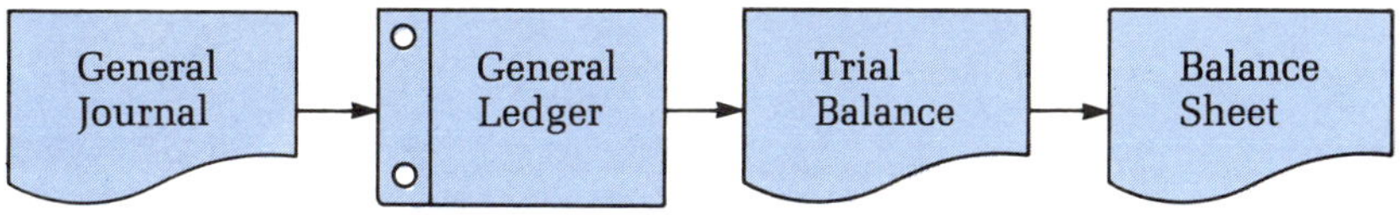

Check and see if you have met the objectives of this chapter. You should be able to

1. journalize in a general journal;
2. post to a general ledger;
3. recognize and use a chart of accounts; and
4. prepare a balance sheet from a trial balance.

Dictionary of Terms

Book of Original Entry A place where accounting transactions are first recorded.

Chart of Accounts A list of the accounts used by a business.

Drawings An amount withdrawn by an owner from a business for personal use.

Explanation The description of an accounting transaction that appears after the debit and credit entries in the general journal.

General Journal A place where accounting transactions are formally recorded.

General Ledger The main ledger with a group of accounts.

Indented Leaving two or three spaces away from the left margin of the journal to record an accounting entry.

Journalizing Recording transactions in a journal.

On Account To buy a good or service without paying for it immediately.

Opening Entry The accounting entry made when a business first starts operations.

Posting Transferring an entry from a journal to a ledger.

Posting Reference Initials and a page number which indicate where an accounting entry has been posted to or has come from.

Trial Balance A listing of the accounts of a business to see if the total debits equal the total credits.

Exercises

1. Paul Stueck started his own upholstery business with $5 000 cash in the bank. Journalize the opening entry for Paul.

2. Rob Gillespie is a student at Central Secondary School in Regina. He has just bought a new home computer system and plans to start his own business. He wants to use his computer to prepare résumés and class reports for students at his school. Given the list of assets and the liability below, journalize the opening entry for Rob as of November 1st.

Assets		**Liability**	
Cash on Hand	125	Bank Loan	500
Supplies	75		
Equipment	1 500		

3. Toni Amaducci is ready to open her own hairdressing salon in one of the rooms in her house. Given the information below, record the opening entry in a 2-column general journal, and then journalize the first four transactions that occurred for her new business.

Feb.	1:	Bank . . . . $3 500/Bank Loan . . . $2 500/Capital . . . ?
	2:	Bought beauty supplies $710, cheque #1.
	2:	Wrote cheque #2 for salon equipment, $1 823.90.
	3:	Bought a filing cabinet for papers, $112.95; cheque #3.
	5:	Bought a cash register on account from Wilson Stationers, cost $325. (*Hint*: Remember the A/P account?)

4. Shown below is a general journal prepared by someone who has no training in accounting. Now that you know all about the general journal, use your notebook and list four things that you see wrong in the way this opening entry was recorded.

GENERAL JOURNAL

PAGE

DATE		PARTICULARS	PR	DEBIT	CREDIT
June	1	Bank		100 —	
June	1	Capital			100 —

5. Shown below are the assets that Ann Hanson used to start her own photography business. Look at the picture and the values below and make the proper opening entry in general journal form. The date is January 1st.

List of Assets

Cash on Hand	$500
Desk	300
Filing Cabinet	120
Camera	975
Table	205

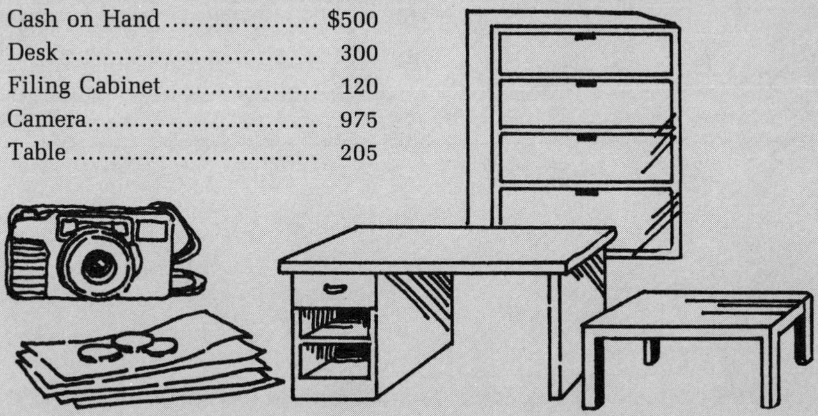

6. Walt Caley has a business cleaning offices in Victoria. He keeps all his equipment in his truck and travels to each job site to do his work. Shown below are the first entries of Walt's business. Journalize them in a general journal, using the rules for journalizing that you have studied in this chapter.

Transactions

Oct. 1: Started the business with $3 000 in the bank, and a van worth about $8 000. (*Opening Entry*).

1: Borrowed $3 000 from the bank and put it into the business Bank account. He plans to repay this loan within one year.

2: Bought some cleaning equipment which cost $1 200. Paid by cheque, #1.

3: Bought more cleaning equipment on account from Office Cleaning Supply at a cost of $650. Walt promised to pay for this equipment in 30 days.

4: Walt decided to pay the bank back $1 000 on the bank loan since he did not really need the money. Cheque #2.

5: Walt withdrew $40 from the business for personal use. Cheque #3.

7. Takeo Mori has just arranged to set up a studio in Vancouver, B.C. to give instruction in karate (Figure 3-3). The opening entry and transactions for Takeo's new business are given below, as well as his chart of accounts. The business name is "Mori Karate."
   (a) Journalize the opening entry (July 1) and the transactions (July 2-6) in general journal form.
   (b) Post to the general ledger accounts.
   (c) Take a formal trial balance.
   (d) Prepare a balance sheet as of July 6, 19 ____.

Transactions

Jul. 1: Owner invested $6 000 cash into the business (Bank a/c).
2: Spent $675 on supplies by writing cheque #1.
4: Bought judo mats, $3 600. Paid by cheque #2.
5: Went to Fitness Design and bought new furniture for the gym, $1 260, on account.
6: Takeo withdrew $240 from the bank for personal use, cheque #3.

Figure 3-3
Takeo has a business teaching karate. He has asked you to help him do his bookkeeping.

Chart of Accounts

Cash on Hand	1
Bank	2
Supplies	3
Equipment	4
Furniture	5
Bank Loan	20
Accounts Payable	21
T. Mori, Capital	30
T. Mori, Drawings	31

8. Karen Miller has just graduated and is opening a practice as a chiropractor. She is renting a small office in the suburbs in Edmonton and is just about ready for her first patients. The opening entry and the transactions are given below, as well as her chart of accounts.
   (a) Journalize the transactions in general journal form.
   (b) Post to the general ledger accounts.
   (c) Take a tape trial balance.
   (d) Prepare a balance sheet dated March 31, 19 ____.

Transactions

Mar. 25: Dr. Miller started with $3 800 in the bank.

26: Bought medical supplies. Paid $800 by writing cheque #1 on the business Bank account.

26: Bought office furniture, a desk, chairs, and filing cabinets for medical records. The cost was $934 (cheque #2).

27: Bought medical equipment costing $3 275, on account from Wells Medical Supply Co. Ltd.

Chart of Accounts

Cash on Hand	1
Bank	2
Medical Supplies	3
Equipment	4
Furniture	5
Accounts Payable	20
Loan Payable	21
K. Miller, Capital	30
K. Miller, Drawings	31

9. Shane Gyorki is a 16-year-old still in school. He has decided to operate his own pool cleaning service for people who hate to open their pools in the spring. The business name is *TEEN POOL-CLEEN*. The information about Shane's new business is given below.
   (a) Journalize the transactions in general journal form.
   (b) Post to the general ledger accounts.
   (c) Take a formal trial balance.
   (d) Prepare a balance sheet as of April 30, 19 ____.

Transactions

Apr. 15: Borrowed $1 500 from his father. Put it into the bank account to set up for the business.

18: Wrote cheque #1 to buy cleaning supplies for business, $89.79.

19: Draws out cash, $25.00. Cheque #2.

20: Bought a vacuum for draining the water off winter covers. Cost was $820. Cheque #3.

26: Bought a 10-speed bike and a special trailer for tools and supplies. Cost $210.90. It was bought on account from Pedal Power.

Chart of Accounts

Cash on Hand	1
Bank	2
Supplies	3
Equipment	4
Bike & Trailer	5
Bank Loan	20
Accounts Payable	21
Loan Payable (Dad)	22
S. Gyorki, Capital	30
S. Gyorki, Drawings	31

Review Questions

1. In a general journal, what do the letters PR stand for?
2. (a) What is an "opening entry"?
   (b) Would an opening entry always have one account to debit and two accounts to credit? Why or why not?
   (c) Would a business have an opening entry at the start of each month? Explain.
3. What always gets written at the top left hand corner of a general journal in the Date column?
4. Why do we indent credit entries in a general journal?
5. Is the wording used on the explanation line of a journal entry very important?
6. Match the terms on the left with their explanations on the right.

(a) Journalizing	(1) A tape or listing which checks to see if the ledger is in balance.
(b) Posting	(2) Recording entries in the GJ.
(c) Taking a trial balance	(3) Transferring entries from a journal to the ledger.

7. Copy the accounts below in your notebook and indicate which side each account increases on, the debit side or the credit side.

Bank	
Increase	

Accounts Payable		Automobile		Bank Loan	

Supplies		Tim Nash, Capital		Equipment	

8. Look at the general journal entries below and write out a clear explanation for each transaction in your notes.

GENERAL JOURNAL

(a) PAGE 5

DATE		PARTICULARS	PR	DEBIT	CREDIT
May	1	Bank Loan		3000 —	
		Bank			3000 —

(b) PAGE 10

DATE		PARTICULARS	PR	DEBIT	CREDIT
Aug.	8	A. Keaton, Drawings		75 —	
		Bank			75 —

(c) PAGE 1

DATE 19—		PARTICULARS	PR	DEBIT	CREDIT
Jan.	2	Truck		18 000 —	
		Accounts Payable - Webber Motors			18 000 —

(d) PAGE 15

DATE		PARTICULARS	PR	DEBIT	CREDIT
Dec.	31	Truck		18 000 —	
		Equipment		12 000 —	
		Gus Pelizzaro, Capital			30 000 —

(e) PAGE 4

DATE		PARTICULARS	PR	DEBIT	CREDIT
April	22	Bank		2500 —	
		Loan Payable – Aunt Sadie			2500 —

Challenge Questions

1. Two friends in grade 12 have just borrowed money from the government on a Student Venture Program. They are planning to operate a bicycle rental business in the city, renting bicycles to local people and tourists during the months of June, July, August, and September. Tell them what an asset is and name the assets you think they will likely need to run their business.

2. We live in a world of initials and symbolic names, such as IBM, GM, and CGE. In Chapter 3 you saw the following initials—GJ, GL, PR, DR, and CR. What do each of them stand for?

3. Look at the account below. The bank account normally has a debit balance, so how could this possibly have happened? Let your mind run wild on this one. There are at least three explanations!

ACCOUNT: Bank NO. 2

DATE		PARTICULARS	PR	DEBIT	CREDIT	DR CR	BALANCE
April	30					CR	125 —

4. Bonus Question—What do the initials in Question 2 mean: IBM, GM, and CGE? (Hint: They are names of famous businesses.)

5. Check the want ads in a newspaper and state the highest salary you can find for a corporation president or chief executive officer. Report back to the class and see if anyone is interested in the job.

Review Case

Josephine Tarsey operates a studio where she paints portraits of people for a fee. She is studying the balance sheet given to her by her accountant shortly after she opened her business. Look at the balance sheet and help Josephine answer the questions she has about her balance sheet.

Jo's Portraits
Balance Sheet
as at October 31, 19 ___

Assets		**Liabilities**	
Cash on Hand	$ 100	Accounts Payable	$ 275
Bank	2 400	Bank Loan	1 125
Painting Supplies	620	Total Liabilities	$1 400
Equipment	500	**Owner's Equity**	
Furniture	900	J. Tarsey, Capital	3 120
	$4 520		$4 520

Questions

1. How many "accounts" does Josephine have?
2. Can Josephine afford to pay off her creditors? Explain.
3. Josephine is wondering if the business is worth $3 120. Explain what her capital figure represents.
4. Explain to Josephine for how long her balance sheet is good.

Challenge Case

Pretend that you are an accountant. A client named Jean Kitchen has come to see you for help. She is starting up a new business at home doing secretarial work for clients on her computer. Listen to her story and then do the accounting work for her. (All of your work will take place November 1st.)

> "I had a great idea about setting up a service in my home using a computer to do secretarial work for clients. This morning I opened a business Bank account with $4 000 cash. Later this morning I went to a computer store and bought a computer system for $2 000 cash. I bought $170 worth of computer supplies—diskettes, paper, and two ribbons for the printer. Since I didn't have quite enough money left to buy a desk for the computer I went to the bank manager and got a loan for $1 700 for the purchase. Finally, I bought a filing cabinet for the business, on account from Grey Sationery for $120. Can you get me started in my business?"

Do the following for your client.

1. Journalize her "opening entry."
2. Journalize the other transactions into a general journal.
3. Set up a general ledger and post the general journal.
4. Take a trial balance of the general ledger.
5. Prepare a formal balance sheet for her as at November 1st.

Take-a-Break

1. **What's Your Theory?**

   Ten students are enrolled in an accounting class. The teacher is so wrapped up in numbers that she seats the students in the order shown to the right. What system does she use?

   1. Don Edwards
   2. Robert Worden
   3. Edith Reed
   4. Rolf Ourster
   5. Jeff Ives
   6. Jessie Xander
   7. Rose Ventnor
   8. Leigh Thompson
   9. Toni Nesbitt
   10. Pete Norris

2. In the grid below, circle 6 numbers that add up to 21 (Hint: Let your mind wander!)

   1 1 1
   3 3 3
   5 5 5
   9 9 9

3. **Three's Company**

   The three columns below all have accounting terms from Chapter 3, but they are all jumbled up. Select a word from each of the three columns so that it makes sense and becomes a useful accounting phrase.

	Column 1	Column 2	Column 3
(a)	chart	each	account
(b)	business	by	owner
(c)	indent	decimals	first
(d)	books	of	used
(e)	bought	of	line
(f)	withdrawn	into	entry
(g)	debit	opening	credit
(h)	no	blank	ledger
(i)	one	entry	account
(j)	post	on	accounts

Chapter 4 Revenue and Expense Transactions

Objectives

By the end of this chapter, you will be able to

1. journalize sales and expense transactions;
2. recognize an expanded chart of accounts; and
3. know how to prepare an Income Statement and a Balance Sheet from a trial balance.

4.1 Service Businesses

The main focus of this textbook is to learn accounting by looking at **service businesses.** These are businesses that sell their services, rather than goods. Here are some examples of service businesses that are taken from the yellow pages of a phone book. All of these people have a skill that they offer to the public, in exchange for money, of course. Many of these service businesses may exist in your own community. And depending on the training and education required for each type of service, you and I will pay what the service demands. Take a look at the list and see if you can mentally decide which type of service or profession would charge us the highest fee and which one might be the cheapest.

Accounting & Bookkeeping Systems

CAPITAL BOOKKEEPING&FINANCIAL SERVICES
See Ad Und Bookkeeping Service
1 Spring ---------- Norwich 863-3711

HORVATH O'MALLEY & CO
GENERAL ACCOUNTING
INCOME TAX SERVICE
56 Ridout W ---------- Tilsnbg 842-9502

Automobile Body Repairing & Painting

A-1 AUTO BODY
COMPLETE COLLISION SERVICE
FIBERGLASS & INSURANCE WORK
OIL UNDERCOATING, FREE ESTIMATES
84 Young ---------- Simcoe 426-2480

After Hours Complete Car Care Service 10 Front -- Norwich 863-2684
(SEE ADVERTISEMENT THIS PAGE)
Bob Jones Collision RR1 Simcoe ---- Simcoe 426-4795
(SEE ADVERTISEMENT THIS PAGE)
BODY WORKS THE 451 QueenswayW -- Simcoe 426-3464

Bathroom Remodelling

ALL-GLO GLAZING
BATHTUB
REFINISHING
IN HOME SERVICE
3 YR WRITTEN GUARANTEE
COLOUR CHANGES AVAILABLE
FREE ESTIMATES
CALL COLLECT
1230 Wilton ---------- London 455-1344

BATHTUB KING REFINISHERS
BATHTUB, SINK & CERAMIC TILE
REGLAZING
A Full Line Of Brass Fixtures
24 Lysanda Av ---------- London 681-5140

Banks

Bank Of Montreal
Branch 160 Broadway ---------- Tilsnbg 842-6467
Commercial Banking ---------- 863-3410
Commercial Banking ---------- Tilsnbg 842-9055
Commercial Banking ---------- Delhi 582-0790
Commercial Banking ---------- Langtn 875-4467
116 King ---------- Delhi 582-2650
30 Main W ---------- Norwich 863-3022
Queen ---------- Langtn 875-4555
Bank Of Nova Scotia 199 Broadway -- Tilsnbg 842-8496
Bank Of Nova Scotia WashingtonGrand&Broadway -- Tilsnbg 842-8496
CANADIAN IMPERIAL BANK OF COMMERCE 200 Broadway -- Tilsnbg 842-7331
Delhi Br 172 Main ---------- Delhi 582-0570
Langton Br Queen ---------- Langtn 875-4465
Norwich Br 15 MainW ---------- Norwich 863-2016

Barbers

ANDRE'S BARBER SHOP
MEN'S HAIRSTYLING
OPEN
TUES TIL THURS 9-5:30
FRI 9-8 SAT 9-5
AMPLE PARKING
APPOINTMENTS NOT NECESSARY
43 Brock E ---------- Tilsnbg 842-7882

Charles Wagner Barber Shop 3–A Potters -- Tilsnbg 842-4025
Debbie's Hair Design RR1 Courtland -- Langtn 875-2696
Generation Gap Mens Hairstyling 21 King -- Delhi 582-3696
John and Jim's Barber Shop 17 BrockE -- Tilsnbg 842-4760
Mountain's Barber Shop 28 MainW -- Norwich 863-2108

The Barber Shop
Men's Hairstyling
169 Broadway ---------- Tilsnbg 842-8185

Baseball–Clubs

Toronto Blue Jays Baseball Club ExhibitionStadium -- Toronto 416 595-0077

Beauty Salons

Angie's Hair Place 171 Second ---------- Delhi 582-3788
Anita's Hair Design 40 Broadway ---- Tilsnbg 842-7292
Beauty Nook Main ---------- PortRowan 586-3933
Cameo Hair Styling NorfolkMall ---------- Tilsnbg 842-7171
(SEE ADVERTISEMENT NEXT PAGE)
Capn Hair Styles 237 Main ---------- Delhi 582-0460

CHARLOTTE'S HAIR SHOP
OPEN TUESDAY TO SATURDAY
NAIL TIPPING
UNISEX STYLING
16 London E ---------- Tilsnbg 842-4006

Clips And Curls 5 MainE ---------- Norwich 863-2047
COLONIAL HAIR FASHIONS 1-D LibraryLn

Contractors–General

A R C INDUSTRIES
INDUSTRIAL SUB CONTRACTING
PALLETS & CRATES
WOODWORKING
126 Concession E ---------- Tilsnbg 842-8406

Cook Mark A Enterprises 14 Andover ---------- 842-6734
Dedrick Bros Excavating Ltd RR1 Delhi

Electric Contractors

Bruce John&Sons 34 NorthcourtW -- Norwich 863-3242
CARROLL ELECTRIC (1982) LTD 25 Spruce -- Tilsnbg 842-8486

D & D ELECTRIC
ALL TYPES OF
MAINTENANCE & CONSTRUCTION
4 Centennial Dr ---------- Tavistock 655-2924
Residence ---------- Woodstock 539-6673

DARLINGTON WIRING & PLUMBING LTD
FARM RESIDENTIAL COMMERCIAL
RENOVATIONS & INSTALLATIONS
Kiln Yards
RR 1 Delhi ---------- Langtn 875-2571

DE WACHTER A ELECTRIC (1984) LTD RR1 Otterville -- Ottervl 879-6636

Insurance Agents

BUTLER JAMES M
Co-Operators Insce Services
HOME - AUTO - FARM
33 Victoria ---------- Norwich 863-2743

Lawn Mowers–Sales & Service

BOLENS LAWN MOWERS—
AUTHORIZED SALES & SERVICE
LANGTON
SINNAEVE EQUIPMENT CENTRE Queen -- Langtn 875-4439

Davidson Motorcycle RR1 Norwich -- Norwich 863-6312
(SEE ADVERTISEMENT THIS PAGE)

Lawyers

Aicken Lois 237 Main ---------- Delhi 582-1552
BATTIN JAMES G 35 Harvey -- Tilsnbg 842-9079
BEATTY&BENNETT 487 Princess -- Woodstock 537-6629
Beatty David J 487 Princess ---- Woodstock 537-6629
Bennett Wm J 487 Princess ---- Woodstock 537-6629

4.2 Sale of Services

Service businesses and professionals will not continue to exist unless they make a profit from selling their services. Until now, we have not mentioned business profits but it is time to do so. We will do this by studying a skilled tradesman, and some of his accounting transactions.

Our example is an electrician, named John Bruce. When John does some wiring in someone's house, for example, to put a new light in the basement, John has "sold his services." In simple terms, John has made a sale. There are two ways customers can pay John for his services—by cash, or by charging the amount owing to a later date. Whether John's customers pay cash or whether they charge may not make much difference to John as long as they pay their bill within a reasonable time (usually 30 days). To record John's sale, we need a new account called **Sales**.

If we use T-accounts to record John's sale of services, the entry in T-accounts would look like this:

Sold services for Cash, $45

Cash		Sales	
45			45

Note: Whenever services are sold we credit Sales.

If John did some electrical wiring for another customer and the customer did not pay in cash, then the entry in the accounts would be:

Sold services on account, $80

Accounts Receivable		Sales	
80			80

Note: Whenever services are sold we credit Sales.

Notice that in each of the transactions above, John made a sale and we credited Sales each time. Only the debit side of the entry was different. The basic rule then is that with cash sales you debit Bank and credit Sales, and with charge sales, you debit Accounts Receivable and credit Sales. If we express this rule formally, it would be:

Sales	
Decrease Debit	Increase Credit

Look carefully at this new rule and commit it to memory—it's an important one. You should notice that the old rules about debit and credit have not changed:

Debit means left and Credit means right.

You may be wondering when you will have a debit in the sales account. This will happen if a customer is not satisfied with the service and we have to refund her/his money from the sale. We will then debit Sales.

"I found him working in the stockroom, J.D. He's perfect!"

4.3 Accounting Rules

You now have five basic rules about accounting entries that you must know in order to make progress in accounting.

Assets	
Incr. Dr	Decr. Cr

Liabilities	
Decr. Dr	Incr. Cr

Capital	
Decr. Dr	Incr. Cr

Drawings	
Incr. Dr	Decr. Cr

Revenue	
Decr. Dr	Incr. Cr

Notice that the term "revenue" is used in the T-accounts above instead of sales. This is because a business can have more than one type of **revenue** and the heading Revenue is a group heading just like Assets is a group heading.

John Bruce is a skilled plumber as well as an electrician (Figure 4-1),

Figure 4-1
A tradesman who is both a plumber and an electrician has two sales accounts in his General Ledger to represent these two services.

and he could keep two Sales accounts. Both of these accounts would be part of the REVENUE group in John's General Ledger.

Sales (Electric Services)	

Sales (Plumbing Services)	

Notice the short forms *Dr* and *Cr* in the T-accounts above. *Dr* is the short form for *Debit* and *Cr* is the short form for *Credit*. It doesn't make sense, does it? The form for *Debit* should be *De*, but it's not; it's *Dr*. Nobody knows why; we just have to accept it. *Debit* is *Dr* and *Credit* is Cr. You will see these short forms all through your study of accounting.

We can update our fundamental accounting equation as well. When we make a sale, this increases the worth of the business and so we can add the heading Revenue to the right hand side of the fundamental equation where the owner's equity is.

Assets = Liabilities + Owner's Equity + Revenue

4.4 General Journal Entries

In the last chapter you learned that businesses do not use T-accounts for their accounting entries. Therefore, the two sales entries for John Bruce's business should be put in general journal form.

GENERAL JOURNAL

PAGE 2

DATE		PARTICULARS	PR	DEBIT	CREDIT
Aug.	5	Bank		45 –	
		Sales			45 –
		Cash sale of service			
	6	Accounts Receivable		80 –	
		Sales			80 –
		Charge sale of service			

4.5 Chart of Accounts

When we use the general journal, we will be posting entries to 3-column accounts, but before we do that, we have to add a new number to the **chart of accounts.** We will number Revenue accounts starting at #40.

Assets	1-19
Liabilities	20-29
Owner's Equity	30-39
Revenue	40-49

4.6 Posting

Look at the general journal entries back in Section 4.4 and see if you understand the posting process into the ledger accounts below.

ACCOUNT: Bank NO. 2

DATE 19__		PARTICULARS	PR	DEBIT	CREDIT	DR CR	BALANCE
Feb.	1		GJ2	45 –		DR	45 –

ACCOUNT: Accounts Receivable NO. 3

DATE 19__		PARTICULARS	PR	DEBIT	CREDIT	DR CR	BALANCE
Feb.	1		GJ2	80 –		DR	80 –

ACCOUNT: Sales NO. 40

DATE 19__		PARTICULARS	PR	DEBIT	CREDIT	DR CR	BALANCE
Feb.	1		GJ2		45 –	CR	45 –
	1		GJ2		80 –	CR	125 –

4.7 Expenses

The second new type of account we need to study is "expenses." The **expenses** of a business are the costs of keeping it running. When John Bruce operates his electrical business, he has many costs to pay to keep his business operating. Some of his costs would be:

van expenses	office expenses	telephone expenses
bank interest	wages expense	accounting expenses

To record the expenses of a business, we need to have new accounts called expense accounts, and we have to know that we debit expense accounts. Here is an expense transaction. Look it over and notice how the expense is recorded in the T-accounts below.

Bought gasoline for the van, $35 and paid by cheque #18.

Van Expense	
35	

Bank	
	35

Another expense might involve interest he has to pay the bank on a bank loan. The entry to record this in T-accounts is:

The bank charged his account with $95 interest on a bank loan.

Bank Interest Expense	
95	

Bank	
	95

You can see from the above two examples that an entry to an expense account is always a debit. The credit side of expense transactions may be a credit to the bank account, when we pay the expense with cash. It could also be an **on account** transaction, an expense the business has incurred that it does not pay immediately. We can use a telephone bill as an example to understand this point. Assume that John Bruce receives a telephone bill for his business for $62. When the bill comes in, John has two choices:

(1) Pay the telephone bill immediately.

(2) Set the telephone bill up as amount owing.

If John pays the bill immediately then the entry would be recorded into his accounts this way:

Telephone Expense	
62	

Bank	
	62

If he wants to show that he has incurred an expense, but will pay for it later, the entry will be recorded this way:

Telephone Expense	
62	

Accounts Payable	
	62

Since we only use T-accounts to learn theory, we should take John's expense transactions and record them in general journal form, just for practice. Three expense transactions for John's business are recorded in general journal form to the right along with the postings to the general ledger accounts.

GENERAL JOURNAL

PAGE 2

DATE 19__		PARTICULARS	PR	DEBIT	CREDIT
Feb.	2	Van Expense		35 –	
		Bank			35 –
		Bought gasoline. Cheque #18			
	5	Bank Interest Expense		95 –	
		Bank			95 –
		Interest on Bank Loan			
	9	Telephone Expense		62 –	
		A/P - Bell Canada			62 –
		To set up telephone bill for			
		January as an amount owing			

GENERAL LEDGER

ACCOUNT Bank NO. 2

DATE 19__		PARTICULARS	PR	DEBIT	CREDIT	DR CR	BALANCE
Feb.	2		GJ2		35 –	DR	145 –
	5		GJ2		95 –	DR	50 –

ACCOUNT Accounts Payable NO. 21

DATE 19__		PARTICULARS	PR	DEBIT	CREDIT	DR CR	BALANCE
Feb.	9		GJ2		62 –	CR	275 –

ACCOUNT Bank Interest Expense NO. 51

DATE 19__		PARTICULARS	PR	DEBIT	CREDIT	DR CR	BALANCE
Feb.	5		GJ2	95 –		DR	180 –

ACCOUNT Telephone Expense NO. 53

DATE 19__		PARTICULARS	PR	DEBIT	CREDIT	DR CR	BALANCE
Feb.	9		GJ2	62 –		DR	62 –

ACCOUNT Van Expenses NO. 58

DATE 19__		PARTICULARS	PR	DEBIT	CREDIT	DR CR	BALANCE
Feb.	2		GJ2	35 –		DR	210 –

4.8 Chart of Accounts

In Section 4.5 we expanded the chart of accounts to include numbers for revenue. We need to add one more group of numbers for expense accounts. Check the new list.

Assets	1-19
Liabilities	20-29
Owner's Equity	30-39
Revenue	40-49
Expenses	50-59

4.9 Accounting Rules

This brings us to the last main rule for accounting. Expense accounts are always debited to increase them.

Expenses

Increase Debit	Decrease Credit

You now have six main rules for recording accounting transactions. Commit these rules to memory. All future accounting is based on these six rules of debit and credit.

Assets

Increase Debit	Decrease Credit

Liabilities

Decrease Debit	Increase Credit

Capital

	Increase Credit

Revenue

	Increase Credit

Expenses

Increase Debit	

Drawings

Increase Debit	

(Part of the rules above were omitted because they are not going to be used very often in this beginning course. Most of the time when you make accounting entries, you will credit *Sales*, debit *Expenses*, debit *Drawings*, and credit *Capital*. You will not normally use the other sides of these accounts.)

We can update our **fundamental accounting equation** for the last time. When a business incurs an expense, this decreases the worth of that business and so we can subtract any Expense accounts from the right hand side of the fundamental equation, where the owner's equity is:

Assets = Liabilities + Owner's Equity + Revenue – Expenses

4.10 The Income Statement

Once we know the figures for revenue and expenses for a business, we can determine if that business has made a **profit**, that is, money for the owner. This is the main reason for a business to exist. The balance sheet does not provide any information about profit since it does not contain the revenue and expense accounts. To calculate the profit for a business, we need to produce another financial statement called the "income statement."

"As most of you know, our company treasurer won't be with us for the next fifteen annual meetings."

An income statement is a financial statement showing the results of the operations of a business over a period of time. It is based on information from revenue and expense accounts.

We can see this more clearly by studying an example. Follow along.

Troy Gage has decided to operate a rental business at a small lake (Figure 4-2). He rents out recreation equipment, canoes, bikes, and windsurfers to customers on an hourly basis. Shown below are the revenue and expense transactions for the first week of July. After a week, Troy is anxious to know if the new business is profitable and he needs our help. Follow the accounting transactions through and you will see whether Troy has made or lost money.

T-accounts will be used instead of a general journal to speed up the recording process and to understand the point of the exercise more quickly.

Figure 4-2
Troy Gage has a business that rents windsurfers. He has hired you to see if his business is going to be profitable.

Transactions

Jul. 1: Opened the business with Rental Equipment worth $4 000, a Bank Loan for $3 000, and T. Gage, Capital $1 000.

1: Wrote cheque #1 for building rent, for one week, $45.

2: Daily cash sales were $95 (cash deposited immediately). (The business uses an account called Rental Income for Sales.)

3: Paid telephone company $62 for installation costs. Cheque #2.

4: Bank charged the business interest on the bank loan, $16.

5: Charge sale to one customer—B. Gregory, $15.

6: Cash sales for the day were $35 (deposited immediately).

8: Cash sales for the day were $65 (deposited immediately).

9: Charge sale to A. Lambton was $22.

10: Cash sales $72 (deposited immediately).

11: Paid part-time wages to a student helper, $60.

These transactions have been entered into T-accounts. They are all numbered so you can follow them from the notes above.

General Ledger

Bank	
(2) 95	45 (1)
(6) 35	62 (3)
(8) 65	16 (4)
(10) 72	60 (11)

Accounts Receivable	
(5) 15	
(9) 22	

Rental Equipment	
(1) 4 000	

Bank Loan	
	3 000 (1)

T. Gage, Capital	
	1 000 (1)

Rental Income	
	95 (2)
	15 (5)
	35 (6)
	65 (8)
	22 (9)
	72 (10)

Loan Interest	
(4) 16	

Rent Expense	
(1) 45	

Wages Expense	
(11) 60	

Telephone Expense	
(3) 62	

Once the entries have been entered into the T-accounts, we can take a trial balance. The formal trial balance for the business is shown below.

Fun-in-the-Sun
Trial Balance
July 6, 19 ___

Account	Debit	Credit
Bank	$ 84.00	
Accounts Receivable	37.00	
Rental Equipment	4 000.00	
Bank Loan		$3 000.00
T. Gage, Capital		1 000.00
Rental Income		304.00
Loan Interest	16.00	
Rent Expense	45.00	
Telephone Expense	62.00	
Wages Expense	60.00	
	$4 304.00	$4 304.00

Detecting Errors

When you take a trial balance of your work, you will often find that your trial balance does not balance. There are several reasons for this, and there are proven methods that can be successfully used to help find your errors. Try this list to detect errors.

1. *Divide the difference by "2".*

   If, for example, your trial balance columns differ by, say, $400, divide this difference by 2 and look for a $200 error. A $200 debit posted as a $200 credit causes double the error to occur.

2. *Divide the difference by "9".*

   This is called a transposition error. Whenever you switch two numbers, the resulting difference is divisible by 9. For example, if you write 85 as 58, the difference (or error) of 27 is divisible by 9. Look in your work for two numbers that you have switched around.

3. *Check your take-down.*

   This means that you may have copied the balance from the ledger account to the trial balance incorrectly. For example, the Bank account in the ledger has a balance of $525.00 and when you took a trial balance, you thought it was $52.50. Check each account balance to see if you "took it down" correctly on the trial balance.

Correcting Errors

Here are two ways to correct errors in accounting.

1. If the error occurs in a Ledger account, for example, the final balance is wrong and if the accounting work was done in pencil, you may just change the account to the correct figure. If the accounting work has been done in ink, the correction method is to draw a line through the wrong figure and write the correct figure above the incorrect one.

ACCOUNT Bank NO. 2

DATE 19__		PARTICULARS	PR	DEBIT	CREDIT	DR CR	BALANCE
Feb.	5		GJ4	50 —		DR	~~375 —~~ 325 —

2. Sometimes a correcting entry should be journalized. For example, if the Automobile Expense account was debited instead of Advertising Expense, the journal entry shown below should be made and posted.

GENERAL JOURNAL

PAGE 7

DATE 19__		PARTICULARS	PR	DEBIT	CREDIT
April	10	Advertising Expense		112 50	
		Telephone Expense			112 50
		To correct journal error			

Once we have recorded all the revenue and expenses for a given time period, it is possible to find out if the business has made any profit. The basic formula to do this is:

Revenue – Expenses = Net Income

Net income is the amount left after expenses have been deducted from revenue.

The term "net income" used to be "net profit" a few years ago but modern accounting now uses the word "income" instead of "profit." They mean the same thing, but we will use the modern word.

Let's put this formula to work on the trial balance that we drew up for Fun-in-the-Sun. We only have to use the revenue and expenses accounts from the trial balance because the other accounts belong on a balance sheet. Here's the Income Statement for Fun-in-the-Sun.

Fun-in-the-Sun
Income Statement
For the Week ended July 7, 19 ___

Revenue:		
Rental Income		$304.00
Expenses:		
Loan Interest	$16.00	
Rent Expense	45.00	
Telephone Expense	62.00	
Wages Expense	60.00	183.00
Net Income		$121.00

Here's the Income Statement again with some special things drawn to your attention about neatness and accounting style. Try to follow these guidelines for work that will impress other people.

Fun-in-the-Sun
Income Statement
For the Week ended July 7, 19 ___

Revenue:		
Rental Income		$304.00
Expenses:		
Loan Interest	$16.00	
Rent Expense	45.00	
Telephone Expense	62.00	
Wages Expense	60.00	183.00
Net Income		$121.00

covers a certain time period, not one day like a Balance Sheet

dollar sign at the top of a column of figures

accounts line up and they are in alphabetical order

dollar sign beside a total

4.11 Financial Statements for a Service Business

Now we need to review two key things you have learned so far.

1. How to prepare a Balance Sheet.
2. How to prepare an Income Statement.

These two documents, both of which you have seen before, are the two most important **financial statements** produced by a business and it will be worthwhile to spend a bit more time looking at them before we finish this chapter.

Let's go back to Chapter 1 to an old item called the fundamental accounting equation. It looked like this:

Assets = Liabilities + Owner's Equity

In this chapter you learned about Revenue and Expense accounts and we expanded the fundamental accounting equation on the right hand side. We can split the fundamental accounting equation into two parts so that each part corresponds to the two main financial statements.

Assets = Liabilities + Owner's Equity + Revenue – Expenses

Balance Sheet (Assets = Liabilities + Owner's Equity)

Income Statement (Revenue – Expenses)

Here is another way of looking at this split.

Dr. B. Fuzzy, Veterinarian
Trial Balance
January 31, 19 ___

Account	Debit	Credit	
Bank	$ 300		Balance Sheet Accounts
Accounts Receivable	1 700		
Supplies	250		
Equipment	8 150		
Accounts Payable		$ 295	
Bank Loan		1 405	
Capital		6 000	
Revenue		9 000	*Income Statement Accounts*
Advertising Expense	390		
Loan Interest	515		
Wages Expense	5 395		
	$16 700	$16 700	

4.12 Financial Statements

Here are the two key financial statements using the trial balance for Dr. Fuzzy from Section 4.11.

Dr. B. Fuzzy, Veterinarian
Income Statement
For the Month Ended January 31, ____

Revenue		$9 000
Expenses:		
Advertising	$ 390	
Loan Interest	515	
Wages Expense	5 395	6 300
Net Income		$2 700

Dr. B. Fuzzy, Veterinarian
Balance Sheet
January 31, 19 ____

Assets		**Liabilities**		
Bank	$ 300	Accounts Payable		$ 295
Accounts Receivable	1 700	Bank Loan		1 405
Supplies	250	Total liabilities		$ 1 700
Equipment	8 150	**Owner's Equity**		
		Dr. B. Fuzzy, Capital	$6 000	
		Add: Net Income	2 700	8 700
	$10 400			$10 400

The net income on the income statement is an important link between the income statement and the balance sheet. Once you find the net income for a business, it is added to the Capital in the Owner's Equity section of the balance sheet. The reason for this is that the net income increases the worth of the business. When we increase the worth of a business, we do it in the Owner's Equity section. Here is the link.

Income Statement

Revenue	$9 000
Expenses	6 300
Net Income	$2 700

Balance Sheet

Owner's Equity		
Dr. B. Fuzzy, Capital	$6 000	
Add: Net Income	2 700	8 700
		$10 400

Look at the balance sheet again. The Owner's Equity section tells us that Dr. Fuzzy had equity of $6 000 at thc start of January, but by the end of January, his equity had increased by $2 700, because of the net income for the month, to $8 700. Therefore, his new Capital at the end of January is now $8 700.

Just a couple of reminders before we finish this section. The income statement shows the results of operations for a certain time period (in this case, one month). The balance sheet shows a financial picture as of a specific day, January 31st. The two financial statements have two different purposes.

4.13 Summary

This chapter is important because it gives you a package of rules for accounting that is very useful (look again at Section 4.6). It reviews the fundamental accounting equation that we studied at the start of the course. And it also shows you where the two main financial statements, the *Balance Sheet* and *Income Statement* come from and the link between these statements. In Chapter 5 you will study another document called a ''worksheet'' which will help you understand the link even better.

By now, you should be able to

1. journalize revenue and expense transactions;
2. recognize an expanded chart of accounts; and
3. know how to prepare an Income Statement and a Balance Sheet from a trial balance.

Dictionary of Terms

Chart of Accounts A list of all the accounts and their numbers used by a business.

Expenses Costs incurred by a business for daily operations.

Fundamental Accounting Equation
Assets = Liabilities + Owner's Equity + Revenue − Expenses

Financial Statements The income statement and the balance sheet.

Income Statement A financial statement showing the results of the operations of a business over a specific time period.

Net Income The amount left after expenses have been deducted from revenue.

On Account A term which refers to an amount owing on goods or services purchased which are not paid for immediately.

Profit A term meaning the same thing as net income.

Revenue A heading referring to all the sales or income accounts of a business.

Service Business A business which sells specific skills as opposed to the sale of merchandise.

Sales A revenue account of a business.

Exercises

1. Identify the following accounts as an Asset (A), Liability (L), Owner's Equity (OE), Revenue (R), or Expense (E).

(a) Accounts Payable	(d) Sales	(g) Bank Interest
(b) Accounts Receivable	(e) Cash on Hand	(h) Wages
(c) Commissions Earned	(f) Drawings	(i) Van

2. Find the missing amounts in these fundamental accounting equations.

	Assets	=	Liabilities	+	Owner's Equity	+	Revenue	–	Expenses
(a)	45 000	=	?	+	37 000	+	8 400	–	6 400
(b)	70 000	=	12 400	+	?	+	12 000	–	10 200
(c)	97 230	=	14 670	+	80 190	+	28 660	–	?
(d)	?	=	57 200	+	13 800	+	95 100	–	69 300
(e)	29 653	=	3 490	+	20 002	+	?	–	18 115

3. Journalize these transactions into a General Journal, page 10.

Jul. 1: Paid the newspaper for advertising, $230. cheque #45.
3: Sold services on account to Trudy Moore, $85.
3: Received the telephone bill for June from Bell Canada. Set it up as an account payable, $75.
6: Cash sale of services, $375.
8: Received the light bill for the month of June, $89. Paid by cheque, #46.
12: Sale on account to J. Webster, $510.
15: Paid for car repairs by cheque, #47, $201.

4. Journalize these transactions into a General Journal, page 4.

Mar. 2: Cash sale of services, $80.
4: Paid the monthly rent by cheque, $700. Cheque #142.
7: Paid the employee wages, $1 200. Cheque #143.
8: Sold services on account to K. Hurlbut, $225.
12: Sold services for cash, $365.
18: Wrote cheque #144 to Texaco for gasoline for business car, $192.
31: Sold services on account to S. Parker for $444.

5. Journalize these transactions into a General Journal, page 1. Post to 3-column ledger accounts and take a trial balance.

Dec. 1:	Jim Ross opened a business with $5 000 in the bank.
1:	Paid monthly rent for the store, $800. Cheque #1.
2:	Sale of services for cash, $450.
6:	Bought some advertising on radio, $205. Cheque #2.
7:	Sale of services on account to L. Hudson, $187.
12:	Cash sale of services, $222.
15:	Bought furniture for the business on account from Patton Furniture, $1 600.
18:	Paid wages to employees, $610. Cheque #3.
20:	Bought some tools on account from Snapp-On, $1 340.
28:	Cash sale of services, $173.

6. Given the trial balance below for a seamstress, use the accounts you need to prepare an income statement in proper form. The trial balance covers the month of September, 19 ____.

Helen Donald
Trial Balance
September 30, 19 ____

Account	Debit	Credit
Bank	$1 776.18	
Accounts Receivable	34.00	
Sewing Equipment	1 480.28	
Accounts Payable		$ 602.41
H. Donald, Capital		1 584.02
H. Donald, Drawings	245.00	
Sewing Income		1 765.92
Accounting Expense	50.00	
Advertising Expense	102.70	
Bank Charges	18.35	
Heat & Light	204.03	
Telephone	41.81	
	$3 952.35	$3 952.35

7. Open the Ledger below in your workbook. Journalize the transactions into a general journal. Post to the ledger, and take a trial balance to check your accuracy. The date is March 31, 19___.

General Ledger

Account	Debit	Credit
Cash on Hand	50	
Bank Balance	1 182	
Accounts Receivable	6 430	
Supplies	1 270	
Equipment	3 990	
Capital		?
Drawings	310	
Accounts Payable		1 675
Sales		8 850
Advertising Expense	820	
Wages Expense	5 240	

Transactions

(1) Received $430 cash for Accounts Receivable. Deposited immediately.

(2) Bought $1 400 worth of supplies from The Factory on account.

(3) Bought supplies costing $100. Wrote a cheque, #1.

(4) Paid $675 cash to the creditors to reduce the Accounts Payable. Cheque #2.

(5) Sold services for $810 cash. Deposited into the bank account.

(6) Paid for radio ads, $400 (station CWIK). Cheque #3.

(7) Sold services on account for $615.00.

(8) Paid employee wages, $118.00, by cheque, #4.

8. Look carefully at the income statement below. Check the rules in Section 4.10 and describe four things wrong with this statement.

Parker's Travel Agency
Income Statement
as at December 31, 19 ___

Revenue:		
Travel Income		$50 000
Expenses:		
Advertising	6 000	
Wages	22 000	
Office	3 000	
Utilities	7 000	
		$12 000

9. Set up a ledger that has eleven 3-column accounts for John Wallet. The ledger should have the following accounts. (Make sure you put the balances on the correct side of the account.)

   Bank $2 000.00; Accounts Receivable $3 225.50; Painting Supplies $2 870.20; Van $12 000.00; Accounts Payable $563.90; John Wallet, Capital, $___?___; Sales $32 556.00; Advertising Expense $310.75; Repairs Expense $123.53; Van Expenses $3 002.94; Wages Expense, $16 485.59.

   (a) Journalize these transactions in general journal form.
   (b) Post to the general ledger.
   (c) Take a tape trial balance of the general ledger.

   Transactions for May

   May 1: Sold services for $620 on account to J. McLellan.
   2: Paid all balances owing on Accounts Payable, by cheque, #1.
   4: Bought gasoline for the van, $32.00. Wrote a cheque, #2.
   7: Wrote a cheque to the local newspaper to cover advertising for the month, $81.30, #3.
   7: Sold services for cash $1 229.00. Deposited into bank.
   8: Repaired a painting gun and the cost was $52.75. Wrote a cheque for the bill, #4.

10. Given the trial balance below, prepare an income statement and a balance sheet for this business. Do not forget that you have to transfer the net income from the income statement to the Owner's Equity section of the balance sheet to complete the balance sheet. The trial balance covers the month of August.

Don's Signs
Trial Balance
August 31, 19 ___

#	Account	Debit	Credit
1	Cash on Hand	50.00	
2	Bank	1 180.50	
3	Accounts Receivable	860.00	
4	Equipment	5 200.00	
9	Van	13 000.00	
20	Bank Loan		3 000.00
21	Accounts Payable		410.20
30	D. Long, Capital		?
40	Sales		8 657.25
41	Advertising Expense	444.02	
44	Supplies Expense	2 387.30	
46	Telephone Expense	102.07	
47	Utilities Expense	88.91	
49	Wages Expense	3 323.23	
		?	?

Review Questions

1. In this chapter you learned about people performing services. Assume that you own your own home; list four skilled people that you could hire for repairs in your home. An example would be an electrician.

2. What are the short forms for "Debit" and Credit"?

3. Draw these six T-accounts in your workbook. Then, without looking at your text, indicate which side each of the accounts increases or decreases on.

Sales | Expenses | Assets

Drawings | Liabilities | Capital

4. A friend of yours is thinking about starting a business making toys in her basement. She knows nothing about accounting but she has heard something about needing a ''ledger'' and a ''chart of accounts.'' Explain to her what these terms mean.

5. Do a balance sheet and an income statement cover the same time period? Explain.

6. List six accounts that we would find on a balance sheet and six accounts that we would find on an income statement.

7. What are the rules about dollar signs on an income statement?

8. Indicate whether each of these accounts normally has a debit (Dr) or a credit (Cr) balance.

   (a) Bank
   (b) Bank Loan
   (c) Bank Charges
   (d) Land
   (e) Accounts Receivable
   (f) Accounts Payable
   (g) Advertising Expense
   (h) K. Kong, Capital
   (i) Sales
   (j) Telephone Expense
   (k) Drawings
   (l) Telephone Expense

9. The sentences below are missing the word '' debit'' or ''credit.'' Write the appropriate missing word in your workbook.

   (a) The only side of the Drawings account we will use will be the __________ side.
   (b) Bank Charges is really an Expense account and therefore we put entries on the __________ side.
   (c) A carpenter who sold his services would __________ the Sales account.
   (d) Decreases in the Bank Loan are __________ entries.
   (e) When a customer makes a cash payment on account we __________ the Accounts Receivable account.
   (f) When the owner invests money into the business it is a __________ to the Capital account.
   (g) If a business borrowed money from the bank, we would have to __________ the liability Bank Loan.

Challenge Questions

1. How could you end up with a
   (a) debit entry in the Sales account?
   (b) credit entry in an Expense account?

2. The accounts below are all mixed up. There are accounts that only belong on a balance sheet and accounts that belong on an income statement. Select the Income Statement accounts and prepare a formal income statement for ''Pat's Hairdressing'' for the year ended December 31, 19 ____.

   Heat Expense $612.67; Bank Loan $600; Property Taxes $555.94; Accounts Payable $231; Hairdressing Income $18 995.67; Light Expense $447.67; Wages $567.70; Bank $182.95; Advertising $333.06; Miscellaneous Expense $58.85; and Equipment $6 754.29.

Review Case

Mike Conlon is a carpenter who will build anything from kitchen cupboards to a new house. His wife Katie keeps the books and makes sure that everything balances. She has just taken off the trial balance below and is about to prepare the financial statements for Mike's business for April. Prepare the income statement for her and then answer the questions.

Mike Conlon, Carpenter
Trial Balance
April 30, 19 ____

Accounts	Debit	Credit
Cash on Hand	$ 50.00	
Bank	3 500.00	
Accounts Receivable	3 330.80	
Tools	4 700.00	
Machinery	8 948.20	
Accounts Payable		$3 555.13
M. Conlon, Capital		?
Sales		7 620.00
Advertising Expenses	78.00	
Bank Charges	24.52	
Heat & Light Expense	220.36	
Telephone Expense	32.07	
Van Expenses	166.88	
Wages Expense	3 822.05	
	?	?

Figure 4-3
Help Mike Conlon decide his financial future by answering the questions on page 97.

Questions

1. How much profit did Mike make in April?
2. If all of Mike's customers paid their accounts, how much money would Mike have?
3. Mike's Accounts Payable figure represents all amounts owing for wood, nails, etc. Can Mike afford to pay off all the Accounts Payable? Explain.
4. Can Mike afford to hire a helper at $2 000 a month? Explain.

Challenge Case

Chris Handler is an 18-year-old student at Fraser S.S. in Penticton, B.C. Chris has a truck-moving business, mostly for short hauls for local businesses in the city. The accounts for the business for last summer are given in alphabetical order. Chris does not know what to do with this information, but he is anxious to have a set of financial statements for his business, to see if he can borrow money for a car. Given the data below, prepare:

1. A formal trial balance with the accounts in proper order.
2. An income statement for the four months ended September 30th.
3. A balance sheet as of September 30, 19 ____.
4. Act as Chris's bank manager and tell him whether you would give him a loan based on his financial statements, and how much.

Accounts Receivable	904.04
Accounts Payable	202.91
Advertising Expense	102.12
Bank	784.48
Computer System	1 299.53
C. Handler, Capital	?
Equipment	900.00
Loan Payable—Mother	50.00
Cash on Hand	20.00
Sales	5 396.15
Small Tools Expense	185.69
Wages	1 538.26

Take-a-Break

1. **Financial Post 500**

Each year *The Financial Post* magazine ranks the top 500 businesses in Canada, by sales, by net income, and other factors. See if you can guess at the leaders in each of the tables below, by picking out #1 in each group. If you really want a challenge, you could try ranking the top five businesses in each category.

Top 5 Companies Ranked by Sales	Top 5 Companies Ranked by Profit
Ford Motor Company	General Motors
General Motors	Bell Canada
Canadian Pacific	Imperial Oil
Bell Canada	Gulf Canada
George Weston	Seagram Company

Top 5 Public Accounting Firms by Revenue	Top 5 Canadian Banks by Assets
Clarkson Gordon	Toronto-Dominion
Thorne, Ernst & Whinney	Bank of Montreal
Price Waterhouse	Bank of Nova Scotia
Touche Ross	Canadian Imperial Bank of Commerce
Coopers & Lybrand	Royal Bank of Canada

2. **Odd Man Out**

In the tables below, the companies are ranked in order by revenue, but one company in each group does not belong there. Can you spot the intruder in each group?

Top 5 Computer Companies by Revenue	Top 5 Energy Companies by Revenue
1. IBM Canada Ltd.	1. Imperial Oil
2. Unisys of Canada Inc.	2. Petro-Canada
3. Mitsubishi	3. Ontario Hydro
4. Control Data Canada Ltd.	4. Shell Canada
5. NCR Canada Ltd.	5. Air Canada

Accounting at Work

Accounts Payable Clerk

Nancy Marynissen graduated from Valleyview Secondary School last month. She was then hired as an accounts payable clerk at the Pine Hills Retirement Home. She is in charge of all the supplier accounts for the nursing home. When the home buys any kinds of goods or services, the bill automatically lands on Nancy's desk. She then takes the supplier's invoice and makes sure that the goods or services were actually received. For example, last month the nursing supervisor ordered 48 new sets of sheets and pillowcases for the nursing home. When the goods arrive, the supervisor checks the quantity against the packing slip in the box to make sure that 48 sets really did arrive. She signs the slip and sends it to the accounting office where Nancy files it. When the invoice from the supplier comes in, Nancy compares the quantity on the invoice to the quantity received, checks the cost to see if it is correct, and extends the invoice to make sure the total amount charged by the supplier is accurate. If everything checks out, Nancy stamps the goods with a special stamp that approves payment, and writes out a cheque to the supplier to pay for the goods.

Nancy keeps accurate records of the amounts owing to suppliers of the nursing home. In general, she divides her records into three major groups so that she can keep track of the purchasing more easily—foods, medical and nursing supplies, and capital equipment. At the end of each month, Nancy prepares a statement for her boss, the nursing home administrator, that shows which suppliers are still owed money, and the total balance owing to all suppliers.

Nancy enjoys her work so far but her boss has hinted that she should be thinking about upgrading her high school diploma with some evening courses in computers. The home is thinking about computerizing some of its records, and the supervisor wants Nancy to learn about computers so she can keep up to date. Nancy enjoys the work in accounting and finds working with figures easy. She will likely upgrade her skills and try to round out her educational background.

Questions for Discussion

1. Given the nature of Nancy's job at the retirement home, do you think she needs to know a lot of complicated mathematics? Explain.
2. If you were Nancy, and wanted to upgrade your knowledge, where would you go?
3. Do you think a computer could replace Nancy at her job?
4. Nancy does not deal directly with the public on her job. Therefore, do you think attitude is very important in her work?

3

Completing the Cycle

Chapter 5
Six-Column Worksheet

Chapter 6
Classified Financial Statement

Chapter 7
Closing Entries/Practice Set I

Chapter 5 Six-Column Worksheet

Objectives

By the end of this chapter, you will be able to

1. complete a 6-column worksheet;
2. prepare an income statement for a business; and
3. prepare an income statement for a business that has a loss.

5.1 The Worksheet

Now that you have seen how a complete set of books is kept, it is time to go one step further and see how we can make the job of preparing financial statements a little easier. This can be done by means of a document called a "worksheet." Before we study the worksheet, however, look at the diagram below to see how the worksheet fits into the accounting cycle.

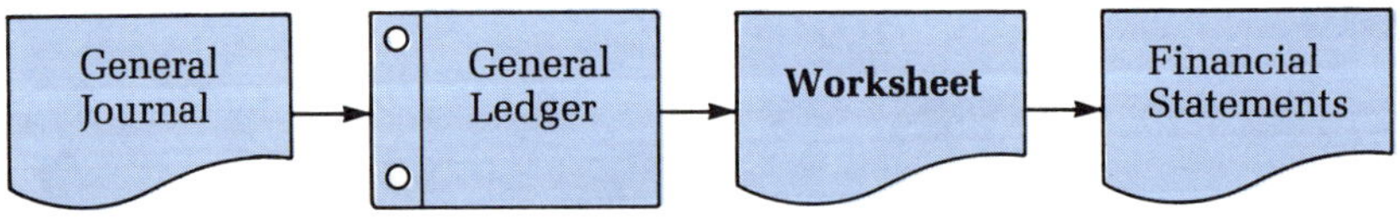

A worksheet is an accountant's working paper used to prepare the financial statements for a business.

You have already learned about the general journal and the general ledger and a bit about financial statements. This chapter introduces you to the worksheet part of the accounting cycle. The worksheet has three pieces of information printed at the top:

1. The name of the business, on the left.
2. The **heading** *Worksheet*, on the right.
3. The time period covered, at the right hand side.

A blank worksheet is shown below so that you can see what this new accounting document looks like. Most of this chapter will be devoted to completing a worksheet for a business.

WORKSHEET

Burke Consulting FOR THE MONTH ENDED *May 31* 19___

	ACCOUNTS	ACCT. NO.	TRIAL BALANCE		INCOME STATEMENT		BALANCE SHEET		
			DR.	CR.	DR.	CR.	DR.	CR.	
1									1
2									2
3									3
4									4
5									5
6									6
7									7
8									8
9									9
10									10
11									11
12									12
13									13
14									14
15									15
16									16
17									17
18									18
19									19
20									20
21									21

The first step is to list balances from accounts in the general ledger. Accounts are taken from the general ledger and are listed in the same order that they appear in the general ledger, that is, Assets, Liabilities, Owner's Equity (Capital and Drawings), Revenue, and Expenses. Each individual account balance is then entered in one of the Trial Balance columns of the worksheet, and **totals** are taken to make sure that the general ledger is in **balance.**

5.2 The *Trial Balance Columns* of the Worksheet

Below is a worksheet with the Trial Balance columns filled in. These balances are taken from the accounts in the general ledger and hopefully the Trial Balance columns will balance the first time you complete the worksheet. If they don't balance, then you must find your errors and correct them before you complete the rest of the worksheet. You will notice that all the figures on the worksheet are in round numbers. In a real business this would not happen, but it makes our study of the worksheet a lot easier.

WORKSHEET

Burke Consulting

FOR THE MONTH ENDED May 31 19 —

	ACCOUNTS	ACCT. NO.	TRIAL BALANCE DR.	TRIAL BALANCE CR.	INCOME STATEMENT DR.	INCOME STATEMENT CR.	BALANCE SHEET DR.	BALANCE SHEET CR.	
1	Cash on Hand		50 —						1
2	Bank		900 —						2
3	Accounts Receivable		3800 —						3
4	Supplies		120 —						4
5	Office Equipment		3000 —						5
6	Automobile		10000 —						6
7	Bank Loan			3000 —					7
8	Accounts Payable			1200 —					8
9	J. Burke, Capital			11000 —					9
10	J. Burke, Drawings		1500 —						10
11	Fees Earned			9800 —					11
12	Advertising Expense		580 —						12
13	Bank Charges		100 —						13
14	Telephone Expense		600 —						14
15	Wages Expense		4350 —						15
16	Totals		25000 —	25000 —					16
17									17
18									18

In the example shown, the Trial Balance columns balance. As long as the general ledger is balanced, then the Trial Balance columns should balance automatically. The most common mistake here is to copy an account balance incorrectly onto the worksheet.

Step 2 on the worksheet is to transfer the amounts in the Trial Balance columns to *one* of the other sets of columns, that is the Income Statement columns or the Balance Sheet columns. For example, the *Cash on Hand* account belongs on a Balance Sheet because it is an asset, so it is written in the Balance Sheet debit column. And since it has a debit balance in the Trial Balance column the amount 50.00 is written in the debit column of the Balance Sheet columns.

WORKSHEET

FOR THE MONTH ENDED May 31 19 —

	ACCOUNTS	ACCT. NO.	TRIAL BALANCE DR.	TRIAL BALANCE CR.	INCOME STATEMENT DR.	INCOME STATEMENT CR.	BALANCE SHEET DR.	BALANCE SHEET CR.	
1	Cash on Hand		50 —				50 —		1
2									2
3									3
4									4

The *Bank* account is also a Balance Sheet account and therefore it is written in the debit column of the Balance Sheet columns.

WORKSHEET

FOR THE MONTH ENDED May 31 19 —

	ACCOUNTS	ACCT. NO.	TRIAL BALANCE DR.	TRIAL BALANCE CR.	INCOME STATEMENT DR.	INCOME STATEMENT CR.	BALANCE SHEET DR.	BALANCE SHEET CR.	
1	Cash on Hand.		50 —				50 —		1
2	Bank		900 —				900 —		2
3									3
4									4
5									5
6									6

Here's one more example, just to emphasize the point. The third account in the Trial Balance columns is *Accounts Receivable*, which is an asset that belongs on a Balance Sheet. Therefore, its debit balance also is written in the Balance Sheet debit column.

WORKSHEET

FOR THE MONTH ENDED May 31 19 —

	ACCOUNTS	ACCT. NO.	TRIAL BALANCE DR.	TRIAL BALANCE CR.	INCOME STATEMENT DR.	INCOME STATEMENT CR.	BALANCE SHEET DR.	BALANCE SHEET CR.	
1	Cash on Hand		50 —				50 —		1
2	Bank		900 —				900 —		2
3	Accounts Receivable		3800 —				3800 —		3
4									4
5									5
6									6
7									7

The next section will transfer all the accounts from the Trial Balance columns to the proper Balance Sheet columns. Note that when they have all been transferred, the assets are debit balances in the debit column of the Balance Sheet columns and the liabilities are credit balances in the credit column of the Balance Sheet columns. The Owner's Equity has two parts—Capital (credit) and Drawings (debit). Note that each of these accounts is placed in its respective column.

5.3 Completing the Worksheet

If the accounts have been entered on the worksheet in the proper order, namely, Assets, Liabilities, Owner's Equity, Revenue, and Expenses, it will be easy to put balances in the correct columns. All Asset, Liability, and Owner's Equity accounts belong and are written in the Balance Sheet columns. All Revenue and Expense balances belong to and are written in the Income Statement columns. Below is the worksheet with all Trial Balance accounts **extended** to either the Income Statement columns or the Balance Sheet columns.

Take another look at the worksheet. Notice that the first 10 accounts, from Cash on Hand down to J. Burke, Drawings, are all Balance Sheet accounts. The rest of the accounts on the left are all Income Statement accounts. This is why it is important to put the accounts in the Trial Balance column in the order of Assets, Liabilities, Owner's Equity (all Balance Sheet accounts), then Revenue and Expense accounts (all Income Statement accounts).

WORKSHEET

Burke Consulting

FOR THE MONTH ENDED May 31 19 —

	ACCOUNTS	ACCT. NO.	TRIAL BALANCE DR.	TRIAL BALANCE CR.	INCOME STATEMENT DR.	INCOME STATEMENT CR.	BALANCE SHEET DR.	BALANCE SHEET CR.	
1	Cash on Hand		50 —				50 —		1
2	Bank		900 —				900 —		2
3	Accounts Receivable		3800 —				3800 —		3
4	Supplies		120 —				120 —		4
5	Office Equipment		3000 —				3000 —		5
6	Automobile		10000 —				10000 —		6
7	Bank Loan			3000 —				3000 —	7
8	Accounts Payable			1200 —				1200 —	8
9	J. Burke, Capital			11000 —				11000 —	9
10	J. Burke, Drawings		1500 —				1500 —		10
11	Fees Earned			9800 —		9800 —			11
12	Advertising Expense		580 —		580 —				12
13	Bank Charges		100 —		100 —				13
14	Telephone Expense		600 —		600 —				14
15	Wages Expense		4350 —		4350 —				15
16									16
17									17
18									18
19									19
20									20
21									21

Next, we should balance the worksheet to check the accuracy of our work. We will do this in Section 5.4.

5.4 Balancing the Worksheet

In the worksheet below the Income Statement columns (debit and credit) are totalled, and the Balance Sheet columns are totalled. You will notice that under the Income Statement columns the credit total is higher than the debit total. The difference is the **net income** of the business, or $4 170.00. You will remember that this is the profit of the business, but the modern trend is to call it the net income.

WORKSHEET

Burke Consulting

FOR THE MONTH ENDED May 31 19 —

	ACCOUNTS	ACCT. NO.	TRIAL BALANCE DR.	TRIAL BALANCE CR.	INCOME STATEMENT DR.	INCOME STATEMENT CR.	BALANCE SHEET DR.	BALANCE SHEET CR.	
1	Cash on Hand		50 —				50 —		1
2	Bank		900 —				900 —		2
3	Accounts Receivable		3800 —				3800 —		3
4	Supplies		120 —				120 —		4
5	Office Equipment		3000 —				3000 —		5
6	Automobile		10000 —				10000 —		6
7	Bank Loan			3000 —				3000 —	7
8	Accounts Payable			1200 —				1200 —	8
9	J. Burke, Capital			11000 —				11000 —	9
10	J. Burke, Drawings		1500 —				1500 —		10
11	Fees Earned			9800 —		9800 —			11
12	Advertising Expense		580 —		580 —				12
13	Bank Charges		100 —		100 —				13
14	Telephone Expense		600 —		600 —				14
15	Wages Expense		4350 —		4350 —				15
16			25000 —	25000 —	5630 —	9800 —	19370 —	15200 —	16
17	Net Income				4170 —			4170 —	17
18					9800 —	9800 —	19370 —	19370 —	18
19									19
20									20
21									21
22									22
23									23
24									24
25									25

The Net Income is written in the debit column of the Income Statement columns and then the two Income Statement columns are totalled to see if they balance. Once these columns are balanced, the Net Income is transferred to the credit column under the Balance Sheet columns, to help balance those columns.

What we are really doing on the worksheet is adding the Net Income to the owner's Capital account. When a business makes a profit, then the worth of the business is increased. This increase is eventually added

to the owner's Capital. Part of the worksheet is shown below. The arrow to the right shows how the Net Income figure is linked to the Capital account.

Figure 5-1
All businesses, big or small, new or established, aim to make a profit.

WORKSHEET

Burke Consulting

FOR THE MONTH ENDED May 31 19 —

	ACCOUNTS	ACCT. NO.	TRIAL BALANCE DR.	TRIAL BALANCE CR.	INCOME STATEMENT DR.	INCOME STATEMENT CR.	BALANCE SHEET DR.	BALANCE SHEET CR.	
1									1
8									8
9	J. Burke, Capital			11000 —				11000 —	9
10	J. Burke, Drawings		1500 —				1500 —		10
11	Fees Earned			9800 —		9800 —			11
12	Advertising Expense		580 —		580 —				12
13	Bank Charges		100 —		100 —				13
14	Telephone Expense		600 —		600 —				14
15	Wages Expense		4350 —		4350 —				15
16			25000 —	25000 —	5630 —	9800 —	19370 —	15200 —	16
17	Net Income				4170 —			4170 —	17
18					9800 —	9800 —	19370 —	19370 —	18
19									19
20									20

Eventually we will add this Net Income figure to the Capital account, but it is not done here on the worksheet itself. Before we finish studying the worksheet, we will do something special with the Capital account, the Drawings account, and the Net Income.

Take another look at the worksheet. You will notice that when you are done, there are *three sets of totals on the worksheet*, the Trial Balance column totals, the Income Statement column totals, and the Balance Sheet column totals. The beauty of the worksheet is that once you are done balancing, you usually know you are right if the three sets of totals are all balanced. It does not guarantee that you are right, but it is a pretty good sign most of the time.

5.5 Net Loss

Unfortunately, not all businesses make a profit. Some lose money at the end of a year and end up with a **net loss.** This section will study how a net loss is handled on a worksheet. To see this, we look at the balancing

"You've just turned this restaurant into a 'non-profit' organization."

totals first because this is where the change occurs from a profit situation.

In the example in Section 5.4, the profit appeared in the debit column of the Income Statement columns and then was transferred to the credit column of the Balance Sheet columns. When a business has a loss, then we do the opposite in the worksheet. Here is an example.

WORKSHEET

G. Reaper

FOR THE MONTH ENDED June 30 19 —

	ACCOUNTS	ACCT. NO.	TRIAL BALANCE DR.	TRIAL BALANCE CR.	INCOME STATEMENT DR.	INCOME STATEMENT CR.	BALANCE SHEET DR.	BALANCE SHEET CR.	
1					43000 —	42000 —	39000 —	40000 —	1
2	Net Loss					1000 —	1000 —		2
3					43000 —	43000 —	40000 —	40000 —	3
4									4
5									5
6									6

Notice that the Net Loss is recorded in the Credit column of the Income Statement columns, and then also in the Debit column of the Balance Sheet columns. Here is the full worksheet for the net loss example above. The business, by the way, is a man who engraves tombstones.

WORKSHEET

G. Reaper

FOR THE MONTH ENDED June 30 19 —

	ACCOUNTS	ACCT. NO.	TRIAL BALANCE DR.	TRIAL BALANCE CR.	INCOME STATEMENT DR.	INCOME STATEMENT CR.	BALANCE SHEET DR.	BALANCE SHEET CR.	
1	Bank		6500 —				6500 —		1
2	Supplies		2500 —				2500 —		2
3	Equipment		10000 —				10000 —		3
4	Truck		20000 —				20000 —		4
5	Bank Loan			13000 —				13000 —	5
6	G. Reaper, Capital			27000 —				27000 —	6
7	Fees Earned			42000 —		42000 —			7
8	Advertising Expense		750 —		750 —				8
9	Office Expense		1250 —		1250 —				9
10	Wages Expense		41000 —		41000 —				10
11			82000 —	82000 —	43000 —	42000 —	39000 —	40000 —	11
12	Net Loss					1000 —	1000 —		12
13					43000	43000 —	40000 —	40000 —	13
14									14
15									15

5.6 Financial Statements

Now for the last step in using the worksheet. The purpose of the worksheet is to make it easier to prepare a set of financial statements for a business, namely, an **income statement** and a **balance sheet.** Remember the fundamental accounting equation from the start of the chapter? We are at the last step!

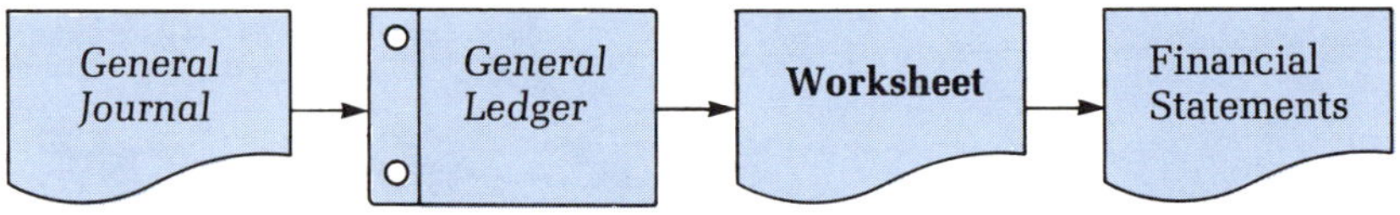

Here is part of the worksheet from Section 5.4. It has all the information needed to prepare the income statement that follows.

WORKSHEET

Burke Consulting — FOR THE MONTH ENDED May 31 19 —

	ACCOUNTS	ACCT. NO.	TRIAL BALANCE DR.	TRIAL BALANCE CR.	INCOME STATEMENT DR.	INCOME STATEMENT CR.	BALANCE SHEET DR.	BALANCE SHEET CR.	
10									10
11	Fees Earned			9800 —		9800 —			11
12	Advertising Expense		580 —		580 —				12
13	Bank Charges		100 —		100 —				13
14	Telephone Expense		600 —		600 —				14
15	Wages Expense		4350 —		4350 —				15
16			25000 —	25000 —	5630 —	9800 —	19370 —	15200 —	16
17	Net Income				4170 —			4170 —	17
18					9800 —	9800 —	19370 —	19370 —	18
19									19
20									20
21									21

Burke Consulting
Income Statement
For the Year Ended May 31, 19 ___

Revenue:		
Fees Earned		$9 800.00
Expenses:		
Advertising	$ 580.00	
Bank Charges	100.00	
Telephone	600.00	
Wages	4 350.00	5 630.00
Net Income		$4 170.00

Back to the fundamental accounting equation now. Let's take another look at it, but we will split the last symbol into its two main parts.

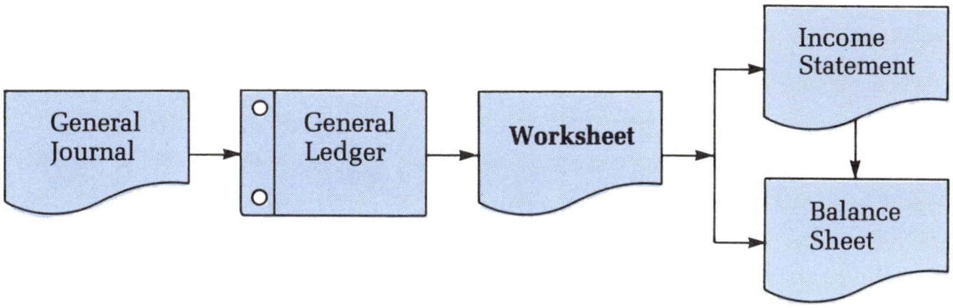

The symbol for Financial Statements has been replaced by the two statements we can produce from the worksheet. But take one more look at this diagram and notice the arrow for the Income Statement to the Balance Sheet. This link is the Net Income figure. Using this information we can now produce the balance sheet from the worksheet.

Here is the part of the worksheet needed to prepare a balance sheet for the same business.

WORKSHEET

Burke Consulting

FOR THE MONTH ENDED May 31 19 —

	ACCOUNTS	ACCT. NO.	TRIAL BALANCE DR.	TRIAL BALANCE CR.	INCOME STATEMENT DR.	INCOME STATEMENT CR.	BALANCE SHEET DR.	BALANCE SHEET CR.	
1	Cash on Hand		50 —				50 —		1
2	Bank		900 —				900 —		2
3	Accounts Receivable		3800 —				3800 —		3
4	Supplies		120 —				120 —		4
5	Office Equipment		3000 —				3000 —		5
6	Automobile		10000 —				10000 —		6
7	Bank Loan			3000 —				3000 —	7
8	Accounts Payable			1200 —				1200 —	8
9	J. Burke, Capital			11000 —				11000 —	9
10	J. Burke, Drawings		1500 —				1500 —		10
11									11
12									12
13			25000 —	25000 —	5630 —	9800 —	19370 —	15200 —	13
14	Net Income				4170 —			4170 —	14
15					9800 —	9800 —	19370 —	19370 —	15
16									16

To prepare a formal balance sheet, we use the last two columns on the right hand side of the worksheet. But in order to balance the new balance sheet, we have to take the Net Income and add it to the Capital balance that appears on the worksheet. This needs some explaining.

The Capital balance on the worksheet is the Owner's Equity at the start of the accounting period. To this, we have to add the Net Income for the time period, and subtract the Drawings for the same time period. The new figure we arrive at is the new Owner's Equity at the end of the fiscal period.

Burke Consulting
Balance Sheet
as at May 31, 19 ___

Assets		**Liabilities**		
Cash on Hand	$ 50.00	Bank Loan		$ 3 000.00
Bank	900.00	Accounts Payable		1 200.00
Accounts Receivable	3 800.00	Total Liabilities		$4 200.00
Supplies	120.00	**Owner's Equity**		
Office Equipment	3 000.00	J. Burke, Capital	$11 000.00	
Automobile	10 000.00	Add: Net Income	4 170.00	
			$15 170.00	
		Less Drawings	(1 500.00)	
		Capital, May 31		13 670.00
	$17 870.00			$17 870.00

5.7 Financial Statements for a Net Loss

If the business has had a loss, like G. Reaper, the man who engraves tombstones, then the procedure for preparing financial statements is the same. Here is G. Reaper's worksheet again and the financial statements that would be produced from it. Notice, again, how the Net Loss situation appears on a worksheet, as opposed to a Net Income situation. The Net

WORKSHEET

G. Reaper — FOR THE MONTH ENDED June 30 19 —

	ACCOUNTS	ACCT. NO.	TRIAL BALANCE DR.	TRIAL BALANCE CR.	INCOME STATEMENT DR.	INCOME STATEMENT CR.	BALANCE SHEET DR	BALANCE SHEET CR	
1	Bank		6500 –				6500 –		1
2	Supplies		2500 –				2500 –		2
3	Equipment		10000 –				10000 –		3
4	Truck		20000 –				20000 –		4
5	Bank Loan			13000 –				13000 –	5
6	G. Reaper, Capital			27000 –				27000 –	6
7	Fees Earned			42000 –		42000 –			7
8	Advertising Expense		750 –		750 –				8
9	Office Expense		1250 –		1250 –				9
10	Wages Expense		41000 –		41000 –				10
11			82000 –	82000 –	43000 –	42000 –	39000 –	40000 –	11
12	Net Loss					1000 –	1000 –		12
13					43000 –	43000 –	40000 –	40000 –	13
14									14

Loss figure appears in the credit column of the Income Statement columns and the debit column of the Balance Sheet columns. The debit in the Balance Sheet column will reduce the owner's Capital figure when we do the balance sheet.

G. Reaper
Income Statement
For the Year Ended June 30, 19 ___

Revenue:		
Fees Earned		$42 000.00
Expenses:		
Advertising	$ 750.00	
Office	1 250.00	
Wages	41 000.00	43 000.00
Net Loss		$(1 000.00)

G. Reaper
Balance Sheet
as at June 30, 19 ___

Assets		**Liabilities**		
Bank	$ 6 500.00	Bank Loan		$13 000.00
Supplies	2 500.00	**Owner's Equity**		
Equipment	10 000.00	G. Reaper, Capital	27 000.00	
Truck	20 000.00	Less: Net Loss	(1 000.00)	
		Capital, June 30		26 000.00
	$39 000.00			$39 000.00

5.8 Summary

The worksheet is an informal accounting document. This means that it is used by the accountant to help gather information to prepare the financial statements for a business. If the worksheet is balanced properly, then the accountant knows it is safe to go ahead and draw up an income statement and a balance sheet for the business. If it does not balance properly, then the errors must be found before the financial statements are prepared. The worksheet is a means of helping the accountant get organized at **year end.** You may learn more about the worksheet in this text or in a follow-up course in accounting.

Here are the chapter objectives again. Check the list and see how well you have done. You should be able to

1. complete a 6-column worksheet;
2. prepare an income statement for a business that has a profit; and
3. prepare an income statement for a business that has a loss.

Dictionary of Terms

Balance Sheet A statement showing the financial condition of a business or person on a specific date.

Balance To ensure that debits equal credits.

Extended The amounts transferred from the Trial Balance columns on a worksheet to either the Income Statement or the Balance Sheet columns.

Heading The description on the top of a worksheet.

Income Statement A financial statement showing the results of the operations of a business over a certain time period.

Net Income The profit made by a business from operations during its fiscal period.

Net Loss The loss incurred by a business from operations during its fiscal period.

Totals The amounts arrived at when the columns on a worksheet are added up.

Worksheet An accountant's working paper used to prepare the financial statements for a business.

Year End The last day of a business fiscal period.

Exercises

1. Given the part worksheet below, calculate whether there is a net income or a net loss, and how much.

WORKSHEET

FOR THE MONTH ENDED ________ 19____

	ACCOUNTS	ACCT. NO.	TRIAL BALANCE		INCOME STATEMENT		BALANCE SHEET		
			DR.	CR.	DR.	CR.	DR.	CR.	
1									1
2									2
3			75000 —	75000 —	35600 —	40000 —	65000 —	60600 —	3
4	Net ?								4
5									5
6									6
7									7

2. Look at the worksheet below. The student who started to do this work has made five errors so far. Describe the errors you see. (*Note:* The heading has been left out on purpose.)

WORKSHEET

FOR THE MONTH ENDED ________ 19____

	ACCOUNTS	ACCT. NO.	TRIAL BALANCE		INCOME STATEMENT		BALANCE SHEET		
			DR.	CR.	DR.	CR.	DR.	CR.	
1	Cash on Hand		40 —					40 —	1
2	Bank		112 —		112 —				2
3	Accounts Receivable		7400 —				7400 —		3
4	Supplies		330 —						4
5	Office Equipment			6500 —			6500 —		5
6	Automobile		9800 —				8900 —		6
7	Bank Loan			38000 —				38000 —	7
8									8
9									9

3. Given the part worksheet below, calculate whether there is a net income or a net loss, and how much.

WORKSHEET

FOR THE MONTH ENDED ________ 19____

	ACCOUNTS	ACCT. NO.	TRIAL BALANCE		INCOME STATEMENT		BALANCE SHEET		
			DR.	CR.	DR.	CR.	DR.	CR.	
1									1
2									2
3			60000 —	60000 —	39000 —	32500 —	57000 —	63500 —	3
4	Net ?								4
5									5
6									6
7									7

4. The worksheet below is missing something. What is missing?

WORKSHEET

FOR THE MONTH ENDED ______ 19 ____

	ACCOUNTS	ACCT. NO.	TRIAL BALANCE		INCOME STATEMENT		BALANCE SHEET		
			DR.	CR.	DR.	CR.	DR	CR	
1	BANK BALANCE								1
2	A/R								2
3	MUSIC SUPPLIES								3
4	AUTO MOBILE								4
5	A/P								5
6	CAPITAL								6
7	DRAWINGS								7
8	MUSIC REVENUE								8
9	ADVERTISING EX								9
10									10
11									11
12									12
13									13
14									14
15									15

5. Josh Keewagin is an artist who paints portraits of people. He was just about to complete his worksheet when he dropped his General Ledger and the accounts fell out. Rearrange and write the accounts in the proper order as they would appear in the Trial Balance columns of his worksheet.

   Rent Expense; Bank Loan; Building; Drawings; Bank; Capital; Accounts Payable; Art Equipment; Advertising; and Revenue.

6. Foothills Tree Service plants trees for customers with a modern mechanical tree planting device. Given the balances below, complete a worksheet for Foothills for the year ended October 31, 19 ____.

   Bank \$3 200; Accounts Receivable \$7 260; Office Equipment \$2 175; Tree Equipment \$18 990; Bank Loan \$20 340; Cam Sass, Capital ?; Cam Sass, Drawings \$3 600; Revenue \$66 550; Advertising Expense \$4 220; Office Expenses \$5 670; Truck Expenses \$12 345; and Wages Expense \$46 600.

7. The trial balance for Ingrid Wierenga, a young pianist who plays at different events, is shown below. The time period covers the year ended December 31, 19 ____. You are to complete the following:

   (a) a worksheet

   (b) an income statement

   (c) a balance sheet

Ingrid Wierenga
Trial Balance
December 31, 19 ___

Account	Debit	Credit
Bank Balance	$ 82.50	
Accounts Receivable	350.00	
Music Supplies	775.00	
Automobile	3 000.00	
Accounts Payable		$ 180.00
I. Wierenga, Capital		3 148.00
I. Wierenga, Drawings	820.25	
Music Revenue		2 325.00
Advertising Expenses	102.50	
Car expenses	404.25	
Miscellaneous	23.00	
Office Expenses	95.50	
	$5 653.00	$5 653.00

8. The trial balance shown belongs to a professional figure skater. Ross gives private lessons for a fee. Unfortunately, Ross has all of his accounts in alphabetical order.
   (a) Put the accounts in the correct order and then complete a worksheet for Ross at his year end.
   (b) Prepare an income statement.
   (c) Prepare a balance sheet.

Ross Garner
Trial Balance
July 31, 19 ___

Account	Debit	Credit
Accounts Payable		$ 765.00
Accounts Receivable	$ 900.00	
Automobile	8 400.00	
Bank Balance	372.00	
Bank Charges	23.60	
Bank Loan		2 375.00
Car Expenses	875.40	
Office Equipment	1 178.30	
Office Expenses	334.45	
Revenue—Lessons		9 223.00
R. Garner, Capital		?
R. Garner, Drawings	3 000.00	
Telephone	486.25	
	?	?

9. Given the General Ledger T-accounts below, prepare a worksheet for the business for the six months ended June 30, 19 ____. The business is run by a cleaning lady named Mrs. Botchley. You will have to calculate the account balances before you enter the accounts on the worksheet.

General Ledger

Bank Balance

200	175
400	
80	

Accounts Receivable

125	125
80	
240	

Office Equipment

2000	

Cleaning Equipment

900	

Automobile

8500	

Accounts Payable

	325
	55
	110

Mrs. Botchley Capital

	?

Mrs. Botchley Drawings

50	
75	
150	

Cleaning Revenue

	200
	125
	400
	80
	320

Automobile Expenses

210	
60	
20	

Bank Charges

10	
5	
15	

Cleaning Supplies

40	
10	
25	

10. Winnipegosis Tours is a business that takes people on boat tours during the summer months. Given the accounts below, complete a worksheet for the business for the month ended October 31, 19 ____.

Cash on Hand, $75; Bank $24 300; Accounts Receivable, $5 672.12; Supplies, $4 302.02; Bank Loan, $12 000; Accounts Payable, $14 812.91; L. Mariner, Capital, $?; L. Mariner, Drawings, $18 500; Sales, $98 334.65; Advertising Expense, $5 608; Bank charges, $210.90; Miscellaneous Expenses, $4 002; Repairs and Maintenance, $8 112.78; and Wages, $42 556.65.

Review Questions

1. (a) List the four steps involved in the accounting cycle.
   (b) What two "statements" does the last step refer to?

2. There are three pieces of information that appear at the top of a worksheet. What are these three pieces?

3. When we list the accounts on a worksheet, they must be set down in a certain order. What is that order?

4. Using your workbook, write beside each of these accounts in what column the amount would be extended to on a worksheet.

		Income Statement (Dr)	Income Statement (Cr)	Balance Sheet (Dr)	Balance Sheet (Cr)
	Example: Cash			Dr	
(a)	Bank Loan				
(b)	R. Cole, Capital				
(c)	Miscellaneous Expense				
(d)	Land				
(e)	R. Cole, Drawings				
(f)	Commissions Earned				
(g)	Accounts Payable				
(h)	Telephone Expense				
(i)	Sales				
(j)	Accounts Receivable				
(k)	Wages				
(l)	Cash on Hand				

5. Has this line on the worksheet been extended properly? Explain.

WORKSHEET

FOR THE MONTH ENDED ________ 19____

	ACCOUNTS	ACCT. NO.	TRIAL BALANCE DR.	TRIAL BALANCE CR.	INCOME STATEMENT DR.	INCOME STATEMENT CR.	BALANCE SHEET DR	BALANCE SHEET CR	
1	Bank Charges		128 17				128 17		1
2									2
3									3
4									4
5									5

6. When we are completing the worksheet, we can split the worksheet into two groups. What does this statement refer to?

7. What is the modern term for ''profit''?

8. (a) When we total the worksheet, the net income is transferred to the credit column of the Balance Sheet columns. Why is this done?

   (b) What happens to a net loss figure?

9. Complete the partial worksheet below in your workbook, by finding the Net Income or the Net Loss.

WORKSHEET

Pat's Paving

FOR THE MONTH ENDED *Nov. 30* 19 —

	ACCOUNTS	ACCT. NO.	TRIAL BALANCE		INCOME STATEMENT		BALANCE SHEET		
			DR.	CR.	DR.	CR.	DR.	CR.	
1					652000 —	724000 —	432000 —	360000 —	1
2									2
3	Totals								3
4									4
5									5

10. The partial worksheet below has five errors. List them.

WORKSHEET

T. Zuskir

FOR THE MONTH ENDED *Nov. 30* 19 —

	ACCOUNTS	ACCT. NO.	TRIAL BALANCE		INCOME STATEMENT		BALANCE SHEET		
			DR.	CR.	DR.	CR.	DR.	CR.	
1					9800 —	7500 —	16700 —	19000 —	1
2						2300 —	3200 —		2
3	Totals				9800 —	9800 —	19000 —	19000 —	3
4									4
5									5

Challenge Questions

1. Why is the net loss on a worksheet entered in the debit column of the two Balance Sheet columns?

2. Look at the partial worksheet below. How much would the Capital account balance be if we were to subtract the Drawings account and the Net Loss from the Capital account?

WORKSHEET

D. Hill

FOR THE MONTH ENDED *May 31* 19 —

	ACCOUNTS	ACCT. NO.	TRIAL BALANCE		INCOME STATEMENT		BALANCE SHEET		
			DR.	CR.	DR.	CR.	DR.	CR.	
1									1
2	D. Hill, Capital			20900 —				20900 —	2
3	D. Hill, Drawings		6700 —				6700 —		3
4	Fees Earned			8500 —		6500 —			4
5	Advertising		120 —		120 —				5
6	Bank Charges		60 —		60 —				6
7	Telephone		410 —		410 —				7
8	Wages Expense		3210 —		8210 —				8
9			30000 —	30000 —			45700 —	48000 —	9
10	Net Loss								10
11	Totals								11
12									12
13									13

Review Case

Rufus the Roofer had his accountant prepare a worksheet for the month ended July 30, 19 ____. It is reproduced below for you. Use only the part of the worksheet you need and prepare an income statement for Rufus for the month of July. After you prepare the income statement, answer the questions Rufus has about his business operations.

WORKSHEET

Rufus FOR THE MONTH ENDED *July 31* 19 —

	ACCOUNTS	ACCT. NO.	TRIAL BALANCE DR.	TRIAL BALANCE CR.	INCOME STATEMENT DR.	INCOME STATEMENT CR.	BALANCE SHEET DR.	BALANCE SHEET CR.	
1	Cash on Hand		80 —						1
2	Bank Balance		240 —						2
3	Accounts Receivable		650 —						3
4	Equipment		4000 —						4
5	Bank Loan			1500 —					5
6	Accounts Payable			670 —					6
7	Rufus, Capital			?					7
8	Rufus, Drawings		300 —						8
9	Sales			8050 —					9
10	Advertising Expense		210 —						10
11	Bank Charges		38 —						11
12	Telephone Expense		40 —						12
13	Truck Expense		412 —						13
14	Wages Expense		7000 —						14
15			?	?					15
16									16
17									17
18									18
19									19
20									20
21									21
22									22
23									23
24									24

Questions

1. His three employees want a 5 percent pay raise. What will that do to Rufus' profit? What should he tell them?
2. How can Rufus improve his financial position?

Challenge Case

Monica Shoebottom sells Real Estate in Victoria, B.C. Last night she was about to prepare a worksheet when she dropped her 3-column ledger accounts on the floor. Help Monica out by rearranging the accounts and completing the worksheet for the month of January, 19 ____.

General Ledger

ACCOUNT: Accounts Payable NO. 21

DATE		PARTICULARS	PR	DEBIT	CREDIT	DR. CR.	BALANCE
May	31					CR	1800 —

ACCOUNT: Accounts Receivable NO. 3

DATE		PARTICULARS	PR	DEBIT	CREDIT	DR. CR.	BALANCE
May	31					DR	3200 —

ACCOUNT: Automobile NO. 11

DATE		PARTICULARS	PR	DEBIT	CREDIT	DR. CR.	BALANCE
May	31					DR	9800 —

ACCOUNT: Bank NO. 2

DATE		PARTICULARS	PR	DEBIT	CREDIT	DR. CR.	BALANCE
May	31					DR	330 —

ACCOUNT: Bank Loan NO. 20

DATE		PARTICULARS	PR	DEBIT	CREDIT	DR. CR.	BALANCE
May	31					CR	5200 —

ACCOUNT: Capital, M. Shoebottom NO. 30

DATE		PARTICULARS	PR	DEBIT	CREDIT	DR. CR.	BALANCE
May	31					CR	6000 —

ACCOUNT: Car Expenses NO. 52

DATE		PARTICULARS	PR	DEBIT	CREDIT	DR. CR.	BALANCE
May	31					DR	1320 —

ACCOUNT: Commissions Earned NO. 40

DATE		PARTICULARS	PR	DEBIT	CREDIT	DR. CR.	BALANCE
May	31					CR	7900 —

ACCOUNT: Drawings, M. Shoebottom NO. 31

DATE		PARTICULARS	PR	DEBIT	CREDIT	DR. CR.	BALANCE
May	31					DR	750 —

ACCOUNT: Office Equipment NO. 12

DATE		PARTICULARS	PR	DEBIT	CREDIT	DR. CR.	BALANCE
May	31					DR	4420 —

ACCOUNT: Office Expenses NO. 54

DATE		PARTICULARS	PR	DEBIT	CREDIT	DR. CR.	BALANCE
May	31					DR	215 —

ACCOUNT: Cash On Hand NO. 1

DATE		PARTICULARS	PR	DEBIT	CREDIT	DR. CR.	BALANCE
May	31					DR	75 —

ACCOUNT: Professional Dues NO. 53

DATE		PARTICULARS	PR	DEBIT	CREDIT	DR. CR.	BALANCE
May	31					DR	300 —

ACCOUNT: Travel Expenses NO. 55

DATE		PARTICULARS	PR	DEBIT	CREDIT	DR. CR.	BALANCE
May	31					DR	490 —

Catch Art

Take-a-Break

1. Which is Canada's oldest company?
2. What do 35 percent of all TV commercials aimed at children flog?
3. In the US they call it the Federal Reserve. What do we call it in Canada?
4. Which department store chain discontinued its catalogue in 1976 after 92 years of publication?
5. How many zeroes are there in a trillion?
6. Which Canadian province ranks first in wheat production?
7. Which Canadian city boasts the most daily newspapers?
8. What is the name of Canada's steel city?
9. Which two cities are home to Canada's Royal Mints?
10. How many maple leafs are there on a penny?
11. What is Canada's largest newspaper chain?
12. What is the Family Allowance better known as?
13. Which company's initials are stamped on one bundle in the canoe on a 1963 Canadian silver dollar?
14. Of what is Mckenzie-Steele-Briggs the largest seller?
15. What are manufactured from white ash and maple in Victoriaville, Quebec?
16. Which way does the beaver on a Canadian nickel face?
17. What was the last year Canada minted dimes with silver?
18. What province is home to Canada's first commercial oil well?
19. What bank does Anne Murray promote?

Chapter 6 Classified Financial Statements

Objectives

At the end of this chapter you will be able to

1. identify two classes of assets and two classes of liabilities;
2. know the difference between an account form and a report form balance sheet;
3. prepare a classified income statement; and
4. have a basic understanding of financial statement analysis.

6.1 Overview

In the first five chapters of this book, you saw a number of formal income statements and balance sheets. This chapter will take those financial statements and present them in a slightly different way, by breaking down the accounts into groups or **classifying** them. If we look at a balance sheet, for example, the assets we list can be broken up into smaller groups. This makes the balance sheet easier to read and provides useful information about the business to the owner. Let's look at the asset classes in Section 6.2.

6.2 Asset Classes

Below you see a partial balance sheet for a small business.

Assets

Cash on Hand	$ 100
Bank	3 900
Accounts Receivable	8 000
Building	74 000
Automobile	14 000
	$100,000

In a real set of statements the assets would be divided into two groups as shown below.

Assets

Current Assets		
Cash on Hand	$ 100	
Bank	3 900	
Accounts Receivable	8 000	$ 12 000
Fixed Assets		
Building	$74 000	
Automobile	14 000	88 000
		$100 000

Current assets are assets which are cash, may be converted to cash, or used up within a year.

Fixed assets are assets which will last longer than one year.

Let us review the current assets and explain what they are.

Current Assets

The asset Cash on Hand is already in cash form and therefore it is as ''current'' as an asset can be (Figure 6-1). The Bank balance is also current since it is in the bank account and can be withdrawn for use at any time. It should be remembered here that assets are listed in the order of their liquidity, the order in which they can be converted to cash.

We learned about liquidity in an earlier chapter but it is a key point to emphasize once more. The Accounts Receivable are current because we expect customers to pay their accounts within 30 days. Some will take longer than 30 days but hopefully all balances will be collected within a year. Therefore, Accounts Receivable meet the second part of the definition—converted to cash within a year.

There is one other way to show the Current Asset section of a balance sheet and that is to show the total current assets on a separate line. Here is the same data that was shown earlier with the total of the current assets on a line by itself and identified as well. Compare this to the earlier method of showing the information.

Assets

Current Assets:		
Cash on Hand	$ 100	
Bank	3 900	
Accounts Receivable	8 000	
Total Current Assets		$12 000

(This method is preferred by accountants because it puts the current asset figure by itself and this is an important figure to accountants...you will see why before the chapter is done.)

Fixed Assets

This class or group of assets is fairly easy to recognize because the assets are all long lasting. The most common "long-lasting" assets you have seen so far in this text would be buildings, automobiles, office equipment, furniture, and shop equipment (Figure 6-2). Fixed assets will also be fairly expensive.

The fixed assets which have the longest life are listed first.

Fixed Assets		
Building	$74 000	
Automobile	14 000	88 000
		$100 000

Figure 6-1
A car and a house are fixed assets. They are long lasting and also expensive.

6.3 Liability Classes

Liabilities of a business are divided into only two groups—Current Liabilities and Long-Term Debt. It would seem to make more sense to say fixed liabilities but this is not the way it is done. If you understood the classification of assets, then you might be able to tell ahead of time what the classification of liabilities is going to be.

Below you see a partial balance sheet that shows all the liabilities of a business.

Liabilities

Bank Loan	$ 5 000
Accounts Payable	2 000
Mortgage Payable	43 000

In the next diagram, these liabilities are split into two groups.

Liabilities

Current Liabilities		
Bank Loan	$5 000	
Accounts Payable	2 000	$ 7 000
Long-term Debt		
Mortgage Payable		43 000

Current liabilities are those debts that will be paid in a year or less.

Long-term debt is any amount owing that will take longer than a year to pay.

It might be worthwhile to note here that there are other liabilities that could be classified as a "long-term debt." One example would be a bank loan that will take longer than a year to pay back. Since it will be hard for you to know when a bank loan is current or long term, it will be noted for you in brackets, as in Bank Loan (current portion) or Bank Loan (long-term portion). When you write the Bank Loan amounts on a balance sheet, do not write the words inside the brackets—they are there only for your information.

Liabilities are usually listed in order of their **liquidation**, that is, the order in which they will be paid back. Hence, because the bank usually gets paid before creditors, it should be shown first under the Current Liabilities section of the balance sheet. Now here is the entire classified balance sheet so that you can see what it looks like when it is all put together.

Sample
Balance Sheet
January 31, 19 ___

Assets			Liabilities	
Current Assets			**Current Liabilities**	
Cash on Hand		$ 100	Bank Loan	$5 000
Bank		3 900	Accounts Payable	2 000
Accounts Receivable		8 000	Total Current Liabilities	$ 7 000
Total Current Assets		$12 000	**Long-Term Debt**	
			Mortgage Payable	43 000
Fixed Assets			**Owner's Equity**	
Building	$74 000			
Automobile	14 000	88 000	A. Sample, Capital	50 000
		$100 000		$100 000

Before you leave this balance sheet, here is a reminder about two of the rules of accounting that you should have mastered by now:

1. There is a dollar sign at the top of each money column, beside subtotals like Total Current Assets, and beside the totals at the bottom of the balance sheet.
2. We draw a single line when we are about to take a total and double lines after we have taken a total.

6.4 Report Form Balance Sheet

Up until this point the balance sheets you have prepared have been **account form** balance sheets, that is, assets on the left side and liabilities and owner's equity on the right side. There is a second way to prepare balance sheets and it is called the **report form** of balance sheet, that is, accounts are listed down the page rather than side by side. This is illustrated in the two diagrams below.

account form **report form**

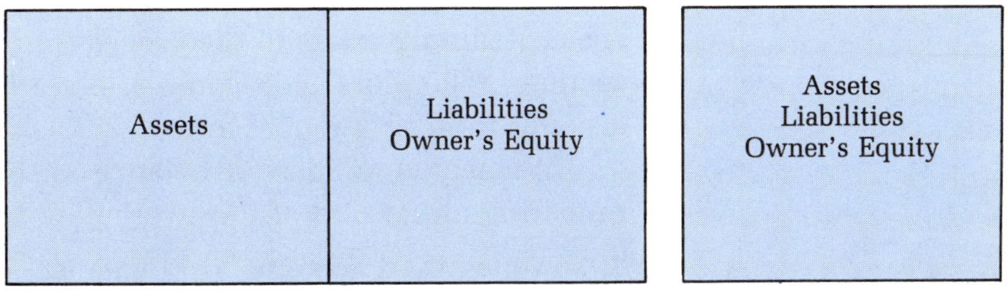

In Section 6.3 of this chapter you saw an example of a classified account form balance sheet. Here is an example of a classified report form balance sheet.

Sample
Balance Sheet
January 31, 19___

Assets		
Current Assets		
Cash on Hand	$ 100	
Bank	3 900	
Accounts Receivable	8 000	
Total Current Assets		$12 000
Fixed Assets		
Building	$74 000	
Automobile	14 000	
		88 000
		$100 000
Liabilities		
Current Liabilities		
Bank Loan	$5 000	
Accounts Payable	2 000	
Total Current Liabilities		$ 7 000
Long-Term Debt		
Mortgage Payable		43 000
Owner's Equity		
A. Sample, Capital		50 000
		$100 000

It does not matter what balance sheet you prepare but you do have to know what each type is. Notice that the term "classified" can be used to describe either an account form balance sheet or a report form balance sheet. It simply refers to the process of dividing the balance sheet into sections. Therefore, you can classify a balance sheet whether it is an account form or a report form.

When you prepare a balance sheet for a business, you can be preparing either one of the two below.

1. A classified account form balance sheet.
2. A classified report form balance sheet.

6.5 Classified Income Statement

While it is very common to classify a balance sheet, it is not as usual to classify an income statement. The usual place to split an income statement into groups is in the Expenses section. The two most common groupings or classes of expenses for a business are "administrative expenses" and "selling expenses." **Administrative expenses** are those expenses that are associated with running the office part of the business. Examples of these expenses would be office salaries, bank charges, office rent, utilities expense, etc. **Selling expenses** are those incurred to sell the service. Examples would include advertising, salespersons' salaries, automobile expenses, etc. Shown below are two income statements—the first is the old model; the second is the new classified model. Note the differences in the two income statements.

Sample

Income Statement

For the Month Ended May 31, 19 ___

Revenue:		
Commissions Earned		$30 000
Expenses:		
Advertising	800	
Automobile Expenses	3 200	
Bank Charges	100	
Office Salaries	4 000	
Office Rent	900	
Salespersons' Salaries	9 000	
Utilities Expense	2 000	
Total Expenses		$20 000
Net Income		$10 000

It is unlikely that a small business would worry about classifying expenses on the income statement, especially with the service type businesses that we are studying in this text. But it is worthwhile for you to see how this classifying would be done. On the next page is the second income statement with the expenses classified, or broken down, into two groups. Note how the right hand column of the income statement looks just like it did in the first sample.

Sample
Income Statement
For the Month Ended May 31, 19 ___

Revenue:		
Commissions Earned		$30 000
Expenses:		
Administrative		
Bank Charges	100	
Office Rent	900	
Office Salaries	4 000	
Utilities	2 000	
Total Administrative	$7 000	
Selling		
Advertising	800	
Automobile	3 200	
Salespersons' Salaries	9 000	
Total Selling	$13 000	
Total Expenses		20 000
Net Income		$10 000

There are different ways to show formal accounting statements, not just the one or two you have seen in this text. If you go on in your studies of accounting, you will see other variations on formal statements, but for the moment, when you prepare statements, use one of the models suggested in this text.

6.6 Financial Statement Analysis

If you have been really thinking about what we have done so far in this chapter, you may be wondering why it is important to ''classify'' financial statements. The reason is that once the financial statements are prepared, an owner or an accountant will study the financial statements to see what they tell about the business. The whole reason for good accounting records is that the data that is obtained tells people about the success or failure of the business. The process of studying financial statements is called *analyzing financial statements*. This is a topic that covers a full course at college but we can take a brief look at it to see what it involves.

There are two key figures that owners, bankers, or investors will look at when they study financial statements. These are **working capital** and **working capital ratio.**

To calculate these figures, we will look at the balance sheet that follows.

Sample
Balance Sheet
January 31, 19 ___

Assets			**Liabilities**		
Current Assets			**Current Liabilities**		
Cash on Hand	$ 100		Bank Loan	$5 000	
Bank	3 900		Accounts Payable	2 000	
Accounts Receivable	8 000		Total Current Liabilities		$ 7 000
Total Current Assets		$ 12 000	**Long-Term Debt**		
Fixed Assets			Mortgage Payable		43 000
			Owner's Equity		
Building	$74 000				
Automobile	14 000	88 000	A. Sample, Capital		50 000
		$100 000			$100 000

Working Capital

The formula used to calculate the working capital is
Current Assets – Current Liabilities

In the sample above, it would be:

Current Assets –	**Current Liabilities** =	**Working Capital**
$12 000	$7 000	$5 000

When the workng capital amount is positive, that is, greater than zero, it means that the business has enough cash or near cash to pay off its current debts. In the sample balance sheet, the business would have $12 000 if it were able to collect all of its Accounts Receivable in cash and add this money to its Cash on Hand and Bank balance. If it were then to pay off the Bank Loan and the Accounts Payable amounts, there would be $5 000 left over. The fact that the working capital figure is positive is a good sign for the business. It is possible for a business to owe more in current liabilities than it could pay with current assets, but this would not be healthy.

Working Capital Ratio

There is a second way to look at the working capital and that is to find the working capital ratio. The formula for this is to divide the current assets by the current liabilities and express the answer as a ratio.

$$\text{Working Capital Ratio} = \frac{\text{Current Assets}}{\text{Current Liabilities}}$$

If we do this for the sample business above, the working capital ratio would be 12 000 : 7 000 or 1.71. As long as this ratio is greater than one, the business is considered to be in good shape financially.

Both the working capital and the working capital ratio must be figured out at the same time. The two balance sheets below will show you why this is so. You will see that both balance sheets have the same amount of (dollar) working capital but the first business is better off because the working capital ratio is higher. The working capital ratio shows that the two businesses are not the same.

Okai

Balance Sheet

January 31, 19 ____

Assets			**Liabilities**		
Current Assets			**Current Liabilities**		
Cash on Hand	$ 100		Bank Loan	$ 4 000	
Bank	28 900		Accounts Payable	11 000	
Accounts Receivable	1 000		Total Current Liabilities		$ 15 000
Total Current Assets		$ 30 000			
			Long-Term Debt		50 000
Fixed Assets					
Building	$70 000		**Owner's Equity**		
Automobile	20 000	90 000	B. Okai, Capital		55 000
		$120 000			$120 000

Working Capital = $15 000

This figure is obtained by taking the current assets and subtracting current liabilities:

$30 000 – $15 000 = $15 000

Working Capital Ratio = 2:1

This ratio is obtained by dividing current assets by the current liabilities:

$$\frac{30\ 000}{15\ 000} = 2:1$$

So-So
Balance Sheet
January 31, 19 ___

Assets			Liabilities		
Current Assets			**Current Liabilities**		
Cash on Hand	$ 100		Bank Loan	$35 000	
Bank	22 900		Accounts Payable	50 000	
Accounts Receivable	77 000		Total Current Liabilities		$ 85 000
Total Current Assets		$100 000			
			Long-Term Debt		75 000
Fixed Assets			**Owner's Equity**		
Building	$50 000				
Automobile	20 000	70 000	Y. So-So, Capital		10 000
		$170 000			$170 000

Working Capital = $15 000

This figure is obtained by taking the current assets and subtracting the current liabilities:

$100 000 – $85 000 = $15 000

Working Capital Ratio = 1.2:1

This ratio is obtained by dividing current assets by the current liabilities:

$$\frac{100\ 000}{85\ 000} = 1.2:1$$

	Okai	So-So
Working Capital	15 000	15 000
Working Capital Ratio	2:1	1.2:1

Both businesses have $15 000 in working capital and because this is a positive amount it is a good sign for both businesses. But, the Okai balance sheet has a working capital ratio of 2:1. This means that the business has twice as many current assets as it does current liabilities. The So-So business has a working capital ratio of only 1.2:1, or 1.17 times as many current assets as current liabilities. Both companies are clearly not in danger according to the analysis but the Okai company has a slight advantage when it comes to the working capital ratio.

Income Statement Analysis

Now let us focus on the income statement. One of the most common things for business people to do with an income statement is to "analyze it vertically." This means that we find out what percentage each expense is of the total revenue. To study this new idea we will use the income statement for Diane's Office Services (Figure 6-3). Look at the income statement and the percentages to the right and then read the explanation that follows.

Diane's Office Services
Income Statement
For the Month Ended May 31, 19 ___

Revenue:			
Sales		$30 000	100.00%
Expenses:			
Advertising Expense	$1 500		5.0%
Automobile Expenses	3 000		10.0
Bank Charges	300		1.0
Office Rent	600		2.0
Office Salaries	13 500		45.0
Utilites	2 100		7.0
Total Expenses		21 000	70.0
Net Income		$ 9 000	30.0

Figure 6-2
By analyzing the income statement of a business, we can tell whether such expenses as the office salaries or office rent are too high.

To find the percentages shown, each Expense figure is divided by the total Revenue figure. Therefore, the Bank Charges of $300 are divided by the total sales figure, or $30 000. Therefore, the Bank Charges are 1.0% of the Revenue earned. Likewise, the office Rent of $600 is 2.0% of Revenue. The final important figure is the Revenue (100%) minus all the Expenses (70.0%) to get the percent of Net Income (30.0%). By comparing the percent of net income from one period to the next, the owner will know if the business is improving from one year to the next. It will also show if expenses have changed from one year to the next and indicate places where financial changes could be made to improve the business.

6.7 Summary

There are two key ideas that you have been exposed to in this chapter:

1. Classified financial statements.
2. Analysis of financial statements.

To classify financial statements means to put accounts into special groups. Assets are classified into current assets, prepaid expenses, and fixed assets. Liabilities are classified into current liabilities and long-term debt. Expenses are classified into two groups—administrative and selling expenses.The reason for classifying the financial statements is to make it easier to read the statements and to perform meaningful analysis of the statements. The most important calculation on a balance sheet has to do with the working capital of a business. Income statements are often analyzed by finding the percent breakdown of the expenses on the income statement.

Here are the chapter objectives again. Check the list and see how well you have done. You should be able to

1. identify two classes of assets and two classes of liabilities;
2. know the difference between an account form and a report form balance sheet;
3. prepare a classified income statement; and
4. have a basic understanding of financial statement analysis.

Dictionary of Terms

Account Form A type of balance sheet where the assets are on the left side and the liabilities and owner's equity are on the right hand side.

Administrative Expenses Expenses which are incurred for the office and general operations of a business, and not sales.

Classifying Breaking down into groups.

Current Assets Assets which are in the form of cash, may be converted to cash, or used up within a year.

Current Liabilities Debts which will paid in less than a year.

Fixed Assets Assets which will last longer than one year.

Liquidation The order in which debts are paid.

Long-Term Debt Any liabilities which are not expected to be paid back in less than a year.

Report Form A type of balance sheet where accounts are listed down the page.

Selling Expenses Expenses incurred as a direct result of trying to sell goods or services.

Working Captial Current assets minus current liabilities.

Working Capital Ratio Current assets divided by current liabilities.

Exercises

1. Identify each of the following assets as a Current Asset (CA), a Fixed Asset (FA), a Current Liability (CL), or a Long-Term Debt (LTD).
   (a) Mortgage Payable
   (b) Land
   (c) Bank
   (d) Furniture
   (e) Computer
   (f) Accounts Receivable
   (g) Bank Loan (due in six months)
   (h) Cash on Hand
   (i) Accounts Payable
   (j) Bank Loan (three-year note)

2. Match the terms on the left to the description on the right.

(a) Fixed Assets	(1) Will be paid within a year.
(b) Current Liabilities	(2) Can be changed to cash or used up in one year.
(c) Long-Term Debt	(3) Lasts longer than one year.
(d) Current Assets	(4) An example would be advertising.
(e) Selling Expenses	(5) Office salaries would be an example.
(f) Administrative Expenses	(6) May take several years to pay off.

3. A student who works for a TV repair person was asked to make a list of all of the fixed assets in the business and came up with the group of items below. Which items are not "fixed assets"? (Be prepared to explain your answers orally.)

   Test equipment; furniture; cash on hand; calculator; typewriter; accounts receivable; sets waiting to be fixed; telephone; land; building; and truck.

4. Given the trial balance at the top of the following page, prepare a report form balance sheet for the business as at November 30, 19 ____. Your balance sheet must be in classified form.

Madame Zenda (Fortune Teller)

Trial Balance

November 30, 19 ___

	Debit	Credit
Cash on Hand	$ 25	
Bank	1 240	
Accounts Receivable	105	
Building	48 000	
Furniture	630	
Bank Loan		$ 1 000
Mortgage Payable		39 000
Y. Zenda, Capital		10 000
	$50 000	$50 000

5. Classify the following expenses as either Administrative Expenses (AE), or Selling Expenses (SE): telephone expense; delivery truck expense; utilities; advertising; office rent; office salaries; postage; salespersons' salaries; and bank changes.

6. Complete the table below by finding the working capital and the working capital ratio for each business.

	Current Assets	Current Liabilities	Working Capital	W.C. Ratio
(a)	$ 48 000	$ 12 000	?	?
(b)	120 000	20 000	?	?
(c)	50 000	100 000	?	?

7. Given the income statement below, analyze the income statement vertically by finding out the percentage of each expense to the revenue. (Notice that since the Students Council is not really a profit-making enterprise, they use the term "Excess Revenue" rather than Net Income.)

Foothills Secondary School

Income Statement

For the month ended September 30, 19 ___

Revenue:		
Student Fees		$5 000
Expenses:		
Student Cards	$ 500	
Dance Expenses	1 250	
Stationery	250	
Bursaries	1 000	3 000
Excess Revenue		$2 000

8. Analyze the income statement for Regina Video by working out each expense as a percent of the revenue.

Regina Video
Income Statement
For the year ended June 30, 19 ___

Revenue:		
Sales		$150 000
Expenses:		
Advertising	$ 1 500	
Bank Charges	7 500	
Utilities	15 000	
Wages	90 000	114 000
Net Income		$ 36 000

9. The trial balance for the New Wave Beauty Salon is shown below.

New Wave Beauty Salon
Trial Balance
March 31, 19 ___

Account	Debit	Credit
Cash on Hand	$ 200	
Bank	4 600	
Accounts Receivable	300	
Beauty Equipment	18 000	
Furniture	900	
Bank Loan (current)		$ 2 700
Accounts Payable		500
Bank Loan (long-term)		5 800
J. Permie, Capital		11 000
J. Permie, Drawings	12 000	
Hairdressing Income		70 000
Advertising	600	
Bank Charges	250	
Rent	8 450	
Telephone Expense	700	
Utilities Expense	1 200	
Wages Expense	42 800	
	$90 000	$90 000

(a) Prepare a worksheet.

(b) Prepare an income statement.

(c) Prepare a classified report form balance sheet.

10. The trial balance for Anne's Coffee Bar is shown below.

Anne's Coffee Bar
Trial Balance
April 30, 19 ___

Account	Debit	Credit
Cash on Hand	$ 25	
Bank	5 975	
Accounts Receivable	500	
Equipment	13 700	
Furniture	1 500	
Bank Loan (current)		$ 500
Accounts Payable		1 800
Bank Loan (long-term)		1 500
A. Wilson, Capital		15 200
A. Wilson, Drawings	13 000	
Sales		46 000
Advertising	1 200	
Bank Charges	300	
Rent	3 600	
Telephone Expense	600	
Utilities Expense	1 800	
Wages Expense	22 800	
	$65 000	$65 000

(a) Prepare a worksheet.

(b) Prepare an income statement.

(c) Prepare a classified report form balance sheet.

11. The trial balance for Fred's Trucking is shown below. Fred lost money last year.

Fred's Trucking
Trial Balance
April 30, 19 ___

Account	Debit	Credit
Cash on Hand	$ 400	
Bank	2 800	
Accounts Receivable	13 800	
Truck	87 800	
Bank Loan (current)		$ 8 000
Accounts Payable		12 000
Bank Loan (long-term)		55 000
F. Bart, Capital		50 000
F. Bart, Drawings	13 000	
Sales		125 000
Advertising	3 200	
Bank Charges/Interest	7 200	
Rent	5 600	
Telephone Expense	2 400	
Truck expenses	71 000	
Wages Expense	42 800	
	$250 000	$250 000

(a) Prepare a worksheet.

(b) Prepare an income statement.

(c) Prepare a classified account form balance sheet.

Review Questions

1. What does the word "classify" mean? Explain in your own words.
2. Name the two asset classes that you learned about in this chapter and write the definition for each one.
3. Assume that you own a business selling real estate and you have an office downtown. List seven fixed assets that the business might have.
4. Explain the difference between a current liability and a long-term debt.
5. How would you decide to classify a bank loan under "Current Liabilities" or "Long-Term Debt"?

6. Why is a mortgage a long-term debt?
7. A friend of yours has been running a bicycle repair business for two years. She says that her current assets are $4 500 and her current liabilities are $2 250. Tell her whether this is good or bad and explain the whole meaning to her.
8. What is the difference between a report form balance sheet and an account form balance sheet? Is there such a thing as an account form income statement?
9. What two classifications are most common on an income statement? Give three examples of expenses that fall into each category.
10. One of the students in the class is having trouble understanding the difference between "Working Capital" and the "Working Capital Ratio." Explain the difference to this student, using dollar figures to show the meaning.
11. The manager of the bank has asked for an income statement that has been "analyzed vertically." What does this mean? Why would the manager be interested in this?

Challenge Questions

1. Which of the two businesses has been more profitable? Be prepared to explain your answer.

Sample 1
Income Statement

Revenue	$80 000
Expenses	75 000
Net Income	$ 5 000

Sample 2
Income Statement

Revenue	$25 000
Expenses	20 000
Net Income	$ 5 000

2. Which of the two businesses below has been more profitable? Be prepared to explain your answer.

Sample 3
Income Statement

Revenue	$40 000
Expenses	30 000
Net Income	$?

Sample 4
Income Statement

Revenue	$60 000
Expenses	48 000
Net Income	$?

3. Darrell opened his auto body repair shop "Mr. Perfect" on January 2, 19 ____. You are going to be Darrell's accountant for the month and perform the following transactions for him:

(a) Record the opening entry for the business.

(b) Journalize the transactions for January.

(c) Post to 3-column ledger accounts.

(d) Prepare and balance a worksheet for the month.

(e) Prepare classified financial statements for the business (use report form for balance sheet).

Use this chart of accounts to set up the general ledger for "Mr. Perfect." (There are no opening balances in the accounts.)

Chart of Accounts

Cash on Hand	1	D. Rope, Drawings	31
Bank	2	Repair Revenue	40
Accounts Receivable	3	Advertising Expense	50
Truck	10	Bank Interest	51
Equipment	11	Heat/Light Expense	52
Small Tools	12	Rent Expense	53
Bank Loan	20	Telephone Expense	54
Accounts Payable	21	Wages Expense	55
D. Rope, Capital	30		

Jan. 2: Borrowed $15 000 from the bank for the business and opened a bank account. Darrell has three years to pay back the bank loan so he regards it as a long-term debt. Darrell also was able to contribute $5 000 from his own savings to the business to use as start-up capital.

2: Paid the monthly rent for the shop, cheque #1, $500.

3: Wrote cheque #2 for $150 to use as cash on hand.

3: Bought painting equipment for the shop, $2 345. Wrote cheque #3 to pay for it.

4: Bought equipment on account from Snap-On Tools, $4 126.17.

6: Sold services (Repair Revenue) for cash, $135. (Note: all cash earned goes into the bank account daily.)

9: Sold services on account to J. McLellan for $1 235.

10: Bought small tools on account, Hobbs Ltd., for $775.

12: Sold services for cash $248, $137, and $400.

14: Darrell withdrew $500 cash for personal use. Cheque #4.

15: Bought a used truck for $6 200 for the business. Put a down payment on the truck for $1 000 by writing cheque #5, and the balance is owed to Rocky Auto Limited.

18: Cash sales $750. Sales on account to J. Hill, $815.

21: Paid wages to part-time help, $515. Cheque #6.

23: Telephone bill came in, $35.12. Set it up as an amount owing to be paid within 30 days.

23: Cheque #7 for newspaper advertising, $228.50.

31: Heating bill was $209.81. Cheque #8.

Review Case

The first income statement for "The Weed Man" is reproduced below. Analyze the income statement vertically and then answer the questions.

The Weed Man
Income Statement
For the Month Ended September 30, 19 ___

Revenue:		
Sale of Services		$98 000
Expenses:		
Administrative		
Bank Charges	$ 200	
Office Rent	3 600	
Office Salaries	18 400	
Utilities	1 800	
Wages	38 000	62 000
		$36 000
Selling		
Advertising	$ 500	
Truck expenses	4 600	
Salespersons' Salaries	10 900	16 000
Net Income		$20 000

1. What percent of revenue is being spent on wages and salaries?
2. In percentage, does the business spend more money on selling expenses or administrative expenses? How much for each?
3. If the advertising expense were doubled, what percent net income would the business have?

Challenge Case

Here is the balance sheet for "The Weed Man." Find the working capital and the working capital ratio, and then answer the questions that follow the balance sheet.

The Weed Man
Balance Sheet
September 30, 19 ___

Assets			**Liabilities**		
Current Assets			**Current Liabilities**		
Cash on Hand	$ 100		Bank Loan	$4 000	
Bank	6 000		Accounts Payable	6 000	
Accounts Receivable	8 900		Total Current Liabilities		$10 000
Total Current Assets		$15 000	**Long-Term Debt**		20 000
Fixed Assets					
Building	$26 000		**Owner's Equity**		
Truck	14 000	40 000	P. Ragg, Capital		25 000
		$55 000			$55 000

Questions

1. If the business paid off the Bank Loan with the money in the bank, what would this do to the working capital and the working capital ratio?
2. If, instead of paying off the bank loan, the business borrowed another $5 000 from the bank, what would this do to the working capital and the working capital ratio?

Take-a-Break

1. **Shred of Trouble**

   The new accounting clerk for S. Spade Investigation Services tossed the sheet with the customer's Chart of Accounts into the office shredder. When she was able to pull out the sheet, only part of each account name remained. Can you identify each account from its partial name?

(a)	sh on h	(f)	ank loa
(b)	unts pa	(g)	ts rece
(c)	ent exp	(h)	quipmen
(d)	very tr	(i)	drawin
(e)	th, capi	(j)	ges exp

2. **Accountants Can Spell Too**

   A first year accounting student really enjoyed working with the numbers in accounting, but had a lot of difficulty spelling some of the words. Scan down the list and see if you can spot all of the spelling errors. Each word has only one error. Time yourself on this and try to run down the list in twenty seconds.

   1. modle
   2. clasify
   3. statment
   4. liqudity
   5. expences
   6. analisis
   7. accoutants
   8. liabillities
   9. owner's equity
   10. addministrative

Chapter 7 Closing Entries/Practice Set I

Objectives

At the end of this chapter you will be able to

1. journalize closing entries;
2. understand the complete accounting cycle; and
3. complete a practice set to consolidate your knowledge of accounting for a service business.

7.1 Overview

The first six chapters have taught you the basic accounting cycle, up to the preparation of classified statements. We have used the diagram below to illustrate what this basic accounting cycle looks like:

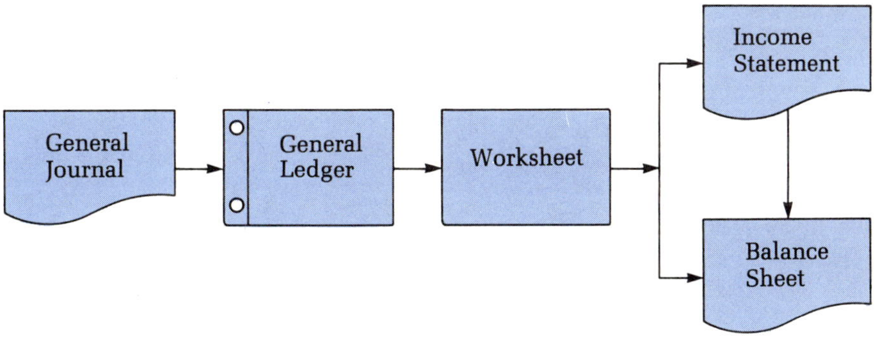

Once a bookkeeper or accountant has prepared the financial statements at the end of a fiscal year, the accounting cycle will start all over again. Before this can happen, however, the books must be **closed out**. Basically, this means two things:

1. We close out the balances in the Revenue and Expense accounts to the Capital account.
2. We close out the balance in the Drawings account to the Capital account.

These accounts are closed out because we want them to be empty when we start the next year's operations. The closing out process has three steps to it and you must know all the steps.

Step 1 Journalize the closing entries.

Step 2 Post the closing entries.

Step 3 Take a post-closing trial balance.

7.2 Closing Out Revenue and Expense Accounts

The trial balance below is for a small welding business owned and operated by Ross Pollock. Ross has a portable welding unit and will do any welding job within a 160 km radius of his hometown. We will look at his trial balance and then journalize the **closing entries** necessary to start Ross off on his second fiscal year.

Figure 7-1
After operating a year, the books of a small welding business will have to be closed out in preparation for the next year's operation.

Ross Pollock
Trial Balance
December 31, 19 ___

No.	Account	Debit	Credit
1	Cash on Hand	$ 25.00	
2	Bank	2 300.00	
3	Accounts Receivable	1 675.00	
10	Truck	14 000.00	
11	Welding Equipment	5 000.00	
20	Bank Loan		$ 4 500.00
21	Accounts Payable		1 500.00
30	R. Pollock, Capital		5 000.00
31	R. Pollock, Drawings	22 000.00	
40	Sales		59 000.00
50	Advertising Expense	1 200.00	
51	Bank Interest Expense	600.00	
52	Office Expenses	575.00	
53	Telephone Expense	720.00	
54	Truck Expense	3 605.00	
55	Wages Expense	18 300.00	
		$70 000.00	$70 000.00

The first step to close out Ross' books is to journalize the closing entry for all the Income Statement accounts, that is, Revenue and Expenses. The closing out entry in general journal form is on page 151.

Sales normally has a credit balance, and therefore in order to close it out to a zero balance, we have to debit the account. The Expense accounts normally have debit balances, and therefore in order to close the Expense accounts out, we have to credit them. The amount left over when we do this is the Net Income, which is $34 000. This Net Income belongs to the owner and therefore it is credited into his Capital account at the end of each fiscal year. (*Note:* If Ross loses money, that is, there is a Net Loss, then we would have had to debit his Capital account instead of crediting it.)

By closing out all the Income Statement accounts, each new fiscal year starts out with a zero balance. This makes sense because we want to keep track of sales and expenses for one year at a time.

GENERAL JOURNAL

PAGE 18

DATE		PARTICULARS	PR	DEBIT	CREDIT
		CLOSING ENTRIES			
Dec	31	Sales		59 000 —	
		Advertising Expense			1 200 —
		Bank Interest Expense			600 —
		Office Expense			575 —
		Telephone Expense			720 —
		Truck Expense			3 605 —
		Wages Expense			18 300 —
		R. Pollock, Capital			34 000 —
		To close out Revenue and Expense			
		accounts at year end.			

7.3 Closing Out the Drawings Account

Next we have to journalize the entry which closes out the Drawings account to the Capital account. We do this because we only want to keep track of the owner's drawings for one year at a time. The Drawings account must have a zero balance at the start of each year.

GENERAL JOURNAL

PAGE 18

DATE		PARTICULARS	PR	DEBIT	CREDIT
Dec.	31	R. Pollock, Capital		22 000 —	
		R. Pollock, Drawings			22 000 —
		To close out Drawings at year end.			

Once we have journalized the closing entries, we must post them into Ross' general ledger. Here is the ledger for Ross' business with the postings completed.

ACCOUNT: Cash On Hand — NO. 1

DATE		PARTICULARS	PR	DEBIT	CREDIT	DR CR	BALANCE
Dec.	31	Balance Forward	—			DR	25 —

ACCOUNT: Bank — NO. 2

DATE		PARTICULARS	PR	DEBIT	CREDIT	DR CR	BALANCE
Dec.	31	Balance Forward	—			DR	2300 —

ACCOUNT: Accounts Receivable — NO. 3

DATE		PARTICULARS	PR	DEBIT	CREDIT	DR CR	BALANCE
Dec.	31	Balance Forward	—			DR	1675 —

ACCOUNT: Truck — NO. 10

DATE		PARTICULARS	PR	DEBIT	CREDIT	DR CR	BALANCE
Dec.	31	Balance Forward	—			DR	14000 —

ACCOUNT: Welding Equipment — NO. 11

DATE		PARTICULARS	PR	DEBIT	CREDIT	DR CR	BALANCE
Dec.	31	Balance Forward	—			DR	5000 —

ACCOUNT: Bank Loan — NO. 20

DATE		PARTICULARS	PR	DEBIT	CREDIT	DR CR	BALANCE
Dec.	31	Balance Forward	—			CR	4500 —

ACCOUNT: Accounts Payable — NO. 21

DATE		PARTICULARS	PR	DEBIT	CREDIT	DR CR	BALANCE
Dec.	31	Balance Forward	—			CR	1500 —

ACCOUNT: R. Pollock, Capital — NO. 30

DATE		PARTICULARS	PR	DEBIT	CREDIT	DR CR	BALANCE
Dec.	31	Balance Forward	—			CR	5000 —
	31		CJE18		34000 —	CR	39000 —
	31		CJE18	22000 —		CR	17000 —

ACCOUNT: R. Pollock, Drawings — NO. 32

DATE		PARTICULARS	PR	DEBIT	CREDIT	DR CR	BALANCE
Dec.	31	Balance Forward	—			DR	22 000 —
	31		CJE18		22 000 —		Ø

ACCOUNT: Sales — NO. 40

DATE		PARTICULARS	PR	DEBIT	CREDIT	DR CR	BALANCE
Dec.	31	Balance Forward	—			CR	59 000 —
			CJE18	59 000 —			Ø

ACCOUNT: Advertising Expense — NO. 50

DATE		PARTICULARS	PR	DEBIT	CREDIT	DR CR	BALANCE
Dec.	31	Balance Forward	—			DR	1 200 —
	31		CJE18		1 200 —		Ø

ACCOUNT: Bank Interest Expense — NO. 51

DATE		PARTICULARS	PR	DEBIT	CREDIT	DR CR	BALANCE
Dec.	31	Balance Forward	—			DR	600 —
	31		CJE18		600 —		Ø

ACCOUNT: Office Expense — NO. 52

DATE		PARTICULARS	PR	DEBIT	CREDIT	DR CR	BALANCE
Dec.	31	Balance Forward	—			DR	575 —
	31		CJE18		575 —		Ø

ACCOUNT: Telephone Expense — NO. 53

DATE		PARTICULARS	PR	DEBIT	CREDIT	DR CR	BALANCE
Dec.	31	Balance Forward	—			DR	720 —
	31		CJE18		720 —		Ø

ACCOUNT: Truck Expense — NO. 54

DATE		PARTICULARS	PR	DEBIT	CREDIT	DR CR	BALANCE
Dec.	31	Balance Forward	—			DR	3 605 —
	31		CJE18		3 605 —		Ø

ACCOUNT: Wages Expense — NO. 55

DATE		PARTICULARS	PR	DEBIT	CREDIT	DR CR	BALANCE
Dec.	31	Balance Forward	—			DR	18 300 —
	31		CJE18		18 300 —		Ø

Notice that the posting reference is CJE which stands for **C**losing **J**ournal **E**ntry. Once we have posted the journal to the ledger, we should take a **post-closing trial balance** of the general ledger. This will be done for you in Section 7.4.

7.4 Post-Closing Trial Balance

Ross Pollock

Trial Balance

December 31, 19 ___

Account	Debit	Credit
Cash on Hand	$ 25–	
Bank	2 300–	
Accounts Receivable	1 675–	
Truck	14 000–	
Welding Equipment	5 000–	
Bank Loan		$ 4 500–
Accounts Payable		1 500–
R. Pollock, Capital		17 000–
	$23 000–	$23 000–

Take a look at the post-closing trial balance above again. You will notice that the only accounts that are left are the Balance Sheet accounts. All the Income Statement accounts and the Drawings account have nil balances. They are empty and ready for the next accounting period. The Balance Sheet accounts carry on from one fiscal period to the next. Here is the accounting cycle again so that you can see how the closing entries affect the cycle, and how the cycle repeats itself each year.

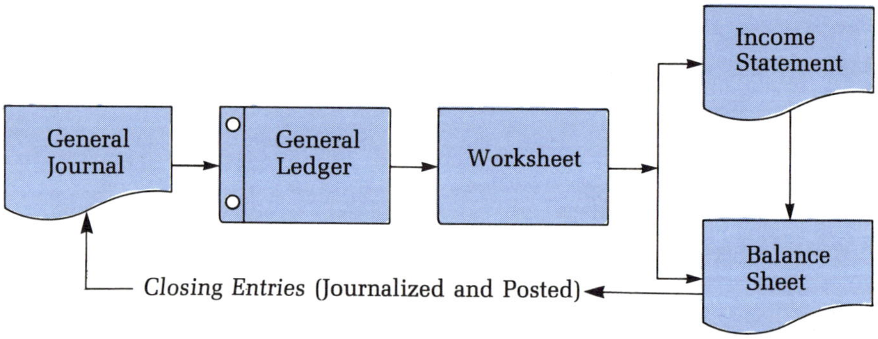

7.5 Summary

The balance of this chapter is devoted to a practice set which will take you through an entire accounting cycle. If you can work through the practice set successfully, you will have mastered the fundamentals of accounting. The practice set will also introduce you to "source documents," that is, the real documents from which accounting entries are made. Pay close attention to the instructions—you should not find this a difficult exercise.

Dictionary of Terms

Closed Out To make an account balance zero.

Closing Entries Entries in the general journal that make an account balance zero.

Post-Closing Trial Balance A trial balance of the general ledger taken after the closing journal entries are posted.

Source Documents

Before you begin work on the practice set, it will be worthwhile to look at some sample "source documents." This term refers to the actual business forms that businesses use and record in their books of account every day. There are five basic source documents that you will see in the practice set. They are shown for you here and briefly explained. In addition, the general journal entry that arises from each source document will be given.

This is a *sales invoice*. This person has sold a story to a children's magazine and this is the bill for that story, $75. The term 30 days means that the author expects to be paid in 30 days.

Creative Books

18 Hogarth Road, London, Ontario 259-3175

SOLD TO CHILDREN'S DIGEST
781 Progress Ave.
Toronto, Ontario

Invoice #1

July 1, 19__

Story Title

" Jake the Snake "

Invoice Amount: $ 75.00

All invoices are net 30 days.

SALES INVOICE

GENERAL JOURNAL

PAGE 1

DATE		PARTICULARS	PR	DEBIT	CREDIT
July	1	A/R - Children's Digest		75 —	
		Sales			75 —
		Sold story to children's magazine			

The second document, a *purchase invoice*, is received by a company when it buys goods or services. In the purchase invoice shown, a new computer is being bought along with a disk drive. This purchase will be charged to an Asset account. See the journal entry.

CLASSY COMPUTER
2020 SPRINGBANK DRIVE
LONDON, ONTARIO
N6K 1A5 275-8945

SOLD TO

PURCHASE INVOICE

ORDER NO. _____
DATE July 2, 19
INVOICE NO. _____
TERMS _____

DESCRIPTION	QUANTITY	UNIT PRICE	AMOUNT
XT Computer	1	$ 995.00	$ 995.00
Disk Drive	1	$ 400.00	$ 425.00
Sub-Total			$ 1420.00
Sales Tax (7%)			$ 99.40
Total			$ 1519.40
All hardware products carry a 90 day guarantee on all parts.			

GENERAL JOURNAL

PAGE 1

DATE		PARTICULARS	PR	DEBIT	CREDIT
July	2	Office Equipment		1519 40	
		A/P-Classy Computer			1519 40
		Bought new computer on account			

The third document, on page 158, is a *cheque*. This sample cheque was written by Bev to pay the regular monthly telephone bill, $50.50.

001

PAY TO THE ORDER OF Bell Canada

July 3 19

$ 50.50

Fifty 50/100 DOLLARS

RE.

PER BEV SAUER Bev Sauer

3030-973 112 5

GENERAL JOURNAL

PAGE 1

DATE		PARTICULARS	PR	DEBIT	CREDIT
July	3	Telephone Expense		50 50	
		Bank			50 50
		Cheque # 001.			

The fourth document is a bank *withdrawal slip* which is filled out when a customer is inside the bank and wishes to take money out of her/his account. The journal entry is also given.

Bank of Montreal **Cash Withdrawal** July 5 19

Received from the **Bank of Montreal** $ 200.00

Two Hundred XX/100 Dollars

MBB Multi-Branch Banking Branch No. Charge to Account No. 3030 – 973

Bev Sauer

To Customer: Please complete this form and sign in presence of teller

GENERAL JOURNAL

PAGE 1

DATE		PARTICULARS	PR	DEBIT	CREDIT
July	5	B. Sauer, Drawings		200 —	
		Bank			200 —
		Withdrew for personal use.			

The final document which we will look at is a *bank debit memo.* This is a notice that the bank sends to us when they have deducted money from our bank account. This may be for service charges, interest on a bank loan, or rental on a safety deposit box.

This bank debit is for interest on a bank loan which the bank has deducted from its customer's bank account.

GENERAL LEDGER DEBIT SLIP Bank of Montreal

BRANCH DEPT.

DATE 07 31 (yr. mth. day)

G.L. ACCT. NO. FUND

INTERNAL/CUSTOMER ACCT. NO. 3030-973

AMOUNT $ 42.00

EXPLANATION This amount represents interest on your bank loan for the previous month.

CONTRA A/C No.

CHEQUE No.

PREPARED BY

CASH RECEIVED – SIGNATURE

APPROVED BY

02-164 (0981)

GENERAL JOURNAL

PAGE 1

DATE		PARTICULARS	PR	DEBIT	CREDIT
July	31	Loan Interest Expense		42 —	
		Bank			42 —
		Bank Debit Memo			

Filing Source Documents

There are several ways to file source documents. In the diagram below there are four copies of the sales invoice. Each copy is filed in a different manner. Copy 1 of the sale invoice is given to the customer because it is the best copy. Copy 2 is filed alphabetically by customer name for quick reference. Copy 3 is filed by date so a daily record of sales can be kept. Copy 4 is filed by number for physical control of all invoices, that is, to make sure none are missing and unaccounted for.

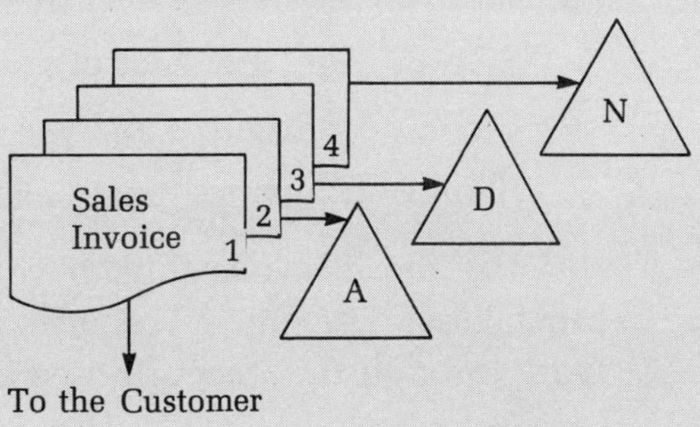

Practice Set I

Figure 7-2
Bev Sauer is setting herself up in business as a children's writer. Help her get her business off to a good start with this practice set.

Bev Sauer is an English teacher who has always thought of writing children's stories for magazines, newspapers, and books (Figure 7-2). This year, she decides to test her dream and has taken a year's leave of absence from her teaching to write children's stories. This practice set will follow Bev's first month at writing to see how successful her venture is. As you go through this practice set, you will have to perform the following steps:

Step 1: Use the chart of accounts to set up a general ledger.

Step 2: Journalize and post the opening entry.

Step 3: Journalize the transactions for July.

Step 4: Post the journal entries for July to the general ledger.

Step 5: Prepare a worksheet as of the end of July.

Step 6: Prepare a set of financial statements.

Step 7: Journalize and post the closing entries.

Step 8: Prepare a post-closing trial balance.

Use the forms set up for you in your workbook to complete the practice set. Remember the basic rules of *neatness* and *accuracy* as you work through this accounting exercise.

Step 1: Set Up the General Ledger

Chart of Accounts

Cash on Hand	1
Bank	2
Accounts Receivable	3
Office Furniture	10
Office Equipment	11
Bank Loan	20
Accounts Payable	21
B. Sauer, Capital	30
B. Sauer, Drawings	31
Sales	40
Advertising	50
Bank Interest	51
Office Supplies	52
Telephone	53
Utilities	54

Note: This is a new business and, therefore, there are no opening balances for CREATIVE BOOKS at this point in time. Set up the accounts with their names and numbers only.

Step 2: Journalize and Post the Opening Entry

Bev has a room in her house that can be used as an office for her new business but she needs to purchase some fixed assets to set up operations. She transfers $2 000 from a personal bank account into her new business bank account. She has also borrowed another $1 500 from the bank to help buy the assets she needs. The bank loan is to be paid back in less than one year. Use one journal entry to start up the business.

Step 3: Journalize the Transactions for July

The transactions for July are given in written form, with the source documents beside them.

CLASSY COMPUTER
2020 SPRINGBANK DRIVE
LONDON, ONTARIO
N6K 1A5 275-8945

SOLD TO

PURCHASE INVOICE

ORDER NO. 859
DATE July 3, 19
INVOICE NO. 3375
TERMS Net 30

DESCRIPTION	QUANTITY	UNIT PRICE	AMOUNT
XT-24 Computer			
- Keyboard	1	$ 299	$ 299.00
- Disk Drive	1	$ 399	$ 399.00
- Monitor	1	$ 399	$ 399.00
- NLQ Printer	1	$ 525	$ 525.00
Sub-Total			$ 1622.00
Sales Tax (7%)			$ 113.54
Total			$ 1735.54
All hardware products carry a 90 day guarantee on all parts.			

Transactions for July

July 3: Bought a computer system from Classy Computer. Bev wrote cheque #1 to pay this invoice.

OFFICE SUPPLY 30 Dundas Street, London, Ontario, N6A 1E7 264-6709

SOLD TO

ORDER NO. 4466
DATE July 5, 19
INVOICE NO. 45279
TERMS Net 30

DESCRIPTION	QUANTITY	UNIT PRICE	AMOUNT
Desk for Computer System, includes adjustable shelf and chair.			$ 129.95
Sales Tax (7%)			$ 9.10
			$ 139.05
Terms: Net 30 days			

PURCHASE INVOICE

July 5: Bought a new desk for the new computer from Office Supply. Set this invoice up as an account payable.

Note: Net 30 means that Bev has 30 days to pay this bill.

The term "purchase invoice" refers to bills that we get from other people or businesses when we buy goods or services from them. Purchase invoices can be paid in cash or set up as an account payable.

CLASSY COMPUTER
2020 SPRINGBANK DRIVE
LONDON, ONTARIO
N6K 1A5 275-8945

PURCHASE INVOICE

SOLD TO

ORDER NO. 865
DATE July 6, 19
INVOICE NO. 3382
TERMS Net 30

DESCRIPTION	QUANTITY	UNIT PRICE	AMOUNT
Fantastic Word Pro by Aster Software House	1	$ 99.95	$ 99.95
Sub-Total			$ 99.95
Sales Tax (7%)			$ 7.00
Total			$ 106.95
All hardware products carry a 90 day guarantee on all parts.			

July 6: Bought word processing software from Classy Computer. Bev wrote cheque #2 to pay this invoice. (Hint: Computer software is an expense.)

Creative Books

18 Hogarth Road, London, Ontario 259-3175

SOLD TO KIDSWORLD Magazine
1452 Yonge Street
Toronto, Ontario

Invoice #1

July 12, 19__

Story Title

" Cory and the Caterpillar "

Invoice Amount: $ 150.00

All invoices are net 30 days.

SALES INVOICE

July 12: Sold a children's story to the magazine KIDSWORLD. Sent a sales invoice (#1) to bill them for the story.

003

July 12 19

PAY TO THE ORDER OF *Classy Computer* $ *54.23*

Fifty-four *23/100* DOLLARS

RE. *Computer supplies*

PER *Bev Sauer*
BEV SAUER

3030-973 112 5

July 12: Wrote cheque #3 to Classy Computer for more computer supplies.

Creative Books

18 Hogarth Road, London, Ontario 259-3175

SOLD TO The LONDON FREE PRESS
1200 King Street W.
London, Ontario

Invoice #2

July 14, 19__

Story Title

" Pokey Bear "

Invoice Amount: $ 75.00

All invoices are net 30 days.

SALES INVOICE

July 14: Sold a story for cash. The cash was immediately put into the Bank account.

July 15: Bev went to the bank and withdrew $50 cash for personal use.

Creative Books

18 Hogarth Road, London, Ontario 259-3175

SOLD TO Toronto Star
1 Bay Street
Toronto, Ontario

Invoice #3

July 17, 19__

Story Title

" Marti goes to the ZOO "

Invoice Amount: $ 225.00

All invoices are net 30 days.

SALES INVOICE

July 17: Sold a story to another newspaper. Set this up as an account receivable.

004

July 20 19

PAY TO THE ORDER OF *Bell Canada* $ *75.00*

Seventy-five *xx*/*100* DOLLARS

RE. *Telephone*

PER *Bev Sauer*
BEV SAUER

3030-973 112 5

July 20: Bell Canada sent a bill for installing the business phone. Bev wrote a cheque (#4) to pay Bell Canada.

Middlesex Printing

Highway 2
Lambeth, Ontario
N0L 1S0
253-6789

INVOICE

SOLD TO

SHIP TO

ORDER NO. ______

DATE July 22, 19

INVOICE NO. ______

TERMS ______

DESCRIPTION	QUANTITY	UNIT PRICE	AMOUNT
Setting up advertising brochure:			$ 138.00
Sales Tax (7%)			$ 9.66
One colour only, one side. 500 copies, light stock.			$ 147.66
Net 30 days			

July 22: Received the bill on the left from Middlesex Printing, for the cost of setting up an advertising brochure, $147.66. Set it up as an amount owing (an account payable).

July 23: KIDSWORLD sent Bev a cheque for $150 to pay invoice #1 dated July 12th.

July 23: The owner of CREATIVE BOOKS, Bev Sauer, invested another $2 000 into her business. It was deposited into the business Bank account.

005

PAY TO THE ORDER OF Royal Bank July 24 19 $ 500.00

Five hundred xx/100 DOLLARS

RE. Bank Loan PER BEV SAUER Bev Sauer

3030-973 112 5

July 24: Wrote the cheque on the left (#5) to the bank to pay part of the Bank Loan.

006

PAY TO THE ORDER OF London P.U.C. July 25 19 $ 22.50

Twenty-two 50/100 DOLLARS

RE. Light bill PER BEV SAUER Bev Sauer

3030-973 112 5

July 25: Wrote cheque #6 to pay the light bill for the office, $22.50.

007

PAY TO THE ORDER OF Royal Bank July 28 19 $ 500.00

Five hundred xx/100 DOLLARS

RE. Inv. 45279 PER BEV SAUER Bev Sauer

3030-973 112 5

July 28: Paid Office Supply for their invoice dated July 5. Cheque #7.

GENERAL LEDGER DEBIT SLIP — Bank of Montreal

BRANCH DEPT.

DATE yr. 07 mth. 31 day

G.L. ACCT. NO. FUND

INTERNAL/CUSTOMER ACCT. NO. 3030-973

AMOUNT $ 10.00

EXPLANATION This amount represents interest on your bank loan for the previous month.

CONTRA A/C No.

CHEQUE No.

PREPARED BY

CASH RECEIVED — SIGNATURE

APPROVED BY

02-164 (0981)

July 31: The bank sent a debit memo charging CREATIVE BOOKS $10 interest on the Bank Loan.

Step 4: Post the Journal Entries to the Ledger

Post all of the journal entries into the general ledger you created for CREATIVE BOOKS back in step 1. You may want to take a tape trial balance before you proceed to the worksheet in step 5.

Step 5: Prepare a Worksheet as of the End of July

The worksheet will be dated July 31st. Balance and cross-balance the worksheet. Use the name CREATIVE BOOKS in the heading.

Step 6: Prepare a Set of Financial Statements

Prepare an income statement and a report form balance sheet for CREATIVE BOOKS for the month ended July 31, 19 ____.

Step 7: Journalize and Post the Closing Entries

When you post the closing entries, use the code CJE, that you learned in this chapter, with an appropriate page number.

Step 8: Prepare a Post-Closing Trial Balance

Your post-closing trial balance will have only balance sheet accounts and will balance if you have carried our your work perfectly.

Note: Closing entries are not normally prepared at the end of one month's operations. It is done in this practice set so that you don't have to carry out a whole year's work. The exercise will simply give you the idea about a full accounting cycle.

Take-a-Break

1. **Accounts Payable**
The answer to each of the following clues is a word or phrase containing the word BILL. For example, the clue "invoice" would give the answer BILL OF SALE. Score yourself out of 12.

(a) pool table game
(b) roadside advertisement
(c) police officer's nightstick
(d) theatre program
(e) prevents discrimination
(f) favourable medical checkup
(g) tin can eater
(h) wallet
(i) restaurant menu
(j) backwards person
(k) rich, rich, person
(l) Australian mammal

2. **Company Names**
Each of the company names below is taken from *The Financial Post* list of the top 500 Canadian companies. Part of the name is missing, namely, the initials that go with the company name. Write down the company initials.

(a) Heinz
(b) Woolworth
(c) Goodrich
(d) Simpson
(e) McDonald Inc.
(f) Canada Ltd.
(g) Sugar Refinery Ltd.
(h) Crain Inc.
(i) Howden & Co.

3. **Company Services**
The companies below are all service-oriented companies that are among the largest 500 in Canada. Match the name of the company to the service it provides.

(a) CN/CP
(b) Clarkson Gordon
(c) Laidlaw
(d) Rogers Communications
(e) Prudential
(f) Ellis-Don
(g) Century 21
(h) Greyhound
(i) Thomson
(j) Mcleod Young Weir

1. stockbrokers
2. construction
3. accounting
4. real estate
5. bus
6. newspapers
7. insurance
8. cable television
9. communications
10. trucking

Accounting at Work

Costing Clerk

Pat Pinnoy is a costing clerk employed by The Medicine Hat Construction Company. Her employer is a general contractor who will take on any construction job if it can be done profitably. Pat's role with the company is to "cost out" jobs to ensure that the company does make money on projects, and therefore she has an important interest in the continued existence of the company.

To understand Pat's job more fully, assume that her boss has been approached by a developer to build a 56-unit townhouse site on the edge of the city. Plans have been selected for the project and the company knows the kind of materials that are to go into the project. At this point in time, Pat can go to work and gather costs for the project. She will have to build up cost estimates for a townhouse based on all the construction materials needed for each unit. This will include concrete foundations, lumber, drywalling, bricking, roofing, painting, and even landscaping. Once Pat has all the costs, her boss can add on a profit margin and make a bid on the project. If Pat makes an error in calculation, it could be disastrous for the company.

Pat received most of her training for the job at the high school she attended. She was able to take three years of accounting courses, one of these a special course in cost accounting. She found this part of her formal education to be most useful. Since coming to work for the Medicine Hat Construction Company, Pat has enrolled in the C.M.A. (Certified Management Accountants) program sponsored by the Society of Management Accountants in her province. Pat has just completed her first year in the program and has four more to go to earn the right to use the C.M.A. designation. Pat takes two courses each year at a nearby community college in the evening. She submits assignments for marking and writes examinations at the end of each year. Her employer pays any tuition and book costs for Pat and has tried to encourage her as much as possible.

Pat has her eye on the organization chart (shown) and hopes to progress up through the management ranks someday. She thinks she might even be the accountant eventually. Since Pat joined the company, she has held the positions of payroll clerk and A/R clerk. She ended up being appointed the costing clerk when her employer found out about her background in cost accounting in high school.

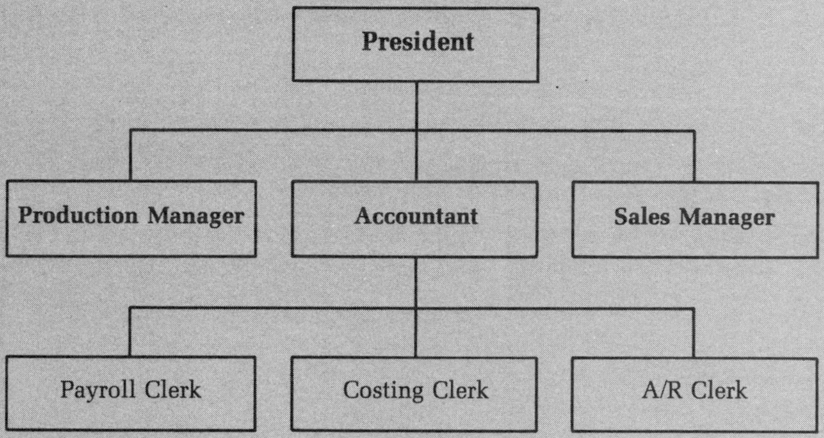

Questions for Discussion

1. Pat's job with Medicine Hat Construction is very important because if she makes a mistake, she can cost the company thousands of dollars. Do you think this is a stressful job?
2. What particular part of Pat's high school training has helped her most in her job?
3. Why are Pat's chances of getting promoted better than the present payroll clerk or the individual who handles the Accounts Receivable?
4. Once Pat earns her C.M.A. designation, would she be disloyal if she looked for a job at another construction company?

4

Multicolumn Journals

Chapter 8
The Multipurpose Journal

Chapter 9
Special Journals

Chapter 8 The Multipurpose Journal

Objectives

At the end of this chapter you will be able to

1. use a multipurpose journal for a small service business;
2. record special entries in the multipurpose journal; and
3. summarize the advantages and disadvantages of the multipurpose journal.

8.1 Overview

The journalizing that you have performed in the text so far has been cumbersome. If a real business recorded every entry in a general journal, it would not have time to carry on its business. A person who owns a small service business will want to spend more time selling his/her services rather than doing the books. Making a profit is the prime concern; it keeps a person in business.

"Take a seat. It'll be about two days."

Figure 8-1
A small business with only one or two owners will most likely not be able to afford a full-time bookkeeper and will use a synoptic journal to record its transactions.

There are many different ways to record accounting transactions in a real business. This chapter is devoted to one key way for a small business to handle all its accounting—the use of a multipurpose columnar journal.

The multipurpose columnar journal is used by a small **proprietorship** (one owner business) or even a small **partnership** (more than one owner) that cannot afford to hire a full-time bookkeeper. A multipurpose columnar journal is sometimes called a **combination journal** or a **synoptic journal**. We will use the name ''Multipurpose Journal'' in this text.

8.2 The Multipurpose Journal

When you look at the column headings in this multipurpose journal, they should be familiar to you. You have seen all of these account headings somewhere in the last seven chapters of the text.

DATE		CUSTOMER/SUPPLIER	NO	BANK DR	BANK CR	ACCOUNTS RECEIVABLE DR	ACCOUNTS RECEIVABLE CR	√			ACCOUNTS PAYABLE DR	ACCOUNTS PAYABLE CR
									1	1		
									2	2		

There are several things to note about the multipurpose journal.

1. Each transaction is written on one line of the journal—both the debit and the credit part of the transaction.
2. The spare column that appears after the Wages column can be used for any Expense account that you will use very often.
3. If there is no special column for the account you want to debit or credit, then the entry goes into the Other Accounts column.
4. You may put entries into this journal that have more than one debit or more than one credit...it can handle multiple entries.
5. The headings chosen for the journal depend on the particular business that uses this journal, and its needs.

Now, let's see how the journal works. This will be much faster than the general journal you have used up until this point. Read on into Section 8.3 and learn how entries are journalized into the multipurpose journal.

8.3 Recording Transactions in the Multipurpose Journal

Transaction 1

July 1: The owner started the business with an investment of \$5 000 cash. The proper entry is to debit *Bank* and credit *Capital*. Here is the entry in the journal.

Note that there is no column for Capital, so we have to use the Other Accounts columns to the right. We write the name Capital in the column so we know where to post this amount later on.

DATE 19—		CUSTOMER/SUPPLIER	NO	BANK DR	BANK CR	ACCOUNTS RECEIVABLE DR	ACCOUNTS RECEIVABLE CR	√			ACCOUNTS PAYABLE DR	ACCOUNTS PAYABLE CR
July	1	Owner Invests		5000 —					1	1		
									2	2		

MULTIPURPOSE JOURNAL

PAGE NO 1

√	Sales CR	Wages DR		OTHER ACCOUNTS ACCOUNT	PR	DR	CR

MULTIPURPOSE JOURNAL

PAGE NO 1

√	Sales CR	Wages DR		OTHER ACCOUNTS ACCOUNT	PR	DR	CR
				Capital			5000 —

Transaction 2

July 2: Cash sale of services for $120. The money is deposited into the business Bank account immediately.

DATE		CUSTOMER/SUPPLIER	NO	BANK DR	BANK CR	ACCOUNTS RECEIVABLE DR	ACCOUNTS RECEIVABLE CR	√			ACCOUNTS PAYABLE DR	ACCOUNTS PAYABLE CR
July	2	Cash Sale		120 —					1	1		
									2	2		

Transaction 3

July 3: Charge sale to a customer Larry Smith, $375. Mr. Smith will pay the account within 30 days.

DATE		CUSTOMER/SUPPLIER	NO	BANK DR	BANK CR	ACCOUNTS RECEIVABLE DR	ACCOUNTS RECEIVABLE CR	√			ACCOUNTS PAYABLE DR	ACCOUNTS PAYABLE CR
July	3	Larry Smith				375 —			1	1		
									2	2		

Transaction 4

July 14: Customer Larry Smith paid his account balance in full.

DATE		CUSTOMER/SUPPLIER	NO	BANK DR	BANK CR	ACCOUNTS RECEIVABLE DR	ACCOUNTS RECEIVABLE CR	√			ACCOUNTS PAYABLE DR	ACCOUNTS PAYABLE CR
July	14	Larry Smith		375 —			375 —		1	1		
									2	2		

Transaction 5

July 18: Bought supplies on account, from Calgary Wholesale, for $810.

DATE		CUSTOMER/SUPPLIER	NO	BANK DR	BANK CR	ACCOUNTS RECEIVABLE DR	ACCOUNTS RECEIVABLE CR	√			ACCOUNTS PAYABLE DR	ACCOUNTS PAYABLE CR
July	18	Calgary Whole							1	1		81
									2	2		

Transaction 6

July 18: Borrowed $8 000 from the bank, to be repaid in less than a year.

DATE		CUSTOMER/SUPPLIER	NO	BANK DR	BANK CR	ACCOUNTS RECEIVABLE DR	ACCOUNTS RECEIVABLE CR	√			ACCOUNTS PAYABLE DR	ACCOUNTS PAYABLE CR
July	18	Royal Bank		8000 —					1	1		
									2	2		

MULTIPURPOSE JOURNAL

PAGE NO 1

	√	Sales CR	Wages DR		OTHER ACCOUNTS: ACCOUNT	PR	DR	CR
		120 —						

MULTIPURPOSE JOURNAL

PAGE NO 1

	√	Sales CR	Wages DR		OTHER ACCOUNTS: ACCOUNT	PR	DR	CR
		375 —						

MULTIPURPOSE JOURNAL

PAGE NO 1

	√	Sales CR	Wages DR		OTHER ACCOUNTS: ACCOUNT	PR	DR	CR

MULTIPURPOSE JOURNAL

PAGE NO 1

	√	Sales CR	Wages DR		OTHER ACCOUNTS: ACCOUNT	PR	DR	CR
—					Supplies Exp.		810 —	

MULTIPURPOSE JOURNAL

PAGE NO 1

	√	Sales CR	Wages DR		OTHER ACCOUNTS: ACCOUNT	PR	DR	CR
					Bank Loan			8000 —

Again, we use the Other Accounts columns for this transaction since we want to credit Bank Loan and there is no special column for it.

Transaction 7

July 20: Wrote cheque #1 to pay part-time wages to employees, $945.

DATE		CUSTOMER/SUPPLIER	NO	BANK DR	BANK CR	ACCOUNTS RECEIVABLE DR	ACCOUNTS RECEIVABLE CR	√			ACCOUNTS PAYABLE DR	ACCOUNTS PAYABLE CR
July	20	Weekly wages	1		945 —				1	1		
									2	2		

Transaction 8

July 24: Owner withdrew $500 cash for his personal use. Cheque #2.

DATE		CUSTOMER/SUPPLIER	NO	BANK DR	BANK CR	ACCOUNTS RECEIVABLE DR	ACCOUNTS RECEIVABLE CR	√			ACCOUNTS PAYABLE DR	ACCOUNTS PAYABLE CR
July	24	Owner withdrew	2		500 —				1	1		
									2	2		

The process of recording transactions into the multipurpose journal is still called journalizing just as it was in earlier chapters.

Here is the whole journal with the eight transactions recorded in it, so that you can have a picture of it in your mind.

DATE 19__		CUSTOMER/SUPPLIER	NO	BANK DR	BANK CR	ACCOUNTS RECEIVABLE DR	ACCOUNTS RECEIVABLE CR	√			ACCOUNTS PAYABLE DR	ACCOUNTS PAYABLE CR
July	1	Owner invests		5000 —					1	1		
	2	Cash Sale		120 —					2	2		
	3	Larry Smith				375 —			3	3		
	14	Larry Smith		375 —			375 —		4	4		
	18	Calgary Whole							5	5		81
	18	Royal Bank		8000 —					6	6		
	20	Weekly wages			945 —				7	7		
	24	Owner withdrew			500 —				8	8		
									9	9		
									10	10		
									11	11		
									12	12		

You should be starting to realize now how efficient such a journal is. Instead of writing the names of the accounts you want to debit and credit each time, as we did in the general journal, we just write the proper figure in the correct column. You still have to write down the account name when you use the Other Accounts columns but overall you do have less writing with the multipurpose journal. The biggest advantage of using this journal will come when we have to post into the general ledger. More on that later...first we have to balance the journal.

MULTIPURPOSE JOURNAL

PAGE NO 1

	√	Sales CR	Wages DR		OTHER ACCOUNTS: ACCOUNT	PR	DR	CR
			945 —					

MULTIPURPOSE JOURNAL

PAGE NO 1

	√	Sales CR	Wages DR		OTHER ACCOUNTS: ACCOUNT	PR	DR	CR
					Drawings		500 —	

MULTIPURPOSE JOURNAL

PAGE NO 1

	√	Sales CR	Wages DR		OTHER ACCOUNTS: ACCOUNT	PR	DR	CR
					Capital			5000 —
		120 —						
		375 —						
—					Supplies Exp.		810 —	
					Bank Loan			8000 —
			945 —					
					Drawings		500 —	

8.4 Balancing the Journal

Once all the entries have been made into the multipurpose journal, we must check to see if the journal is in balance. To do this we take totals of all of the debit and credit columns. The total of all debit columns must be the same as the total of all the credit columns.

DATE 19—		CUSTOMER/SUPPLIER	NO	BANK DR	BANK CR	ACCOUNTS RECEIVABLE DR	ACCOUNTS RECEIVABLE CR	√	ACCOUNTS PAYABLE DR	ACCOUNTS PAYABLE CR
July	1	Owner invests		5000 —						
	2	Cash sale		120 —						
	3	Larry Smith				375 —				
	14	Larry Smith		375 —			375 —			
	18	Calgary Whole								81
	18	Royal Bank		8000 —						
	20	Weekly wages			945 —					
	24	Owner withdrew			500 —					
		Balancing Totals		13495 —	1445 —	375 —	375 —		0	81

Notice that the money columns in the journal have a single ruled line before totals are taken and a double ruled line underneath each column total. This is consistent with earlier accounting rules you learned.

Notice also that the two blank columns in the journal, (Accounts Payable Debit, and the one to the right of *Wages*) have a 0 balance recorded at the bottom. This is helpful in case you end up looking for errors later and you wonder whether this column has been totalled or not. It is a good habit to get into.

If we need to use two pages in a multipurpose journal, then balancing totals must be taken at the bottom of the first journal page and carried forward to the top of the next journal page, like this:

DATE 19—		CUSTOMER/SUPPLIER	NO	BANK DR	BANK CR	ACCOUNTS RECEIVABLE DR	ACCOUNTS RECEIVABLE CR	√	ACCOUNTS PAYABLE DR	ACCOUNTS PAYABLE CR
		Sub-totals		13495 —		375 —	375 —			81

DATE 19—		CUSTOMER/SUPPLIER	NO	BANK DR	BANK CR	ACCOUNTS RECEIVABLE DR	ACCOUNTS RECEIVABLE CR	√	ACCOUNTS PAYABLE DR	ACCOUNTS PAYABLE CR
		Balances Forward		13495 —		375 —	375 —		0	81

MULTIPURPOSE JOURNAL

PAGE NO 1

√	Sales CR	Wages DR		Other Accounts: Account	PR	DR	CR
				Capital			5000 —
	120 —						
	375 —						
				Supplies Exp.		810 —	
				Bank Loan			8000 —
		945 —					
				Drawings		500 —	
	495 —	945 —	0 —			1310 —	13000 —

MULTIPURPOSE JOURNAL

PAGE NO 1

√	Sales CR	Wages DR		Other Accounts: Account	PR	DR	CR
	495 —		0 —			810 —	13000 —

MULTIPURPOSE JOURNAL

PAGE NO 1

√	Sales CR	Wages DR		Other Accounts: Account	PR	DR	CR
	495 —		0 —			810 —	13000 —

Totals in the multipurpose journal should be balanced at the bottom of a page, before sub-totals are carried forward to the next page. This can be done with a calculator and a tape trial balance. Total debits must equal total credits, as usual.

8.5 Posting the Journal

Once the multipurpose journal is balanced we can post to the General Ledger accounts. The special columns, like Bank, have only their final totals posted to the Ledger account, that is, the debit total and the credit total. The special accounts that were written under the Other Accounts column have to be posted individually. First we post all of the column totals, except Other Accounts.

DATE 19—		CUSTOMER/SUPPLIER	NO	BANK DR	BANK CR	ACCOUNTS RECEIVABLE DR	ACCOUNTS RECEIVABLE CR	√			ACCOUNTS PAYABLE DR	ACCOUNTS PAYABLE CR
									1	1		
									2	2		
		Balancing Totals		134 95 —	14 45 —	3 75 —	3 75 —		3	3	0	8
									4	4		
									5	5		

ACCOUNT: Bank NO. 2

DATE		PARTICULARS	PR	DEBIT	CREDIT	DR CR	BALANCE
July	31		MJ1	134 95 —	14 45 —	DR	120 50 —

ACCOUNT: Accounts Payable NO. 21

DATE		PARTICULARS	PR	DEBIT	CREDIT	DR CR	BALANCE
July	31		MJ1		8 10 —	CR	8 10 —

ACCOUNT: Wages Expense NO. 58

DATE		PARTICULARS	PR	DEBIT	CREDIT	DR CR	BALANCE
July	31		MJ1	9 45 —		DR	9 45 —

MULTIPURPOSE JOURNAL

PAGE NO 1

✓	Sales CR	Wages DR		OTHER ACCOUNTS ACCOUNT	PR	DR	CR
	495 —	945 —	0 —			1310 —	13000 —

ACCOUNT: Accounts Receivable NO. 3

DATE		PARTICULARS	PR	DEBIT	CREDIT	DR CR	BALANCE
July	31		MJ1	375 —	375 —	DR	0 —

ACCOUNT: Sales NO. 40

DATE		PARTICULARS	PR	DEBIT	CREDIT	DR CR	BALANCE
July	31		MJ1		495 —	CR	495 —

Note: The posting reference that is used in the accounts is MJ1 which stands for **M**ultipurpose **J**ournal Page **1**.

Once the column totals have been posted to their respective Ledger accounts, we have to go back to the multipurpose journal and place posting references beneath each column total. Under each total that was posted, we write the account number (in brackets) to which that total was posted. Here is the last line of the journal showing the column totals and the posting references.

DATE 19—		CUSTOMER/SUPPLIER	NO	BANK DR	BANK CR	ACCOUNTS RECEIVABLE DR	ACCOUNTS RECEIVABLE CR	√			ACCOUNTS PAYABLE DR	C
									1	1		
									2	2		
		Balancing Totals		13495 —	1445 —	375 —	375 —		3	3	0	8
									4	4		
				(2)	(2)	(3)	(3)		5	5		(:
									6	6		

Here is the multipurpose journal again! The last step is to post the special accounts from the Other Accounts columns on the right hand side of the journal. If you look at the Sample shown, you should see that there are four entries that will have to be posted to Ledger accounts—Capital (Cr), Supplies Expense (Dr), Bank Loan (Cr), and Drawings (Dr).

DATE 19—		CUSTOMER/SUPPLIER	NO	BANK DR	BANK CR	ACCOUNTS RECEIVABLE DR	ACCOUNTS RECEIVABLE CR	√			ACCOUNTS PAYABLE DR	C
July	1	Owner invests		5000 —					1	1		
	2	Cash sale		120 —					2	2		
	3	Larry Smith				375 —			3	3		
	14	Larry Smith		375 —			375 —		4	4		
	18	Calgary Whole							5	5		8
	18	Royal Bank		8000 —					6	6		
	20	Weekly wages			945 —				7	7		
	24	Owner withdrew			500 —				8	8		
		Balancing Totals		13495 —	1445 —	375 —	375 —		9	9	0	8
									10	10		
				(2)	(2)	(3)	(3)		11	11		(:

ACCOUNT: Bank Loan NO. 20

DATE		PARTICULARS	PR	DEBIT	CREDIT	DR CR	BALANCE
July	31		MJ1		810 —	CR	810 —

ACCOUNT: Drawings NO. 31

DATE		PARTICULARS	PR	DEBIT	CREDIT	DR CR	BALANCE
July	31		MJ1	500 —		DR	500 —

MULTIPURPOSE JOURNAL

PAGE NO 1

√	Sales CR	Wages DR		Other Accounts: Account	PR	DR	CR
	495 —	945 —	0 —			1310 —	13000 —
	(40)	(58)					

MULTIPURPOSE JOURNAL

PAGE NO 1

√	Sales CR	Wages DR		Other Accounts: Account	PR	DR	CR
				Capital			5000 —
	120 —						
	375 —						
				Supplies Exp.		810 —	
				Bank Loan			8000 —
		945 —					
				Drawings		500 —	
	495 —	945 —	0 —			1310 —	13000 —
	(40)	(58)					

ACCOUNT: Capital NO. 30

DATE		PARTICULARS	PR	DEBIT	CREDIT	DR. CR	BALANCE
July	31		MJ1		5000 —	CR	5000 —

ACCOUNT: Supplies Expense NO. 56

DATE		PARTICULARS	PR	DEBIT	CREDIT	DR. CR	BALANCE
July	31		MJ1	810 —		DR	810 —

Once the individual accounts have been posted, we must go back to the multipurpose journal and enter individual account numbers in the posting reference column to show that these other accounts have been posted to the general ledger. Here is the journal with the account numbers entered in the PR column.

Date 19—		Customer/Supplier	No	Bank DR	Bank CR	Accounts Receivable DR	Accounts Receivable CR	√			Accounts Payable DR	Accounts Payable CR
July	1	Owner invests		5000 —					1	1		
	2	Cash sale		120 —					2	2		
	3	Larry Smith				375 —			3	3		
	14	Larry Smith		375 —			375 —		4	4		
	18	Calgary Whole							5	5		81
	18	Royal Bank		8000 —					6	6		
	20	Weekly wages			945 —				7	7		
	24	Owner withdrew			500 —				8	8		
		Balancing Totals		13 495 —	1445 —	375 —	375 —		9	9	0	81
									10	10		
				(2)	(2)	(3)	(3)		11	11		(2

The Other Accounts columns have the disadvantage that each of the accounts which has been debited or credited must be posted individually to its proper Ledger account. This is time-consuming but there is no way to avoid this. It might be possible to have a multipurpose journal that has more than one spare column, but it is difficult, if not impossible, to have one with columns for every account possible. This is why the spare column in the multipurpose journal is used for an account which will be used fairly often.

8.6 The Accounting Cycle

Look at the accounting cycle in the diagram. Here the general journal is taken out and the multipurpose journal inserted in its place. The accounting cycle really remains much the same as before. A business may still find it needs a general journal when it uses a multipurpose journal, but only for closing entries or very unusual entries.

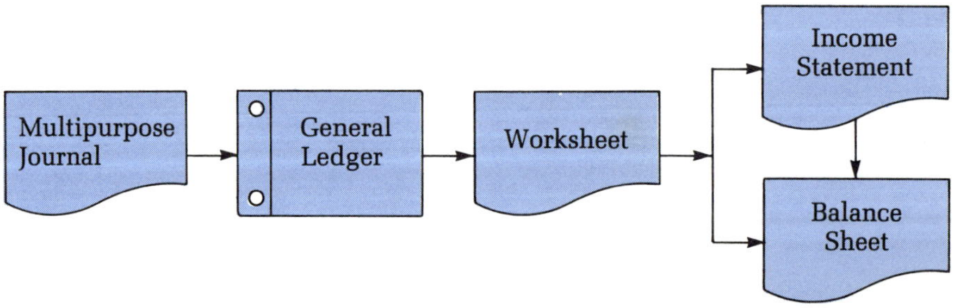

MULTIPURPOSE JOURNAL

PAGE NO 1

	√	Sales CR	Wages DR		Other Accounts: Account	PR	DR	CR
					Capital	30		5000 –
		120 –						
		375 –						
–					Supplies Exp.	56	810 –	
					Bank Loan	20		8000 –
			945 –					
					Drawings	31	500 –	
–		495 –	945 –	0 –			1310 –	13000 –
		(40)	(58)					

"If you want your money back, say so! Don't give me that guff about it being too noisy."

8.7 Special Entries

It is possible to record special entries in the multipurpose journal. Assume that a customer is unhappy with our services, or product, and we decide to refund the cash that we have received for the sale. The entry to record this refund would be a credit to the Bank account and a debit to Sales (to remove the sale). This refund entry can be recorded in the multipurpose journal by putting a credit in the Bank credit column and putting the debit in the Sales column. Since the Sales column normally has a credit entry, we can make a debit entry there by putting the amount in that column and circling it. This means that the number inside the circle is the opposite of what the column usually is. Since the Sales column is usually a credit, the entry becomes a debit. The same effect can be achieved by putting the number in the column in red ink. At the top of the following page is the accounting entry for the cash refund, using the circling technique.

DATE		CUSTOMER/SUPPLIER	NO	BANK DR	BANK CR	ACCOUNTS RECEIVABLE DR	ACCOUNTS RECEIVABLE CR	√			ACCOUNTS PAYABLE DR	ACCOUNTS PAYABLE CR
July	5	Cash refund			75 —				1	1		
									2	2		
									3	3		

The transaction below is for a refund of $20 which we received from a supplier for overpaying our account. It is not necessary to circle it.

DATE		CUSTOMER/SUPPLIER	NO	BANK DR	BANK CR	ACCOUNTS RECEIVABLE DR	ACCOUNTS RECEIVABLE CR	√			ACCOUNTS PAYABLE DR	ACCOUNTS PAYABLE CR
July	9	Refund - overpaid		20 —					1	1		
									2	2		
									3	3		

It is also possible to record a **multiple entry** (more than one debit or credit on one line of the multipurpose journal). Here is an example. Bought a new car from Zitt Motors for $15 000. We wrote a cheque for $2 000 as a down payment and promised to pay the rest in 30 days.

DATE		CUSTOMER/SUPPLIER	NO	BANK DR	BANK CR	ACCOUNTS RECEIVABLE DR	ACCOUNTS RECEIVABLE CR	√			ACCOUNTS PAYABLE DR	ACCOUNTS PAYABLE CR
July	13	Bought car on account			2000 —				1	1		130
									2	2		
									3	3		

Finally, you may use the Other Accounts section for a multiple entry. Assume you are in a stationery store and need to buy two things—some calculating pads and a new office desk. The debit for this transaction is split because the supplies are an expense debit and the office desk is a fixed asset. This entry requires two debits in the Other Accounts columns.

DATE		CUSTOMER/SUPPLIER	NO	BANK DR	BANK CR	ACCOUNTS RECEIVABLE DR	ACCOUNTS RECEIVABLE CR	√			ACCOUNTS PAYABLE DR	ACCOUNTS PAYABLE CR
July	20	Bought stationery							1	1		3
		+ desk							2	2		
									3	3		
									4	4		

MULTIPURPOSE JOURNAL

PAGE NO 1

√	Sales CR	Wages DR		OTHER ACCOUNTS			
				ACCOUNT	PR	DR	CR
	75 —						

MULTIPURPOSE JOURNAL

PAGE NO 1

√	Sales CR	Wages DR		OTHER ACCOUNTS			
				ACCOUNT	PR	DR	CR

MULTIPURPOSE JOURNAL

PAGE NO 1

√	Sales CR	Wages DR		OTHER ACCOUNTS			
				ACCOUNT	PR	DR	CR
				Automobile		15000 —	

MULTIPURPOSE JOURNAL

PAGE NO 1

√	Sales CR	Wages DR		OTHER ACCOUNTS			
				ACCOUNT	PR	DR	CR
				Supplies Exp.		24 —	
				Furniture		300 —	

8.8 Locating Errors in the Multipurpose Journal

You can use any **one** of the following ways to locate errors in the multipurpose journal.

1. Find the amount you are out by subtracting the debit total from the credit total. Divide the difference by 9 to see if the error is a **transposition error**, that is, the digits of an amount are reversed.
2. Divide the error by 2 and look for this amount in the wrong column of the multipurpose journal.
3. If you have used an adding machine with a tape to add the columns, check the tape takedown to see if you have entered the correct figures into the adding machine,
4. Check each line in the journal to see if each line balances itself. This will be easy to check, except for multiple entries, but it will take some time.

8.9 Advantages of the Multipurpose Journal

1. It is faster to record transactions because the transactions are entered in special columns and account names do not usually have to be written down in the journal.
2. Only the column totals are posted thus reducing significantly the posting required to the general ledger.
3. All business transactions are entered in one book. This means that one person can do the recording and also it is easy to find certain transactions because they are entered in chronological order.

8.10 Disadvantages of the Multipurpose Journal

1. It may be easy to make errors making entries in a large journal, if for example, a number is entered in the wrong column by mistake.
2. The journal is best suited to a small business where the number of transactions is not very large and can easily be entered by one person.
3. It may be cumbersome to record special entries in the multipurpose journal and thereby increase the chance of errors being made.

8.11 Summary

This whole chapter has been dedicated to learning about the multipurpose journal, which is very useful to a small business. Many businesses in Canada are "small businesses," that is they are owned by one person, or are family type businesses. They are too small to have fancy accounting systems and they need something that will provide the accountant with a balanced set of books that is neat and orderly. The multipurpose journal is very useful this way because everything is self-contained. The biggest advantages are that it cuts down writing account names, and it saves time when posting to the general ledger. A student of accounting must, however, keep in mind that the multipurpose journal will vary from business to business in terms of the setup used. If a student understands why the multipurpose journal works, rather than just how to use it, it will be easier to appreciate the real usefulness of such a journal.

Dictionary of Terms

Combination Journal A multicolumn journal used for recording accounting transactions, sometimes called a synoptic journal.

Multiple Entry An accounting transaction which has more than one debit, and/or more than one credit.

Multipurpose Journal A multicolumn journal for recording accounting transactions, sometimes called a synoptic journal.

Partnerhsip A business owned by two or more people.

Proprietorship A business owned by one person.

Transposition Error An accounting error where digits are reversed (e.g., 48 written as 84).

Exercises

1. Record the following transactions in a multipurpose journal. Balance and rule the journal.

Dec. 1: Sold services to P. Hamstrung on account, $234.50.
3: Owner K. Ford invested $14 000 cash into her business.
3: Bought a new desk for the business, $345.00. Cheque #1.
5: Sold services for cash, $75.20.
8: Paid weekly wages to employees, $715.20. Cheque #2.
11: Received telephone bill, $52.19. Set up as an A/P.
13: Sold services for cash, $1 235.02.
14: Paid $200 toward the bank loan. Cheque #3.
20: Customer W. Earp paid the business $802 on account.

2. Medicine Hat Moving and Storage Company has the chart of accounts given below. Use these accounts to record the transactions given in a multipurpose journal. Balance and rule the journal.

Chart of Accounts

Cash on Hand	1	B. Bos, Capital	30
Bank	2	B. Bos, Drawings	31
Accounts Receivable	3	Revenue	40
Trucks	10	Advertising	50
Building	11	Bank Interest	51
Equipment	12	Office Expense	52
Bank Loan	20	Repairs & Maintenance	53
Accounts Payable	21	Truck Expenses	54
Mortgage Payable	25	Wage Expenses	55

Transactions

Oct. 1: Paid monthly mortgage payment, cheque #234, $550.
3: Borrowed $12 000 from the Bank of Montreal to purchase new word processing equipment for the business.
4: Sold services for $580 cash.
4: Charge sale to J. Beattie in the amount of $1 245.
5: Wrote cheque #235 to employee L. Lambert for wages. Amount was $462.35.
6: Cash sale of services, $112.50.
7: Bought the new word processing equipment for the business. Total cost was $14 820. We wrote a cheque (#236)

for $12 000 and the balance will be paid to Micro Sales in 30 days.

8: Charge sale to Peter Roberts, $772.10.

10: A customer bought $600 worth of services. She paid us a deposit of $150 and promised to pay the rest in 30 days.

11: Wrote cheques for the following expenses:

#238: Repairs to building......................	$802.31
#239: Radio station CTKO.....................	87.95
#240: Gasoline for truck	234.78

12: Cash sale, $546.78; Charge sale to G. Park, $718.12.

3. The multipurpose journal below has five errors, both in accounting technique and in the calculations. List the five errors in your notes.

DATE 19__		CUSTOMER/SUPPLIER	NO	BANK DR	BANK CR	ACCOUNTS RECEIVABLE DR	ACCOUNTS RECEIVABLE CR	✓			ACCOUNTS PAYABLE DR	ACCOUNTS PAYABLE C
May	1	P. Henderson							1	1		
	2	Bank of Nova Scotia		3500 —					2	2		
	4	World Suppliers			476 —				3	3		4
	9					1820 —			4	4		
	13	Firestone Tire			992 —				5	5		
									6	6		
									7	7		

4. The multipurpose journal below has been totalled but is *out of balance*. Find any errors in the journal that have caused the imbalance.

DATE 19__		CUSTOMER/SUPPLIER	NO	BANK DR	BANK CR	ACCOUNTS RECEIVABLE DR	ACCOUNTS RECEIVABLE CR	✓			ACCOUNTS PAYABLE DR	ACCOUNTS PAYABLE C
Nov.	1	Cash Sale		482 —					1	1		
	1	J. Jamieson				1385 —			2	2		
	4	Canada Trust			2225 —				3	1		
	6	Sutherlands							4	4		7
	14	Konig Motors			418 —				5	5		76
	18	Weekly sales		1764 —		2380 —			6	6		
		Balancing Totals		2246 —	2643 —	3765 —	0 —		7	7	0 —	
									8	8		
									9	9		

MULTIPURPOSE JOURNAL

PAGE NO 5

	√	Sales CR	Wages DR		OTHER ACCOUNTS ACCOUNT	PR	DR	CR
		230 —						
					Bank Loan			3000 —
—								
		1820 —						
							992 —	

MULTIPURPOSE JOURNAL

PAGE NO 11

	√	Sales CR	Wages DR		OTHER ACCOUNTS ACCOUNT	PR	DR	CR
		482 —						
		1385 —						
					Bank Loan		2225 —	
—					Supplies Exp.		718 —	
—					Automobile		8030 —	
		4144 —						
—		6011 —	0 —				10973 —	

5. Journalize the following in a multipurpose journal.

Feb. 1: Eva Bell opened her business with a bank balance of $18 000.

2: Charge sale to Joe Brady, $42.50.

4: Borrowed $12 000 from the Canadian Imperial Bank of Commerce to buy office furniture and equipment.

5: Bought furniture that cost $7 500. Cheque #1.

8: Charge sale to D. Lust, $385.

12: Wrote cheque #2 to Bell Canada, for the installation of the phone system, $125.

12: Cash sale of services, $90.50.

13: Bought a new electronic typewriter for the business, on account from Forest City Business Equipment, $1 050.

14: Charge sale to T. Streef, $235.40.

14: Wrote cheque #3 to the bank to reduce the bank loan by $4 000.

16: Sold $815 worth of services to J. Brady on account.

20: Wrote cheques for the following expenses:

#4: Forest City Business Equipment	$1 050.00
#5: Radio Station CFPL.....................	333.75
#6: Consumers Gas...........................	189.16

25: Cash sales, $489.72; Charge sale to M. Godden, $400.00.

28: J. Brady paid his account in full.

28: Eva Bell, the owner, withdrew $200 for her personal use.

6. Ralph Ward is a carpenter who builds fine furniture to customers' specifications. On the following page are his trial balance for March 31 and his transactions for April.

Ralph Ward, Carpenter

Trial Balance

March 31, 19 ___

#	Account	Debit	Credit
1.	Cash in Hand	$ 75.00	
2.	Bank	215.80	
3.	Accounts Receivable	400.00	
10.	Shop Building	27 500.00	
12.	Tools & Equipment	8 985.00	
22.	Accounts Payable		$ 567.18
25.	Bank Loan		2 300.00
31.	R. Ward, Capital		7 844.34
32.	R. Ward, Drawings	2 800.00	
41.	Carpentry Revenue		32 440.90
51.	Advertising	224.35	
52.	Bank Interest	178.91	
53.	Office Expense	339.96	
54.	Repairs & Maintenance	1 435.78	
55.	Truck Expenses	776.67	
56.	Utilities Expense	220.95	
		$43 152.42	$43 152.42

(a) Use the trial balance to open a general ledger.

(b) Journalize the transactions into a multipurpose journal.

(c) Post the journal into Ralph's General Ledger.

Transactions for April

2: Cheque #34: to Pro hardware for small tools, $312.41.

2: Cheque #35: to *London Free Press*, advertising, $22.50

4: Sale of Service: to A. Lossing for $890 cash.

8: Bank Debit Memo: in the amount of $25.62, interest on loan.

10: Sale of Services: $1 245 for carpentry work for B. Hartley, on account.

14: Cheque #36: to Canadian Tire on account, $67.28.

15: Cheque #37: for drawings by R. Ward, $300.

18: Cash Receipt: Customer, D. Irving, paid his account, $420. The money was put into the bank immediately.

18: Cash Receipt: Customer, G. Hartley paid his account from April 10th in full.

20: Purchase: Bought new tools for the business, on account

from Modern Industrial Supply, $1 024.

21: Sale of Services: to D. Pite, $310 cash.

22: Cheque #38: to Township for business tax, $35.

29: Cheque #39: Wages to his wife for doing the books, $300.

30: Bank Debit Memo: Interest deducted from account, $41.75.

30: Cheque #40: Repairs to shop furnace, J. Bruce & Sons, $280.

Review Questions

1. True or False? (Answer in your notebook.)
   (a) Most businesses use a general journal to record their daily business transactions.
   (b) The multipurpose journal is used mainly by small businesses that do not have a lot of daily transactions.
   (c) The words ''synoptic'' and ''combination'' mean the same thing when referring to journals.
   (d) The multipurpose journal can be used by one person in a business and this is an advantage for a small business.
   (e) A multipurpose journal cuts down posting to the ledger.
   (f) A multipurpose journal is much less work than a general journal because many account names are not written.
   (g) A multipurpose journal cannot be used for accounting entries that take more than one line.
2. How many lines in a multipurpose journal does a transaction normally take to record?
3. A multipurpose journal may have one or more spare (or blank) columns. What is the spare column(s) used for?
4. Why is it necessary to have the Other Accounts columns in the multipurpose journal?
5. What kind of information do you write in the Particulars column of the multipurpose journal?
6. What do we call the process of entering transactions into the multipurpose journal?

7. What do we have to do to "balance" a multipurpose journal? Explain this process briefly but carefully indicating any accounting rules that must be followed in the process.

8. There are two ways to take a trail balance of a multipurpose journal, a formal way and an informal way. Explain each method.

9. Explain the "posting process" from the multipurpose journal including how the amounts posted are cross-referenced.

10. Some of the transactions you studied in this chapter were called special entries. List the four types of special entries that were explained in the chapter and describe them briefly.

11. List the rules for locating errors in the multipurpose journal in your notebook.

12. Draw up a table like the one below and summarize the advantages and disadvantages of the multipurpose journal in table form. Use your own words as much as possible.

Advantages	Disadvantages
(a) SAMPLE	
(b)	
(c) ONLY	

13. A friend in class cannot seem to balance her multipurpose journal. She is out by exactly $1 000. Indicate three ways your friend might be able to find this error and balance her journal.

Challenge Questions

1. The following entries do not fit "neatly" into a multipurpose journal, but they do fit. In order to show a debit entry in a credit column, you can either circle the entry (see example below), or enter the figure in red. Take a multipurpose journal form and record these "unusual" transactions. Balance and cross-balance the journal when you are done just to see if you have recorded properly.

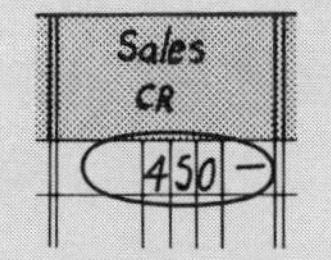

Jan. 3: The bookkeeper made a clerical error and charged the phone bill cheque to Supplies expense, instead of Telephone expense. The amount was $43.20.

9: A customer, Jack Trent, was overcharged $80 on a bill we sent to him last week for services rendered.

15: We overpaid an employee by $25.00 and she returned the extra money to the business, in cash.

28: Sales Invoice #50, in the amount of $42.00, was entered into the multipurpose journal but should have been cancelled because it was a wrong figure and a new bill was made out. Inv. #50 needs to be taken out of the journal.

31: The extra blank column has been used for the Asset account called Supplies (Dr). Last week a transposition error occurred when the accounting clerk wrote down $370.21 instead of $307.21 to record a purchase of supplies made by cheque. A correcting entry needs to be made into the journal to correct this error.

Review Case

1. Susan Pasqualli operates a bridal consulting service. Her husband helps her by recording the entries in the multipurpose journal each week. Look at the work he has done so far, and list five errors that he has made.

DATE 19__		CUSTOMER/SUPPLIER	NO	BANK		ACCOUNTS RECEIVABLE		✓			ACCOUNTS PAYABLE	
				DR	CR	DR	CR				DR	CR
Sept.	1	Opening entry		5000 —					1	1		
	2	Bought equipment	1		2400 —				2	2		
	6		2		12 —				3	3		
	8	Sold services				800 —			4	4		
	9	Paid creditor	3		190 —				5	5	190 —	
	10	Paid creditor			75 —				6	6	75 —	

2. The husband does not seem to know the basic rules of accounting. Write him a short letter explaining the six basic rules of accounting that you learned in this course, so that he can improve his bookkeeping. Use T-accounts to show him the rules for debit and credit for these accounts:

Assets; Liabilities; Capital; Drawings; Revenue; and Expenses.

Challenge Case

Alex Dobreenin operates a shoe repair business called "Moneysave Repair" in a new shopping mall. He has just been in business a few days and he knows it is time to set up his books. He has heard about the multipurpose journal but he doesn't know what it is. Alex has hired you as a consultant to tell him about the journal. Write Alex a report, less than a page, using the style shown below. In the report, tell him about the journal, how it works, what its advantages are, and show him what the journal would look like for his business. Use up the special columns for any expenses that you feel would occur regularly for Alex's shoe repair business.

Sample Report Form

TO: Mr. Alex Dobreenin

FROM: Your Name

RE: Using a Multipurpose Journal

DATE: (*Today's Date*)

MULTIPURPOSE JOURNAL

PAGE NO 1

	√	Sales CR	Wages DR		OTHER ACCOUNTS			
					ACCOUNT	PR	DR	CR
					Capital		5000 —	
					Equipment		5000 —	
					Cdn. Tire		12 —	
			800 —					

Take-a-Break

1. **Count on It**

   Start counting from one. How high will you have to count before you reach a number with the letter *a* in it?

2. **A Penny Saved**

   If you put one penny in the bank on the first day of the month, two pennies the next day, four pennies the next day and so on, doubling the number of pennies each day, how much will you have saved after 31 days not counting interest?

   (a) less than $100

   (b) about $21.5 million

   (c) about $135 000

3. **Change-Up**

   Without looking at a real coin, on what side of a quarter does the word "Canada" apppear, heads or tails?

4. **The Name Game**

   The names below are real shops or businesses with unusual names. Can you guess what type of business establishment each one is?

   Out to Lunch
   (a) family couselling service
   (b) 24-hour bookstore
   (c) caterer

   Shelf Esteem
   (a) building restoration company
   (b) gift boutique
   (c) closet shop

   Get It Together
   (a) health food store
   (b) women's apparel
   (c) plumbing

   The Way We Wore
   (a) reweaving shop
   (b) military memorabilia store
   (c) vintage clothing

   You Name It
   (a) used auto parts
   (b) second-hand clothes
   (c) vintage phonograph record store

   Suspended Animation
   (a) kite store
   (b) wine tasting
   (c) belt and suspenders store

Chapter 9 Special Journals

Objectives

At the end of this chapter you will be able to

1. recognize how special journals fit into the accounting cycle; and
2. record accounting transactions in a cash receipts journal, cash payments journal, purchases journal, and sales journal.

9.1 Overview

In the last chapter you learned all about a useful accounting book of entry called the multipurpose columnar journal. When a business is either new or small, the multipurpose journal is an extremely good way to record transactions. Once a business starts to grow, however, the accounting paperwork grows (Figure 9-1). A bigger number of entries means more work and it could be that more accounting clerks will be needed to handle the work. This chapter will show you how to use extra clerks by using four special books of account or ''special journals.''

Special journals are books of account which handle only certain accounting functions, and are used by larger businesses.

Figure 9-1
The special journals that you will learn about in this chapter are used in larger businesses, which have more paperwork and more staff to deal with it.

9.2 The Accounting Cycle

These new special journals are an addition to the general journal. Here is the accounting cycle, with the new special journals, to help you frame a picture of the accounting process in your mind.

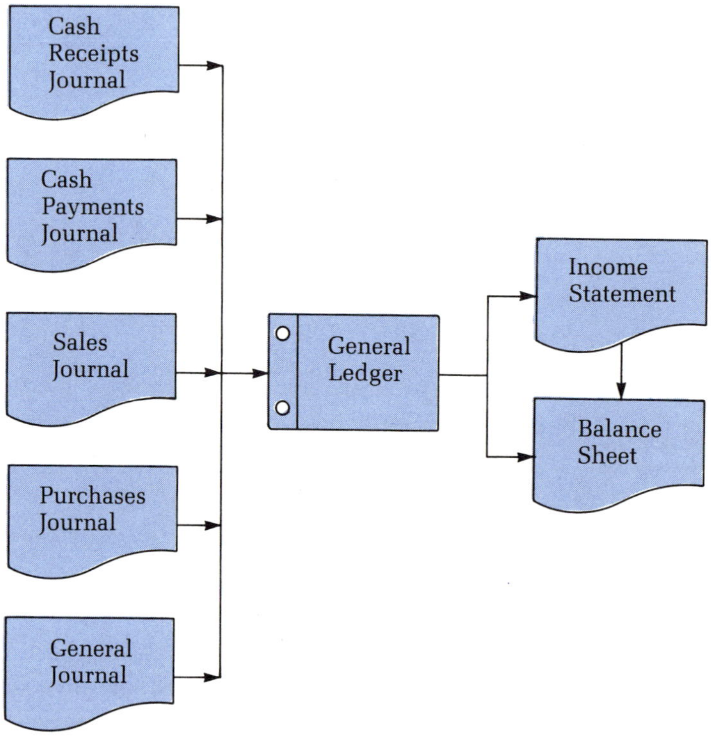

9.3 Cash Receipts Journal

All transactions which result in cash coming into the business are put into the **cash receipts journal.** There are so few ways in which cash can come into a business that we can list them very briefly:

1. Cash sale of services.
2. Customer pays cash on account.
3. Owner invests cash into the business.
4. Business borrows money from the bank.

Here are these transactions journalized into a cash receipts journal.

CASH RECEIPTS JOURNAL

PAGE NO 2

DATE		PARTICULARS	OTHER ACCOUNTS CR.			√	ACCTS. REC. CR.	SALES CR	INV. NO					BANK DR
19—			ACCOUNT	PR	AMOUNT									
Feb.	1	Cash sale						32 10						32 10

PAGE NO 2

DATE		PARTICULARS	OTHER ACCOUNTS CR.			√	ACCTS. REC. CR.	SALES CR	INV. NO					BANK DR
			ACCOUNT	PR	AMOUNT									
Feb.	3	Jenny Wilford					85 —							85 —

PAGE NO 2

DATE		PARTICULARS	OTHER ACCOUNTS CR.			√	ACCTS. REC. CR.	SALES CR	INV. NO					BANK DR
			ACCOUNT	PR	AMOUNT									
Feb.	15	Owner invests cash	H. Todd, – Capital		900 —									900 —

PAGE NO 2

DATE		PARTICULARS	OTHER ACCOUNTS CR.			√	ACCTS. REC. CR.	SALES CR	INV. NO					BANK DR
			ACCOUNT	PR	AMOUNT									
Feb.	29	Business borrows	Bank Loan		500 —									500 —

Here is the cash receipts journal with all four transactions shown.

DATE 19—		PARTICULARS	OTHER ACCOUNTS CR. ACCOUNT	PR	AMOUNT	√	ACCTS. REC. CR.	SALES CR.	INV. NO.		
Feb.	1	Cash sale						32 10			
	3	Jenny Wilford					85 –				
	15	Owner invests cash	H. Todd, – Capital	31	900 –						
	29	Business borrows	Bank Loan	21	500 –						

There are four things to note about the cash receipts journal:

1. All entries in the cash receipts journal involve a debit to the Bank account.
2. There are extra blank columns in case the business has special cash receipts and needs an extra column. It may, for example, have two types of revenue.
3. Only cash sales are entered directly into the cash receipts journal. (Charge sales are entered in another journal.)
4. There is an Other Accounts column for entries which have not been anticipated or which do not occur very often.

The whole cash receipts journal with the journal cross-balanced and with posting notations is shown below. When posting to the ledger, the notation CRJ is used, coming from the first three letters of the **C**ash **R**eceipts **J**ournal. The numbers below the columns show that the column totals have been posted.

DATE 19—		PARTICULARS	OTHER ACCOUNTS CR. ACCOUNT	PR	AMOUNT	√	ACCTS. REC. CR.	SALES CR.	INV. NO.		
Feb.	1	Cash sale						32 10			
	3	Jenny Wilford					85 –				
	15	Owner invests cash	H. Todd, – Capital	30	900 –						
	29	Business borrows	Bank Loan	20	500 –						
					1400 –		85 –	32 10			
							(3)	(40)			

CASH RECEIPTS JOURNAL

PAGE NO 2

		BANK DR
		32 10
		85 —
		900 —
		500 —

ACCOUNT: Bank NO. 2

DATE		PARTICULARS	PR	DEBIT	CREDIT	DR. CR	BALANCE
Feb.	29		CRJ2	1 517 10		DR	1 517 10

ACCOUNT: Accounts Receivable NO. 3

DATE		PARTICULARS	PR	DEBIT	CREDIT	DR. CR	BALANCE
Feb.	29		CRJ2	85 —		DR	85 —

ACCOUNT: Bank Loan NO. 20

DATE		PARTICULARS	PR	DEBIT	CREDIT	DR. CR	BALANCE
Feb.	29		CRJ2		500 —	CR	500 —

CASH RECEIPTS JOURNAL

PAGE NO 2

		BANK DR
		32 10
		85 —
		900 —
		500 —
		1 517 10
		(1)

ACCOUNT: H. Todd, Capital NO. 30

DATE		PARTICULARS	PR	DEBIT	CREDIT	DR. CR	BALANCE
Feb.	29		CRJ2		900 —	CR	900 —

ACCOUNT: Sales NO. 40

DATE		PARTICULARS	PR	DEBIT	CREDIT	DR. CR	BALANCE
Feb.	29		CRJ2		32 —	CR	32 10

9.4 Cash Payments Journal

The second major special journal is the **cash payments journal.** All accounting transactions which involve a credit (or a decrease) to the Bank account are entered in this journal. Most of the entries in this journal will come from writing out a cheque in payment of something. You may also find an entry that is a credit to the bank which comes from an action taken by the bank (Figure 9-2). For example, when the bank deducts

Figure 9-2
When the owner of a business withdraws cash or when action is taken by a bank to deduct payment for a loan, the transaction is recorded in the cash payments journal.

DATE 19—		PARTICULARS
Feb.	1	L. Fraser

DATE		PARTICULARS
Feb.	8	Office Outfitters

DATE		PARTICULARS
Feb.	9	Canada Supply Ltd.

DATE		PARTICULARS
Feb.	19	Owner withdrew funds

money from a business account for interest on a bank loan, this is entered in the cash payments journal. Here are four sample transactions:

1. Paid cash for an expense.
2. Paid cash for the purchase of an asset.
3. Paid cash to reduce an account payable.
4. Owner withdrew cash from the business for personal use.

CASH PAYMENTS JOURNAL

PAGE NO. 2

OTHER ACCOUNTS DR.			√	ACCTS. PAY. DR.	OFFICE EXP. DR.	REPAIR EXP. DR.	WAGES EXP. DR.			CH. NO.	BANK CR.
ACCOUNT	PR	AMOUNT									
							240 —			23	240 —

PAGE NO. 2

OTHER ACCOUNTS DR.			√	ACCTS. PAY. DR.	OFFICE EXP. DR.	REPAIR EXP. DR.	WAGES EXP. DR.			CH. NO.	BANK CR.
ACCOUNT	PR	AMOUNT									
Furniture		2000 —								24	2000 —

PAGE NO. 2

OTHER ACCOUNTS DR.			√	ACCTS. PAY. DR.	OFFICE EXP. DR.	REPAIR EXP. DR.	WAGES EXP. DR.			CH. NO.	BANK CR.
ACCOUNT	PR	AMOUNT									
				132 —						25	132 —

PAGE NO. 2

OTHER ACCOUNTS DR.			√	ACCTS. PAY. DR.	OFFICE EXP. DR.	REPAIR EXP. DR.	WAGES EXP. DR.			CH. NO.	BANK CR.
ACCOUNT	PR	AMOUNT									
J. Hill, —		600 —								26	600 —
Drawings											

There are four things to note about the cash payments journal:

1. All entries in the cash payments journal have a credit to the Bank account.
2. The special columns are used for those items which occur most frequently in a business. In this sample, it is assumed that office expenses, repairs expenses, and wages will be the expense accounts that are debited most often.
3. As with the CRJ, there is an Other Accounts column for any items which do not have their own special column.
4. At the end of the month, the cash payments journal is totalled, cross-balanced, and posted just like the cash receipts journal.

Here is the cash payments journal, balanced and posted to the ledger. The posting reference is CPJ, coming from **C**ash **P**ayments **J**ournal.

DATE 19__		PARTICULARS	OTHER ACCOUNTS DR.			√	ACCTS. PAY. DR.	OFFICE EXP DR.	REPAIR EXP. DR.	WAGES EXP. DR.	
			ACCOUNT	PR	AMOUNT						
Feb.	1	L. Fraser								240 —	
	8	Office Outfitters	Furniture	11	2 000 —						
	9	Canada Supply Ltd.					132 —				
	18	Owner withdrew funds	J. Hill, — Drawings	31	600 —						
					2 600 —		132 —	0 —	0 —	240 —	
							(21)			(58)	

CASH PAYMENTS JOURNAL

PAGE NO. 2

		CH. NO.	BANK CR
		23	240 —
		24	2000 —
		25	132 —
		26	600 —
		26	2972 —

GENERAL LEDGER

ACCOUNT: Bank NO. 2

DATE		PARTICULARS	PR	DEBIT	CREDIT	DR CR	BALANCE
Feb.	29		CPJ1		2972 —	DR	1384 90

ACCOUNT: Accounts Payable NO. 21

DATE		PARTICULARS	PR	DEBIT	CREDIT	DR CR	BALANCE
Feb.	29		CPJ	132 —		CR	2644 —

ACCOUNT: J. Hill, Drawings NO. 30

DATE		PARTICULARS	PR	DEBIT	CREDIT	DR CR	BALANCE
Feb.	18		CPJ2	600 —		DR	600 —

ACCOUNT: Repairs Expense NO. 57

DATE		PARTICULARS	PR	DEBIT	CREDIT	DR CR	BALANCE

ACCOUNT: Wages Expense NO. 58

DATE		PARTICULARS	PR	DEBIT	CREDIT	DR CR	BALANCE
Feb.	29		CPJ2	240 —		DR	240 —

9.5 Sales Journal

The third special journal is the simplest of the four you will study. Here is what the headings on the sales journal look like.

Date		Particulars	Other Accounts Cr.							Sales Cr.
			Account	PR	Amount					

The **sales journal** has only charge sales entered into it. (Remember that cash sales are entered into the cash receipts journal.) Usually no other transactions get entered into the sales journal. Therefore, this special journal only needs the columns you see above because all charge sales are a credit to Sales and a debit to the Accounts Receivable account. If we look at one sample transaction it will give you the idea about how this journal is used.

Sale on account to J. Gleeson, $124.00.

Date 19—		Particulars	Other Accounts Cr.							Sales Cr.
			Account	PR	Amount					
Aug.	3	J. Gleeson								124 –

The sample sales journal below shows four such entries. All the entries in the sales journal will be identical.

Date 19—		Particulars	Other Accounts Cr.							Sales Cr.
			Account	PR	Amount					
Aug.	3	J. Gleeson								124
	4	A. Bell								300
	5	H. Kinick								52
	5	G. Richardson								476
										952
										(40)

SALES JOURNAL

PAGE NO 8

INV NO.		√	ACCTS. REC. DR.

SALES JOURNAL

PAGE NO 8

INV NO.		√	ACCTS. REC. DR.
81			124 —

SALES JOURNAL

PAGE NO 8

INV NO.		√	ACCTS. REC. DR.
81			124 —
82			300 —
83			52 —
84			476 —
			952 —
			(3)

There are only three things to note about the sales journal:

1. Even though there is an Other Accounts section in this journal, it will seldom be used.
2. The columns which are blank will not be needed, unless the business has two different types of sales and wants to keep track of each type. For example, a person who is a plumber and an electrician might have two Sales columns, one for plumbing services and one for electrical services.
3. The sales journal is balanced and posted exactly like the other two journals you have studied in this chapter.

9.6 Purchases Journal

The fourth and final special journal is the purchases journal. It is more common to find this used in a business which sells goods rather than services, but we can study its usefulness here. The **purchases journal** is used to record any bills received by our business which we want to set up as an account payable. Here are the headings of the journal.

DATE		PARTICULARS	OTHER ACCOUNTS DR.			ADVERT. EXP. DR.	OFFICE EXP. DR.	REPAIRS EXP. DR.	WAGES EXP. DR.	
			ACCOUNT	PR	AMOUNT					

DATE 19—		PARTICULARS
Aug.	1	Bought band saw

DATE		PARTICULARS
Aug.	7	Andy the Plumbe

DATE 19—		PARTICULARS
Aug.	1	Bought band sav
	7	Andy the Plumbe
	9	Pete's Garage
	12	Station CTKO
	13	Stafford Motors
	28	The Town Crier

In this chapter we shall restrict the purchases journal entries to two types of transactions.

1. Purchase of assets on account.
2. Bills for expenses incurred.

PURCHASES JOURNAL

PAGE NO. ______

INV. NO.		√	ACCTS. PAY. CR.

Here are two sample transactions to show what is meant by each of these two types of transactions.

Bought some shop equipment on account $8 000.

PURCHASES JOURNAL

PAGE NO. 8

	OTHER ACCOUNTS DR. ACCOUNT	PR	AMOUNT	ADVERT. EXP. DR.	OFFICE EXP. DR.	REPAIRS EXP. DR.	WAGES EXP. DR.		INV. NO.		√	ACCTS. PAY. CR.
	Shop Equip.		8000 –						667			8000 –

Note that the column labelled "Inv.#" refers to the invoice number which appears on the invoice or bill which our business receives. It is the supplier's (creditor's) number, not ours.

Received a bill for repairs to plumbing, $330.

PURCHASES JOURNAL

PAGE NO. 8

	OTHER ACCOUNTS DR. ACCOUNT	PR	AMOUNT	ADVERT. EXP. DR.	OFFICE EXP. DR.	REPAIRS EXP. DR.	WAGES EXP. DR.		INV. NO.		√	ACCTS. PAY. CR.
						330 –			75			330 –

Here is the purchases journal with the two entries shown together, some other entries added in for flavouring, the journal totalled, balanced, and completed with posting references.

PURCHASES JOURNAL

PAGE NO. 8

	OTHER ACCOUNTS DR. ACCOUNT	PR	AMOUNT	ADVERT. EXP. DR.	OFFICE EXP. DR.	REPAIRS EXP. DR.	WAGES EXP. DR.	Truck EXP. DR	INV. NO.		√	ACCTS. PAY. CR.
	Shop Equip.	12	8000 –						667			8000 –
						330 –			75			330 –
								265 –	123			265 –
				80 –					97			80 –
	Delivy. Truck	13	9500 –						C42			9500 –
				42 –					330			42 –
			17500 –	122 –	0 –	330 –	0 –	265 –				18217 –
			(51)	(51)	(54)	(55)		(57)				(21)

The special points you must remember about the purchases journal are:

1. Every entry in the purchases journal has a credit to Accounts Payable. You just have to decide where the debit goes. (This journal would be better called the Accounts Payable journal, but it isn't.)
2. The columns can be used for any expense item that you wish and this will depend on which expenses will be used most often by the business.
3. The Other Accounts column is used for any debit items which do not have their own special column.
4. A purchase of some kind that was partly paid for in cash would have to be entered in the cash payments journal.

9.7 Summary

Once a business starts to grow, the accounting system must grow with the business. This means that the work will expand and may have to be done by more than one clerk or bookkeeper. This can only be accomplished if the business uses several different books of original entry. This chapter shows you samples of special journals that can be used to divide up the accounting work among several employees in a business. Only certain transactions are entered in special journals and this makes it easier to find certain entries. The larger a business becomes the more the accounting work will have to be broken down into small components and handled by several people.

Check and see if you have met the chapter objectives. You should be able to

1. recognize how special journals fit into the accounting cycle; and
2. record accounting transactions in a cash receipts journal, cash payments journal, purchases journal, and sales journal.

Dictionary of Terms

Cash Payments Journal A journal used to record all transactions that decrease (credit) the Bank account.

Cash Receipts Journal A journal used to record all transactions that increase (debit) the Bank account.

Purchases Journal A journal used to record all transactions which result in an increase (credit) to the Accounts Payable account.

Sales Journal A journal used to record all charge sales.

Special Journals A term that refers to journals that handle only certain accounting transactions.

Exercises

1. What do the letters CRJ, CPJ, SJ, PJ, and GJ stand for?
2. What special journal is this?

DATE	PARTICULARS	OTHER ACCOUNTS DR.			ADVERT. EXP. DR.	OFFICE EXP. DR.	REPAIRS EXP. DR.	WAGES EXP. DR.	
		ACCOUNT	PR	AMOUNT					

3. All of the transactions below belong in the cash receipts journal. Indicate what account has to be debited and what account has to be credited to record the transaction properly.
   (a) The bank loaned our business $13 000 to buy a new computerized lathe for the shop.
   (b) Cash sales for the week (that were deposited in the bank) totalled $2 546.18.
   (c) Our customer, Ralph Schoendienst, paid us $875 cash which he has owed for four months. We deposited the money.
   (d) The owner put $5 000 into the business from personal funds, and it was deposited in the bank.
4. These transactions below belong in the cash payments journal. Indicate the account to debit and credit for each entry.
   (a) Cheque #91, to Bell Canada for the monthly phone bill, $167.72.
   (b) Cheque #92, to Loeb Ltd., to reduce our account, $3 385.31.
   (c) Cheque #93, to the bank, $3 000 to reduce our bank loan.
   (d) The bank sent a debit memo indicating they had deducted $125.02 from our account for interest on our bank loan.
   (e) Cheque #94, to Joe Palmer for repairs to cover wind damage to the premises, $1 486.09.
   (f) Cheque #95 to the owner, Jason Fiorotto, for a personal withdrawal of funds from the business, $500.
5. All of the transactions below belong in the purchases journal. Indicate what account has to be debited and what account has to be credited to record the transaction properly.
   (a) Bought two hectares of land on which to erect a building. Cost was $75 000. Seller was Campeau Properties.
   (b) Received an invoice from a supplier, Medway Shippers, in the amount of $810.23. Their invoice #M662.

(c) The telephone bill came in the mail and we set it up as an account payable, $88.07, to Bell Canada.

(d) Our lawyer, G. Bishop, sent us a bill for $500 for legal services in connection with buying the land.

INV NO.		√	ACCTS. PAY. CR.

(e) We received an invoice from the television station, CHOO for last month's TV commercials, $1 560, #CH679.

6. For each of the transactions below, indicate by writing down the letters CRJ (Cash Receipts Journal), CPJ (Cash Payments Journal), PJ (Purchases Journal), or SJ (Sales Journal), into which journal the transaction would be entered.

(a) Sold services on account to J. Tupper for $245.50.

(b) Bought a new automobile for the business and wrote a cheque for $18 750.

(c) Cash sales for the day totalled $1 874.25.

(d) Borrowed $5 600 from a trust company to meet business cash needs, and deposited funds in our bank account.

(e) Cheque #1893 in the amount of $8 359 was paid to our supplier Magyar Distributing Ltd.

(f) Rewired our customer's old home and billed him $480 for the service. He promised to pay in two weeks.

(g) The bank sent up a memo saying they had deducted $23.95 from our business Bank account for monthly service charges.

(h) We deposited $4 803.03 into the business Bank account. This represented cash sales for the week.

(i) Bought supplies for the business, paper bags, and wrapping paper. Total cost was $902.01. Wrote cheque #1894.

7. Record the following accounting transactions in the Sales Journal used by ''Lozingers Realty.'' For the journal page use ''9.''

Sept. 1: Sold services to D. Peters, $450.00. Invoice #2673.

3: Sold services to T. Hanson, $1 200.00. Invoice #2674.

4: Invoice #2675 to M. Bishop, for services $128.00.

10: Services sold to J. Held, $1 040.00, invoice #2677.

12: Sold services to Y. Chin, $770.00, invoice #2678.

15: Services sold to Col. H. Watterston, $1 500.00, invoice #2679.

Total, balance, and rule the journal when you have done the journalizing.

8. Record the following transactions in a cash receipts journal. The business transactions relate to Mr. Tiffany Stain, an artist. The journal page you are using is "3."

Mar. 1: Borrowed $2 000 from the bank to buy art supplies. The loan is to be paid back in six months.

4: Sold two paintings for cash, $750 and $475. (This may be entered as one transaction.)

7: Tiffany was left $5 000 as an inheritance in her uncle's will. She decided to put this into her business and deposited the money. Treat it as an investment by the owner.

10: Sale of another painting for $1 350 cash. The money was deposited immediately into the business Bank account.

18: Sale of small painting, $70 cash. Deposited.

20: Received a cheque from a customer, I. Grewal, on account for $325.00.

28: Cash sale of $340 for a painting. Deposited.

31: Another customer, D. Kasparav, paid the balance of her account, $210 cash. Deposited.

Total, balance, and rule the journal when you have done the journalizing.

9. Record the following transactions for S. Kuyper, who has a shoe repair business, in a cash payments journal. Start on page "6."

Jun 2: Cheque #102, to Hodge Realty for the monthly rent, $315.

4: Paid the bank part of the bank loan, $300. Cheque #103.

5: Cheque #104 to Shopping News for advertising, $17.50.

5: Cheque #105 to Tony Cervini, $75.00, part-time wages.

8: Paid the light bill of $119.95. Cheque #106.

12: Payment on account to Canada Last, $75.62. Cheque #107.

18: Monthly bank statement shows a debit memo of $16.10 for interest on the business loan.

20: Cheque #108 to owner, S. Kuypert, drawings of $1 400.00.

20: Cheque #109 to Ken's siding for repairs to the eavestrough on the storefront, $98.20.

29: Paid $52.40 for bags to put customers' shoes in. Cheque #110.

10. The following transactions relate to the purchases journal of Brenda Butkowski who operates a travel agency. Start on page 3 and record the following entries for Brenda's business for March.

Mar. 5: Bought new computer equipment for the business, to provide immediate access to reservation information, at cost of $8 600. (Set this up as a fixed asset—computer equipment.) Invoice #2265.

8: New desks to hold the computer terminal, disk drive, and printer cost $820.00. (Charge to furniture.) Invoice #265.

12: Received bill for electricity for the previous month, $210. Invoice #873.

13: Newspaper advertising invoice in the amount of $125.00 was received in the mail. Invoice #FP82.

15: Bought supplies for the new computer system from Data Pro Supplies, $234.25. Invoice #2-0069.

20: An invoice was received from Reliable Electric for repairs to the air conditioning system—cost $314.00. Invoice #RE331.

28: Bought some keychains, rulers, and wallets to hand out as gifts to travel clients at a cost of $515.00. (Charge to miscellaneous expense.); Mr. Advertising, invoice #A39621.

29: Received an invoice from the accountant, J. Jamieson, for services rendered in doing year-end accounting work, $1 200. Invoice #BL746.

29: Received an invoice from Imperial Oil for gasoline and other car expenses, $872.38. Invoice #88-2661.

31: Bell Canada sent its phone bill for February, $376.01. Invoice #5891.

11. Here are some short descriptions of accounting transactions. Given this very brief information, indicate in your notes into which of the special journals (CRJ, CPJ, SJ, or PJ) you think each entry should be entered.

(a) Cash sales slip.
(b) Charge sales slip.
(c) Bill from supplier.
(d) Bank debit memo.
(e) Cheque #1410.
(f) Credit note to customer.
(g) Credit note from supplier.
(h) Note from the bank indicating that loan was approved.
(i) Bill from city for property taxes.

Review Questions

1. What is another name for the combination journal?
2. Does the general journal get replaced when we use special journals?
3. Name the five journals that you have learned in this chapter.
4. List the four transactions that can be entered in a cash receipts journal.
5. What is the purpose of the Other Accounts column in a special journal?
6. What is one thing every entry in a CRJ has in common?
7. Identify a service business that would split its revenue into two groups.
8. What do all entries in a cash payments journal have in common?
9. List the four transactions that are entered in a cash payments journal.
10. How does a business know what names to put at the top of the blank columns in a cash payments journal?
11. Assume that you bought a car for $18 000. You paid $5 000 down and promised to pay the rest in 60 days.
    (a) In what journal would you record this transaction?
    (b) What accounts would you debit and credit for this entry?
12. What do the following notations mean?
    CPJ8; CRJ9; SJ2; PJ10; GJ4; MJ
13. There is only one type of accounting entry that goes into a sales journal. What entry is that?
14. What two basic entries are recorded in a purchases journal?
15. To what does the notation "Inv.#" refer in a purchases journal? In what other journal do you see the same notation?
16. Every item in the purchases journal has one side that is the same. What is this? Because of this, what would a better name be for the purchases journal?
17. When does a business begin to consider seriously using special journals.?
18. Without looking back in your text, draw the accounting cycle in your notebook. Use the following outline to jog your memory.

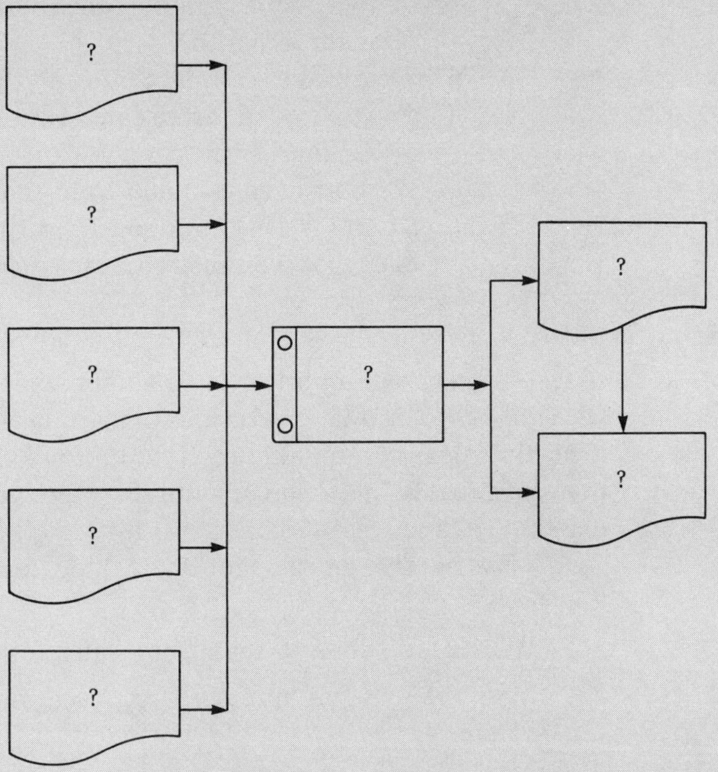

Challenge Questions

1. If you were going to make entries in each of the special journals below, there is one column that always has a figure entered into it. Look up each journal if you have to, and indicate what column in each of these journals always has an entry in it. (*Note*: In the case of one journal, there is more than one column that always has an entry. Name all the columns in this case.)

   Cash Receipts Journal

   Cash Payments Journal

   Sales Journal

   Purchases Journal

2. The following transactions are "weird" or "unusual" accounting entries. Indicate into which special journal they would best fit.

   Nov. 1: The owner donated a desk, which had been sitting at home and had not been used, to the business.

   5: Bought a new computer for the business. Half was paid

for by cheque, and the other half will be owed to the supplier for a month.

8: We owed a supplier $200 and the supplier owed us $200 so we decided just to cancel out these entries in our books rather than swap cheques for nothing.

20: We borrowed $40 000 from the bank. Of the total loan, $3 500 is for a mortgage and the rest is for a short term loan that we must pay back in 90 days.

Review Case

Arkley's Welding Emporium is a small business that has grown quickly. Up until now, the owner, who knows nothing about accounting, has used a multipurpose columnar journal for his books. His wife is complaining that she needs help to keep up with the paperwork and suggests that they use the "five-journal system" and hire another employee.

Name the five journals for Mr. Arkley, and answer these questions that he has:

1. "Where do I look to see all my sales for the month?"
2. "Are the cheque numbers recorded anywhere with this new system?"
3. "How many new people do I have to hire for this fancy new system?"
4. "How many general ledgers do I need with this new system?"

Challenge Case

Given the four special journals below, record the following transactions for a new secretarial services business that has just opened up. *Balance* each journal when you have finished journalizing. (*Note*: Some of the entries are tricky, so go carefully!)

Mar. 1: The business was started with $5 000 capital, a bank loan for another $20 000, and a donation to the business of a computer system worth $2 000 by the owner, Lana Lang.

4: Sale of services to Firestone Co., on account, $1 800. Invoice #1.

4: Bought new software, costing $810.00, on account from Land of Software. Invoice #LS2288.

6: Bought new filing cabinets on account from Wilson Stationers (four cabinets @ $69.95 each). Invoice #WS4785.

8: Sale of services, cash $240. Invoice #2.

8: Cheque #1, to pay $500 toward the bank loan.

12: Cheque #2, monthly rent $750.

12: Cheque #3, telephone installation, $102.95.

14: Sale of services: cash, $80 invoice #3; on account to Jason Mfg., $450. Invoice #4.

17: Bought a new car for the business, $18 000 full price. Paid

CASH RECEIPTS JOURNAL

PAGE NO 5

CULARS	OTHER ACCOUNTS CR.			√	ACCTS. REC. CR.	SALES CR	INV. NO					BANK DR.
	ACCOUNT	PR	AMOUNT									

CASH PAYMENTS JOURNAL

PAGE NO. 8

	OTHER ACCOUNTS DR.			√	ACCTS. PAY. DR.	OFFICE EXP. DR.	REPAIR EXP. DR.	WAGES EXP. DR.			CH. NO.	BANK CR.
	ACCOUNT	PR	AMOUNT									

SALES JOURNAL

PAGE NO. 6

ULARS	OTHER ACCOUNTS CR.							SALES CR.	INV. NO.		√	ACCTS. REC. DR.
	ACCOUNT	PR	AMOUNT									

PURCHASES JOURNAL

PAGE NO. 7

	OTHER ACCOUNTS DR.			ADVERT. EXP. DR.	OFFICE EXP. DR.	REPAIRS EXP. DR.	WAGES EXP. DR.		INV. NO.		√	ACCTS. PAY. CR.
	ACCOUNT	PR	AMOUNT									

$1 000 down, cheque #4, and promised to pay the rest over a period of six months to Stauffer Motors.

18: There was an error on our invoice to Jason Mfg. It should have been for $480. We phoned and apologized and they promised to destroy the original invoice. We will correct this on our books and make out a new invoice.

20: Bought some paint for the business to finish the repairs being made, on account from "Colour Your Office," $115.25.

22: Sales invoice on account to K. Henderson, $75.

24: The Firestone Co. and Jason Mfg. both paid their accounts in full.

31: Cheque to the owner, $400 drawings, #5.

31: Advertising bill received from the Evening Star, $333. Set it up as an account payable. Invoice #ES77125.

Take-a-Break

1. **Couplets**

The 30 three-letter words below can be paired to make 15 accounting words. Each pair of words is only used once.

PRO	ALS	UNT	POS	REF	QUE
COL	FIT	OME	CRE	URE	ITS
REC	GER	LED	BER	TOT	FIG
AMO	ORD	AID	INC	DIT	UMN
DIG	CHE	UND	NUM	REP	TED

2. **The Buck Stops Here**

Although it is proper to say one dollar when talking about currency, many people say ''buck'' when referring to a dollar. For each clue below, you are looking for a word or phrase that contains the word ''buck'' in it.

(a) Sci-fi hero of the 25th century.

(b) Shift responsibility to another.

(c) Author of ''The Good Earth.''

(d) Sword-wielding pirate.

(e) The home of Queen Elizabeth.

(f) Slang for cowboy.

(g) Old horse drawn vehicle.

(h) Hunting ammunition.

(i) Annie's rich guardian.

(j) Purchase at a driving range.

3. **Funny Business**

If big business lived up to the promise of their company names, you might expect Sunkist to make tanning lotion. Here are some other goods and services that companies might provide if their names were a literal indication of their business. Can you match each hypothetical product with its most likely corporate name?

(1) Canadian Pacific	(a) weightlifting equipment
(2) Canada Packers	(b) calendars
(3) Goodyear	(c) shipping containers
(4) Husky	(d) bottled gases
(5) Air Canada	(e) salmon fishing

Accounting at Work

Bookkeeper

Kim Chan has been working for Student Movers for a year and a half. She handles all the accounting and secretarial work for the business, since it is fairly new and still growing. The accounting records are kept in a multipurpose columnar journal that looks like this:

DATE		CUSTOMER/SUPPLIER	NO	BANK		ACCOUNTS RECEIVABLE		√			ACCOUNTS PAYABLE	
				DR	CR	DR	CR				DR	CR
									1	1		
									2	2		

Kim uses this journal to record all accounting transactions for the business. Because she studied accounting in high school, she has an excellent grasp of how to keep a set of books for a small service business. Since Student Movers is fairly new, there are only a few entries each month. By the time Kim gets to month end, she has about two pages of journal entries. Her main task is to make sure the journal is balanced at month end before she posts it into the General Ledger accounts. As a precaution, Kim balances the journal at the end of each week and puts pencil totals into the journal. Because she is careful and neat, the balancing at month end has never been a problem in the time Kim has been the bookkeeper. Kim's accounting job is important to the success of Student Movers since all sales, purchases, payroll payments, and deposits are recorded into the multicolumn journal. Kim had studied how to use this journal in her high school accounting courses and this was part of the reason that Student Movers hired her. Kim also knows that as the business grows, her boss will want to split the duties she now performs between a secretary and a full time bookkeeper. If Kim has to choose between two careers, she knows she will want to do the accounting for the business. She feels confident that she can handle the new bookkeeping duties full time, and her boss regards her as a valuable employee of the business.

Questions for Discussion

1. What two characteristics does Kim use at her job that make her a valuable employee?
2. Kim never has any trouble balancing her books at month end. Why is that?

3. Could you do Kim's job with the training you have received so far in accounting? Explain.
4. Assume that you are the boss of Student Movers. You have decided to make Kim the Head Bookkeeper and to hire two more accounting clerks. Where do you look for these new clerks? Why?

MULTIPURPOSE JOURNAL

PAGE NO 1

	√	Moving Income CR			OTHER ACCOUNTS			
					ACCOUNT	PR	DR	CR

5

Introduction to Payroll

Chapter 10
Understanding Payroll

Chapter 10 Understanding Payroll

Objectives

At the end of this chapter you will

1. know the four basic ways employees are paid;
2. be able to calculate a person's net pay; and
3. recognize some key payroll documents, such as a time card, statement of earnings, employee earnings record card, and a payroll journal.

10.1 Reasons for Payroll Accuracy

The calculation of payroll in the workplace is an important accounting function for two main reasons:

1. Employees will expect, and are entitled, to be paid accurately for their work.
2. The government requires by law that certain deductions be taken from a paycheque.

10.2 Methods of Paying Employees

We can assume in this textbook that there are four basic methods to pay employees. These are listed below and will be explained in the following notes.

1. Salary 2. Piece Rate 3. Hourly Rate 4. Commission

Salary

Cindy Post has been hired as a travel agent for a travel agency in Regina. Her starting salary is \$24 000 a year. Even though Cindy's salary is quoted to her as an annual salary, Cindy will most likely be paid once a month. Her monthly salary will be calculated like this:

$$\frac{\$24\ 000}{12 \text{ months}} = \$2\ 000 \text{ per month}$$

The \$2 000 per month is Cindy's **gross pay**. There are certain payroll deductions that will be made from Cindy's gross pay to arrive at the **net pay** she takes home. Net pay is commonly called take-home pay.

Piece Rate

Tyler Kavitz has a job in a factory making children's toys. He is paid \$0.75 for each toy he produces. Therefore, if Tyler makes 150 toys in one day his gross pay would be:

150 parts x \$0.75 = \$112.50

The more parts Tyler makes, the higher his daily gross pay will be. Like Cindy, Tyler will have certain money deductions taken from his gross pay to arrive at his take-home pay. Tyler receives his cheque every two weeks. The employer determines whether employees get paid weekly, every two weeks, or monthly.

Hourly Rate

Cara Beatty works at a shoe store part-time after school and on Saturday. She is paid \$3.75 for each hour she works. Last week she worked 15 hours. Therefore, her gross pay was:

15 hours x \$3.75 = \$56.25

(Many teenagers today have part-time jobs and you will probably be aware of how ''hourly-rate payroll'' works.)

Commission Rate

Rusty Bender sells used cars in Victoria and is paid on a commission basis, which depends on how many cars he sells. For each car he sells he gets a percent of the selling price of the car. For example, if Rusty sells a car for \$18 000, his commission (gross pay) is:

\$18 000 x 2% = \$360.

The more cars Rusty sells, the higher his gross pay will be.

The method used for paying employees will vary depending on the type of work the employees do. Here are some examples of jobs and the method of paying employees that might be used.

Lawyer	Salary
Store Clerk	Hourly Rate
Worm Picker	Piece Rate
Real Estate Sales	Commisssion
Press Operator	Hourly Rate
Dog Food Sales	Commission
Pilot	Salary
Tomato Picker	Piece Rate

Figure 10-1
There are different methods of paying employees, depending on the job. Which of these people do you think would be paid a salary and which an hourly rate of pay? Are there some jobs illustrated here that you think would be paid by commission or by piece rate?

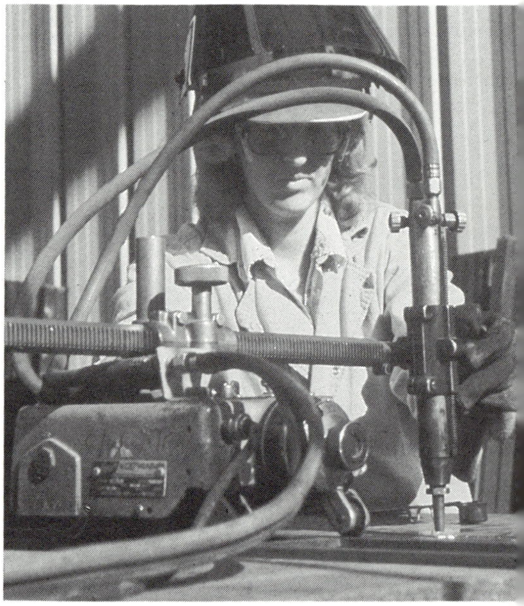

10.3 Time Cards

Employees paid on an hourly rate basis may have to complete a time card to show the regular and the overtime hours they have worked in a given week. The time card may be completed by hand or punched in a time clock device located in a plant or office. If a time clock is used, the worker inserts a card into the clock and the time clock automatically punches the time the employee starts work on the card. At the end of the day, the employee inserts the time card into the time clock and punches again. The number of hours worked by the employee is recorded automatically.

The time card below shows actual hours worked in one week by an employee. In this business all employees work a 40 hour week from Monday to Friday. Any time over 40 hours per week is *overtime* and employees are paid *time-and-a-half* for overtime. In the time card shown for Kate Allison, you will notice that she has worked two overtime hours on Wednesday. She will be paid time-and-a-half for the two hours.

TIME CARD

NO. 20

NAME Kate Allison

PAY PERIOD ENDING April 4, 19__

DAY	HOURS		
	TOTAL	REGULAR	OVERTIME
M	8	8	
T	8	8	
W	10	8	2
T	8	8	
F	8	8	
TOTALS	42	40	2

	HOURS	RATE	GROSS PAY
REGULAR			
OVERTIME			
		GROSS PAY	

"I know it's your first time in 38 years, but what would happen if everyone was ten minutes late for work?"

Once we have the time card totalled, we can calculate Kate's gross pay for the week. Here is the calculation for the regular hours:

40 regular hours x $4.00 per hour = $160.00 gross pay

For every hour overtime Kate works, she collects *time-and-a-half*. This means that she gets her regular hourly rate plus half of that rate for every overtime hour she works. Since Kate makes $4.00 per hour, her overtime rate is $6.00 per hour ($4.00 x 1.5). *Note:* The 1.5 refers to *time-and-a-half*.) Therefore, her overtime pay will be:

2 overtime hours x $4.00/hr x 1.5 = $12.00

Before we leave this idea of time cards, we should look at another example of a time card to see how overtime works when there is an odd number of overtime hours. Shown below is a time card for an office employee, Bart Garner. The payroll calculation is completed on the right hand side. Double-check the calculations given in order to understand how Bart's gross pay is calculated. Think of this as your own paycheque and make sure that you are paid the correct amount.

TIME CARD

NO. 20

NAME Bart Garner

PAY PERIOD ENDING August 12, 19—

DAY	HOURS		
	TOTAL	REGULAR	OVERTIME
M	8	8	
T	8	8	
W	8	8	
T	8.5	8	.5
F	9	8	1.0
TOTALS	41.5	40	1.5

	HOURS	RATE	GROSS PAY
REGULAR	40	7.50	300.–
OVERTIME	1.5	11.25	16.88
		GROSS PAY	316.88

Regular Pay

$ 7.50/hour
x 40
$300.00

Overtime Pay

$ 7.50/hour
x 1.5
11.25/hour
x 1.5 hours
$16.88

Gross Pay = 300.00 + 16.88
= $316.88

10.4 Payroll Deductions

Earlier in the chapter it was mentioned that the gross pay is not the same as your net pay (take-home pay). There are several deductions that can be taken from your gross pay by the employer. These can be divided into two groups, "statutory deductions" and "voluntary deductions." **Statutory deductions** are deductions which the employer is required by law to deduct from an employee's paycheque. It refers mainly to three deductions, each of which will be discussed carefully for you in this text:

(1) Canada Pension Plan Deduction

(2) Unemployment Insurance Deduction

(3) Income Tax Deduction

Canada Pension Plan

This refers to an amount deducted from an employee's gross pay for contributions to the Canada Pension Plan. This plan provides retirement income for all of us when we reach retirement age. Only employees who are 17 years of age or over are required to have deductions taken from their paycheque for the Canada Pension Plan. The amount deducted is calculated from a table provided by **Revenue Canada**. The most recent table is reproduced for you here and will show you how to look up the correct deduction for CPP (Canada Pension Plan). The only figure you need to know, to be able to use the table, is the employee's gross pay. If we use Bart's gross pay above as an example then we are looking for a CPP deduction of $316.88. The Revenue Canada table for Canada Pension Plan contributions is shown below. All you have to do is fit the employee's gross pay into the remuneration column and read the CPP deduction. For example, if the gross pay is $316.88, then look down the Remuneration column until you can fit the number 316.88 into a range of numbers, that is, $316.69–$317.23. Then look at the CPP column and you will see that the deduction for Canada Pension Plan this week is $4.84.

Remuneration *Rémunération* From-*de*	To-*à*	C.P.P. *R.P.C.*	Remuneration *Rémunération* From-*de*	To-*à*	C.P.P. *R.P.C.*	Remuneration *Rémunération* From-*de*	To-*à*	C.P.P. *R.P.C.*	Remuneration *Rémunération* From-*de*	To-*à*	C.P.P. *R.P.C.*
232.80 -	233.34	3.33	272.80 -	273.34	4.05	312.80 -	313.34	4.77	352.80 -	353.34	5.49
233.35 -	233.90	3.34	273.35 -	273.90	4.06	313.35 -	313.90	4.78	353.35 -	353.90	5.50
233.91 -	234.45	3.35	273.91 -	274.45	4.07	313.91 -	314.45	4.79	353.91 -	354.45	5.51
234.46 -	235.01	3.36	274.46 -	275.01	4.08	314.46 -	315.01	4.80	354.46 -	355.01	5.52
235.02 -	235.56	3.37	275.02 -	275.56	4.09	315.02 -	315.56	4.81	355.02 -	355.56	5.53
235.57 -	236.12	3.38	275.57 -	276.12	4.10	315.57 -	316.12	4.82	355.57 -	356.12	5.54
236.13 -	236.68	3.39	276.13 -	276.68	4.11	316.13 -	316.68	4.83	356.13 -	356.68	5.55
236.69 -	237.23	3.40	276.69 -	277.23	4.12	316.69 -	317.23	4.84	356.69 -	357.23	5.56
237.24 -	237.79	3.41	277.24 -	277.79	4.13	317.24 -	317.79	4.85	357.24 -	357.79	5.57

Unemployment Insurance

This refers to a sum deducted from an employee's gross pay for contributions made to the Unemployment Insurance Plan. The Unemployment Insurance table is also provided by Revenue Canada and appears in the same booklet as the CPP deduction. The only figure you need to calculate the U.I. deduction is the employee's gross pay. If an employee had a gross pay of $316.88, for example, the Unemployment Insurance deduction (premium) would be $7.45. Check this out on the table below.

Remuneration *Rémunération*		U.I. Premium *Prime d'a.-c.*	Remuneration *Rémunération*		U.I. Premium *Prime d'a.-c.*	Remuneration *Rémunération*		U.I. Premium *Prime d'a-c.*	Remuneration *Rémunération*		U.I. Premium *Prime d'a.-c.*
From-*de*	To-*à*		From-*de*	To-*à*		From-*de*	To-*à*		From-*de*	To-*à*	
252.98 -	253.40	5.95	283.62 -	284.04	6.67	314.26 -	314.68	7.39	344.90 -	345.31	8.11
253.41 -	253.82	5.96	284.05 -	284.46	6.68	314.69 -	315.10	7.40	345.32 -	345.74	8.12
253.83 -	254.25	5.97	284.47 -	284.89	6.69	315.11 -	315.53	7.41	345.75 -	346.17	8.13
254.26 -	254.68	5.98	284.90 -	285.31	6.70	315.54 -	315.95	7.42	346.18 -	346.59	8.14
254.69 -	255.10	5.99	295.32 -	285.74	6.71	315.96 -	316.38	7.43	346.60 -	347.02	8.15
255.11 -	255.53	6.00	285.75 -	286.17	6.72	316.39 -	316.80	7.44	347.03 -	347.44	8.16
255.54 -	255.95	6.01	286.18 -	296.59	6.73	316.81 -	317.23	7.45	347.45 -	347.87	8.17
255.96 -	256.38	6.02	286.60 -	297.02	6.74	317.24 -	317.65	7.46	347.88 -	348.29	8.18
256.39 -	256.80	6.03	287.03 -	287.44	6.75	317.66 -	318.08	7.47	348.30 -	348.72	8.19

Income Tax Deductions

So far, for Bart, we have found two deductions, Canada Pension Plan and Unemployment Insurance. The next step is to subtract both of these from his gross pay to find an amount called "taxable income." (This figure is needed to calculate Bart's income tax deduction.)

Gross Pay		$316.88
Less:		
CPP	$4.84	
UI	7.45	12.29
Taxable Income		$304.59

Taxable income is the income from which income tax is deducted.

Employees do not pay tax on their gross pay, but they do pay on their taxable income. Income tax is deducted from paycheques for many Canadians, and the tax deducted is sent to the Receiver General in Ottawa.

The Income Tax table is partly shown below. Bart's tax deduction is found in column 1. Use his taxable income figure of $304.59 and look up his tax deduction in column 1. Bart would have $51.75 deducted from his paycheque for income tax, if his Net Claim Code was "1".

WEEKLY PAY Use appropriate bracket — PAIE PAR SEMAINE Utilisez le palier approprié	IF THE EMPLOYEE'S "NET CLAIM CODE" ON FORM TD1 IS – SI LE «CODE DE DEMANDE NETTE»								
	1	2	3	4	5	6	7	8	9
	DEDUCT FROM EACH PAY – *RETENEZ SUR CHAQ*								
$ 295.00 - 299.99	50.30	48.25	44.45	40.75	36.75	33.55	31.65	28.70	24
300.00 - 304.99	51.75	49.65	45.85	42.15	38.20	34.95	33.00	30.05	25
305.00 - 309.99	53.15	51.10	47.30	43.60	39.60	36.35	34.35	31.40	27
310.00 - 314.99	54.60	52.50	48.70	45.00	41.05	37.80	35.75	32.75	28
315.00 - 319.99	56.00	53.95	50.15	46.45	42.45	39.20	37.20	34.10	30
320.00 - 324.99	57.45	55.35	51.55	47.85	43.90	40.65	38.60	35.50	31
325.00 - 329.99	58.85	56.80	53.00	49.30	45.30	42.05	40.05	36.90	32
330.00 - 334.99	60.30	58.20	54.40	50.70	46.75	43.50	41.45	38.35	34
335.00 - 339.99	61.70	59.65	55.85	52.15	48.15	44.90	42.90	39.75	35
340.00 - 344.99	63.15	61.05	57.25	53.55	49.60	46.35	44.30	41.20	36

10.5 Personal Exemptions

When you start work, you will be required by law to fill out a TD1 form. This form allows you to claim personal exemptions to help reduce your income tax payments. Basically taxpayers are allowed personal exemptions whether they are single, married, or have children.

Personal exemptions are amounts deducted from yearly income before paying income tax.

Any employee who is single is allowed a basic personal exemption of $4 180. This means that the first $4 180 that a single person earns is tax free. A married person is allowed to claim an additional $3 660 for a spouse who is not working. A child under 18 is worth an exemption of $710 and each child over 18 is worth an exemption of $1 420.

Bart is married with two children aged 16 and 18 years. Bart's wife is not working outside the home and Bart can claim for the married exemption.

This is the calculation for Bart's total exemption:

Basic Personal Exemption		$4 180
Married Exemption		3 660
Exemption for Children:		
1 child age 16	$ 710	
1 child age 18	1 420	2 130
Total Exemption		$9 970

Once we know Bart's total exemption figure, we can use the table given below to figure out his Net Claim Code. The Net Claim Code corresponds to the number at the top of the Income Tax Deduction table. Use the table of Net Claim Codes below and plug in Bart's total exemption figure of $9 970. His Net Claim Code is "10." We now have the two pieces of information we need to find his Income tax deduction., Read on to Section 10.6.

Table of Net Claim Codes 1986 ***Table des codes de demande nette***

Net Claim - *Demande nette* Exceeding - Not exceeding *Excédant - N'excédant pas*	Net Claim Code *Code de demande nette*	Net Claim - *Demande nette* Exceeding - Not exceeding *Excédant - N'excédant pas*	Net Claim Code *Code de demande nette*
For use re: Tables 11 and 12 *Utilisation: Tables 11 et 12*	0	$ 7,800 — 8,570	8
$4,179 — 4,230	1	8,570 — 9,370	9
4,230 — 4,890	2	9,370 — 10,250	10
4,890 — 5,610	3	10,250 — 11,110	11
5,610 — 6,240	4	11,110 — 11,930	12
6,240 — 7,060	5	11,930 — 12,570	13
7,060 — 7,430	6	12,570 and up — *et plus*	X
7,430 — 7,800	7	No tax withholding required *Aucune retenue d'impôt requise*	E

10.6 Income Tax Deduction

Look at the Income Tax table. The column on the left is " Weekly Pay" which means "Taxable Income." The Net Claim Code is the number at

WEEKLY PAY Use appropriate bracket — PAIE PAR SEMAINE Utilisez le palier approprié	IF THE EMPLOYEE'S "NET CLAIM CODE" ON FORM TD1 IS — SI LE «CODE DE DEMANDE NETTE» DE L'EMPLOYÉ									
	1	2	3	4	5	6	7	8	9	10
	DEDUCT FROM EACH PAY — *RETENEZ SUR CHAQUE PAIE*									
$ 295.00 - 299.99	50.30	48.25	44.45	40.75	36.75	33.55	31.65	28.70	24.60	20.30
300.00 - 304.99	51.75	49.65	45.85	42.15	38.20	34.95	33.00	30.05	25.95	21.60
305.00 - 309.99	53.15	51.10	47.30	43.60	39.60	36.35	34.35	31.40	27.30	22.95
310.00 - 314.99	54.60	52.50	48.70	45.00	41.05	37.80	35.75	32.75	28.65	24.30
315.00 - 319.99	56.00	53.95	50.15	46.45	42.45	39.20	37.20	34.10	30.00	25.65
320.00 - 324.99	57.45	55.35	51.55	47.85	43.90	40.65	38.60	35.50	31.35	27.00
325.00 - 329.99	58.85	56.80	53.00	49.30	45.30	42.05	40.05	36.90	32.70	28.35

the top of each column in the Income Tax table. Using a "Taxable Income" for Bart of $304.59, and a Net Claim Code of 10, the amount to be deducted from Bart's paycheque for income tax is $21.60.

Gross Pay		$316.88
Less:		
CPP	$4.84	
UI	7.45	12.29
Taxable Income		$304.59
Less:		
Income Tax		21.60
Net Pay		$282.99

10.7 Voluntary Deductions

The three deductions shown in the calculation above are all required by law. A 16-year-old student will have only Unemployment Insurance deducted, because CPP starts at age 17. And a part-time student may not make enough to pay income tax.

Some businesses have other **voluntary deductions.** These will vary from business to business, but a few typical ones are described here for you:

Union Dues

If the employees in a business belong to a union, it is common practice to have union dues automatically deducted from an employee's paycheque. The employer then remits the union dues deducted, directly to the union, on behalf of the employee. This process is called *checkoff*.

Bonds

Some employees have difficulty saving money and will voluntarily sign up for a payroll savings plan. This plan allows the employer to deduct a certain amount from the employee's paycheque. At the end of a given time period, say a year, the funds accumulated will be used to buy Canada Savings Bonds for the employee.

Health Insurance Plans

Some provinces have government-run insurance plans. In Ontario, the OHIP scheme covers doctor or hospital bills. In British Columbia, the

M.S.A. plan provides similar coverage. A deduction may be made from an employee's paycheque to cover the payments into this plan. Rates depend on whether a person is single or married and supporting a family.

Voluntary deductions are deductions that an employee allows to be deducted from his or her paycheque.

Let's go back to the calculation of Bart's paycheque and add some "voluntary deductions." Here is some new information about Bart:

1. The store where Bart works is unionized. The union contract calls for $4.50 per week to be deducted from each employee's paycheque for union dues.
2. Bart has signed up for the Canada Savings Bond payroll deduction plan. He has asked his employer to deduct $20.00 a week for Canada Savings Bonds.
3. Bart is married and pays $22.00 to a provincial health insurance plan. This is taken from his weekly paycheque as well.

These new deductions will further reduce Bart's net pay. Here is the new calculation which gives effect to the three new voluntary deductions we have just discussed.

"Did you get your raise?"

Gross Pay			$316.88
Less:			
CPP	$4.84		
UI	7.45		12.29
Taxable Income			$304.59
Less:			
Income Tax			21.60
Less:			282.99
Union Dues		$ 4.50	
Bonds		20.00	
Health Insurance		22.00	46.50
Net Pay		=	$236.49

Of all the deductions recorded for Bart, his employer is only required to contribute toward two of these—the Canada Pension Plan and the Unemployment Insurance Plan deduction. The employer does not normally contribute any money toward income tax, union dues, bonds, or OHIP.

The three voluntary deductions we discussed in the last section are only samples of the many types of deductions that are sometimes taken from employee paycheques. Here are some others, just for your information.

Retirement Pension Plan: Money is deducted which is put toward a pension plan that you can collect on when you retire from work.

Blue Cross: Some businesses have joined this plan which provides payment for medical expenses not covered by OHIP.

Group Life Insurance: A business may have insurance which pays benefits on retirement or on the death of an employee. This is called a group plan.

Charitable Donations: Employees may have money deducted from their paycheque for their favourite charity, for example, the Cancer Society, Heart Fund, or United Way.

Credit Union: Some larger companies have a credit union for their employees. Employees can then have money deducted from their paycheques to deposit into a savings account.

We will not go into a lot of detail about these other plans because they vary considerably from one business to another. It is sufficient to know that they exist, that most are good plans, and that they can be paid for by regular deductions from a paycheque.

10.8 Statement of Earnings

When an employee is paid by the employer, it is good accounting practice to give the employee a "statement of earnings." This is a record, for the employee, of the gross pay, deductions, and net pay for the payroll time period. This statement can be provided as a separate form along with the payheque, or it is attached with a perforated line so the employee can detach and keep it for his/her personal records.

A statement of earnings explains to an employee how the pay is calculated.

Figure 10-2
Statement of earnings with employee paycheque attached.

STATEMENT OF EARNINGS

EMP NO	HOURS		EARNINGS		DEDUCTIONS						
	REG	OT	REGULAR	OVERTIME	CPP	UI	TAX	DUES	BONDS	OHIP	NET PAY
8	40	3	300.00	16.88	4.84	7.45	21.60	4.50	20.00	22.00	236.49

2654

PAY TO THE ORDER OF: Bart Garner $236.49

THE SUM OF Two hundred and thirty-six 49/100 DOLLARS

MANAGER – THE VIDEO STORE
2020 MAIN STREET

10.9 Employee Earnings Record Card

After the employees' paycheques are completed, details for each employee's pay should be entered into another document, called the "employee earnings record card." This card is kept by the employer and is used to prepare a "T4 slip" for each employee at the end of the year. The T4 slip is used by employees to complete their personal income tax return by the end of April each year.

The employee earnings record card records all pay and deductions for an employee for the whole year.

A T4 slip is a statement of earnings and deductions given to an employee by the employer each year to enable him or her to complete a tax return.

EMPLOYEE EARNINGS RECORD CARD

EMPLOYEE NAME: Garner, Bart — BIRTHDATE: Feb. 12/62
ADDRESS: R.R. 7 — S.I.N.: 445-278-201
TOWN: Woodstock, Ontario — TEL. NO.: 485-1282
POSTAL CODE: NOJ ILO — DATE HIRED: July 1/81

PAY PERIOD ENDING	GROSS PAY	DEDUCTIONS						NET PAY
		CPP	U.I.	TAX	DUE	BONDS	OHIP	
August 5	350.00	5.00	7.62	23.90	4.50	20.00	0.00	288.98
12	316.88	4.84	7.45	21.60	4.50	20.00	22.00	236.49
19	330.00	4.92	7.51	22.40	4.50	20.00	0.00	270.67
26	316.88	4.84	7.45	21.60	4.50	20.00	0.00	258.49
Totals	1313.76	19.60	30.03	89.50	18.00	80.00	22.00	1054.63

Figure 10-3 Employee Earnings Record Card

As with all payroll documents, an EERC (Employee Earnings Record Card) must be completed accurately. It should be cross-balanced at regular monthly intervals. You will notice that Bart's EERC has been balanced and cross-balanced.

10.10 The Payroll Journal

When employees' paycheques are calculated, they should be recorded immediately into a *payroll journal*. Look at the payroll journal on page 245. It has been balanced and cross-balanced for you. All columns from Gross Pay to Net Pay have been added. The gross pay total minus each deduction total must equal the total of the Net Pay column. Check it out!

PAYROLL JOURNAL

EMP. NO	EMPLOYEE NAME	TAX CODE	GROSS PAY	DEDUCTIONS C.P.P.	DEDUCTIONS U.I.	DEDUCTIONS TAXABLE INCOME	DEDUCTIONS TAX	NET PAY
1	Adams, Robert		450.00	25 40	6 75		34 90	382.95
2	Baker, Fran		500.00	32 10	7 20		42 12	418.58
3	Cooper, Clem		650.00	38 90	8 13		50 —	552.97
4	Drew, Abigail		485.00	26 10	6 90		30 —	442.00
		Totals	2085.00	122 50	28 98		157 02	1776.50

In many businesses today, payroll calculations are computerized. More will be said on this in a later chapter.

10.11 Employment Standards Act

Many provinces in Canada have enacted legislation to protect employees. Three basic areas usually covered by this type of legislation include laws regarding overtime pay, minimum wages, and vacation pay.

One provincial employment act provides the following:

Hours of Work

"Hours are normally not to exceed 8 in a day or 48 in a week. Overtime at time and one half is payable on all hours over 44 in a week (not, however, for working over 8 hours in a day)."

Holidays

There are "seven public holidays: New Year, Good Friday, Victoria Day, Canada Day, Labour Day, Thanksgiving Day, and Christmas Day."

Vacation Pay

"The employer must give two weeks vacation with pay after each year worked, or 4% of total wages for the year or each part thereof."

Maternity Leave

A woman may qualify for pregnancy leave if she "has worked for the employer for at least twelve months and eleven days before the estimated delivery date. She then has a right to 11 weeks leave before the estimated date...and up to six weeks leave after the delivery."

Equal Pay for Equal Work

"Women should not be paid less than men for substantially the same kind of work performed in the same establishment, the performance of which requires substantially the same skill, effort, and responsibility."

10.12 Summary

Payroll is an important accounting topic because it directly affects all people who work. We want to be paid for our services, and we want our pay to be calculated correctly. There are four main methods of paying employees—hourly rate, piece rate, salary, and commission. Whether employees are paid weekly, bi-weekly, or monthly depends on the employer. If there is a union involved, many employment conditions will be negotiated and appear in the union contract. In other businesses, employees may sign a personal contract with their employer. In all provinces legislation has been passed to protect both employers and employees. The goal of a payroll system is to follow the law, to provide employees with the correct pay, and to have good accounting records.

Time to check the chapter objectives. You should be able to

1. know the four basic ways employees are paid;
2. calculate a person's net pay; and
3. recognize some key payroll documents, such as a time card, statement of earnings, employee earnings record card, and a payroll journal.

Dictionary of Terms

Employee Earnings Record Card A payroll document in which the employer keeps track of an employee's earnings for the whole year.

Gross Pay An employee's wage before deductions, statutory and voluntary, have been taken from it.

Net Pay An employee's pay after all deductions have been taken from gross pay.

Personal Exemptions The amounts an employee is allowed to deduct from income before paying income tax.

Revenue Canada The government department in Canada that handles the revenues of the country.

Statement of Earnings The portion of an employee's paycheque that explains how the pay is calculated.

Statutory Deductions Deductions that employers are required by law to calculate—Canada Pension Plan, Unemployment Insurance, and Income Tax.

Taxable Income Income from which income tax is deducted.

T4 Slip Statement of earnings and deductions given to each employee to complete a tax return.

Voluntary Deductions Payroll deductions that an employee allows to be deducted from a paycheque. Blue Cross and Canada Savings Bonds are examples.

Exercises

1. For each employee below, find his/her gross pay.
   (a) Sandra Tuttle is a receptionist for Moncton Cable TV. Her salary is $19 500 a year, and she is paid on a monthly basis. How much a month does she earn?
   (b) Donna Town picks tomatoes in Southwestern Ontario. She is paid $2.15 a peck. The number of pecks she picked last week was: Mon. (16); Tues.(18); Wed. (12); Thurs. (14); Fri. (17). Find her gross pay.
   (c) Karen Zvanitas works in a dry cleaning store for a part-time pay rate of $3.75/hour. If she works over 40 hours she is paid time-and-a-half. Last week she put in 43 hours. Find her gross pay.
   (d) Michael Fox has a job at the Calgary Stampede selling cowboy hats and other clothing items. He is paid on a commission rate of 8% of all sales he makes. During the first week of the Exhibition, he sold $7 856 in goods. Find his gross pay.

2. All of the employees for the High River Riding School are paid on an hourly basis. Any time over 40 hours is overtime at time-and-a-half. Given the table below, find the gross pay for all the employees in your workbook.

Employee Name	Hours	Pay Rate	Gross Pay
1. Kurt Vaggart	40.0	5.00	?
2. Leslie Petranko	42.0	5.10	?
3. Cy Sparlinton	44.5	5.15	?
4. Vicki Laekman	37.0	5.20	?

TIME CARD

NO. 2

NAME Sonny Hamerton

PAY PERIOD ENDING July 8, 19—

DAY	HOURS		
	TOTAL	REGULAR	OVERTIME
M	8		
T	9		
W	10.5		
T	8.5		
F	9.5		
TOTALS		?	?

	HOURS	RATE	GROSS PAY
REGULAR			
OVERTIME			
		GROSS PAY	

3. The employees who clean the stables on the Rockey Farm are paid on an hourly basis. They are required to punch a time clock each day when they start work and when they finish at the end of the day. Calculate the number of regular and overtime hours worked by employee #2, Sonny Hamerton. (All hours over 8 each day are overtime.)

4. Pete's Garage has four employees who are paid on an hourly basis. Complete the time cards (below, and on page 250) in your student workbook.

TIME CARD

NO. 1

NAME Greg Gonzo

PAY PERIOD ENDING Dec. 8, 19—

DAY	HOURS		
	TOTAL	REGULAR	OVERTIME
M	9		
T	10		
W	8.5		
T	8.5		
F	8		
TOTALS	?	?	?

	HOURS	RATE	GROSS PAY
REGULAR			
OVERTIME			
		GROSS PAY	

TIME CARD

NO. 2

NAME Al Barbutto

PAY PERIOD ENDING Dec. 8, 19—

DAY	HOURS		
	TOTAL	REGULAR	OVERTIME
M	8		
T	8		
W	8		
T	8		
F	12		
TOTALS	?	?	?

	HOURS	RATE	GROSS PAY
REGULAR			
OVERTIME			
		GROSS PAY	

TIME CARD

NO. 3

NAME Hank Murk

PAY PERIOD ENDING Dec. 8, 19 —

DAY	HOURS		
	TOTAL	REGULAR	OVERTIME
M	8		
T	9		
W	10.5		
T	8		
F	9		
TOTALS	?	?	?

	HOURS	RATE	GROSS PAY
REGULAR			
OVERTIME			
		GROSS PAY	

TIME CARD

NO. 4

NAME Sonny Sideup

PAY PERIOD ENDING Dec. 8, 19 —

DAY	HOURS		
	TOTAL	REGULAR	OVERTIME
M	10		
T	10		
W	8		
T	8		
F	9.5		
TOTALS	?	?	?

	HOURS	RATE	GROSS PAY
REGULAR			
OVERTIME			
		GROSS PAY	

5. Add and cross-add this payroll journal in your student workbook. Make sure it cross-balances!

PAYROLL JOURNAL

EMP. NO.	EMPLOYEE NAME	TAX CODE	GROSS PAY	DEDUCTIONS				NET PAY
				C.P.P.	U.I.	TAXABLE INCOME	TAX	
1	Adams, Robert		600.00	28 40	7 76		45 62	?
2	Baker, Fran		620.00	33 —	7 90		38 20	?
3	Cooper, Clem		710.00	34 35	8 12		51 —	?
4	Drew, Abigail		840.00	42 10	8 48		62 10	?
			?	?	?		?	?

6. Complete the time cards on page 251 in your workbook. Any time worked over 8 hours in one day is overtime and is to be paid at time-and-a-half.

TIME CARD

NO. 1

NAME Anthony Cobb

PAY PERIOD ENDING

DAY	HOURS		
	TOTAL	REGULAR	OVERTIME
M	8		
T	8		
W	9		
T	8		
F	8		
TOTALS	?	?	?

	HOURS	RATE	GROSS PAY
REGULAR	?	$6.00	?
OVERTIME	?		?
		GROSS PAY	?

TIME CARD

NO. 2

NAME Lorne Little

PAY PERIOD ENDING

DAY	HOURS		
	TOTAL	REGULAR	OVERTIME
M	8		
T	9		
W	9		
T	8		
F	10		
TOTALS	?	?	?

	HOURS	RATE	GROSS PAY
REGULAR	?	$6.20	?
OVERTIME	?		?
		GROSS PAY	?

TIME CARD

NO. 3

NAME Pamela Fram

PAY PERIOD ENDING

DAY	HOURS		
	TOTAL	REGULAR	OVERTIME
M	9		
T	9		
W	9		
T	8		
F	8		
TOTALS	?	?	?

	HOURS	RATE	GROSS PAY
REGULAR	?	$7.00	?
OVERTIME	?		?
		GROSS PAY	?

TIME CARD

NO. 4

NAME Zakk Zitt

PAY PERIOD ENDING

DAY	HOURS		
	TOTAL	REGULAR	OVERTIME
M	8		
T	8		
W	9		
T	8		
F	9		
TOTALS	?	?	?

	HOURS	RATE	GROSS PAY
REGULAR	?	$8.50	?
OVERTIME	?		?
		GROSS PAY	?

7. Find the Canada Pension Plan deductions, using the tables in a Revenue Canada deductions booklet.

Gross Pay	Pay Period	CPP
$216.13	weekly	______
$307.25	weekly	______
$361.00	weekly	______

8. Find the Unemployment Insurance deductions using the tables in a Revenue Canada deductions booklet.

Gross Pay	Pay Period	CPP
$225.00	weekly	______
$300.00	weekly	______
$361.00	weekly	______

9. Complete the payroll journal below in your workbook, using the Revenue Canada deduction tables at the end of the chapter.

PAYROLL JOURNAL

EMP. NO.	EMPLOYEE NAME	TAX CODE	GROSS PAY	DEDUCTIONS C.P.P.	U.I.	TAXABLE INCOME	TAX	NET PAY
1	Bouton, Jacques	12	550.00					
2	Farreaux, Gilles	1	600.00					
3	Garneau, Annette	8	495.00					
4	Manon, Michelle	10	525.00					
			?	?	?		?	?

Review Questions

1. What are the two main reasons for making sure a payroll has been accurately prepared?
2. List the four main methods for paying employees. Give examples of each method in your answer.
3. Indicate by which of the four payroll methods each of the following employees would probably be paid:

   Company president; school custodian; store clerk; student picking cucumbers; teacher; and salesperson.
4. (a) What is a time card?

   (b) Name two methods of completing a time card.

5. What do "time-and-a-half" and "double time" mean?
6. Explain the difference between statutory and voluntary deductions. Give three examples of statutory deductions and six examples of voluntary deductions.
7. What do the initials CPP and UI stand for?
8. What is the name of the government department that handles payroll (CPP, UI, and Income Tax) deductions?
9. Explain how we arrive at taxable income.
10. A friend of yours has just started a part-time job at a local bowling alley. Your friend is 18 years old. Tell her/him what deductions are likely to be taken from the first paycheque.
11. What would the total exemption be for an employee who has a spouse as a dependant and three children ages 10, 15, and 19?
12. What is the significance of the term "Net Claim Code"?
13. Name two pieces of information a bookkeeper would need to find an employee's income tax deduction.
14. A co-worker has just received a T4 slip from her employer. Explain to her what this is.
15. You have just been hired to work for a company in Halifax. The personnel manager explains that there are several voluntary deductions that you can select on your paycheque, if you wish. If you wanted to do each of the following, what would be the name of the "voluntary deduction" you would choose in each case?
    (a) Provide protection for your spouse in case you die.
    (b) Save money on a weekly basis.
    (c) Donate money to the Cancer Society regularly.
    (d) Set aside money for your eventual retirement.
16. Describe the following payroll items—a statement of earnings; an employee earnings record card; and a payroll journal.

Challenge Questions

1. Name four service businesses in your area and find out, by phoning two of them, which payroll method they use for their employees.
2. An employee worked the hours last week that you see below. If

Saturday is double time; Monday was a holiday and requires payment at triple time; and time over 40 hours from Monday to Friday is paid at time-and-a-half, find the employee's gross pay.

		Hours Worked						Pay
No.	**Employee Name**	**M**	**T**	**W**	**T**	**F**	**S**	**Rate**
26	Blubber, K.M.	8	9	8	8	9	5	6.20

3. Consult a Revenue Canada deduction booklet and find out about the following:
   (a) For how long does a person contribute to the Canada Pension Plan?
   (b) What is the age at which a person has to stop paying into the Canada Pension Plan?
   (c) Are there any employees who do not have to pay into the Unemployment Insurance Plan?
   (d) What is the maximum amount that a person has to pay into Unemployment Insurance weekly?

Review Case

TIME CARD

NO. 5

NAME C. Sinatra

PAY PERIOD ENDING April 30, 19—

DAY	HOURS		
	TOTAL	REGULAR	OVERTIME
M	9		
T	9		
W	10		
T	10		
F	8		
TOTALS		?	?

	HOURS	RATE	GROSS PAY
REGULAR	?	$7.00	?
OVERTIME	?		?
		GROSS PAY	?

The time card shown belongs to Carmen Sinatra who works at an income tax office called Quicktax.

Carmen is paid "time-and-a-half" for any hours worked over 40 each week. Using the form in your workbook, calculate the gross pay for Carmen by completing her time card. Use the Revenue Canada tables.

Challenge Case

You have just started your first job as a payroll clerk for the City Linen Company. The company has two employees who pick up dirty laundry around the city and bring it back to the plant to be washed. Two workers inside the plant, with computerized washing machines, do all the laundry that same night. The two truck drivers are hourly rated employees and the two inside workers are salaried. Your first task is to figure out the payroll for the employees for the week ended August 7th. Follow the steps below and see if you can complete the payroll calculations accurately. Complete the payroll journal in your workbook. (If you make any mistakes, you will lose your job.)

1. The inside workers are salaried. Hans Gruber earns $315 week. Lucy Pinot earns $335 week. The time cards for the two truck drivers are shown below. Any time over 40 hours per week is overtime at time-and-a-half.

2. The following information about dependants is needed to calculate each employee's tax exemption.

Hans: Married, claims his wife:

Bruce: Claims only the children, ages 5 and 12

Lucy: Single

Henry: Single

TIME CARD

NO. 1

NAME Bruce Sanyo

PAY PERIOD ENDING ________

DAY	HOURS		
	TOTAL	REGULAR	OVERTIME
M	9		
T	8		
W	8		
T	8		
F	8		
TOTALS	?	?	?

	HOURS	RATE	GROSS PAY
REGULAR	?	$8.50	?
OVERTIME	?		?
		GROSS PAY	?

TIME CARD

NO. 2

NAME Henry Kotter

PAY PERIOD ENDING ________

DAY	HOURS		
	TOTAL	REGULAR	OVERTIME
M	10		
T	10		
W	8		
T	9		
F	8		
TOTALS	?	?	?

	HOURS	RATE	GROSS PAY
REGULAR	?	$9.50	?
OVERTIME	?		?
		GROSS PAY	?

3. Complete the payroll journal below. Find each employee's net pay. Use your Revenue Canada deduction tables to find deductions. Total and cross-balance the payroll journal. (Show your work to your boss.)

PAYROLL JOURNAL

EMP. NO.	EMPLOYEE NAME	TAX CODE	GROSS PAY	DEDUCTIONS				NET PAY
				C.P.P.	U.I.	TAXABLE INCOME	TAX	

Take-a-Break

Wacky Words

The object here is to discover the familiar word, phrase, or proper name represented by its arrangement of letters and/or symbols. The example to the left below is "circular reasoning" and the one to the right is "mixed bag." The other wacky words below are all related to accounting or finance terms in one way or another. Have fun!

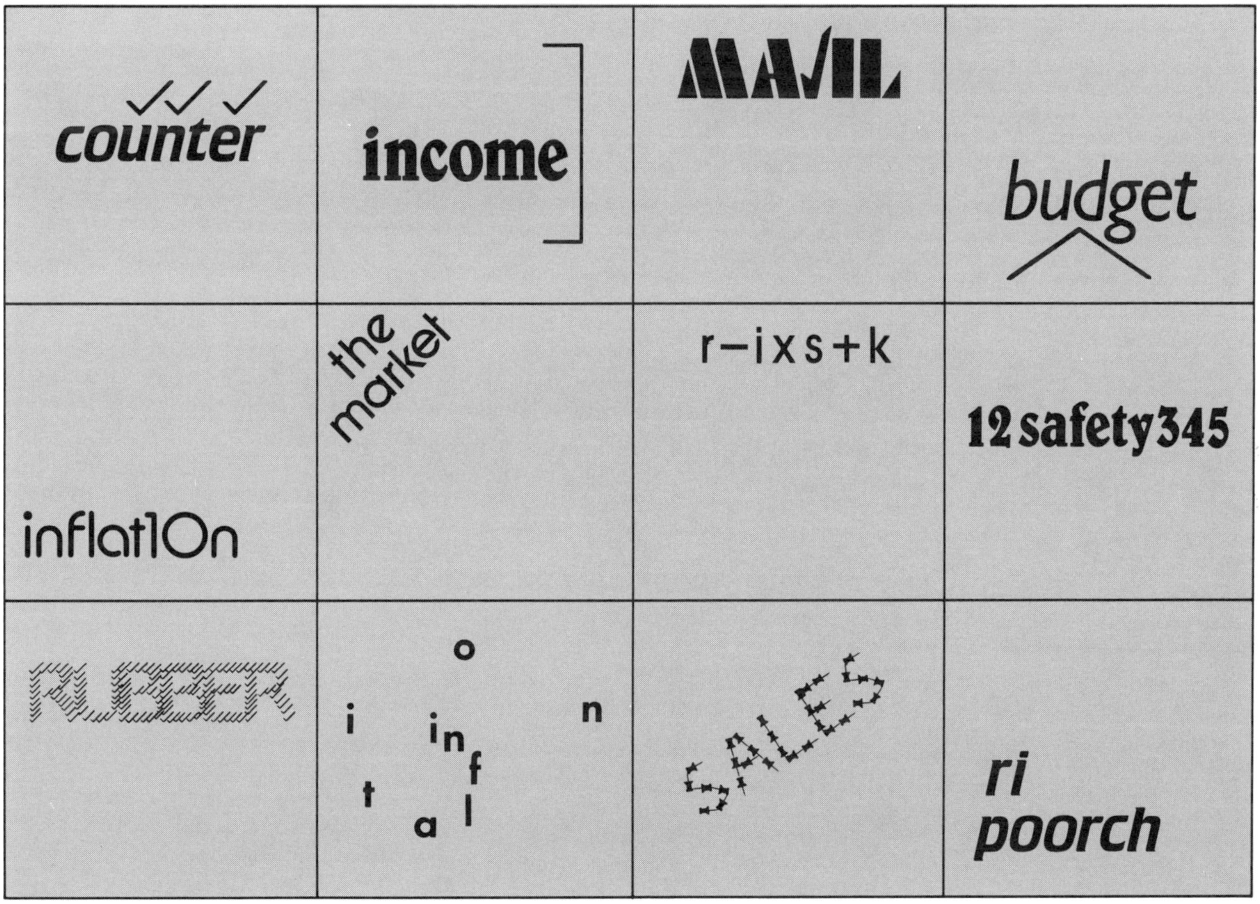

Accounting at Work

Payroll Clerk

Canada-Haul is a trucking company owned and operated by the Southfork Family. Randy Verbruggen is the payroll clerk for the business and has total responsibility for all payroll operations. His duties in this job are:

1. Check all time cards, submitted by the truck drivers, for completeness and accuracy.
2. Calculate the gross pay for each driver.
3. Use Revenue Canada deduction tables to calculate deductions for CPP, UI, and Income Tax.
4. Make out cheques for each truck driver, based on his (Randy's) net pay calculations.
5. Keep up-to-date Employee Earnings Record Cards for each employee.
6. Submit payroll deductions to the government.
7. Prepare T4 slips for the truck drivers at year end for their tax returns.

Randy reports directly to the chief accountant for the business, and has had his position for the past three years.

Randy was hired as payroll clerk after he graduated from a community college with an accounting degree. As you can see from the partial organization chart, there are several other employees in the accounting department with similar positions of responsibility. All of the people junior and senior to Randy are community college graduates, and, therefore, if Randy wants to get promoted he will have lots of competition.

Chief Accountant
R. Cougler, CMA

- A/R Clerk (Deena Stone)
- A/P Clerk (Chris Snyder)
- Payroll Clerk (R. Verbruggen)
- General Acctng. (Sue Coderre)

Randy's job is a very responsible one as the total company payroll, at the end of a two-week period, is usually about $40 000. The payroll money is put into a special bank account and Randy writes all the payroll cheques for the trucking business. His boss, the chief accountant, reconciles the payroll bank account each month as an accounting check on Randy's work.

Randy's boss filed a report on his work with the president of the trucking company. In short, the chief accountant praised Randy for his attendance at work, his punctuality, neatness, attitude, and accuracy. He suggests that Randy "has every right to expect to be promoted as soon as possible."

Questions for Discussion

1. Look at the partial organization chart again. Can you tell from the chart if any of the four accounting positions are more important than the others?
2. What payroll method is used to pay the truckers for Pacific Rent-Alls?
3. Check over the list of duties that Randy has to perform in his job. How many of these do you think you could perform right now?
4. Is there anything Randy can do to enhance his chances for promotion, considering the great report he got from his boss?

6

Cash and Banking

Chapter 11
Cash and Banking

Chapter 12
Practice Set II

Chapter 11 Cash and Banking

Objectives

At the end of this chapter you will be able to

1. know the elements of good cash control;
2. recognize key banking documents;
3. reconcile a bank account;
4. know how to set up a petty cash fund; and
5. know how to make journal entries from a bank reconciliation statement.

11.1 Cash Control

In a business the control over cash is one of the most important accounting activities that takes place. Cash is the most ''liquid'' asset a business has, and if proper accounting and physical controls are not in place, then a lot of money can be lost by the business. To understand this point, think about a fast food outlet (Figure 11-1). A fast food outlet deals mainly in cash—when people eat take away food they are expected to pay in cash. The employees who are handling the cash may be tempted to steal if proper controls are not in place at the fast food outlet. Here are some suggestions for effective control of cash.

Figure 11-1
A fast food outlet, like any business, must keep careful control over cash.

Physical Controls

1. Use a cash register to record all sales.
2. Allow only one person, a cashier, to use the cash register.
3. Transfer cash from the cash register to a business safe regularly.
4. Transfer cash from the business safe to a bank account daily.

Accounting Controls

1. Use the cash register tape to prepare a ''daily balance form'' for the business.
2. Do not allow the person who handles the cash register to record any accounting entries in the books of the business. They can record fraudulent figures.
3. Reconcile the bank account regularly (once a month) to ensure that all receipts are eventually deposited into the bank account.

Figure 11-2a
A modern cash register

The picture shows a modern electronic cash register. Most of the newer models are now computerized and can do many accounting entries, other than just recording cash received and paid out in business transactions.

The cash register provides a tape at the end of the day which lists all of the important amounts that the business needs to balance its cash. A sample cash register tape called an "audit tape" is reproduced below to show you the codes that can appear on a tape. The meaning of the codes is also given to you.

TX	$	85.65
SA	$	810.20
RA	$	325.00
CH	$	327.50
CA	$	568.35

TX = Sales TaX
SA = All SAles
RA = Received on Account (from customers)
CH = CHarge sale total
CA = CAsh sale total

Figure 11-2b
A modern cash register provides an accurate and speedy record of cash sales.

An audit tape is the tape produced by a cash register that summarizes daily cash transactions.

From the tape, the store owner or the accountant can prepare a "daily balance form," like the one below, to see if the cash balances at the end of the day. Cash may be short or over, as the form will show.

A daily balance form is drawn up from the audit tape each day to see if the cash balances.

DAILY BALANCE FORM

ACTUAL CASH IN DRAWER

24	x $1.00 =	24.00
40	x 2.00 =	80.00
11	x 5.00 =	55.00
23	x 10.00 =	230.00
24	x 20.00 =	480.00
	CHANGE =	23.10
	TOTAL =	892.10

CASH SUMMARY

CASH SALES (CA)	568.35
REC'D ON ACCOUNT (RA)	325.—
CASH COUNT SHOULD BE	893.35
ACTUAL CASH IN DRAWER	892.10
CASH (SHORTAGE) OVER	1.25

GENERAL JOURNAL

	DEBIT	CREDIT
BANK	892.10	
ACCTS. REC. (CH)	327.50	
CASH SHORT	1.25	
ACCTS. REC (RA)		325.—
SALES (SA)		810.20
SALES TAX (TX)		85.65
CASH OVER		
TOTALS	1220.85	1220.85

Note that the codes on the audit tape are shown on the daily balance form to help you put the amounts in the right place. A couple of arrows are also added to make the flow clearer for you. When the cash register is balanced at the end of the day, the cash register will either be short or over. Therefore, when you draw up the general journal entry, there will either be a debit to "Cash Short" *or* a credit to "Cash Over," but not both.

11.2 Banking

Once a business has balanced its daily cash, it is wise to deposit the cash into the bank account. This should be done daily as a matter of good cash control. In some businesses, as in a busy supermarket, it is wise to make a deposit more than once a day, depending on how much cash has been taken in. For those businesses which close their doors after normal banking hours, there are two banking options:

1. Put a deposit into the Night Depository (a slot in the front of the bank through which deposits can be made after banking hours).
2. Open the business Bank account in a bank or trust company that has extended hours, e.g., 8 a.m. to 8 p.m.

Figure 11-3
A night depository

There are many different types of bank accounts that may be used by individuals or businesses, but there are three basic bank accounts—the savings account, a personal chequing account, and a current account.

The savings account is an account that individuals put money in to earn interest.

The personal chequing account is an account that individuals use to write cheques to pay household bills.

The current account is a chequing account that businesses use to make regular daily deposits and write cheques.

"I wanna open a joint-account with someone who's got plenty of dough."

11.3 Bank Documents

When you open a bank account, you will be asked to fill out a **signature card** similar to the one shown below. This helps the bank to verify your signature and to ensure that people do not write cheques on your account fraudulently.

SURNAME	GIVEN NAMES		TRANSIT
SURNAME	GIVEN NAMES		SIGNATURE CODE
ACCOUNT NO.	ACCOUNT TYPE	DATE OPENED	DATE CLOSED

Specimen Signature(s)

OTHER SERVICES
- ☐ MBB
- ☐ PLoC
- ☐ Other

(See reverse)

SIGNATURE CODE
✓ - Single
1 - Either
2 - Both
3 - Multiple
4 - Non-Writer

Bank of Montreal

See reverse for additional signatures

Figure 11-4
A bank signature card

The deposit slips used by banks, credit unions, and trust companies vary in format. The sample below, from the Bank of Montreal, is a fairly common type. This depositor is putting bills, coins, and two cheques into her account.

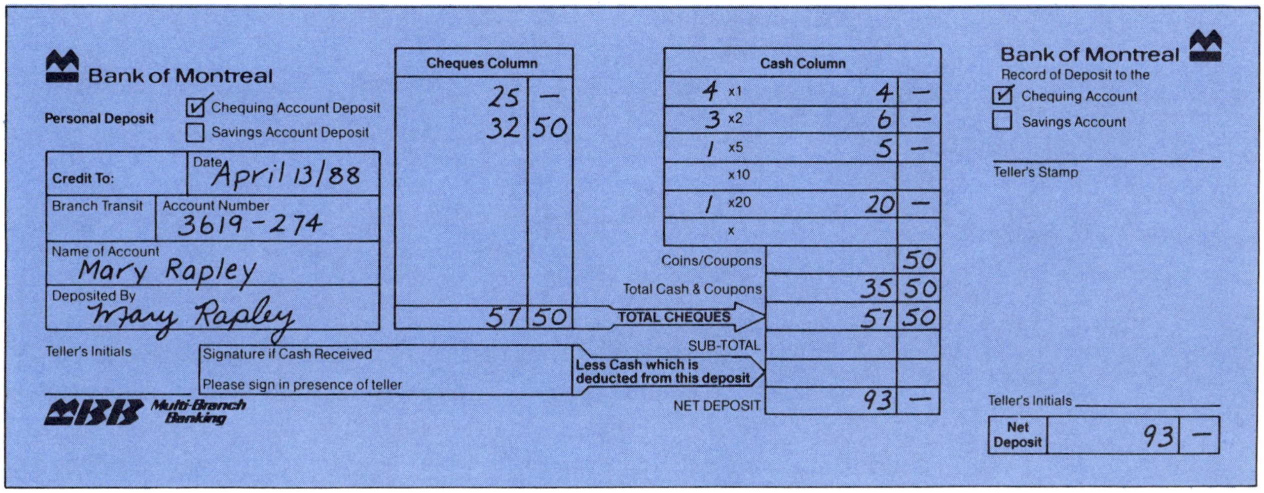
Bank of Montreal
Personal Deposit
☑ Chequing Account Deposit
☐ Savings Account Deposit
Credit To: Date April 13/88
Branch Transit | Account Number 3619-274
Name of Account: Mary Rapley
Deposited By: Mary Rapley
Teller's Initials
Signature if Cash Received — Please sign in presence of teller
MBB Multi-Branch Banking

Cheques Column	
25	—
32	50
57	50

Cash Column		
4 x1	4	—
3 x2	6	—
1 x5	5	—
x10		
1 x20	20	—
x		
Coins/Coupons		50
Total Cash & Coupons	35	50
TOTAL CHEQUES	57	50
SUB-TOTAL		
Less Cash which is deducted from this deposit		
NET DEPOSIT	93	—

Bank of Montreal
Record of Deposit to the
☑ Chequing Account
☐ Savings Account
Teller's Stamp
Teller's Initials
Net Deposit 93 —

Figure 11-5
A bank deposit slip

A third document you should be familiar with is the withdrawal slip. It is filled out when you are in the bank and want to take some money out of your account.

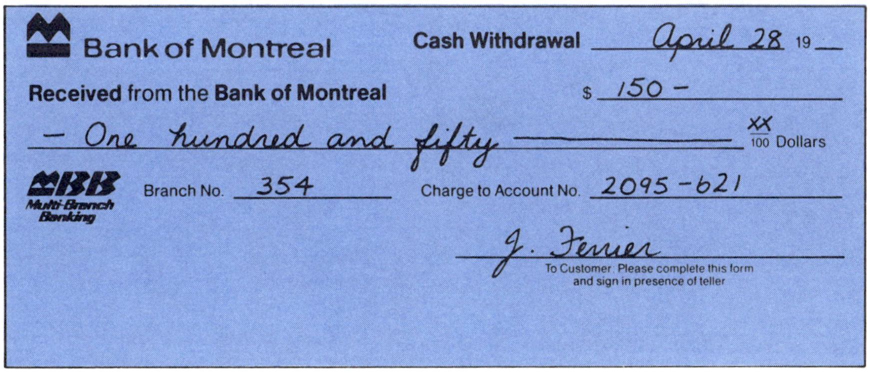
Bank of Montreal
Cash Withdrawal April 28 19__
Received from the Bank of Montreal $ 150 –
– One hundred and fifty ———— xx/100 Dollars
MBB Multi-Branch Banking
Branch No. 354 Charge to Account No. 2095-621
J. Ferrier
To Customer: Please complete this form and sign in presence of teller

Figure 11-6
A cash withdrawal slip

Finally, if you want to pay someone for a good or service you write out a cheque. Cheques are the most common method for making payments and the banks in Canada process thousands of these each day.

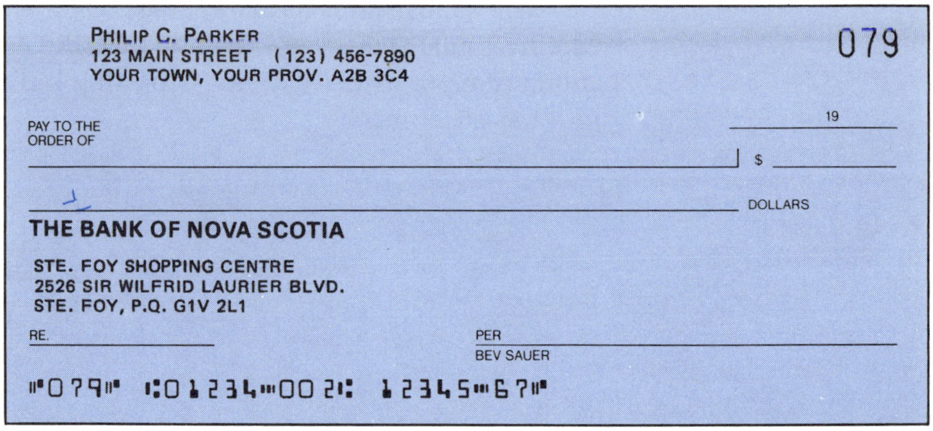

You may have noticed that the cheque has special numbers on the bottom so that it can be processed by a computer. These special characters are referred to as *magnetic ink characters*. They are read by a machine called a *Magnetic Ink Character Reader* (MICR), which reads the cheque numbers directly into a computer. Such cheques have been in existence for many years now and your bank will probably insist that you use these since MICR coding speeds up the processing of cheques. Because so many cheques are written by people and business each day, it is important to write a cheque as accurately as possible. Look at the cheque below and note the special points that people should follow when they write out cheques:

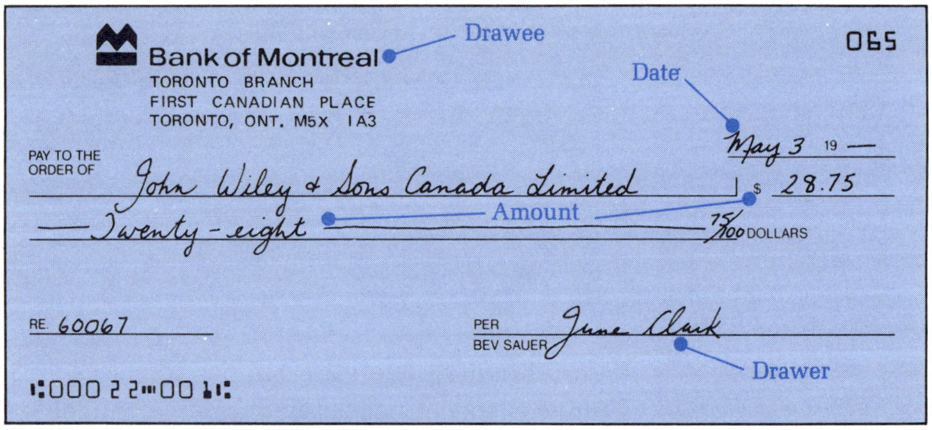

1. All cheques should be numbered, 1,2,3 etc.
2. Write the dollar figure close to the dollar sign so that the amount cannot be altered.

3. Put a line before and after the written amount so that it cannot be altered.

If you receive a cheque that you want to deposit into your bank account, for example, a paycheque, you must endorse it on the back. To endorse a cheque is to sign it on the back. There are two types of cheque endorsements you should know—the *restrictive* endorsement and the *simple* endorsement.

Figure 11-8a
Restrictive endorsement

Figure 11-8b
Simple endorsement

A restrictive endorsement is wise because if you lose the cheque and someone finds it, that person cannot cash the cheque. This is a form of personal cash control. A simple endorsement should only be used in the bank, or when you are personally handing a cheque over to another person. A cheque that has been endorsed with a simple endorsement may be cashed by anyone who finds it.

Finally, if you have your own personal chequing account, you should prepare a paper called a Bank Reconciliation Statement. This calculation will help you to check up on the bank and keep track of exactly how much is in your bank account.

Bank reconciliation is the process of calculating the true balance of a bank account.

11.4 Reconciling a Personal Bank Account

It often happens that the balance shown on your bank statement does not agree with the balance shown in your personal records. Notice in the two documents below that the balance on the bank statement, $200.00, does not agree with the balance shown in Jenny's personal cashbook. We need to know why this has happened.

BANK STATEMENT

Bank of Montreal

Jenny Gray
R.R.1
Woodstock, Ontario

ACCOUNT NUMBER

BRANCH

FWD: $50.00

STATEMENT OF FROM TO PAGE

DESCRIPTION	DEBITS	CREDITS	DATE	BALANCE
		50 00	1 8	100 00
	50 00		1 10	50 00
	SC 1 00		1 12	49 00
	12 50		1 20	36 50
	5 00		1 20	31 50
		80 00	1 22	111 50
		58 50	1 31	170 00

DATE		PARTICULARS	DEBIT	CREDIT	BALANCE
Jan.	1	Balance Forward			50 —
	8	Paycheque	50 —		100 —
	8	Eaton's		50 —	50 —
	13	A + A Records		12 50	37 50
	15	D. Gray		5 —	32 50
	22	Paycheque	80 —		112 50
	31	Birthday Gift	32 —		144 50
	31	Mappins		11 25	133 25
	31	Paycheque	58 50		191 75

The first step in reconciling is to look for amounts on the cashbook that have not been entered by the bank. These are highlighted for you. There is a deposit that the bank has not recorded yet, and a cheque that has not yet been cashed by the bank.

DATE		PARTICULARS	DEBIT	CREDIT	BALANCE
Jan.	1	Balance Forward			50 —
	8	Paycheque	50 —		100 —
	8	Eaton's		50 —	50 —
	13	A + A Records		12 50	37 50
	15	D. Gray		5 —	32 50
	22	Paycheque	80 —		112 50
	31	Birthday Gift	32 —		144 50
	31	Mappins		11 25	133 25
	31	Paycheque	58 50		191 75

The second step is to look for items on the bank statement that do not appear in Jenny's cashbook. There is one item, the bank service charge of $1.00 and it has been highlighted on the statement.

BANK STATEMENT

Bank of Montreal

Jenny Gray
R.R.1
Woodstock, Ontario

ACCOUNT NUMBER

BRANCH

FWD: $50.00

STATEMENT OF FROM TO PAGE

DESCRIPTION	DEBITS	CREDITS	DATE	BALANCE
		50 00	1: 8	100 00
	50 00		1:10	50 00
	SC 1 00		1:12	49 00
	12 50		1:20	36 50
	5 00		1:20	31 50
		80 00	1:22	111 50
		58 50	1:31	170 00

Once we have this information, we can prepare a formal bank reconciliation. Jenny's bank reconciliation as at the end of January is prepared in the same account form format that we used for balance sheets back in Chapter 1.

Jenny Gray
Bank Reconciliation Statement
as at January 31, 19 ____

Balance Per Bank	$170.00	Balance per Books	$191.75
Add:		*Less:*	
Outstanding Deposit	32.00	Service Charge	1.00
	202.00	*True Balance*	$190.75
Less:			
Outstanding Cheque	(11.25)		
True Balance	$190.75		

The true balance that Jenny has in her bank account is not the bank figure, nor is it the figure in her cashbook. The true balance is $190.75. This is because there are amounts on the cashbook that the bank has not yet recorded, and the bank has a service charge figure that is not shown in Jenny's cashbook.

An *outstanding deposit* is one which Jenny has in her cashbook but the bank has not recorded it yet. This can happen if the deposit is on the last day of the month or if it was mailed in and delayed. Likewise, an *outstanding cheque* is one which Jenny has written and given to someone but that person has not yet cashed the cheque. The three reconciling items you see here are common to most bank reconciliation problems.

11.5 Reconciling a Business Bank Account

Here is a multipurpose journal and a bank statement for a business. Look at both and see if you can follow the reconciliation process.

DATE		CUSTOMER/SUPPLIER	NO	BANK DR	BANK CR	ACCOUNTS RECEIVABLE DR	ACCOUNTS RECEIVABLE CR	√			ACCOUNTS PAYABLE DR	ACCOUNTS PAYABLE CR
Aug.	1	Sales		94 —					1	1		
	5	L. Lewis		75 —					2	2		
	10	Payroll	68		310 —				3	3		
	12	Hay Electric	69		75 —		75 —		4	4		
	15	Owner invested		300 —					5	5		
	17	Sales		125 —					6	6		
	18	Bell Canada	70		50 —				7	7		
	19	Taxi	71		10 —				8	8		
	22	Sales		400 —					9	9		
	24	Beauty Supply Co.	72		90 —				10	10		
	24	Sales		500 —					11	11		
	26	Office Outfitters	73		4 50				12	12		
	27	Ajax Holdings	74		700 —				13	13		
	28	Beauty Council	75		16 30				14	14		
	31	Sales		100 —					15	15		
		Balancing Totals		1594 —	1255 80	NIL	75 —		16	16	NIL	N
									17	17		

BANK STATEMENT

Bank of Montreal

Linda's Hair Salon
2356 Queen St. West
Toronto, Ontario

ACCOUNT NUMBER

BRANCH

FWD: $121.95

STATEMENT OF | FROM | TO | PAGE

DESCRIPTION	DEBITS	CREDITS	DATE	BALANCE
		94.00	8 1	215.95
		75.00	8 6	290.95
	310.00	300.00	8 17	280.95
		125.00	8 20	405.95
	75.00	400.00	8 22	
	10.00		8 22	720.95
	90.00	500.00	8 25	
	50.00		8 25	1080.95
	700.00		8 28	380.95
	SC 5.75		8 31	375.20

If we follow four basic steps, we can reconcile the bank account for Linda's Hair Salon, the way we reconciled Jenny's personal account.

Step 1: Tick the deposits in the multipurpose journal against the bank statement to see if there are any outstanding deposits not ticked (✓).

Step 2: Tick the cheques in the multipurpose journal against the bank statement to see if there are any outstanding cheques not ticked (✓).

Step 3: Look for any items on the bank statement which have not been ticked off. These are reconciling items that Linda does not have on her books.

Step 4: Prepare the bank reconciliation statement.

MULTIPURPOSE JOURNAL

PAGE NO 8

√	Sales CR	Wages DR		OTHER ACCOUNTS: ACCOUNT	PR	DR	CR
	94 —						
		310 —					
				Repairs		75 —	
				Capital			300 —
	125 —						
				Telephone Exp.		50 —	
				Misc. Expense		10 —	
	400 —						
				Supplies		90 —	
	500 —						
				Office Expense		4 50	
				Rent Expense		700 —	
				Licence Exp.		16 30	
	100 —						
	1219 —	310 —				945 80	300 —

DATE		CUSTOMER/SUPPLIER	NO	BANK DR	BANK CR	ACCOUNTS RECEIVABLE DR	ACCOUNTS RECEIVABLE CR	✓			ACCOUNTS PAYABLE DR	ACCOUNTS PAYABLE CR
Aug.	1	Sales		✓ 94 —					1	1		
	5	L. Lewis		✓ 75 —					2	2		
	10	Payroll	68		✓ 310 —				3	3		
	12	Hay Electric	69		✓ 75 —		75 —		4	4		
	15	Owner invested		✓ 300 —					5	5		
	17	Sales		✓ 125 —					6	6		
	18	Bell Canada	70		✓ 50 —				7	7		
	19	Taxi	71		✓ 10 —				8	8		
	22	Sales		✓ 400 —					9	9		
	24	Beauty Supply Co.	72		✓ 90 —				10	10		
	24	Sales		✓ 500 —					11	11		
	26	Office Outfitters	73		O 4 50				12	12		
	27	Ajax Holdings	74		✓ 700 —				13	13		
	28	Beauty Council	75		O 16 30				14	14		
	31	Sales		O 100 —					15	15		
		Balancing Totals		1594 —	1255 80	NIL	75 —		16	16	NIL	NI
									17	17		

BANK STATEMENT

Bank of Montreal

Linda's Hair Salon
2356 Queen St. West
Toronto, Ontario

ACCOUNT NUMBER

BRANCH

FWD: $121.95

STATEMENT OF FROM TO PAGE

DESCRIPTION	DEBITS	CREDITS	DATE	BALANCE
		✓ 94 00	8 1	215 95
		✓ 75 00	8 6	290 95
	✓ 310 00	✓ 300 00	8 17	280 95
		✓ 125 00	8 20	405 95
	✓ 75 00	✓ 400 00	8 22	
	✓ 10 00		8 22	720 95
	✓ 90 00	✓ 500 00	8 25	
	✓ 50 00		8 25	1080 95
	✓ 700 00		8 28	380 95
	SC O 5 75		8 31	375 20

The ticking process will show you that there are four items that have circles beside them. This means that there are four reconciling items. Here is the formal reconciliation that tells us what the real or *true balance* is in the bank account:

PAGE NO 8

√	Sales CR	Wages DR		OTHER ACCOUNTS: ACCOUNT	PR	DR	CR
	94—						
		310—					
				Repairs		75—	
				Capital			300—
	125—						
				Telephone Exp.		50—	
				Misc. Expense		10—	
	400—						
				Supplies		90—	
	500—						
				Office Expense		4 50	
				Rent Expense		700—	
				Licence Exp.		16 30	
	100—						
	1219—	310—				945 80	300—

Linda's Hair Salon
Bank Reconciliation Statement
August 31, 1986

Balance Per Bank	$375.20	Balance Per Books	$460.15
Add:		*Less:*	
Outstanding Deposit	100.00	Service Charge not on books	(5.75)
	475.20	*True Balance*	$454.40
Less:			
Outstanding Cheque			
#73 4.50			
#75 16.30	(20.80)		
True Balance	$454.40		

Note the following explanations for the reconciliation.

1. The *balance per bank* comes from the balance shown on the bank statement on August 31st.
2. The *outstanding deposit* is the only deposit not ticked off on the Bank Statement as having been received by the bank as of August 31st.
3. The *outstanding cheques* are the two cheques that were not ticked off in the multipurpose journal.
4. The *balance per books* comes from the general ledger Bank account balance on August 31st.
5. The *service charge* is an entry on the bank statement that the business

does not have on its books (labelled SC on the bank statement).

6. The *true balance* is the amount of money that the business would really have in its bank account if all reconciling items had gone through the bank books and business books.

As a general rule of thumb, there will usually be some reconciling items when bank reconciliations have to be done. The true balance of the bank account will usually be neither the bank balance nor the general ledger balance, but some other figure.

The bank reconciliation statement is usually produced for someone in the business, such as the owner or the accountant, and would rarely be seen by outsiders. It is a ''cash control'' feature of a business and it will be a good control if someone other than the person who handles the daily cash does it.

11.6 Banking Terminology

Linda's bank statement for September is reproduced below to illustrate three new items that might appear on a bank statement. These are items that you often find in a bank reconciliation.

BANK STATEMENT

Bank of Montreal

Linda's Hair Salon
2356 Queen St. West
Toronto, Ontario

ACCOUNT NUMBER

BRANCH

FWD: $375.20

STATEMENT OF FROM TO PAGE

DESCRIPTION	DEBITS	CREDITS	DATE	BALANCE
		100.00	9 1	475.20
	4.50		9 4	
	16.30		9 4	454.40
	30.00	180.00	9 10	604.40
	DM 540.00		9 15	64.40
		CM 800.00	9 20	864.40
	110.00	130.00	9 21	754.40
	120.00		9 21	764.40
	28.00		9 26	
	32.00		9 26	704.40
	NSF 35.20		9 30	669.20

DM stands for Debit Memo.

CM is a Credit Memo.

NSF means Non-Sufficient Funds.

NSF Cheque

The initials NSF stand for **N**on-**S**ufficient **F**unds. An **NSF cheque** is a cheque for which there are not enough funds in the account of the payer to cover the amount of the cheque. Therefore, the cheque is charged back against Linda's bank account and a notation, NSF, is put beside the cheque on the bank statement.

Debit Memo

When the bank processes a **debit memo**, it is taking money out of the business bank account. On the bank statement the debit memo (DM) shows in the withdrawal section. It is to pay for interest on a business loan. The bank automatically takes $540.00 out of Linda's business bank account as part payment on a business loan each month. (Linda would have to approve of this when she first took out the loan with the bank.)

Credit Memo

When the bank processes a **credit memo**, it is putting money into an account for a customer. In Linda's bank statement, the credit memo (CM) is an amount that has been put into Linda's bank account. This is a loan to Linda's business because she was running out of money to pay bills for her hairdressing business.

Other Bank Services

Banks provide other services to their customers, such as

1. electronic transfer of funds instantaneously from one branch to another;
2. overdraft protection in case a customer writes cheques for more money than he/she has in a bank account;
3. purchase of travellers cheques and money orders;
4. purchase of foreign currency; and
5. automated teller machines for immediate cash withdrawal any time of day or night.

11.7 Journal Entries from a Reconciliation

Let's go back to the bank reconciliation for a moment. It is important to understand what happens after the reconciliation is prepared, because both the bank books and Linda's books are incorrect. The bank will correct this near the start of the next month when they record the outstanding deposit and the outstanding cheques. Notice the entries in the September bank statement shown.

Linda's Hair Salon
Bank Reconciliation Statement
August 31, 1986

Balance Per Bank	$375.20	Balance Per Books	$460.15
Add:		*Less:*	
Outstanding Deposit	100.00	Service Charge not recorded on books	(5.75)
	475.20	*True Balance*	$454.40
Less:			
Outstanding Cheque			
#73 4.50			
#75 16.30	(20.80)		
True Balance	$454.40		

BANK STATEMENT

Bank of Montreal

Linda's Hair Salon
2356 Queen St. West
Toronto, Ontario

ACCOUNT NUMBER

BRANCH

FWD: $375.20

STATEMENT OF FROM TO PAGE

DESCRIPTION	DEBITS	CREDITS	DATE	BALANCE
		100.00	9 1	475.20
	4.50		9 4	
	16.30		9 4	454.40
	30.00	130.80	9 10	604.40
	DM 540.00		9 15	64.40
		CM 800.00	9 20	864.40
	110.00	130.00	9 21	
	120.00		9 21	764.40

Linda will have to adjust her books for the service charge which the bank has charged her (and she hasn't recorded). The entry to adjust for this is shown in general journal form and posted into the general ledger Bank account on the right.

GENERAL JOURNAL

PAGE 3

DATE		PARTICULARS	PR	DEBIT	CREDIT
Aug.	31	Bank Charges		5 75	
		Bank			5 75
		Service Charge on bank statement			

GENERAL LEDGER

ACCOUNT: Bank NO. 2

DATE		PARTICULARS	PR	DEBIT	CREDIT	DR CR	BALANCE
Aug.	31	Balance Forward				DR	460 15
	31		GJ3		5 75	DR	454 40

Notice that the bank's books and Linda's books agree in amount in early September. In reality this does not always happen, but we can make it work out neatly here to understand the procedure.

11.8 Petty Cash

In many of the earlier problems in this text, we saw the term ''Cash on Hand.'' This is a small amount of cash on hand, say, $50 that a business keeps to pay small bills, rather than write cheques for payment. This is also called *petty cash*, and it is used to pay for such things as a delivery charge or to purchase some office supplies like pens and pencils. If we set up a petty cash fund of $50 for a business, the journal entry for this would be:

GENERAL JOURNAL

PAGE 1

DATE		PARTICULARS	PR	DEBIT	CREDIT
Jan.	1	Petty Cash	1	50 —	
		Bank	2		50 —
		Cheque #1. To set up original fund.			

When this cheque is cashed, the person who cashes it puts the $50 cash into a small petty cash box in the office, and this amount becomes the petty cash fund.

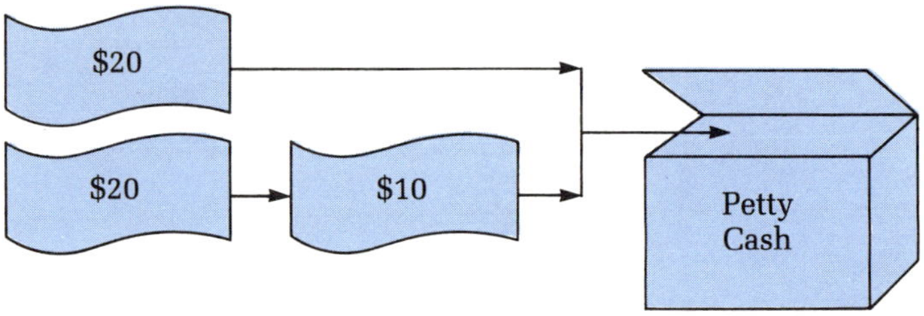

Good cash control requires that only one person has access to and control over this fund. Other employees must go to that person to have a bill paid from the petty cash fund. Whenever money is taken out of the petty cash fund, a receipt or bill must be put back into the box to show where the money has gone.

At any given point in time, the box must contain either $50 cash or $50 in cash and receipts. In the diagram below, you can see that there is only $5 in cash inside the box but there are small bills which add up to another $45. Once the fund gets very low in cash, it can be replenished (filled up again).

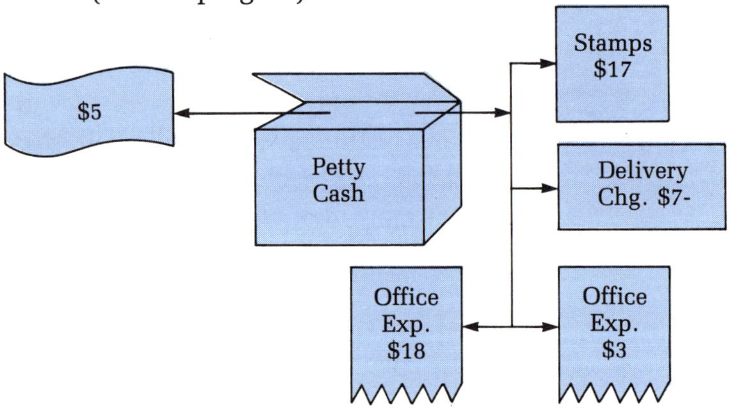

We do this by writing a cheque out for $45, taking it to the bank and cashing it, and putting the $45 back in the petty cash box to bring the fund back up to its original $50. The accounting entry to do this is given below. Notice that the debits for the accounting entry are all the expenses that were paid out of the petty cash fund. Therefore, the debits for this entry show what was paid for out of the petty cash fund.

GENERAL JOURNAL

PAGE 1

DATE		PARTICULARS	PR	DEBIT	CREDIT
Jan.	31	Delivery Expense	53	17 —	
		Office Expense	55	7 —	
		Postage Expense	56	21 —	
		Bank	2		45 —
		Cheque #87 to reimburse the Petty Cash fund.			

Every time the petty cash fund needs to be replenished, an entry must be made in the books just like the one above. Finally, we may find down the road that the petty cash fund is too small, and that it gets to be replenished too often. If this happens, we can increase the petty cash amount, say to $200. When we increase its size, another accounting entry is needed, just like the original one. The entry shows an increase in the petty cash fund by $150 to bring it up to $200.

GENERAL JOURNAL

PAGE 1

DATE		PARTICULARS	PR	DEBIT	CREDIT
Mar.	1	Petty Cash fund	1	150 —	
		Bank	2		150 —
		Cheque #181 to increase the fund to $200.			

The person who operates the petty cash fund may have to follow certain rules, as follows:

Petty Cash Rules

1. An authorized voucher or bill (Figure 11-9) must be put into the box for every cash payment.
2. When the fund falls below a certain amount, for example, $10, it must be replenished.
3. No payments larger than a set sum, for example, $20.00, may be made from the petty cash fund.
4. Vouchers and cash must be turned in to the bookkeeper (or accountant) when the fund is turned in to be replenished.

PETTY CASH VOUCHER

NO.__________ DATE __________

AMOUNT __________

FOR __________

____

CHARGE TO: __________

APPROVED BY: __________

RECEIVED BY: __________

Figure 11-9
A Petty Cash Voucher

11.9 Summary

Cash control is one of the most important functions for businesses and for individuals as well. Good accounting methods will help to control cash on hand to cut down on losses due to theft by employees. There are many ways to control cash, one of the most important being a bank reconciliation to check on cash balances in any bank accounts. This is particularly important nowadays when money is being withdrawn or deposited into bank accounts automatically, without our having to write cheques. All we need are special cards with security code numbers to feed into money machines and we are able to access our bank accounts and carry out banking transactions instantaneously.

See if you have met the chapter objectives. You should be able to

1. know the elements of good cash control;
2. recognize key banking documents;
3. reconcile a bank account;
4. know how to set up a petty cash fund; and
5. know how to make journal entries from a bank reconciliation statement.

Dictionary of Terms

Audit Tape The tape showing daily cash transactions produced on a cash register, used to prepare the daily balance form.

Bank Reconciliation A calculation which determines the true balance of a bank account.

Credit Memo A memo from the bank putting funds into a customer's account.

Current Account A chequing account that businesses use to make regular daily deposits and write cheques.

Daily Balance Form A form used by a business to balance its cash on hand with transactions at the end of a business day.

Debit Memo A memo from the bank withdrawing funds from a customer's account.

NSF Cheque A cheque for which there is not enough money in an account to cover the amount made out on the cheque.

Personal Chequing Account An account that individuals use to write cheques to pay household bills.

Savings Account An account that individuals put money into to earn interest.

Signature Card The card completed by a customer when a bank account is opened to show a specimen signature.

Exercises

1. High River Drycleaning wants to set up a petty cash fund for paying small bills. The owner wants to start the fund with $100, but the bookkeeper is not sure how to make the entry. Journalize the entry to set up this petty cash fund, in a general journal.

2. Look at the diagram below, and answer these questions:
   (a) With how much money did the petty cash fund start?
   (b) How much of the fund has been spent?
   (c) Record the general journal entry that is needed to replenish this petty cash fund.

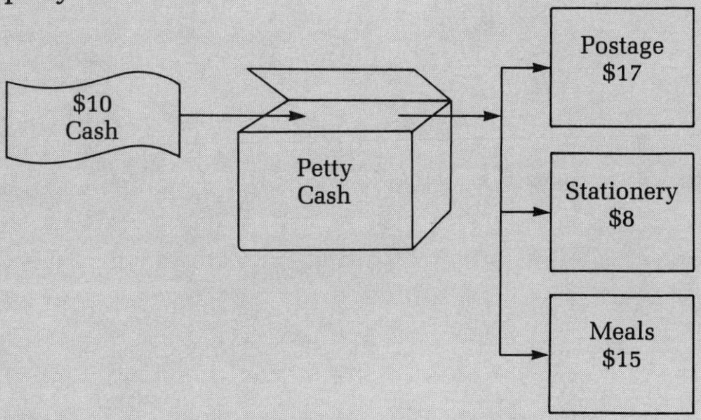

3. An insurance office has a small petty cash fund of $25. The staff have been replenishing it too often and have decided to raise the fund to $200. Journalize the entry that will raise their petty cash fund to the new $200 limit.

4. You are the accountant in the main office of a large newspaper, *The Daily Planet*. The office manager has brought you the petty cash box and the vouchers that are in it. Journalize the enty to replenish the fund.

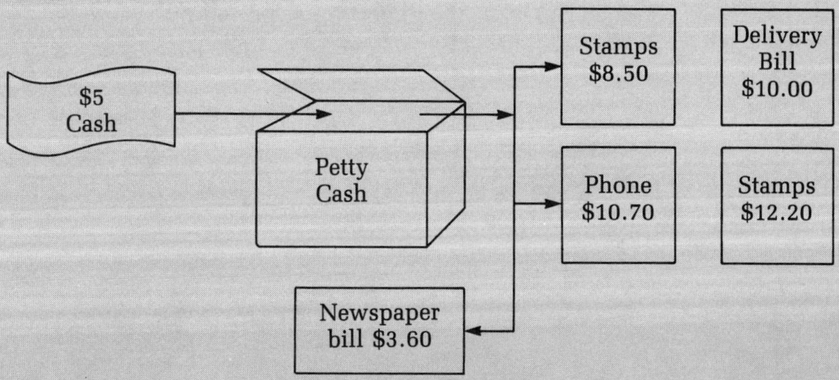

5. Dinosaur Valley Secondary School has been having a problem with the collections at their school dances. The school treasurer reports that not all the money collected for the dances is being turned in at the end of the night. Look at the door setup for the gym in the diagram and see if you can suggest better control at the doors, so that all the cash collections are turned in.

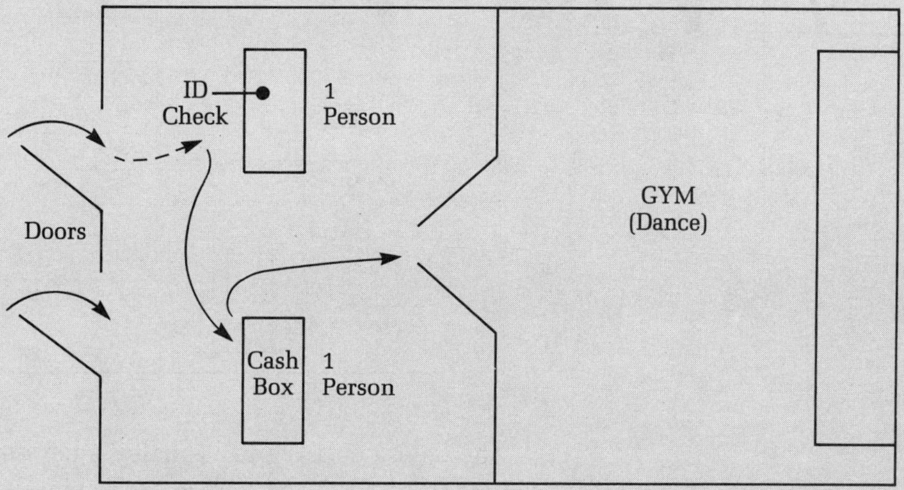

TX $ 45.65
SA $ 810.20
RA $ 325.00
CH $ 327.50
CA $ 568.35

6. The cash register audit tape shown to the left is the one that you saw earlier. Without looking back in the book, can you remember what each code means? If you get stuck, go back to the chapter.

7. Use the cash register audit tape given and the cash count on the daily balance form to complete the form. Make sure that the general journal entry balances when you are done. (*Note:* A business will have a cash shortage or an overage, but not both.)

DAILY BALANCE FORM

ACTUAL CASH IN DRAWER
28 x $1.00 =
56 x 2.00 =
52 x 5.00 =
16 x 10.00 =
25 x 20.00 =
CHANGE = 22.90
TOTAL =

CASH SUMMARY	
CASH SALES (CA) REC'D ON ACCOUNT (RA)	
CASH COUNT SHOULD BE ACTUAL CASH IN DRAWER	
CASH (SHORTAGE) OVER	

GENERAL JOURNAL	DEBIT	CREDIT
BANK		
ACCTS. REC. (CH)		
CASH SHORT		
ACCTS. REC (RA)		
SALES (SA)		
SALES TAX (TX)		
CASH OVER		
TOTALS		

TX $ 65.50
SA $935.50
RA $450.00
CH $372.10
CA $628.90

8. Use the audit tape given and the cash count on the daily balance form to complete the form. Make sure that the general journal entry balances when you are done. (*Note*: A business will have a cash shortage or an overage, but not both.)

TX $ 80.00
SA $920.00
RA $118.00
CH $142.88
CA $857.13

DAILY BALANCE FORM

ACTUAL CASH IN DRAWER
28 x $1.00 =
56 x 2.00 =
52 x 5.00 =
16 x 10.00 =
25 x 20.00 =
CHANGE = 15.12
TOTAL =

CASH SUMMARY

CASH SALES (CA) REC'D ON ACCOUNT (RA)	
CASH COUNT SHOULD BE ACTUAL CASH IN DRAWER	
CASH (SHORTAGE) OVER	

GENERAL JOURNAL

	DEBIT	CREDIT
BANK		
ACCTS. REC. (CH)		
CASH SHORT		
ACCTS. REC (RA)		
SALES (SA)		
SALES TAX (TX)		
CASH OVER		
TOTALS		

9. The balance in Wendy Hartley's personal cashbook as of June 30th was $568.12. The balance per the bank statement was $600.12. The following items were outstanding at the end of the month:

   Outstanding deposits: $400.00

   Outstanding cheques: $45.00; $24.50; $72.00; $300.00

   Service charge not recorded on Wendy's books: $9.50

   Prepare a formal bank reconciliation as of June 30.

10. The bank statement balance for "Willy's Welding" as of January 31st was $1 015.00. The bank balance per the business General Ledger was $1 326.35. The following items were found to be outstanding:

    Outstanding deposits: $80.00; $175.00; $94.00

    Outstanding cheques: $12.80; $33.00; $84.25

    Service charge: $12.40

    NSF cheque not recorded on the books: $80.00

    Prepare a formal bank reconciliation for the business as of June 30th.

11. Morty Mortar, a stone mason, was trying to find out how much money was really in his bank account. He has the following information: balance per bank statement, $2 450.00; balance per the general ledger bank account, $2 808.25. The following items are outstanding:

    O/S deposits: $242.00; $200.00
    O/S cheques: $10.80; $65.00; $24.00; $52.20
    Service charge: $8.25
    NSF cheque: $60.00

    Prepare a bank reconciliation as of June 30th.

12. The bookkeeper for ''Wonderworld Amusement Park'' is trying to reconcile the bank account at the end of April. Help her finish the job. The Bank account balance in the general ledger was $4 300. The bank statement from the Royal Bank showed a balance of $7 742.18 at month end. The outstanding items were:

    O/S cheques: $180; $245; $102.10; $21.12; $50; $12.21

    O/S deposit: $2 100.00

    NSF cheque: $60.00

    Service charge: $8.25

    Bank credit memo for a loan advanced to the business (not recorded on company books): $5 000

    Prepare a bank reconciliation as of June 30th.

Challenge Questions

1. The petty cash fund shown needs to be replenished. Look at the vouchers and the balance and journalize a replenishing entry in a multipurpose journal.

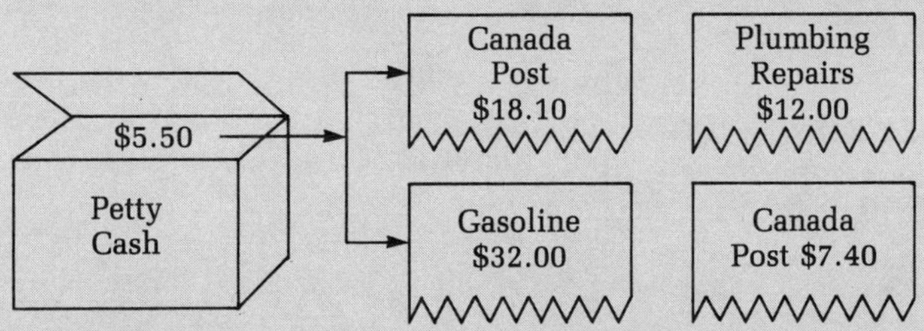

2. Use the information below to prepare a bank reconciliation statement for Lazlo Beta as of December 31, 19 ___.

Balance Per Bank	$12 265.12
Balance Per Books	11 679.27
Credit Memo	1 800.00
Debit Memo	450.00
N.S.F. Cheque	175.00
Outstanding Cheque	251.27
Outstanding Deposit	830.00
Service Charge	10.42

Review Questions

1. Explain briefly what a petty cash fund is.
2. Name three items that could be paid out of a petty cash fund.
3. One of the company salespersons came into the main office and was complaining about a $50 speeding ticket. He has asked the person in charge of the petty cash fund to reimburse him for the ticket. If you were the person in charge of the fund, what would you say to him?
4. (a) What is a replenishing cheque?
   (b) How often is a replenishing entry made?
5. List the five pieces of information on a petty cash voucher.
6. List the five physical controls that can be used to make sure no cash is lost or stolen in a business.
7. What do these codes from an audit tape mean?
   TX SA RA CH CA
8. When is a daily balance form prepared in a business?
9. What does the term ''Cash Over'' mean?
10. Where is a night depository located? For what is it used?
11. Name the three main types of bank accounts that people and businesses can open at a bank. Describe each type briefly, in your own words.

12. You mention to your mother, who does the family books, that you have just learned how to reconcile a bank account. She has never done this and wants to know what you mean. Bring her up to date and tell her how to do this with a synoptic journal and the bank statement.

13. Indicate if these statements about reconciling a bank statement are true or false.
    (a) A business Bank account should be reconciled every day.
    (b) The ''balance per books'' comes from the general ledger Bank account.
    (c) The real balance in the bank is called the true balance.
    (d) The term ''debit memo'' means that the business has had money taken out of its bank account.
    (e) When a cheque is NSF, it means that money has been taken out of a business Bank account.
    (f) It is usually necessary to prepare journal entries for the general ledger Bank account after a bank reconciliation has been prepared.

14. What do the initials MICR mean?

15. Write out an example of a restrictive endorsement for a cheque you have received.

Review Case

Copy! Copy! Copy! is a new small business in Moncton that duplicates and reproduces any kind of business documents for its customers. The firm has been operating now for two months and the boss thinks it would be nice to have a Petty Cash Fund for paying out small bills. She doesn't really know how it works and she wants you to write down, in point form, how a Petty Cash Fund operates. She thinks probably $100 will be large enough to start and she wonders about the General Journal entry needed to set up this account. Journalize this for her in General Journal form. Explain to her as well, how the fund gets filled up again when it gets down near the empty point.

Challenge Case

1. The bank statement, general ledger Bank account, and multipurpose journal for Pyke's Paving are shown below.
   (a) Prepare a bank reconciliation statement as of February 29.
   (b) Once you have reconciled the Bank account, prepare the entries that are needed for the books to bring them in line with the true balance on the reconciliation.

BANK STATEMENT

Bank of Montreal

Pyke's Paving Service
3452 Victoria Street
Burnaby, B.C.

ACCOUNT NUMBER

BRANCH

FWD: $77.50

STATEMENT OF FROM TO PAGE

DESCRIPTION	DEBITS	CREDITS	DATE	BALANCE
		110.00	2:1	187.50
		80.00	2:5	267.50
	75.00		2:8	
	13.50		2:8	179.00
	22.00	300.00	2:12	457.00
	40.00	220.00	2:13	637.00
	90.00		2:20	
	10.20		2:20	536.80
	300.00		2:22	236.80
	SC 6.80		2:29	230.00

DATE		CUSTOMER/SUPPLIER	NO	BANK DR	BANK CR	ACCOUNTS RECEIVABLE DR	ACCOUNTS RECEIVABLE CR	√	
Feb.	1	Sale of Services		110 —					1
	3	Willson Stationers	24		75 —				2
	5	Sale of Services		80 —					3
	7	Canada Post	25		13 50				4
	11	Willson Stationers	26		22 —				5
	12	K. Shyster		300 —			300 —		6
	13	Sale of Services		220 —					7
	13	P. Desborough	27		40 —				8
	15	A. Potter	28		90 —				9
	20	Modern Office Supplies	29		10 20				10
	21	Canada Post	30		5 90				11
	22	Burnaby Electric	31		60 —				12
	22	Owner Withdrew	32		300 —				13
	23	Bell Canada	33		18 30				14
	25	F. Tardy		195 —			195 —		15
		Totals		905 —	634 90	0 —	495 —		16
									17

ACCOUNT: Bank NO. 2

DATE		PARTICULARS	PR	DEBIT	CREDIT	DR/CR	BALANCE
Aug.	31	Balance Forward				DR	69 90
	31		SY2	905 —	634 90	DR	340 —

MULTIPURPOSE JOURNAL

PAGE NO ______

ACCOUNTS PAYABLE DR.	ACCOUNTS PAYABLE CR	√	Sales CR	Wages DR		OTHER ACCOUNTS ACCOUNT	PR	DR.	CR
			110 —						
					75 —				
			80 —						
						Postage Exp.		13 50	
					22 —				
			220 —						
				40 —					
				90 —					
					10 20				
						Postage Exp.		5 90	
						Light Expense		60 —	
						P. Pike, Dwgs.		300 —	
						Telephone Exp.		18 30	
0 —	0 —		410 —	130 —	107 20			100 70	

Take-a-Break

Business Trivia

1. What is the champagne of ginger ales?
2. How many bends are there in a standard paper clip?
3. What western province boasted Canada's first health insurance scheme?
4. How many weeks a year does a typical office worker spend on coffee breaks.
5. What are the first three Arabic numerals?
6. Whose picture is on a $5 bill?
7. What did NDP leader David Lewis call those Canadian corporations whom he felt got undeserved tax breaks?
8. Which board game did Parker Brothers originally reject claiming it had "52" fundamental errors?
9. What is the most popular colour for tennis balls judging by sales?
10. Which is the only Canadian newspaper sold in Moscow?
11. What is the highest denomination of Canadian Tire money?
12. Who presided over the closing of the Iron Ore Company of Canada in Quebec?
13. What Winnipeg newspaper did J.W. Dafoe edit for 43 years?
14. What is the main commercial fish of Canada's west coast?
15. What Canadian city boasts the oldest shopping street in North America?
16. What was the serial number of all Canadian centennial dollar bills?

Source: Trivial Pursuit, Genus II edition

Chapter 12 Practice Set II

Objectives

At the end of this chapter you will have worked through a practice set for a small service business called Jones Electronics. You will have performed the following accounting operations:

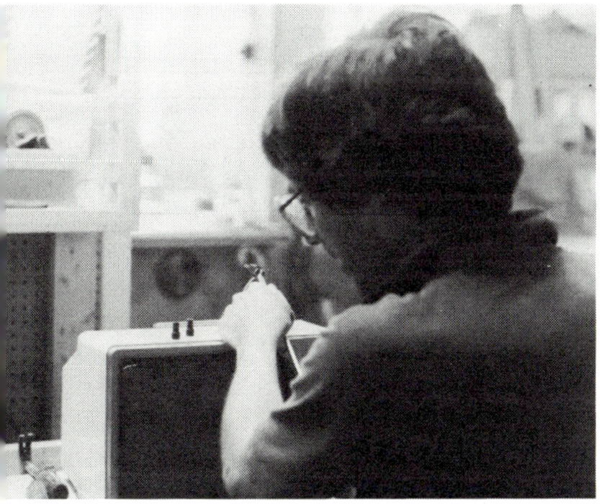

Figure 12-1
Jones Electronics—a small business

Step Operation

1. Set up a general ledger.
2. Record the opening entry for the business.
3. Journalize transactions into a multipurpose journal.
4. Post to a general ledger.
5. Reconcile the bank account at month end.
6. Prepare a worksheet.
7. Prepare a set of classified financial statements.
8. Journalize and post the closing entries.
9. Prepare a post-closing trial balance.

12.1 Overview

Jones Electronics is a small electronics repair business owned and operated by Rick Jones, a skilled TV and VCR technician. Rick's business is located in a small town called Norwich, and this practice set will take you through Rick's first month of operations. The project is set out in steps for you to follow—your teacher may want to check your work after certain steps of the project.

12.2 Step 1

Before we record any transactions, we must set up the General Ledger for Jones Electronics. To do this, we need a Chart of Accounts. Open 3-column accounts for each of the accounts in the chart. Record only the name and the number of each account, since Jones Electronics is just starting its first month of operations.

Chart of Accounts

1.	Petty Cash	40.	Sales-TV Repairs
2.	Bank	41.	Sales-VCR Repairs
3.	Accounts Receivable	50.	Accounting Fee
10.	Repair Equipment	51.	Advertising Expense
11.	Office Equipment	52.	Bank Interest Expense
12.	Delivery Van	53.	Heat & Light Expense
20.	Bank Loan	54.	Rent Expense
21.	Accounts Payable	55.	Parts Supplies
30.	R. Jones, Capital	56.	Telephone Expense
31.	R. Jones, Drawings	57.	Wages Expense

The first account should look like this after you have set it up—name, number, but no opening balance.

GENERAL LEDGER

ACCOUNT: *Petty Cash* NO. *1*

DATE	PARTICULARS	PR	DEBIT	CREDIT	DR. CR	BALANCE

12.3 Step 2

The next step in the practice set is to record the opening entry for the business. When Rick started the business, near the first of January, he had some cash but he had to borrow from Canada Trust. Journalize the opening entries in the Multipurpose Journal (Page 1).

Jan. 2: Rick invested $20 000 into his new business from his personal savings. Money was deposited into the business Bank account.

2: Borrowed $10 000 from Canada Trust and put it into the business Bank account for Jones Electronics.

Jones Electronics

DATE	CUSTOMER/SUPPLIER	NO	BANK		ACCOUNTS RECEIVABLE		√			ACCOUNTS PAYABLE	
			DR	CR	DR	CR				DR	CR
								1	1		
								2	2		

12.4 Step Three

The Multipurpose Journal for Jones Electronics should be set up as in the example below.

The business transactions are given below for the first month of business. Journalize the transactions for January into Jones Electronics' Multipurpose Journal. The transactions have all been labelled to assist you with your entry into the journal. When you have journalized all the transactions, add and cross-add the journal at the end of January, and proceed to step 3 of the practice set.

Transactions

Jan. 2: *Cheque*
Bought a new computer system for the business, which includes a keyboard, monitor, disk drive, and printer. Total cost was \$1 518.75. Cheque #1.

2: *Cheque*
Set up a Petty Cash Fund for small payments, \$100.00. Cheque #2.

Jan. 3: *Cash Sales*
Repaired TVs for customers for cash, \$235.00. (All cash received is deposited daily into the business Bank account through the night depository at the bank.)

Jan. 4: *Purchase Invoice*
Bought service parts from Hitachi, for \$872.16. Set this up as an account payable. Invoice #H7513.

Jan. 5: *Sales Invoices*
Sold services to H. Cornwell on account, \$85, and J. Snoddy, \$42.50. Invoices #1 and #2.

Jan. 8: *Cheque*
Monthly rent was due. Wrote cheque #3 to pay this in advance, \$350.00.

8: *Cash Sales*
Cash sales for the day totalled \$310.75.

MULTIPURPOSE JOURNAL

PAGE NO 1

√				OTHER ACCOUNTS			
				ACCOUNT	PR	DR	CR

8: *Cheque*
Bell Canada sent a bill for installing the new business phone, $112.79. Cheque #4.

Jan. 8: *Cheque*
Rick's employee—Jeff Harrison—handed in his time card. He is paid $4.50/hour. (OT = Time-and-a-half over 40 hours/week)

TIME CARD

NO 1

NAME Jeff Harrison

PAY PERIOD ENDING Jan. 8, 19—

DAY	HOURS		
	TOTAL	REGULAR	OVERTIME
M	8		
T	8		
W	8		
T	9		
F	10		
TOTALS			

	HOURS	RATE	GROSS PAY
REGULAR			
OVERTIME			
		GROSS PAY	

(*Note:* You will have to calculate his Net Pay using the tables for Tax, CPP, and UI. Jeff is single, and therefore his tax code is "1".) Record the monthly payroll in a payroll journal set out like the one below. The cheque number is 5.

PAYROLL JOURNAL

EMP. NO.	EMPLOYEE NAME	TAX CODE	GROSS PAY	DEDUCTIONS				NET PAY
				C.P.P.	U.I.	TAXABLE INCOME	TAX	
			200.25	2 74	4 71		21 25	?

Jan. 9: *Cash Receipt*
H. Cornwell sent a cheque to pay his account in full, $85.00.

9: *Purchase Invoice*
Bought some repair equipment on account from the supplier, Hi-Tech Supply, $2 200. Invoice #00039.

Jan. 10: *Sales Invoices*
To J. Ferris for VCR repairs, $67.20 and Dr. L. Ferraro, television repairs $62.75. Invoices #3 and #4.

10: *Cash Receipt*
J. Snoddy paid his account in cash.

10: *Cash Sales*
Sales for the past two days were put into the night depository, $402.90 cash.

Jan. 12: *Cheque*
Cheque #6 to the Norwich Gazette for newspaper advertising, $182.45.

12: *Purchase Invoice*
Bought a new service van for the business on account from Fidlin Motors. Total cost was $16 800.

12: *Cash Receipt*
Received cash payment from Dr. Ferraro for the invoice sent out on January 10 for TV repairs.

Jan. 15: *Cheque*
Cheque #7 to Jeff Harrison for weekly wages.

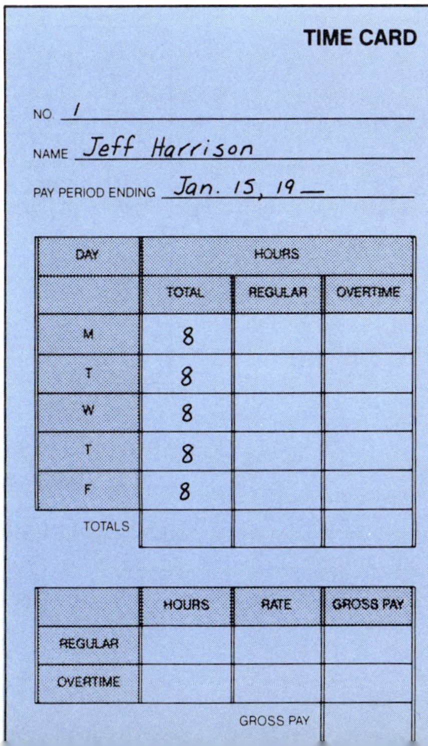

TIME CARD

NO. 1

NAME Jeff Harrison

PAY PERIOD ENDING Jan. 15, 19__

DAY	HOURS		
	TOTAL	REGULAR	OVERTIME
M	8		
T	8		
W	8		
T	8		
F	8		
TOTALS			

	HOURS	RATE	GROSS PAY
REGULAR			
OVERTIME			
		GROSS PAY	

Jan. 15: *Sales Invoice*
Fixed a VCR and a TV for Ralph Crittenden, on account, $50.74. Invoice #5.

Jan. 15 *Cheque*
Wrote cheque #8 for $300 to Fidlin Motors, monthly payment on the van.

Jan. 16: *Cash Sales*
Deposited the money from cash sales into the Bank account, $620.10

16: *Cheque*
Cheque #9 to J. Symons, C.A. This was fee payment for setting up the multipurpose journal and the general ledger for the business, $125.00.

Jan. 17: *Cash Sales*
Total was $102.70.

Jan. 18: *Purchase Invoice*
Bought parts supplies from Geo. Peterson & Co. Invoice total was $513.81.

Jan. 19: *Cash Receipt*
Received $50.74 from Ralph Crittenden to pay his account in full from January 15th.

Jan. 21: *Debit Memo*

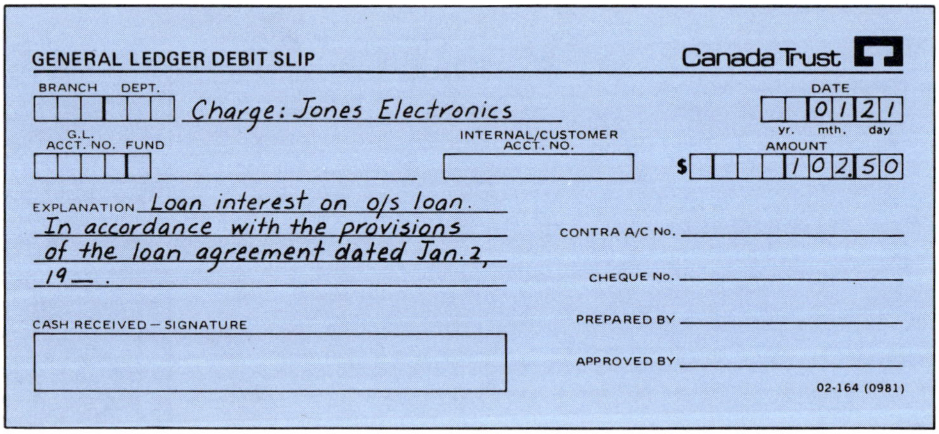
GENERAL LEDGER DEBIT SLIP — Canada Trust

BRANCH DEPT. — Charge: Jones Electronics — DATE yr. mth. day: 01 21

G.L. ACCT. NO. FUND — INTERNAL/CUSTOMER ACCT. NO. — AMOUNT $ 102.50

EXPLANATION Loan interest on o/s loan. In accordance with the provisions of the loan agreement dated Jan. 2, 19__.

CONTRA A/C No.

CHEQUE No.

CASH RECEIVED — SIGNATURE

PREPARED BY

APPROVED BY

02-164 (0981)

Jan. 22: *Cash Sales*
Total was $745.68.

Jan. 23: *Cheque*
Owner withdraws $180 from the business for his personal use, by writing out cheque #10, payable to himself.

Jan. 24: *Sales Invoice*
Charge sale for repairs to Lois Ward, $44.00. Invoice #6.

Jan. 25: *Cheque #11 to Jeff Harrison.*

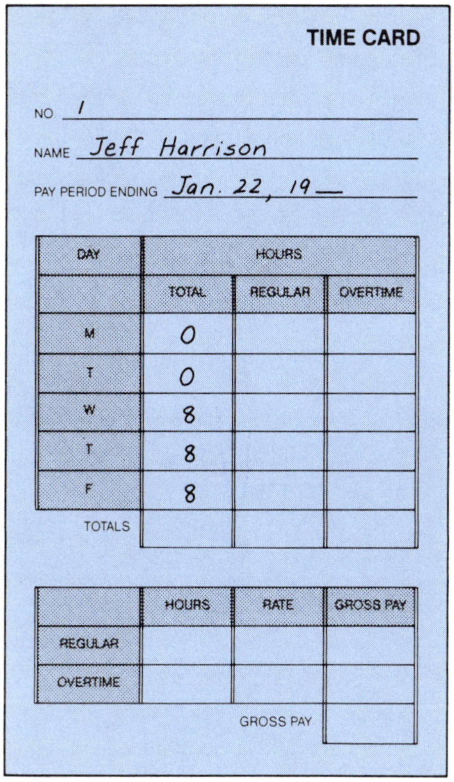

TIME CARD

NO 1

NAME Jeff Harrison

PAY PERIOD ENDING Jan. 22, 19—

DAY	HOURS		
	TOTAL	REGULAR	OVERTIME
M	0		
T	0		
W	8		
T	8		
F	8		
TOTALS			

	HOURS	RATE	GROSS PAY
REGULAR			
OVERTIME			
		GROSS PAY	

Jan. 28: *Cash Sales*
Total-to-date was $717.42.

Jan. 29: *Cheque*
Wrote cheque #12 to Geo. Peterson to pay for the parts bought on account on January 18th.

Jan. 29: *Sales Invoice*
Charge sale to David Irving, TV repair, $30. Invoice #7.

Jan. 30: *Purchase Invoice*
Received the monthly bill from Union Gas for hydro, $142.99.

Jan. 31: *Cheque*
Paid Andrews Service Station for gasoline and oil bought for the van for the month, $107.25. Cheque #13.

31: *Cash Sales*
Total deposited was $1 454.02.

31: *Cheque*
Rick wrote out cheque #14, to replenish the Petty Cash Fund

at month end. The following vouchers were inside the petty cash box.

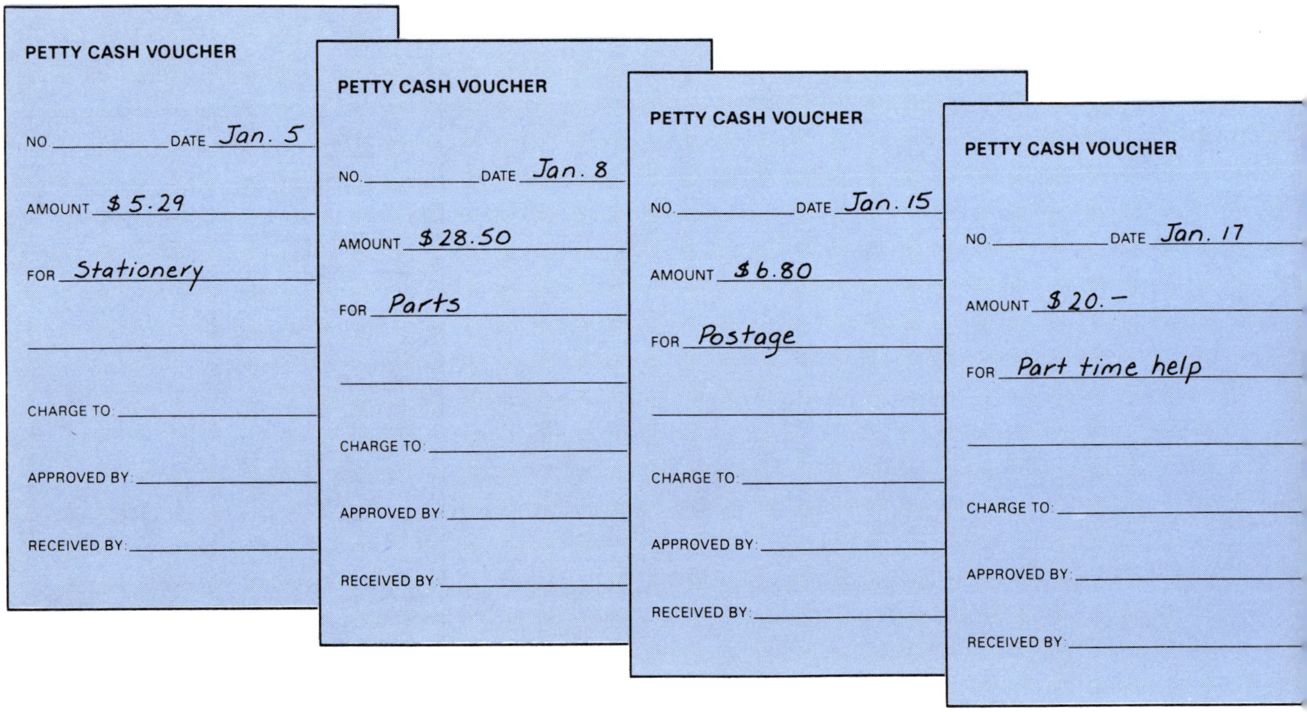
PETTY CASH VOUCHER

NO. ______ DATE Jan. 5

AMOUNT $5.29

FOR Stationery

CHARGE TO:

APPROVED BY:

RECEIVED BY:

PETTY CASH VOUCHER

NO. ______ DATE Jan. 8

AMOUNT $28.50

FOR Parts

CHARGE TO:

APPROVED BY:

RECEIVED BY:

PETTY CASH VOUCHER

NO. ______ DATE Jan. 15

AMOUNT $6.80

FOR Postage

CHARGE TO:

APPROVED BY:

RECEIVED BY:

PETTY CASH VOUCHER

NO. ______ DATE Jan. 17

AMOUNT $20.—

FOR Part time help

CHARGE TO:

APPROVED BY:

RECEIVED BY:

12.5 Step Four

Rick Jones received his bank statement for January. Use it to prepare a bank reconciliation statement for his bank account at the end of January. Journalize any entries that arise from the reconciliation.

12.6 Step Five

Take an adding machine tape of your multipurpose journal to make sure it cross-balances. Post the journal to the general ledger for Jones Electronics.

12.7 Step Six

Take the balances in the general ledger at the end of January and record them on a worksheet for the business. Extend, balance, and rule the worksheet.

BANK STATEMENT

Canada Trust

Jones Electronics
Main Street
Norwich, Ontario

ACCOUNT NUMBER

BRANCH

FWD: $0.00

STATEMENT OF FROM TO PAGE

DESCRIPTION	DEBITS	CREDITS	DATE	BALANCE
		20 000:--	1:2	20 000:--
		10 000:--	1:2	30 000:--
	1 518:75		1:3	28 381:25
	100:00		1:3	
		235:--	1:3	28 616:25
		310:75	1:8	28 927:--
	171:55		1:8	28 755:45
	350:00		1:9	
	112:79		1:9	28 292:66
		85:--	1:9	28 377:66
		445:40	1:10	28 823:06
		62:75	1:12	28 885:81
	182:45		1:13	28 703:36
	300:00		1:15	28 403:36
	157:25		1:15	28 246:11
	125:00	620:10	1:16	28 741:21
	SC 3:00	102:70	1:17	28 840:91
		50:74	1:19	28 891:65
	DM 102:50		1:21	28 789:15
		745:68	1:22	29 534:83
	180:00		1:23	29 354:83
	103:58		1:25	29 251:25
		717:42	1:28	29 968:67
		1 454:02	1:31	31 422:69

12.8 Step Seven

Use the worksheet to prepare

1. an income statement for January;
2. a classified report form balance sheet as at the end of January.

12.9 Step Eight

Journalize and post the closing journal entries at the end of January.

12.10 Step Nine

Take a post-closing trial balance of the general ledger.

Accounting at Work

General Accounting Clerk

Craig Majernik works for a store in a donut chain in a small city. Craig's title is Accounting Clerk, but in effect he handles most of the accounting functions of the business. In particular, one of his duties is to balance the cash at the end of the day. Waiters and waitresses are allowed to use the cash register, but they do not have access to the audit tape inside the cash register. At the end of the day, Craig counts the cash in the cash register drawer and balances it against the audit tape inside the machine. If the cash shortage or overage is too great, Craig is expected to inform the store manager, and help his boss find out what went wrong. Once

the daily cash is balanced, Craig makes up the bank deposit slip and takes all the cash to the bank to deposit it into the night depository. A copy of the cash report, and the deposit slip are left for Craig's boss to see in the morning. Craig also makes up the entry in the books to show that the deposit has been made.

The other accounting duty that Craig does in this business is to look after the employee payroll. Each employee punches in a time card in the back of the store and Craig's duties are to:

1. calculate regular and overtime hours and gross pay;
2. record deductions for Canada Pension Plan, Unemployment Insurance, and Income Tax;
3. write out a cheque for each employee's net pay;
4. record the payroll information in the store Payroll Journal; and
5. update each employee's Statement of Earnings.

Of all his duties, Craig finds this one the most interesting because he likes to ensure that employees are paid accurately for their work.

Craig was hired by the donut shop from among several high school applicants. Craig took two accounting courses at high school, but his employer was most impressed with his personality and his attitude. Craig has management ambitions and feels that starting in an accounting career will help him later when he searches for more responsibility.

Questions for Discussion

1. Craig is lucky that he got this accounting position. What was the main reason Craig got the job?
2. Name four other courses that Craig could have taken at high school that would help him in his work.
3. For the past three days, the cash register has been short $20 each day. Craig has noticed that his friend, who also works at the store has been acting suspiciously and feels he may be the culprit. What would you do at this point if you were Craig?
4. How can Craig let his boss know that he wants to ''get ahead'' in the business?

7

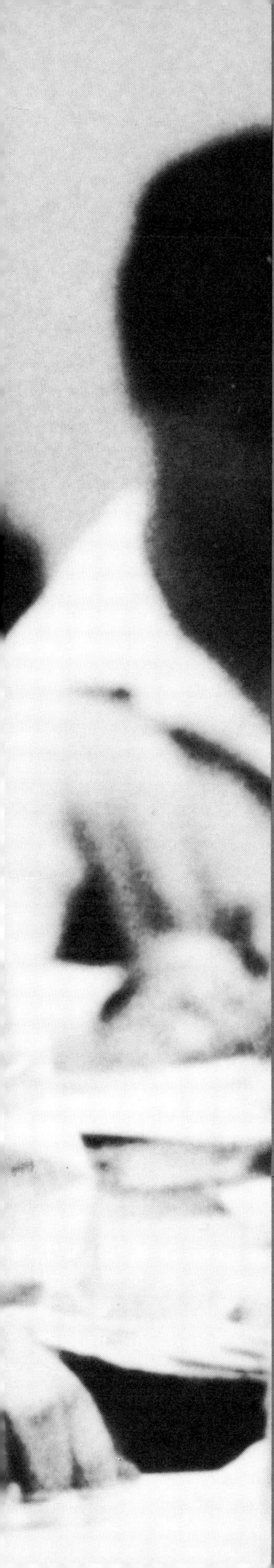

Advanced Accounting Functions

Chapter 13 Adjusting and Closing Entries

Chapter 14 Accounting for a Merchandise Business

Chapter 15 Subsidiary Ledgers

Chapter 13 Adjusting and Closing Entries

Objectives

At the end of this chapter you will be able to

1. identify the need for adjusting entries;
2. understand the preparation of three types of adjusting entries;
3. know how to complete an 8-column worksheet; and
4. journalize and post adjusting and closing entries and prepare a post-closing trial balance.

13.1 Overview

One of the problems that occurs with accounting entries is that they may benefit more than one time period. If, for example, a business bought a car for a salesperson to use, it should last more than one year. Therefore, the business will want to spread the cost of that car over a period of time longer than one year. This is adjusting for depreciation on the car. Adjusting entries are made on an 8-column worksheet which you will study in this chapter.

13.2 Depreciation —Automobile

When a business buys a new car, it will set the car up as a fixed asset, and then credit either Bank or Accounts Payable, depending on whether the business paid cash for the car.

GENERAL JOURNAL

PAGE

DATE		PARTICULARS	PR	DEBIT	CREDIT
Jan.	1	Automobile		15 000 —	
		Bank			15 000 —
		Bought new car Cheque #1.			

We know that the car will last longer than a year but we have charged the whole cost of the car into an asset account. What we have to do with the cost of the car, is to spread the cost over the expected life of the car. This is the process called "depreciation." Since it is hard to tell how long a car will last, accountants use a percentage to spread the cost of the car over a few years. This percentage rate in accounting is called rate of depreciation. For any vehicles like cars, trucks, and vans, we say they have a rate of depreciation of 30% per year. Here is how the calculation works:

Cost of Automobile = $15 000
Depreciation Rate = x 30% (per year)
Depreciation = $4 500

Depreciation is the process of allocating the cost of an asset over its useful life.

Let's take another look at the calculation above and say it in words. "The car originally cost $15 000. We depreciate the car 30%, or $4 500 in one year." This calculation, then, requires an entry (or an adjustment) on the worksheet. Here is a worksheet with a new set of columns in it called "Adjustments." This new worksheet is called an 8-column worksheet. You will remember that the worksheet you studied in Chapter 5 is a 6-column worksheet.

	ACCOUNTS	ACCT. NO.	TRIAL BALANCE		ADJUSTMENTS	
			DR.	CR.	DR.	CR.
1						
2						
3						
4						
5						
6						
7						

To record depreciation on a car, we put an entry in the Adjustments column of the worksheet. We know from our calculations that the depreciation on the car is $4 500 for the first year. To record this, we must debit an account called "Depreciation Expense—Automobile" and credit an account called "Accumulated Depreciation—Automobile." Here is the entry as it is made on the worksheet in the Adjustments column.

	ACCOUNTS	ACCT. NO.	TRIAL BALANCE		ADJUSTMENTS	
			DR.	CR.	DR.	CR.
1	Depreciation Exp.-Auto.				(1) 4500 —	
2	Accumulated Deprecn.-Auto.					(1) 4500 —
3						
4						
5						
6						
7						
8						

Notice that the adjusting entry in the Adjustments column has a number beside it—"1". Every entry in the Adjustments column is numbered. This is done to make it easier to keep track of adjustments, and to double-check your work later, if necessary.

Once you have recorded the adjusting entry in the two Adjustments columns, the amounts can be transferred to either the Income Statement

WORKSHEET

FOR THE MONTH ENDED ________ 19____

INCOME STATEMENT		BALANCE SHEET		
DR.	CR.	DR.	CR.	
				1
				2
				3
				4
				5
				6
				7

WORKSHEET

FOR THE MONTH ENDED ________ 19____

INCOME STATEMENT		BALANCE SHEET		
DR.	CR.	DR.	CR.	
				1
				2
				3
				4
				5
				6
				7
				8

columns or the Balance Sheet columns. Since depreciation is an expense, the debit goes to the Income Statement columns. The Accumulated Depreciation is part of the Balance Sheet because this account is paired with the Automobile account. More on this concept later.

This is a good time to look at the whole worksheet and see how the entry for depreciation looks, with all of the other accounts in place on the worksheet.

	ACCOUNTS	ACCT. NO.	TRIAL BALANCE DR	TRIAL BALANCE CR	ADJUSTMENTS DR.	ADJUSTMENTS CR.	INCOME STATEMENT DR.	INCOME STATEMENT CR.
1	Bank		480 —					
2	Accounts Receivable		4120 —					
3	Automobile		15000 —					
4	J. Eidt, Capital			12000 —				
5	J. Eidt, Drawings		2000 —					
6	Fees Earned			19600 —				19600 —
7	Advertising Expense		1200 —				1200 —	
8	Office Expenses		5300 —				5300 —	
9	Telephone Expense		3500 —				3500 —	
10			31600 —	31600 —				
11	Depreciation Exp.– Auto.				(1) 4500 —		4500 —	
12	Accumulated Deprecn.-Auto					(1) 4500 —		
13								
14								

The worksheet is not finished because we still have other adjusting entries to record. It will be finished in another section. Notice how the Depreciation Expense—Automobile amount gets written in the Income Statement columns and becomes an expense just like regular expense entries. What we are really doing here is expensing $4 500 of the car cost. We can also say that we are writing off $4 500 of the car cost.

Test yourself on your understanding of this chapter so far. Answer these questions.

1. How much did the car cost?
2. What rate did we "depreciate" it?
3. How much was the depreciation for one year?

Answers

1. 15 000
2. 30%
3. 4 500

13.3 Depreciation—Other Assets

There are four main groups of assets that you should know. The government groups assets into *classes* and assigns each class a certain annual depreciation rate. The four shown are the most common rates and classes of fixed assets.

Class	Description	Rate
3	Buildings (Brick)	5%
5	Buildings (Frame)	10%
8	Furniture, Equipment	20%
10	Automotive	30%

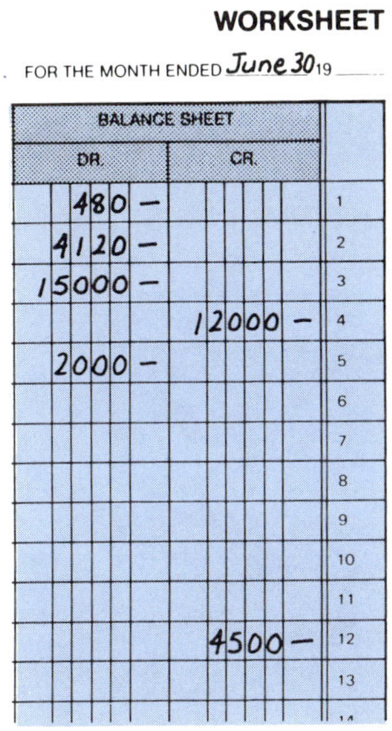

Assume that a business bought three new office typewriters for its secretarial staff, and the total cost was $2 400. The depreciation on these new typewriters for the first year would be calculated the same way as we calculated the depreciation on the automobile, except that the rate is 20% instead of 30%.

Cost of Typewriters	=	$2 400	
Depreciation Rate	=	x 20%	(per year)
Depreciation	=	$ 480	

A brick building has a rate of 5% because it lasts much longer than cars or office equipment. The calculation for depreciation on a new building that cost $150 000 would be:

Cost of Building	=	$150 000	
Depreciation Rate	=	x 5%	(per year)
Depreciation	=	$ 7 500	

There are other classes of assets with different rates of depreciation, but you need only to master these four for the accounting problems we will tackle in this book.

13.4 Prepaid Expenses

Our second set of adjustments to the worksheet is for an asset account called "prepaid expenses." This is a new account that has not yet been mentioned in this book. It refers to money spent on something which will last longer than one time period. The two examples of this are Insurance and Supplies.

Prepaid expenses are expenses that will benefit more than one time period.

13.5 Prepaid Insurance

If you owned a video store and had a lot of expensive equipment, you would want to have it properly insured. Sometimes the insurance company will sell a policy that lasts longer than one year. This can be shown in a line diagram.

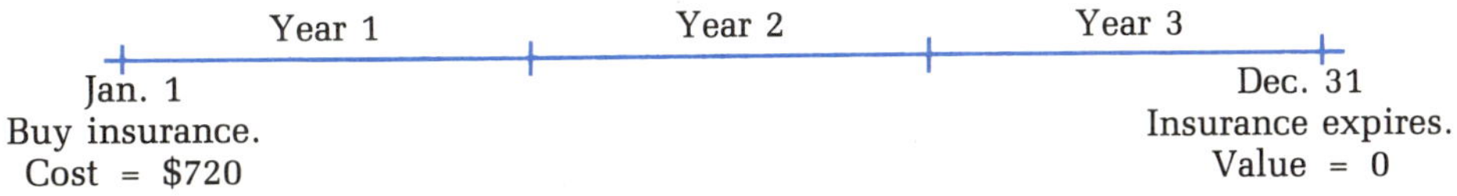

Because the policy lasts three years, we have to spread the cost of the insurance over the three years. This means that somehow we have to debit the Insurance Expense account with $240 for one year. When we buy the insurance, this is the journal entry.

GENERAL JOURNAL

PAGE 1

DATE		PARTICULARS	PR	DEBIT	CREDIT
Jan.	1	Prepaid Insurance		720 —	
		Bank			720 —
		Bought 3-yr. policy. Cheque # 42			

The account Prepaid Insurance is an asset account and appears on the balance sheet. Here is part of the same worksheet with the Prepaid Insurance listed with the other assets in the Trial Balance columns.

	ACCOUNTS	ACCT. NO.	TRIAL BALANCE		ADJUSTMENTS		INCOME STATEMENT	
			DR.	CR.	DR.	CR.	DR.	CR.
1	Bank		480 —					
2	Accounts Receivable		1600 —					
3	Prepaid Insurance		720 —					
4								
5								

When we get to the end of the year, we will have to adjust the Prepaid Insurance because we will have used up only one year's worth of insurance, $240.00. We have to adjust for the amount we have used with a credit to Prepaid Insurance, and a debit to Insurance Expense. Here is the adjustment on the worksheet.

	ACCOUNTS	ACCT. NO.	TRIAL BALANCE		ADJUSTMENTS		INCOME STATEMENT	
			DR.	CR.	DR.	CR.	DR.	CR.
1	Prepaid Insurance		720 —			(2) 2240 —		
2								
3	Insurance Expense				(2) 2240 —		240 —	
4								
5								

The adjustment you see above is taking $240 out of the asset account, Prepaid Insurance, and putting it into the Insurance Expense account. The $240 is the amount of insurance that has been "used up" in one year. The next year there will be another entry to expense $240 for year 2, and a final adjustment in the last year of the policy.

After the adjusting entry is placed in the Adjustments column of the worksheet, the accounts affected are extended to the right. The new balance for Prepaid Insurance is $480 because the insurance policy still has two years to run. The Insurance Expense is $240 because this is the cost of insurance for one year. In the next year, an identical adjustment will have to be made. (Notice that this second adjustment is numbered "2".)

13.6 Prepaid Supplies

The last adjustment we shall study in this text is an adjustment for the purchase of supplies (Figure 13-1). This is very similar to the adjustment you just studied for insurance and, in fact, works the same way because it is also a prepaid expense.

WORKSHEET

FOR THE MONTH ENDED *June 30* 19

BALANCE SHEET		
DR.	CR.	
		1
		2
		3
		4

WORKSHEET

FOR THE MONTH ENDED *June 30* 19 ___

BALANCE SHEET		
DR.	CR.	
480 —		1
		2
		3
		4

Figure 13-1 Adjustments must be made for the supplies used in an office.

	ACCOUNTS	ACCT. NO.	TRIAL BALANCE DR	TRIAL BALANCE CR	ADJUSTMENTS DR	ADJUSTMENTS CR	INCOME STATEMENT DR	INCOME STATEMENT CR
1	Bank		480 —					
2	Accounts Receivable		4 120 —					
3	Prepaid Insurance		720 —			(2) 240 —		
4	Prepaid Supplies		1 800 —			(3) 1 680 —		
5								
6	Insurance Expense				(2) 240 —		240 —	
7	Supplies Expense				(3) 1 680 —		1 680 —	

Assume that the worksheet we are studying is for a doctor, and that on July 1 the doctor bought $1 800 worth of medical supplies for the office. This would be such items as bandages, gauzes, medicines, crutches, etc. These supplies may last beyond the end of the year. When it comes to December 31st, someone will have to take an **inventory** of supplies on hand to see what has been used up. This means that someone will made a list of supplies still on hand at the end of the fiscal year and then attach a dollar value to these supplies. When the doctor first purchased the supplies, the doctor could have debited the asset account Prepaid Supplies. At the end of the year the doctor should credit the asset account with the amount of supplies still on hand and debit this amount into a Supplies Expense account. The worksheet above shows prepaid expense adjustments.

J. Eidt

	ACCOUNTS
1	Bank
2	Accounts Receivable
3	Prepaid Insurance
4	Prepaid Supplies
5	Automobile
6	J. Eidt, Capital
7	J. Eidt, Drawings
8	Fees Earned
9	Advertising Expense
10	Office Expense
11	Telephone Expense
12	
13	Depreciation Exp.-Auto
14	Accumulated Deprecn.-Auto
15	Insurance Expense
16	Supplies Expense
17	
18	Net Income
19	

WORKSHEET

FOR THE MONTH ENDED June 30 19__

BALANCE SHEET DR.	BALANCE SHEET CR.	
		1
		2
480 —		3
120 —		4
		5
		6
		7

After the adjusting entry is placed in the Adjustments column of the worksheet, accounts affected are extended to the right. The balance for Prepaid Supplies is $120 because the supplies inventory showed that there was still $120 worth of medical supplies on hand at year end. Therefore $1 680 is transferred out of the asset account and charged into an expense account since these supplies are *used up*. Note that this adjustment is #3 on the worksheet.

13.7 Balancing the Worksheet

Once all the adjusting entries have been entered into the Adjustments columns of the worksheet, the worksheet can then be balanced. The first step in balancing now is to make sure the Adjustments columns are balanced.

Once this is done, we can extend the worksheet and find out if the business has had a profit or a loss. Below is the entire worksheet with the adjustments extended and with the worksheet balanced and ruled properly.

Notice that after the adjustments are made and the Adjustments columns are balanced, the balancing procedure for the worksheet is exactly as you learned it before in Chapter 5.

WORKSHEET

FOR THE MONTH ENDED June 30 19__

ACCT. NO.	TRIAL BALANCE DR	TRIAL BALANCE CR	ADJUSTMENTS DR.	ADJUSTMENTS CR.	INCOME STATEMENT DR.	INCOME STATEMENT CR.	BALANCE SHEET DR.	BALANCE SHEET CR.	
	480 —						480 —		1
	1600 —						1600 —		2
	720 —			(2) 240 —			480 —		3
	1800 —			(3) 1680 —			120 —		4
	15000 —	12000 —					15000 —		5
								12000 —	6
	2000 —						2000 —		7
		19600 —				19600 —			8
	1200 —				1200 —				9
	5300 —				5300 —				10
	3500 —				3500 —				11
	31600 —	31600 —							12
			(1) 4500 —		4500 —				13
				(1) 4500 —				4500 —	14
			(2) 240 —		240 —				15
			(3) 1680 —		1680 —				16
			6420 —	6420 —	16420 —	19600 —	19680 —	16500 —	17
					3180 —			3180 —	18
					19600 —	19600 —	19680 —	19680 —	19

13.8 Journalizing Adjusting and Closing Entries

Once the adjustments have been entered on the worksheet, they must be formally recorded in a general journal. The worksheet is not a formal accounting document and the adjustments that are made on it must be entered into the books of account. This is done by recording them in general journal form. Before we see the general journal entries, here is the accounting cycle once again, in an expanded version.

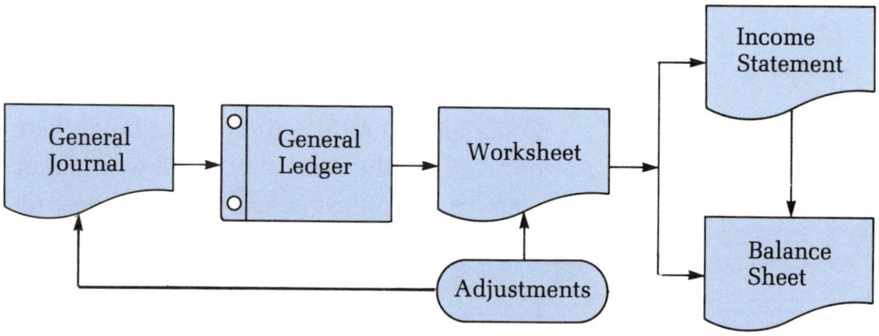

The diagram is showing you that once the worksheet has been balanced you can journalize the **adjusting entries** and post them into their respective general ledger accounts. The financial statements will be correct, but the adjusting entries have to be posted to make the general ledger agree with the worksheet balances.

GENERAL JOURNAL

PAGE 1

DATE		PARTICULARS	PR	DEBIT	CREDIT
		ADJUSTING JOURNAL ENTRIES			
June	30	Depreciation Expense - Automobile	51	4 500 —	
		Accumulated Depreciation - Auto.	11		4 500 —
		Annual depreciation on automobile.			
	30	Insurance Expense	52	240 —	
		Prepaid Insurance	4		240 —
		Year-End adjustment for 3-year insurance policy.			
	30	Supplies Expense	54	1 680 —	
		Prepaid Supplies	5		1 680 —
		To adjust for supplies used during the year.			

GENERAL LEDGER

ACCOUNT: Bank — NO. 2

DATE		PARTICULARS	PR	DEBIT	CREDIT	DR/CR	BALANCE
June	30	Balance Forward	—			DR	480 —

ACCOUNT: Accounts Receivable — NO. 3

DATE		PARTICULARS	PR	DEBIT	CREDIT	DR/CR	BALANCE
June	30	Balance Forward	—			DR	1 600 —

ACCOUNT: Prepaid Insurance — NO. 4

DATE		PARTICULARS	PR	DEBIT	CREDIT	DR/CR	BALANCE
June	30	Balance Forward	—			DR	720 —
	30		AJE		240 —	DR	480 —

ACCOUNT: Prepaid Supplies — NO. 5

DATE		PARTICULARS	PR	DEBIT	CREDIT	DR/CR	BALANCE
June	30	Balance Forward	—			DR	1 800 —
	30		AJE		1 680 —	DR	120 —

ACCOUNT: Automobile — NO. 10

DATE		PARTICULARS	PR	DEBIT	CREDIT	DR/CR	BALANCE
June	30	Balance Forward	—			DR	15 000 —

ACCOUNT: Accumulated Depreciation - Automobile — NO. 11

DATE		PARTICULARS	PR	DEBIT	CREDIT	DR/CR	BALANCE
June	30	Balance Forward	—				
	30		AJE		4 500 —	CR	4 500 —

ACCOUNT: Bank Loan — NO. 20

DATE		PARTICULARS	PR	DEBIT	CREDIT	DR/CR	BALANCE
June	30	Balance Forward	—				0 —

ACCOUNT: J. Eidt, Capital — NO. 30

DATE		PARTICULARS	PR	DEBIT	CREDIT	DR/CR	BALANCE
June	30	Balance Forward	—			CR	12 000 —

ACCOUNT: J. Eidt, Drawings — NO. 31

DATE		PARTICULARS	PR	DEBIT	CREDIT	DR. CR	BALANCE
June	30	Balance Forward	—			DR	2000 —

ACCOUNT: Fees Earned — NO. 40

DATE		PARTICULARS	PR	DEBIT	CREDIT	DR. CR	BALANCE
June	30	Balance Forward	—			CR	19600 —

ACCOUNT: Advertising Expense — NO. 50

DATE		PARTICULARS	PR	DEBIT	CREDIT	DR. CR	BALANCE
June	30	Balance Forward	—			DR	1200 —

ACCOUNT: Depreciation Expense – Automobile — NO. 51

DATE		PARTICULARS	PR	DEBIT	CREDIT	DR. CR	BALANCE
June	30	Balance Forward	—				0 —
	30		AJE			DR	4500 —

ACCOUNT: Insurance Expense — NO. 52

DATE		PARTICULARS	PR	DEBIT	CREDIT	DR. CR	BALANCE
June	30	Balance Forward	—			DR	0 —
	30		AJE	240 —		DR	240 —

ACCOUNT: Office Expense — NO. 53

DATE		PARTICULARS	PR	DEBIT	CREDIT	DR. CR	BALANCE
June	30	Balance Forward	—			DR	5300 —

ACCOUNT: Supplies Expense — NO. 54

DATE		PARTICULARS	PR	DEBIT	CREDIT	DR. CR	BALANCE
June	30	Balance Forward	—			DR	0 —
	30		AJE	1680 —		DR	1680 —

ACCOUNT: Telephone Expense — NO. 55

DATE		PARTICULARS	PR	DEBIT	CREDIT	DR. CR	BALANCE
June	30	Balance Forward	—			DR	3500 —

Once the adjusting journal entries have been posted, we must attend to **closing entries**. This means two things:

1. We transfer (close out) the balance in the Drawings account to the Capital account.
2. We make all balances in the Sales and Expense accounts zero (0) and transfer (close out) their balances to the Capital account. Then we prepare a **post-closing trial balance.**

These accounts are closed out because we want them to be empty when we start the next year's operations. The closing out process has three steps:

Step 1 Journalize the closing entries.

Step 2 Post the closing entries.

Step 3 Take a post-closing trial balance.

Step 1

GENERAL JOURNAL

PAGE 1

DATE		PARTICULARS	PR	DEBIT	CREDIT
		CLOSING ENTRIES			
June	30	J. Eidt, Capital	30	2000 —	
		J. Eidt, Drawings	31		2000 —
		To close out account at year end.			
June	30	Fees Earned	40	19600 —	
		Advertising Expense	50		1200 —
		Depreciation Expense – Automobile	51		4500 —
		Insurance Expense	52		240 —
		Office Expense	53		5300 —
		Supplies Expense	54		1680 —
		Telephone Expense	55		3500 —
		J. Eidt, Capital	30		3180 —
		To close out Revenue and Expense accounts to Capital at year end.			

Step 2

GENERAL LEDGER

ACCOUNT J. Eidt, Capital NO. 30

DATE		PARTICULARS	PR	DEBIT	CREDIT	DR CR	BALANCE
June	30		—			CR	12000 —
	30		CJE	2000 —		CR	10000 —
	30		CJE			CR	13180 —

ACCOUNT: J. Eidt, Drawings — NO. 31

DATE		PARTICULARS	PR	DEBIT	CREDIT	DR CR	BALANCE
June	30	Balance Forward	—			DR	2000 —
	30		CJE		2000 —		0 —

ACCOUNT: Fees Earned — NO. 40

DATE		PARTICULARS	PR	DEBIT	CREDIT	DR CR	BALANCE
June	30	Balance Forward	—			CR	19600 —
	30		CJE	19600 —			0 —

ACCOUNT: Advertising Expense — NO. 50

DATE		PARTICULARS	PR	DEBIT	CREDIT	DR CR	BALANCE
June	30	Balance Forward	—			DR	1200 —
	30		CJE		1200 —		0 —

ACCOUNT: Depreciation Expense - Automobile — NO. 51

DATE		PARTICULARS	PR	DEBIT	CREDIT	DR CR	BALANCE
June	30	Balance Forward	—			DR	0 —
	30		AJE	4500 —		DR	4500 —
	30		CJE		4500 —		0 —

ACCOUNT: Insurance Expense — NO. 52

DATE		PARTICULARS	PR	DEBIT	CREDIT	DR CR	BALANCE
June	30	Balance Forward	—			DR	0 —
	30		AJE	240 —		DR	240 —
	30		CJE		240 —		0 —

ACCOUNT: Office Expense — NO. 53

DATE		PARTICULARS	PR	DEBIT	CREDIT	DR CR	BALANCE
June	30	Balance Forward	—			DR	5300 —
	30		CJE		5300 —		0 —

ACCOUNT: Supplies Expense — NO. 54

DATE		PARTICULARS	PR	DEBIT	CREDIT	DR CR	BALANCE
June	30	Balance Forward	—			DR	0 —
	30		AJE	1680 —		DR	1680 —
	30		CJE		1680 —		0 —

ACCOUNT: Telephone Expense NO. 55

DATE		PARTICULARS	PR	DEBIT	CREDIT	DR CR	BALANCE
June	30	Balance Forward	—			DR	3500–
	30		CJE		3500–		0–

Note: All of the revenue and expense accounts and the drawings account now have zero balances. All accounts after "Capital" are now closed out to zero and ready for the next accounting cycle!

Step 3

J. Eidt
Post-Closing Trial Balance
June 30, 19 ____

Account	Debit	Credit
Bank	$ 480–	
Accounts Receivable	1 600–	
Prepaid Insurance	480–	
Prepaid Supplies	120–	
Automobile	15 000–	
Accumulated Depreciation—Automobile		4 500–
J. Eidt, Capital		13 180–
	$17 680–	$17 680–

13.9 Summary

In this chapter you have learned that accounting is not as neat and tidy as a lot of people like to believe. There are adjustments made at the end of a business fiscal year. Although you only learned how to make three adjustments—depreciation, insurance, and supplies—you should remember that there are many other types of adjustments that do exist. If you go on in your study of accounting, you will learn more of them. If you have followed the diagram of the accounting cycle, it should help you understand how these adjustments fit in. The adjusting entries help match revenues and expenses for the appropriate time periods and this is why they are so important.

Check out the chapter objectives. You should be able to

1. identify the need for adjusting entries;
2. understand the preparation of three types of adjusting entries;
3. complete an 8-column worksheet; and
4. journalize and post adjusting and closing entries and prepare a post-closing trial balance.

Dictionary of Terms

Adjusting Entries Accounting entries made on a worksheet to adjust accounts at year end.

Closing Entries Accounting entries that close out drawings, sales, and expense accounts to zero at the end of a fiscal year.

Depreciation A process of allocating the cost of an asset over its useful life.

Inventory A list of supplies or merchandise on hand.

Post-Closing Trial Balance A listing of all the accounts in the general ledger after all the closing entries have been made.

Prepaid Expenses Expenses which will benefit more than one time period.

Exercises

1. An automobile costs $17 872. Find the depreciation if the depreciation rate is 30%.

2. Given the government rates of depreciation as outlined in Section 13.2, what are the rates for these assets?
   (a) Photocopier (c) Garbage truck (e) Brick warehouse
   (b) Frame Shed (d) Delivery van (f) Tables

3. Copy the table below in your notebook and using government rates for depreciation, complete the table below by finding the net book value (the cost of an asset less depreciation.)

Asset	Cost	Rate of Deprec.	Annual Deprec.	Net Book Value
1. Equipment	6 800			
2. Automobile	12 750			
3. Brick Building	324 000			
4. Furniture	8 050	SAMPLE ONLY		
5. Delivery Van	16 663			
6. Frame Building	82 000			

4. The insurance policies below all run for a 3-year period. When each policy was purchased, it was charged into the Prepaid Insurance account. Find out how much the adjustment will be for each policy if our year end is December 31, 19 ____. (*Note*: Calculate your answers by using months, not days.)

Coverage	Policy Cost	Date Bought	Adjustment
Building	124 000	Jul. 1st	?
Furniture	82 000	Oct. 1st	?
Automobiles	51 000	Dec. 1st	?

5. The insurance policies below have different terms. Use the same technique as in Question 4 above and find the adjustment that will have to be recorded for each insurance policy. Our year end is Dec. 31.

Coverage	Policy Cost	Date Bought	Term	Adjustment
Delivery Trucks	120 000	Apr. 1st	2 yrs	?
Liability Ins.	500 000	July 1st	3 yrs	?
Furn. & Equip.	380 000	Dec. 1st	1 yr	?

6. Given the partial worksheet below, calculate the depreciation for each fixed asset for one year. Record the amount in your workbook. It is not necessary to extend the worksheet.

	ACCOUNTS	ACCT. NO.	TRIAL BALANCE		ADJUSTMENTS		INCOME STATEMENT	
			DR.	CR.	DR.	CR.	DR.	CR.
1	Building (Brick)		128000 –					
2	Building (Frame)		680000 –					
3								
4								
5								
6								

7. Place this trial balance on a worksheet and then record the adjustments for the business. Balance and extend the worksheet.
   (a) Depreciation is at government rates.
   (b) The insurance policy was bought on Apr. 1—it will last two years.
   (c) Supplies on hand at year end are worth $200.

Allan Flowers
Trial Balance
May 31, 19 ____

Account	Debit	Credit
Bank	250	
Accounts Receivable	21 900	
Prepaid Insurance	450	
Prepaid Supplies	480	
Building (brick)	120 000	
Automobile	18 300	
Bank Loan		5 000
A. Flowers, Capital		?
Commissions Earned		38 000
Advertising Expense	1 200	
Heat & Light	2 800	
Office Expenses	6 520	
Wages Expense	28 100	
	200 000	200 000

WORKSHEET

FOR THE MONTH ENDED ________ 19____

BALANCE SHEET		
DR.	CR.	
		1
		2
		3
		4
		5
		6
		7

8. Cam Nighthawk is a hunting guide who runs his business in Banff National Park. Using his ledger after one year of operations:
   (a) Take a trial balance on a worksheet.
   (b) Record the year end adjustments indicated.
   (c) Extend, balance, and rule the worksheet.
   (d) Prepare an income statement and balance sheet.
   (e) Journalize and post the adjusting entries.
   (f) Journalize and post the closing entries.
   (g) Prepare a post-closing trial balance.

ACCOUNT: Petty Cash NO. 1

DATE		PARTICULARS	PR	DEBIT	CREDIT	DR CR	BALANCE
Dec.	31	Balance Forward	—			DR	50—

ACCOUNT: Bank NO. 2

DATE		PARTICULARS	PR	DEBIT	CREDIT	DR CR	BALANCE
Dec.	31	Balance Forward	—			DR	8450—

ACCOUNT: Accounts Receivable NO. 3

DATE		PARTICULARS	PR	DEBIT	CREDIT	DR CR	BALANCE
Dec.	31	Balance Forward	—			DR	3775—

ACCOUNT: Prepaid Insurance NO. 4

DATE		PARTICULARS	PR	DEBIT	CREDIT	DR CR	BALANCE
Dec.	31	Balance Forward	—			DR	600—

ACCOUNT: Prepaid Supplies NO. 5

DATE		PARTICULARS	PR	DEBIT	CREDIT	DR CR	BALANCE
Dec.	31	Balance Forward	—			DR	500—

ACCOUNT: Van NO. 10

DATE		PARTICULARS	PR	DEBIT	CREDIT	DR CR	BALANCE
Dec.	31	Balance Forward	—			DR	14500—

ACCOUNT: Accumulated Depreciation - Van NO. 11

DATE		PARTICULARS	PR	DEBIT	CREDIT	DR CR	BALANCE

ACCOUNT: Equipment NO. 12

DATE		PARTICULARS	PR	DEBIT	CREDIT	DR CR	BALANCE
Dec.	31	Balance Forward	—			DR	6200—

ACCOUNT: Accumulated Depreciation - Equipment NO. 13

DATE		PARTICULARS	PR	DEBIT	CREDIT	DR CR	BALANCE

ACCOUNT: Bank Loan NO. 20

DATE		PARTICULARS	PR	DEBIT	CREDIT	DR CR	BALANCE
Dec.	31	Balance Forward	—			CR	0—

ACCOUNT: Accounts Payable NO. 20

DATE		PARTICULARS	PR	DEBIT	CREDIT	DR CR	BALANCE
Dec.	31	Balance Forward	—			CR	2680—

ACCOUNT: C. Nighthawk, Capital NO. 30

DATE		PARTICULARS	PR	DEBIT	CREDIT	DR CR	BALANCE
Dec.	31	Balance Forward	—			CR	38195—

ACCOUNT: C. Nighthawk, Drawings NO. 31

DATE		PARTICULARS	PR	DEBIT	CREDIT	DR CR	BALANCE
Dec.	31	Balance Forward	—			DR	1500—

ACCOUNT: Fees Earned NO. 40

DATE		PARTICULARS	PR	DEBIT	CREDIT	DR CR	BALANCE
Dec.	31	Balance Forward	—			CR	18400—

ACCOUNT: Advertising Expense NO. 50

DATE		PARTICULARS	PR	DEBIT	CREDIT	DR. CR.	BALANCE
Dec.	31	Balance Forward	—			DR	1600 —

ACCOUNT: Bank Interest / Charges NO. 51

DATE		PARTICULARS	PR	DEBIT	CREDIT	DR. CR.	BALANCE
Dec.	31	Balance Forward	—			DR	90 —

ACCOUNT: Depreciation – Building NO. 52

DATE		PARTICULARS	PR	DEBIT	CREDIT	DR. CR.	BALANCE

ACCOUNT: Depreciation – Equipment NO. 53

DATE		PARTICULARS	PR	DEBIT	CREDIT	DR. CR.	BALANCE

ACCOUNT: Depreciation – Van NO. 54

DATE		PARTICULARS	PR	DEBIT	CREDIT	DR. CR.	BALANCE

ACCOUNT: Insurance Expense NO. 55

DATE		PARTICULARS	PR	DEBIT	CREDIT	DR. CR.	BALANCE

ACCOUNT: Miscellaneous Expenses NO. 56

DATE		PARTICULARS	PR	DEBIT	CREDIT	DR. CR.	BALANCE
Dec.	31	Balance Forward	—			DR	340 —

ACCOUNT: Supplies Expense NO. 57

DATE		PARTICULARS	PR	DEBIT	CREDIT	DR. CR.	BALANCE

ACCOUNT: *Telephone Expense* NO. *58*

DATE		PARTICULARS	PR	DEBIT	CREDIT	DR CR	BALANCE
Dec.	31	Balance Forward				DR	755 —

ACCOUNT: *Van Expenses* NO. *59*

DATE		PARTICULARS	PR	DEBIT	CREDIT	DR CR	BALANCE
Dec.	31	Balance Forward	—			DR	1640 —

The following adjustments are to be made at year end:

(a) Depreciation of all assets is at government rates.

(b) The insurance policy was purchased on July 1st and will last for two years.

(c) The inventory count at year end shows supplies of $180 on hand.

Review Questions

1. What does "accounting entries benefit more than one time period" mean?
2. What is the difference between the term "adjustments" and the term "adjusting entries"?
3. If you bought a car for $20 000 and it depreciated 30% after the first year, what would its net book value be?
4. Define "depreciation."
5. Name the two prepaid expense accounts that you studied in this chapter.
6. Where are adjustments recorded on a worksheet?
7. Which accounts get closed out at year end?
8. Give the class number and the depreciation rates for these assets:

   Computer; Bulldozer; Tool Shed; Hearse; Tables.
9. Classify each of these accounts as either asset (A), liability (L), owner's equity (OE), revenue (R), or expense (E):

Prepaid Insurance; Drawings; Accumulated Depreciation; Supplies; Account Payable; Truck; Commissions Earned.

10. A business bought an insurance policy to protect them from being sued. The cost of the policy, which had coverage for $1 000 000, was $1 360 for three years. If the policy was bought on May 1st and the company year end is Oct. 31st, how much insurance is used up in the year the policy is purchased?
11. A doctor said to her nurse, ''Take an inventory of our medical supplies on hand. My accountant needs the figure.'' What does the doctor mean by the word ''inventory''?
12. Draw a picture in your notes of the accounting cycle.
13. What are the three steps in the closing out process?

Challenge Questions

1. A car is bought for $23 000. Given the government rate of depreciation for cars, how much will the net book value of the car be after two years?
2. When we talk about accounts which are paired in accounting, we refer to them as contra accounts. What were the two contra accounts you learned about in this chapter?
3. A friend has just opened a new entertainment centre, complete with mini golf, driving range, and baseball batting cages. Now that you have studied all about depreciation in accounting, list for your friend all the items in the entertainment centre which will have to be adjusted for depreciation at year end.
4. You have just got the bright idea to buy a car and use it as a taxi. The car costs $15 000 and will be depreciated according to government rates. You have calculated that you could drive the car six days a week, eight hours a day for 50 weeks. How much an hour do you have to earn to cover depreciation?

Review Case

Sharon Harrison operates the ''School of Grooming'' for pets. You have just handed her the first balance sheet for her business. Assume that you are her accountant and answer the questions she has about the balance sheet at the top of page 330.

School of Grooming
Balance Sheet
December 31, 19 ___

Assets			Liabilities	
Petty Cash		$ 75	Bank	$12 000
Bank		2 615	Accounts Payable	1 450
Accounts Receivable		3 220	Total Liabilities	$13 450
Prepaid Expenses		840		
Automobile	$13 800			
Less: Acc. Dep.	(4 140)	9 660		
Furniture/Equipment	$32 000		**Owner's Equity**	
Less: Acc. Dep.	(5 400)	26 600	S. Harrison, Capital	29 560
		$43 010		$43 010

Questions

1. What does ''Acc. Dep.'' mean?
2. How much is the business car worth?
3. Can I repay the bank loan?

Challenge Case

Bob Bailey is a repair technician who repairs electronic typewriters and computers. He operates out of his own home and has just finished his second year of business.

Bailey Technical Repair
Income Statement
For the Year Ended March 31, 19 ___

Revenue:		
Service Income		$48 752
Expenses:		
Advertising	$ 185	
Bank Interest	75	
Heat & Light	480	
Miscellaneous	212	
Telephone	366	
Wages	24 779	26 097
Net Income		$22 655

Draw up a new Income Statement after these changes:

1. He bought a new van for $19 000. This changes depreciation.
2. His sole employee got an 8% pay raise.
3. He borrowed the money from the bank to buy the van. Interest is at 12% (expense).

Take-a-Break

Make a list in your note book of the names of each of these 13 assets. Then, indicate whether each asset would be found in a home, a business, or both.

	No	Name of Asset	Home	Business	Both
Example	1	Carpet	?	?	?

Chapter 14 Accounting for a Merchandise Business

Objectives

At the end of this chapter you will be able to

1. distinguish between a service business and merchandise business;
2. recognize and know the rules for special accounts for a merchandise business;
3. journalize, post, and prepare a set of financial statements for a merchandise business; and
4. calculate and record Ontario Sales Tax.

14.1 Overview

The main focus of this text has been to deal exclusively with service businesses—hairdressing salons, auto body repair shops, golf courses, plumbers, etc. The second group of people who are in business are those who sell goods—jewellery, clothes, groceries, baked goods, furniture, etc. These businesses are called **merchandise businesses** because they buy goods and resell them for a profit.

Figure 14-1
Small merchandise businesses line a busy city street.

14.2 Purchases and Inventory

The most important difference between a service business and a merchandise business is the need for a merchandise business to have inventory. **Inventory** is stock that a business has on hand at any given time. A new car dealership must have cars on its lot, or people won't be interested in looking or buying. The dealer makes **purchases** or buys goods from suppliers to display them to the buyers. The dealer below has 12 cars in stock (in inventory) to sell to customers, varying in sizes, shapes, power, and prices.

The accounting entry used when a car dealer buys cars to sell is given in general journal form. We will need a new account called Purchases to record the purchase of the new cars.

GENERAL JOURNAL

PAGE

DATE		PARTICULARS	PR	DEBIT	CREDIT
Oct.	1	Purchases		180 000 —	
		A/P – Ford Ltd.			180 000 —
		Bought 12 new cars for resale.			

(The cars purchased will, of course, have been bought at different prices, but they can be lumped together into one debit for purposes of learning the correct accounting.)

14.3 Gross Profit

When a car dealer buys a car, we know that the dealer will sell the car for more than it costs; otherwise, the dealer would soon be out of business. The difference between the selling price of cars and the cost of buying those cars is called "gross profit." We can put this in mathematical form to see what this means a little more clearly.

Sold (3 Cars):	\$12 000 + 18 000 + 20 000 =	50 000
Cost of Goods Sold:	\$10 000 + 15 000 + 16 000 =	41 000
	Gross Profit =	9 000

You may have noticed that each car was sold for more than it cost to buy it. This is only good business sense. The other important point to note is that the gross profit does not all go to the owner of the car dealership. There are other expenses to pay to run the business—advertising, wages, telephone, interest on bank loans, and so forth. These are familiar expenses that you have seen earlier in the text. On page 335 is the data for the car dealership, expressed in the form of an income statement.

Al's Cars
Income Statement
For the week ended October 7, 19 ___

Revenue:		
Sale of Cars		$50 000
Cost of Goods Sold:		41 000
Gross Profit		$ 9 000
Expenses:		
Advertising	$ 200	
Loan Interest	70	
Office	190	
Telephone	40	
Wages	1 000	1 500
Net Income		$ 7 500

The term ''cost of goods sold'' is new. It shows how much the cars cost when the dealer eventually sold to its customers. The Cost of Goods Sold section is like an expense, but it gets its own section on the income statement because it is so important.

Cost of goods sold is the amount it cost to purchase goods that have been sold.

Gross profit is the money from sales minus the purchase price.

14.4 Inventory

You may suspect that a car dealership's books are more complicated than is shown above and you are right, but this example will help explain how gross profit is derived. Let's explore this purchase idea a bit further and get closer to a real car dealership.

If you have driven by a car lot, you know that there are usually lots of new cars on the lot. When dealers buy cars, they do not usually sell them immediately. Therefore, when a car dealer gets to a year end, say December 31st, there will be cars left over on the lot to be sold next year. This complicates the Cost of Goods Sold section of the income statement. But we can understand it with a little work. Here are some data for a car dealership for the six months ended June 30th.

Inventory January 1 20 cars $300 000	+	Purchases 50 cars $900 000	−	Inventory June 30th 30 cars $400 000	=	Cost of Goods Sold 40 cars $800 000

Here is the same information in income statement form:

Anderson Pontiac Buick
Income Statement
For the Six Months Ended June 30, 19___

Revenue:		
Sale of Cars		$1 000 000
Cost of Goods Sold:		
Inventory, January 1	$ 300 000	
Purchases	900 000	
Goods Available for Sale	$1 200 000	
Inventory, June 30	(400 000)	800 000
Gross Profit		$ 200 000

The income statement shows us that the business sold cars for one million dollars. Those cars that were sold cost $800 000 to buy and, therefore, the gross profit from the sale of the cars was $200 000. The "inventory" figures on January 1st and on June 30th are obtained by going out to the car lot and taking physical listing of all of the cars, along with their cost and obtaining a total.

Figure 14-2
The inventory of a car dealership

14.5 Purchases Account

When the dealership buys cars, the debit is always to the Purchases account. The credit entry will either be Accounts Payable or Cash.

(1) *On Account:*

Purchases		A/P Ford Ltd.	
900 000			900 000

(2) *Paying Cash:*

Purchases		Bank	
900 000			900 000

14.6 More New Accounts

There are several new accounts that we should learn at this point, all of them arising from the new merchandise business we are studying in this chapter.

Sales Returns and Allowances

One customer returned a car to the dealership because it was defective. Selling price, $25,000.

A/R		Sales Returns & Allowances	
	25 000	25 000	

Freight-In

Paid freight costs on the most recent shipment of cars to the dealership. (Freight-In can also be called Transportation-In.)

Freight-In		Bank	
2 300			2 300

Purchase Returns and Allowances

The dealership returned one car to the manufacturer because it was the wrong model.

Accounts Payable	
9 400	

Purchase Returns & Allowances	
	9 400

Delivery Expense

A car was delivered to a customer out-of-town. Delivery cost, $45.

Delivery Expense	
45	

Bank	
	45

Just a brief explanation of the new accounts before we look at a long example on this new idea of purchases and inventory.

Sales Returns and Allowances

This account is used when customers return goods that they have bought, or when we reduce the price of a product in order to sell it. This is a contra account because it belongs with the Sales account as a pair of accounts. The word "contra" simply means two accounts that belong together. The reason we do not put sales returns and allowances as a debit to the Sales account is that the business will have a separate record of all sales returns and allowances. This will be useful information to management. Here are the contra accounts shown together.

Sales Returns and Allowances	
Debit	////
	////

Sales	
////	Credit
////	

Freight-In

This account is used for the cost of shipping goods from the manufacturer to the place of business. It could be for truck costs, train costs, shipping, or air freight. Freight-in is an expense of the business, but it is shown as part of the Cost of Goods Sold, as we shall see shortly.

Purchase Returns and Allowances

This account is used for purchases which the business makes and which will be eventually returned to the supplier. Usually this will happen when all or part of the goods that are bought are defective. Like the Sales Returns and Allowances account, this separate account will indicate to management if it is buying too many defective goods. It is also a contra account because it is paired with Purchases.

Purchases	
Debit	////
	////

Purchases Returns and Allowances	
////	Credit
////	

Delivery Expense

This account is used to record the cost of delivering goods to the customers. A good example of this would be large department stores like Eaton's, the Bay, or Sears, which make home deliveries to customers. Delivery costs can be fairly substantial for these businesses and they want to record these costs as a separate expense, so as to keep a record of this cost.

The Purchases account, the Sales Returns and Allowances account, the Freight-In account, the Purchases Returns and Allowances account, and the Delivery Expense account are all new accounts used in merchandise businesses.

14.7 Set of Books

This section will take you through a short set of books for a small store that sells washers, dryers, stoves, and refrigerators, to show you how these new accounts are handled in a real merchandise business. As you read through this section, you will see all of the steps you have learned for the accounting cycle. You will also see a multipurpose journal, since this is more realistic than a general journal.

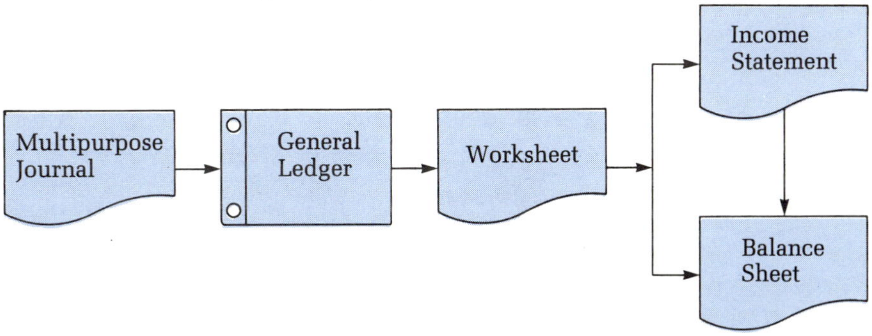

Transactions

Apr. 1: Opened the business with $50 000 cash, deposited into bank.

1: Set up a petty cash fund, $50.00. Cheque #1.

1: Bought washers & dryers for resale for $26 000. Cheque #2.

2: Paid freight on Apr. 1 purchase, cost $700. Cheque #3.

2: Sold a refrigerator for $1 200, cash.

3: Sold a washer and dryer set for cash, $1 350 total.

5: Bought a used delivery truck for the business, $7 500. Cheque #4.

5: Bought gas and oil for the delivery truck, $32.50 on account from Andrews Service Station.

7: Sold a stove on account to G. Hartley, $1 100.

7: Mr. Hartley complained about a defective timer on his stove. His account was credited with $39.95.

9: We returned a defective stove to the manufacturer for credit to our account, $750, Canadian Distributors.

12: Cash sales, $3 560. Deposited into the bank immediately.

15: Owner withdrew $200 for personal use. Cheque #5.

Snyder's Household Appliances

DATE		CUSTOMER/SUPPLIER	NO	BANK DR	BANK CR	ACCOUNTS RECEIVABLE DR	ACCOUNTS RECEIVABLE CR	✓
April	1	Owner Invested		50000 —				
	1	Set up Fund	1		50 —			
	1	Bought appliances	2		26000 —			
	2	Freight charges	3		700 —			
	2	Sold refrigerator		1200 —				
	3	Sold washer/dryer		1350 —				
	5	Bought Truck	4		7500 —			
	5	Andrews Service Station						
	7	G. Hartley				1100 —		
	7	G. Hartley					39 —	
	9	Inglis Manufacturing						
	12	Cash Sales		3560 —				
	15	Owner withdrew	5		200 —			
	17	Inglis Manufacturing						
	18	J. McLellan				1340 —		
	24	Cash Sales		840 —				
	25	Monthly Rent	7		500 —			
	26	Bell Canada					54 —	
	27	Wages	8		810 —			
	28	Cash Sales		1600 —				
	30	P.U.C.	9		229 —			
	31	Replenish fund	10		44 —			
		Balancing Totals		58550 —	36033 —	2440 —	93 —	

17: Bought another shipment of refrigerators from the Inglis company, on account, $6 400.

18: Sale on account to J. McLellan, $1 340.

24: Cash Sale, $840.

25: Cheque for monthly store rent, Cheque #6, $500.

26: Telephone bill-set up as an A/P, $54.40.

27: Part-time wages to one employee, $810. Cheque #7.

28: Sale of another washer and dryer set, $1 600, cash.

30: Cheque #8 to Public Utilities for heat and light, $229.50.

31: Replenished the petty cash fund. Cheque #9. The vouchers were: Canada Post — $18.00; Office Expense — $26.00.

You will notice that the multipurpose journal has a new column called Purchases. This is normal for a merchandise business because this account is used frequently. The second new thing to notice is the last entry which replenishes the petty cash fund. There are two debit entries needed to replenish the petty cash fund and, therefore, they have to be written in the "Other Accounts" section and take up two lines. The multipurpose journal is posted to the ledger next.

MULTIPURPOSE JOURNAL

PAGE NO 1

	Accounts Payable		√	Sales	Wages	Purchases	Other Accounts			
	DR	CR		CR	DR	DR	Account	PR	DR	CR
1							Capital	31		50000 —
2							Petty Cash	1	50 —	
3						26000 —				
4							Freight-In	53	700 —	
5				1200 —						
6				1350 —						
7							Truck	10	7500 —	
8		32 —					Truck Expense	67	32 —	
9				1100 —						
10							Sales Ret.	42	39 —	
11	750 —						Purchases Ret.	52		750 —
12				3560 —						
13							Drawings	32	200 —	
14		6400 —				6400 —				
15				1340 —						
16				840 —						
17							Rent Expense	65	500 —	
18							Telephone Exp.		54 —	
19					810 —					
20				1600 —						
21							Heat/Light	62	229 —	
22							Postage Exp.	64	18 —	
23							Office Exp.	63	26 —	
24	750 —	6432 —		10990 —	810 —	32400 —			9348 —	50750 —
25										
26										

ACCOUNT: Petty Cash NO. 1

DATE		PARTICULARS	PR	DEBIT	CREDIT	DR CR	BALANCE
Apr.	30		SY1	50 —			50 —

ACCOUNT: Bank NO. 2

DATE		PARTICULARS	PR	DEBIT	CREDIT	DR CR	BALANCE
Apr.	30		SY1	58550 —	36033 —	DR	22517 —

ACCOUNT: Accounts Receivable NO. 3

DATE		PARTICULARS	PR	DEBIT	CREDIT	DR CR	BALANCE
Apr.	30		SY1	2440 —	93 —	DR	2347 —

ACCOUNT: Merchandise Inventory NO. 4

DATE		PARTICULARS	PR	DEBIT	CREDIT	DR CR	BALANCE

ACCOUNT: Truck NO. 10

DATE		PARTICULARS	PR	DEBIT	CREDIT	DR CR	BALANCE
Apr.	30		SY1	7500 —		DR	7500 —

ACCOUNT: Accounts Payable NO. 21

DATE		PARTICULARS	PR	DEBIT	CREDIT	DR CR	BALANCE
Apr.	30		SY1	750 —	6432 —	CR	5682 —

ACCOUNT: E. Snyder, Capital NO. 30

DATE		PARTICULARS	PR	DEBIT	CREDIT	DR CR	BALANCE
Apr.	30		SY1		50000 —	CR	50000 —

ACCOUNT: E. Snyder, Drawings NO. 31

DATE		PARTICULARS	PR	DEBIT	CREDIT	DR CR	BALANCE
Apr.	30		SY1	200 —		DR	200 —

ACCOUNT: Sales NO. 40

DATE		PARTICULARS	PR	DEBIT	CREDIT	DR. CR	BALANCE
Apr.	30		SY1		10 990 —	CR	10 990 —

ACCOUNT: Sales Returns and Allowances NO. 41

DATE		PARTICULARS	PR	DEBIT	CREDIT	DR. CR	BALANCE
Apr.	30		SY1	39 —		DR	39 —

ACCOUNT: Purchases NO. 51

DATE		PARTICULARS	PR	DEBIT	CREDIT	DR. CR	BALANCE
Apr.	30		SY1	32 400 —		DR	32 400 —

ACCOUNT: Purchases Returns and Allowances NO. 52

DATE		PARTICULARS	PR	DEBIT	CREDIT	DR. CR	BALANCE
Apr.	30		SY1		750 —	CR	750 —

ACCOUNT: Freight-In NO. 53

DATE		PARTICULARS	PR	DEBIT	CREDIT	DR. CR	BALANCE
Apr.	30		SY1	700 —		DR	700 —

ACCOUNT: Heat/Light Expense NO. 62

DATE		PARTICULARS	PR	DEBIT	CREDIT	DR. CR	BALANCE
Apr.	30		SY1	229 —		DR	229 —

ACCOUNT: Office Expense NO. 63

DATE		PARTICULARS	PR	DEBIT	CREDIT	DR. CR	BALANCE
Apr.	30		SY1	10 —		DR	10 —

ACCOUNT: Postage Expense NO. 64

DATE		PARTICULARS	PR	DEBIT	CREDIT	DR. CR	BALANCE
Apr.	30		SY1	18 —		DR	18 —

ACCOUNT: Rent Expense NO. 65

DATE		PARTICULARS	PR	DEBIT	CREDIT	DR CR	BALANCE
Apr.	30		SY1	500 —		DR	500 —

ACCOUNT: Telephone Expense NO. 66

DATE		PARTICULARS	PR	DEBIT	CREDIT	DR CR	BALANCE
Apr.	30		SY1	54 —		DR	54 —

ACCOUNT: Truck Expense NO. 67

DATE		PARTICULARS	PR	DEBIT	CREDIT	DR CR	BALANCE
Apr.	30		SY1	32 —		DR	32 —

ACCOUNT: Wages Expense NO. 68

DATE		PARTICULARS	PR	DEBIT	CREDIT	DR CR	BALANCE
Apr.	30		SY1	810 —		DR	810 —

Snyder's Household Appliances

	ACCOUNTS	ACCT. NO.	TRIAL BALANCE DR.	TRIAL BALANCE CR.	ADJUSTMENTS DR.	ADJUSTMENTS CR.	INCOME STATEMENT DR.	INCOME STATEMENT CR.
1	Petty Cash	1	50 —					
2	Bank	2	22517 —					
3	Accounts Receivable	3	2347 —					
4	Merchandise Inventory	4	0 —				0 —	25000 —
5	Truck	10	7500 —					
6	Accounts Payable	21		5682 —				
7	E. Snyder, Capital	30		50000 —				
8	E. Snyder, Drawings	31	200 —					
9	Sales	40		10990 —				10990 —
10	Sales Returns + Allowances	41	39 —				39 —	
11	Purchases	51	32400 —				32400 —	
12	Purchases Returns + Allow.	52		750 —				750 —
13	Freight-In	53	700 —				700 —	
14	Heat/Light Expense	62	229 —				229 —	
15	Office Expense	63	26 —				26 —	
16	Postage Expense	64	18 —				18 —	
17	Rent Expense	65	500 —				500 —	
18	Telephone Expense	66	54 —				54 —	
19	Truck Expense	67	32 —				32 —	
20	Wages Expense	68	810 —				810 —	
21	Totals		67422 —	67422 —			34808 —	36740 —
22	Net Income						1932 —	
23							36740 —	36740 —

Inventory Adjustment

Note the adjustment for the month-end inventory. The procedure is to take the old inventory in the Trial Balance debit column, extend it to the Income Statement debit column, and put the new inventory at the month end (or year end) in the Income Statement credit column and the Balance Sheet debit column. The new inventory at the end of the month is obtained by listing all of the appliance inventory, washers, dryers, refrigerators, and stoves, along with their unit and total cost. In this example the total inventory cost is $25 000. Once the worksheet is balanced we can prepare the financial statements.

Snyder's Household Appliances

Income Statement

For the Month Ended April 30, 19 ___

Revenue:			
Sales			$10 990
Less: Sales Returns and Allowances			39
Net Sales			$10 951
Cost of Goods Sold:			
Inventory, April 1		Nil	
Purchases	$32 400		
Add: Freight-In	700		
	$33 100		
Less: Purchase Returns and Allowances	750	$32 350	
Goods Available for Sale		$32 350	
Inventory, April 30		(25 000)	7 350
Gross Profit			$ 3 601
Expenses:			
Heat and Light Expense		$ 229	
Office Expenses		26	
Postage Expense		18	
Rent Expense		500	
Telephone Expense		54	
Truck Expense		32	
Wages Expense		810	1 669
Net Income			$1 932

WORKSHEET

FOR THE MONTH ENDED April 30 19 ___

BALANCE SHEET DR.	BALANCE SHEET CR.	
50 —		1
22517 —		2
2347 —		3
25000 —		4
7500 —		5
	5682 —	6
		7
200 —		8
		9
		10
		11
		12
		13
		14
		15
		16
		17
		18
		19
		20
57614 —	55682 —	21
	1932 —	22
57614 —	57614 —	23

Snyder's Household Appliances
Balance Sheet
as at April 30, 19 ___

Assets		Liabilities		
Current Assets:		**Current Liabilities:**		
Petty Cash	$ 50	Accounts Payable		$ 5 682
Bank	22 517			
Accounts Receivable	2 347	**Owner's Equity**		
Merchandise Inventory	25 000	**E. Snyder, Capital**		
Total Current Assets	$49 914	Balance, Apr. 1	$ 0	
		Add: Investment	50 000	
		Net Income	1 932	
Fixed Assets:			$51 932	
Truck	7 500	Less: Drawings	(200)	51 732
	$57 414			$57 414

14.8 Sales Tax

When a business is a merchandise business, it has the added complication of having to calculate sales tax when sales are made. In a shoe store, for example, a sales tax is charged to the customers for every pair of shoes sold. The rate charged varies from province to province in Canada, 0% tax in Alberta to 10% in Newfoundland. We will use the rate of 7% sales tax in this example. (In this entry the sales tax is calculated at 60.00 x 0.07 = $4.20)

GENERAL JOURNAL

PAGE 1

DATE		PARTICULARS	PR	DEBIT	CREDIT
Aug.	1	Accounts Receivable		64 20	
		Sales			60 00
		Sales Tax Payable			4 20
		Sales Invoice # 812.			

The *Sales Tax Payable* Account is a current liability account which must be paid to the provincial government, usually monthly. Here is the entry to clear out the sales tax account for the last month.

GENERAL JOURNAL

PAGE 1

DATE		PARTICULARS	PR	DEBIT	CREDIT
Sept.	1	Sales Tax Payable		675 00	
		Bank			675 00
		Wrote a cheque to the Provincial			
		Treasurer for August sales tax.			

In a business where sales tax is fairly common, one of the blank columns on a multipurpose journal would be used for sales tax. Here is a sample page with some entries to show this to you.

MULTIPURPOSE JOURNAL

PAGE NO 7

...NTS RECEIVABLE CR	√			ACCOUNTS PAYABLE DR	ACCOUNTS PAYABLE CR	√	Sales CR	Sales Tax CR	Wages DR	OTHER ACCOUNTS ACCOUNT	PR	DR	CR
		1	1				200 —	14 —					
		2	2				40 —	2 80					
		3	3										
		4	4					(16 80)					
		5	5										
		6	6										

14.9 Summary

There are two basic kinds of businesses that we have studied—service type businesses and merchandise businesses. The accounting for a merchandise business is more complex because it has to keep track of inventory. You have learned all about six new accounts in this chapter, and they are set up in T-account form for you to review.

Purchases	
Dr. Incr	

Purchase Returns & Allowances	
	Cr. Incr

Sales Returns & Allowances	
Dr. Incr	

Freight In	
Dr. Incr	

Delivery Expense	
Dr. Incr	

Merchandise Inventory	
Dr. Incr	

Here is another way of remembering the new accounts—by their proper place on the financial statements:

Purchases	Income Statement
Purchase Returns and Allowances	Income Statement
Sales Returns and Allowances	Income Statement
Freight-In	Income Statement
Delivery Expense	Income Statement
Merchandise Inventory	Income Statement *and* the Balance Sheet

The most important part of the chapter is probably the Cost of Goods Sold section of the Income Statement, because it has so many accounts to it. Concentrate your efforts on this section and it will pay off for you if you go on to other accounting courses.

Check the objectives out again. You should be able to

1. distinguish between a service business and a merchandise business;
2. recognize and know the rules for special accounts for a merchandise business;
3. journalize, post, and prepare a set of financial statements for a merchandise business; and
4. calculate and record Ontario Sales Tax.

Dictionary of Terms

Cost of Goods Sold The purchase price of inventory that has been sold.

Gross Profit Sales price minus cost of goods sold

Inventory The stock of goods that a business has to sell.

Merchandise Business A business that sells goods rather than services.

Purchases Goods that a merchandise business buys from suppliers and resells for a profit.

Exercises

1. The owner of a new computer store took this inventory. Find the total inventory at month end.

Inventory Listing

Decription	Qty	Price	Total
disk drives	12	$299	?
printers	10	525	?
keyboards	18	399	?
monitors	18	199	?
		TOTAL	??

2. Indicate if these accounts have a debit or credit balance.

   Merchandise Inventory; Purchases; Purchase Returns and Allowances; Sales Returns and Allowances; Freight-In; Delivery Expense.

3. Record these transactions in general journal form:

   Jan. 2: Bought $4 500 worth of goods for resale. Cheque #1.

   3: Sold $800 worth of goods to customers, on account.

   4: Cash sales of merchandise were $1 480.00. The money was immediately deposited into the business Bank account.

   5: Bought $6 100 worth of merchandise for resale, on account from Andre Gagnon et Fils.

   6: Sales on account, $4 900. Cash sales were $3 250. It was immediately deposited.

4. If a car dealership sold 25 cars for a total sales figure of $312 000, and the cost of goods sold was $268 000, what was the gross profit?

5. Unscramble the accounts below, put them in their proper order, and prepare an income statement for the store for the month ended February 28, 19 ____.

Wages Expense	42 000
Sales	138 000
Cost of Goods Sold	78 000
Advertising Expense	4 400
Telephone Expense	2 100
Office Expenses	4 500

6. Use the accounts below to prepare the Cost of Goods Sold section of an income statement.

Inventory, January 1, 19 ____, $80 000; Purchases, $260 000; Inventory, December 31, 19 ____, $55 000.

7. Use the accounts below to prepare the Cost of Goods Sold section of an income statement.

   Inventory, Janaury 1, 19 ____, $150 000; Purchases, $490 000; Inventory, December 31, 19 ____, $85 000.

8. Find the balances of these T-accounts.

Purchases	
45 000	
22 000	
35 000	

Purchase Returns & Allowances	
	500
	750
	225

Sales Returns & Allowances	
15	
60	
180	

Freight-In	
35	
27	
48	

9. Find the balances in these T-accounts and then use them to prepare a partial income statement down to the gross profit line. The business name is "Remember" (it's a card shop), and the month is June 19 ____.

Sales	
	55 000
	38 000
	44 000

Sales Returns & Allowances	
80	
20	
200	

Purchases	
13 200	
67 300	
45 145	

Purchase Returns & Allowances	
	230
	415

Merchandise Inventory	
36 000	

(The closing inventory figure is $43 000)

10. Given the balances in the T-accounts below and on page 352, use them to prepare a partial income statement, down to the gross profit line. The business name is "Smiths Men's Wear," and the month is May.

Sales	
	80 000

Sales Returns & Allowances	
590	

Purchases	
67 500	

Purchase Returns & Allowances	
	820

Merchandise Inventory	
32 500	

(The closing inventory figure is $45 000)

11. Journalize these transactions in a general journal:

Nov. 1: Sold goods on account to customers, $815.

1: Bought merchandise for resale for $8 000, on account from Arnott Wholesale.

2: Cash sales: $2 300. (The money is always deposited daily into the store bank account when cash sales are made.)

3: A customer returned $120 worth of goods that were defective. Her account was credited, Shirley Avery.

4: Paid delivery expenses to a customer, $18.75. Cheque #80.

5: Cheque #81 to CP express for freight-in on goods bought, $52.50.

12. Set up a 3-column accounts ledger with these accounts.

Bank	

Accounts Receivable	

Sales	

Sales Tax	

Sales Returns & Allowances	

Record these transactions in general journal form and then post them to the ledger accounts you have set up. Find the balance for each of the accounts and then take a trial balance to make sure your work is correct. (Use the sales tax rate that is applicable to your province.)

Aug. 1: Sold goods for cash, $900 plus sales tax.

2: Sold goods on account to customers, $1 200 plus sales tax.

5: $80 worth of goods were returned because they were broken. The customer's account was credited (don't forget the sales tax). Customer was C. Robinson.

8: Customers paid the business $550 in cash for amounts

previously owing on account. The money was deposited immediately into the bank.

10: Sold goods for cash, $420 plus sales tax.

14: Sold goods on account, $30 plus sales tax, D. Ropp.

13. Set up a 3-column account ledger with these accounts:

    Bank (2); Accounts Receivable (3); Sales Tax Payable (22); Sales (40); Sales Returns & Allowances (41); Purchases (54); Purchase Returns & Allowances (55); Freight-In (56); Delivery Expense (57).

    Journalize these transactions in a general journal; post to the ledger; and take a trial balance. Use the sales tax rate for your province.

    Dec. 1: Bought goods for resale $3 000 on account, Fisher Supply.

    2: Sold goods for $500 cash, plus sales tax, R. Miller.

    5: Paid freight on goods purchased, $82. Cheque #579.

    5: We returned $110 of defective goods (bought on Dec. 1).

    7: Sold goods on account to a customer $1 400 plus sales tax, R. Oreskovich.

    8: Cash sales, $750 plus sales tax.

    12: Cash refund to a customer for a defective good, $60 (don't forget the sales tax), R. Oreskovich.

    18: Bought goods for resale $740, cheque #580, Kindree Mfg.

Review Questions

1. In your notebook, indicate if each of the businesses below is a service business or a merchandise business.

(a) bakery	(f) drycleaners	(k) jewellery store
(b) lawyer	(g) auto body	(l) hardware store
(c) plumber	(h) video store	(m) insurance agent
(d) video arcade	(i) golf course	(n) furniture store
(e) garage	(j) accountant	(o) cable television

2. If you were a jewellery retailer, what are ten items that would be purchases (goods you would buy to resell)?

3. In the journal entry below, the business has bought goods for resale. If the business had paid cash for the goods, what would change in the entry?

GENERAL JOURNAL

PAGE

DATE		PARTICULARS	PR	DEBIT	CREDIT
June	1	Purchases		8 000 —	
		Accounts Payable			8 000 —
		Bought shipment of watches			

4. Use the model income statement in Section 14.3 to prepare an income statement for Reed Flowers for the year ended December 31, 19 ____. Sales were $265 000; Cost of Goods Sold, $190 000; Advertising Expense, $1 370; Bank Interest, $3 400; Heat & Light Expense, $4 800; Office Expenses, $1 200; Telephone Expense $1 850; and Wages, $22 400.

5. In the income statement you prepared for Question 4, what is the net income as a percent of sales?

6. Explain the term "Cost of Goods Sold" in your own words.

7. Fill in the missing amounts in this partial Income Statement:

Amanda's Variety Store
Income Statement
For the Six Months Ended June 30, 19____

Revenue:		
Sales		$380 000
Cost of Goods Sold:		
Inventory, January 1	$ 75 000	
Purchases	250 000	
Goods Available for Sale	$?	
Inventory, June 30	(110 000)	?
Gross Profit		$?

8. Indicate whether these new accounts have a debit (Dr) or credit (Cr) balance:

Purchases; Sales Returns and Allowances; Freight-In; Purchase Returns and Allowances; and Delivery Expense.

Briefly explain for what type of transaction each of the new accounts is used.

9. Go back and take another look at the financial statements in Section 14.7. Try this review of the financial statements to see how well you understand the new points. Answer all of the questions to yourself and then check the answers given on the right. The answers are in reverse order to help keep you from cheating on yourself.)

Questions on Income Statement

1. What time period does the income statement cover?
2. How many sets of contra accounts are on the income statement?
3. What was the value of goods returned by customers during the month?
4. Did Al Craig return any goods to his suppliers during the month?
5. What was the cost of the merchandise that could have been sold in April?
6. What was Al's gross profit?
7. What were total "expenses" for April?
8. What percent profit did Al make?

Answers:

8. 17.64%
7. 1 669
6. 3 601
5. $32 350 (Goods available for sale).
4. Yes...$750 worth (Purchase Returns & Allowances).
3. $39 (Sales Returns and Allowances).
2. Two sets (Sales/ S.R.A. and Purchases/P.R.A.)
1. One Month.

Questions on Balance Sheet

1. Calculate Al's working capital (current assets – current liabilities).
2. Is the merchandise inventory shown from the start of the month, or the end of the month?
3. Did Al's equity position go up or down in April?
4. How much money did Al have to start his new business?

Answers:

4. $50 000
3. Up—Al had $50 000 at the start of April and $51 732 at the end of the month.
2. The end of the month.
1. $44 232. ($49 914)

Challenge Question

This question will take you through a problem from journalizing into a multipurpose journal, through the posting process, the completion of a worksheet, and the preparation of financial statements.

Step 1

Set up the following General Ledger for *The Bootery*, a shoe store in Toronto. Use 3-column accounts and show balances as of November 30th.

Account	Debit	Credit
1. Petty Cash	100	
2. Bank	25 000	
3. Accounts Receivable	12 800	
4. Merchandise Inventory	37 000	
10. Office Equipment	3 000	
11. Store Equipment	7 000	
21. Bank Loan		11 000
22. Accounts Payable		8 000
23. Sales tax Payable		375
31. L. Girard, Capital		?
32. L. Girard, Drawings	11 000	
41. Sales		265 000
42. Sales Returns & Allowances	350	
50. Advertising	3 840	
51. Bank Charges	830	
52. Car Expense	3 375	
53. Freight-In	2 440	
54. Miscellaneous Expense	670	
55. Purchases	170 300	
56. Purchase Returns & Allowances		625
57. Repairs	3 125	
58. Telephone Exp.	1 690	
59. Wages Expense	42 480	
	325 000	325 000

Step 2

Journalize these transactions for December, 19 ___ in a multipurpose journal. Use page 15 for the journal.

Dec. 1: Paid the bank loan. Cheque #812.

1: Customer, B. Gorbould, paid $1 800 to reduce his account balance.

2: Bought goods for resale, $1 860, on account from Henri Belanger.

3: Paid telephone bill for last month, $75.50. Cheque #813.

4: Wrote cheque #814 for $600 to reduce accounts payable to Henri Belanger.

7: Cash sales, $8 000.00 plus sales tax (use your provincial rate).

11: Increased the Petty Cash Fund from $100 to $200. Cheque #815.

12: A customer returned a blouse valued at $64.00 (plus tax). Her account was credited. (Use the S.R.A. account as well.) Sue Gardiner.

14: Sales on account, $2 400 plus sales tax, to R. Karlinski.

15: We returned $300 worth of goods to Henri Belanger. Our account was credited by him.

20: Cash sales, $5 500 plus sales tax.

21: Received a bill for repairs to the store window, $235.00. Set it up as an account payable to D. Miller.

24: Sales on account, $1 200 plus sales tax, H. Wagler.

25: Customer returned a jacket, $110 plus sales tax. Her account was credited, Liz McDannold.

Step 3

Total and balance the multipurpose journal for December.

Step 4

Post the journal to your general ledger.

Step 5

Complete a worksheet for the business as of December 31. The year end inventory figure that you will need for the income statement is $27 000.

Step 6

Prepare an income statement and a balance sheet for the business.

Review Case

Pete Pollowski is an 18-year-old teenager who sells popsicles from a refrigerated bicycle stand at all Toronto Blue Jays home games. Look over his Income Statement and answer the questions that follow:

Pete Pollowski
Income Statement
For the Four Months Ended September 30, 19 ___

Revenue:		
Sale of Popsicles		$22 700
Cost of Goods Sold:		
Inventory, June 1st	0	
Purchases	$12 000	
Goods available for sale	$12 000	
Inventory, Dec. 31st	(500)	$11 500
Gross Profit		$11 200
Expenses:		
Advertising	$ 1 350	
Bank Charges	700	
Bicycle Repairs	650	2 700
Net Income		$ 8 500

Questions

1. If Pete had sold all of his inventory at the end of September, how much would his net income be?
2. The Toronto Blue Jays want Pete to advertise in their program and will charge him $1 000 for the whole season. Can he afford this? Should he?
3. Does Pete have a good business here? Explain.
4. Pete is thinking about hiring another employee to sell as well. The new bike will cost $5 000 and he will give the employee 50% of the profits. Is this a good idea?

Challenge Case

Art Halley's Garden Centre is just finishing up another fiscal year, ended February 28, 19 ____. Given the Trial Balance below, prepared by his bookkeeper, prepare an Income Statement for the business, and answer all the questions Art has about his Income Statement.

Account	Debit	Credit
1. Petty Cash	100	
2. Bank	5 000	
3. Accounts Receivable	16 800	
4. Merchandise Inventory	53 000	
10. Garden Equipment	16 000	
22. Accounts Payable		19 000
23. Sales Tax Payable		500
31. A. Halley, Capital		?
32. A. Halley, Drawings	11 000	
41. Sales		300 000
42. Sales Returns & Allowances	850	
50. Advertising	5 200	
51. Bank Charges	1 200	
52. Freight-In	2 440	
53. Miscellaneous Expense	710	
54. Purchases	190 000	
55. Purchase Returns & Allowances		500
56. Telephone Expenses	1 100	
58. Truck Expense	3 000	
58. Wages Expense	73 600	
	380 000	380 000

(The year end inventory figure is $46 000.)

Questions

1. What percent profit am I making on sales?
2. Can I afford to hire another gardener at an annual cost of $25 000?
3. Can I afford the gardener and spend another $12 000 on television advertising as well?
4. Should I pay off the bank loan?

Take-a-Break

The business cards below have all been cut in half and re-dealt, that is, the top halves do not match the bottom halves. See if you can pair up the business tops and bottoms by matching letters to numbers.

1.

TALLY, SUM & COST

56789012
34567890
12345678
90123456

"Serving Regina Since 1925"
Sprayed in Place
Urethane Foam
52 Valley Drive
Regina, Sask.
452-1818

a.

2.

Ricardo's Carpet

Lawyers
1st. Canadian Place
Toronto, Ontario
H5L 1J2
(416) 825-6000

b.

3.

WALKER COMMUNICATION

"Fumigation for the nation"
2525 Winnipegosis Ave.
Winnipeg, Manitoba G5L 6F6
352-8200

c.

4.

LITT, GATE and SUE

"Our work is on sail."
C. Highliner, Owner
Harbour Road, Port Dover, Ont.
263-0001

d.

5.

BRAKE STOP

REPAIRS TO ALL MAKES
18 STAMPEDE ROAD
CALGARY, ALBERTA
B3C 3B1
351-6000

e.

6.

LAKE ERIE
BOAT REPAIR

"We cover all your needs"
Home . Fire . Auto . Life
1200 Maison Blvd.
Montreal, P.Q.
623-4040

f.

7.

PETER'S
PEST CONTROL >>>>>>

"Give your car a brake"
Exclusive Brake Shop
1500 Dundas St., London, Ontario 452-6379

g.

8.

ROCKY
VIEW
GARAGE

Chartered Accountants
2910 Oulette Ave., Windsor, Ont. 579-6241

h.

9.

Ireland
Insulation
Company

Beeper Services for the Greater Vanvouver Area
702-BEEP
2520 Quay Blvd., Vancouver, B.C. A2B3B5

i.

10.

UMBRELLA INSURANCE

"You'll be floored by our service"
1800 Queen St., Toronto, Ontario J25 7V9
653-1800

j.

Chapter 15 Subsidiary Ledgers

Objectives

At the end of this chapter you will be able to

1. know what a sub-ledger is;
2. post to accounts receivable and accounts payable sub-ledgers;
3. take a trial balance of the A/R and A/P sub-ledgers; and
4. understand the need for keeping accurate records of amounts owing by customers and to suppliers.

15.1 Overview

If you have covered most of the chapters in the text by now, you will recognize the basic **accounting cycle** in the diagram below. Accounting starts when we journalize entries in the *general journal*, post to the *general ledger*, take a *trial balance* on a worksheet, and prepare the *income statement* and *balance sheet*.

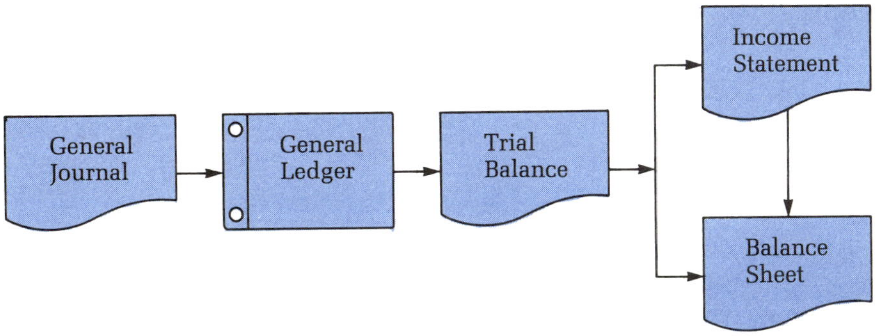

This chapter will add another dimension to this cycle, by creating two new ledgers. Here's a diagram to show how they fit into the regular accounting cycle.

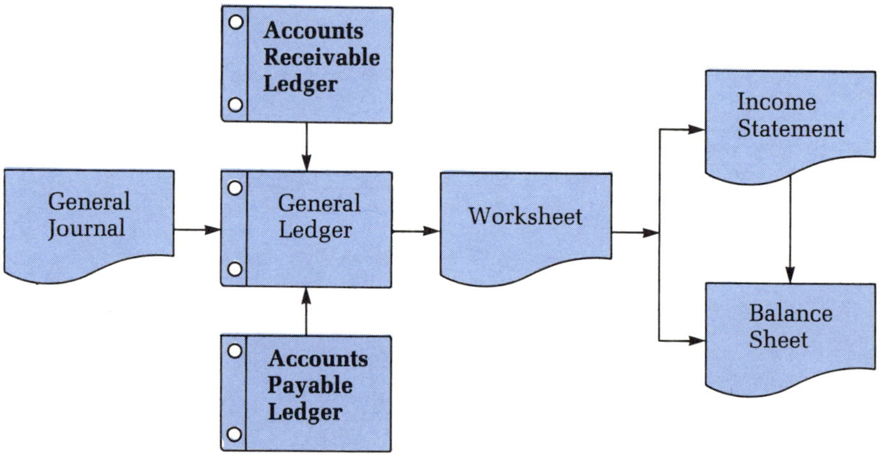

15.2 Accounts Receivable Ledger

In all of the general journal entries we have made up to this point, we have recorded debits into **Accounts Receivable** and we have noted who each of the customers is. A typical journal entry has been:

GENERAL JOURNAL

PAGE 3

DATE		PARTICULARS	PR	DEBIT	CREDIT
Mar.	1	A/R F. Nutt	3	150 —	
		Sales	40		150 —
		Sold services to F. Nutt.			

When this journal entry is posted, we have been debiting the Accounts Receivable account and crediting Sales like this:

ACCOUNT: Accounts Receivable NO 3

DATE		PARTICULARS	PR	DEBIT	CREDIT	DR CR	BALANCE
Mar.	1		GJ3	150 —		DR	150 —

ACCOUNT: Sales NO. 40

DATE		PARTICULARS	PR	DEBIT	CREDIT	DR. CR	BALANCE
Mar.	1		GJ3		150 —	CR	150 —

This is a problem because if we put all of our customers' debts into Accounts Receivable, the customer balances will be all mixed up. We will not know how much each of our customers owes us. A better way to do this is to have a 3-column account for each customer. Then, when we sell goods or services to that customer, we can record the amount of the sale in her/his account.

15.3 Customer Accounts Balances

Before we do any accounting entries on this new theory, just think of a couple of examples of how people keep track of their customer account balances. If you have ever had your own paper route, you know that it's a simple matter to keep track of customers. You are given a card for each customer and you put all the cards on rings. Each card has a stub, and when you get paid, the customer gets the stub. The remaining stubs are your Accounts Receivable.

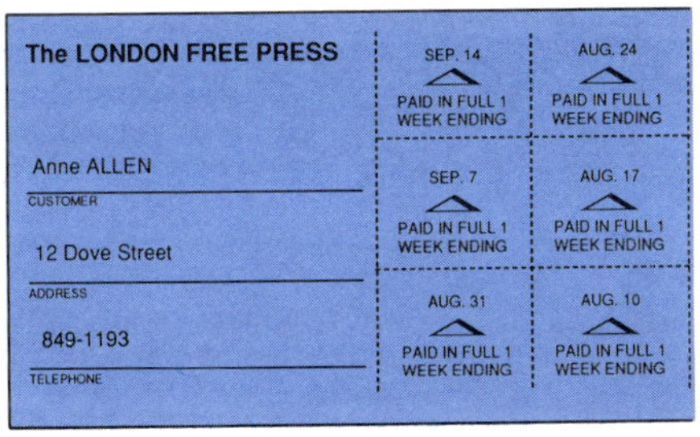

In the second diagram, assume that today is August 31st. How many weeks' payment does Jack owe for his newspaper? If the paper costs $2.00 weekly, then your A/R balance from Jack is $8.00.

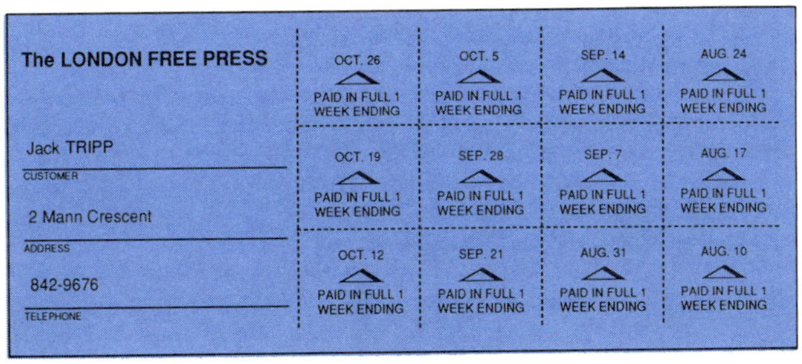

Some businesses keep track of their customer accounts using a filing tray that has cards with customer balances on them. In the diagram to the left, the tray is divided into alphabetical sections from A to Z. Each customer has an account card showing all of his/her transactions. The cards of all the customers are then filed in alphabetical order. The ''A'' section, for example, would have accounts for Adams, Arbuck, and Azblaster, in that order. The tray may also be on wheels so that it can be easily moved around the office and then stored in a vault at night for safekeeping.

Here is an example of one of the cards for a customer named Keith Adams. Notice that the information at the top is fairly complete. This is needed so that a statement can be sent out to the customer at the end of each month, to pay the bill. Note as well that Keith has a **credit limit** of $1 500. This means that Keith can charge up to $1 500 worth of services at any one time. However, Keith cannot charge for services over this amount.

ACCOUNTS RECEIVABLE LEDGER CARD

NAME: Keith Adams
ADDRESS: 654 Parkinson Road
Charlottetown POSTAL CODE: P2R 6L1
TELEPHONE NUMBER: 772-5142 CREDIT LIMIT: $1500

DATE		PARTICULARS	DEBIT	CREDIT	BALANCE
June	1	Invoice #26	45 —		45 —
	3	Invoice #31	120 —		165 —
	5	Received Payment		45 —	120 —
	12	Invoice #40	80 —		200 —

From the entries in Keith's account, you can tell that he owes the business $200. You can also tell that this amount comes from two different invoices, #31 and #40.

15.4 The Accounts Receivable Ledger

Now, let's go back to the theory we started to talk about in Section 15.2. The journal entry we saw in that section was:

GENERAL JOURNAL

PAGE 3

DATE		PARTICULARS	PR	DEBIT	CREDIT
Mar.	1	A/R F. Nutt	3	150 —	
		Sales	40		150 —
		Sold services to F. Nutt			

Notice that the debit side of this entry has two parts to it, the A/R part (Accounts Receivable) and the customer's name—F. Nutt. When we have sales to customers, it is common to have a group of accounts for such customers called an **accounts receivable ledger.** We use 3-column accounts in this ledger and they are the same 3-column accounts that we use in the general ledger. Here is what an accounts receivable ledger looks like.

GENERAL LEDGER

ACCOUNT: Adams, Keith NO.

DATE		PARTICULARS	PR	DEBIT	CREDIT	DR CR	BALANCE
June	1		GJ7	45 —		DR	45 —

ACCOUNT: Arbuck, Sally NO.

DATE		PARTICULARS	PR	DEBIT	CREDIT	DR CR	BALANCE
June	1		GJ7	80 —		DR	80 —

ACCOUNT: Azblaster, Giff NO.

DATE		PARTICULARS	PR	DEBIT	CREDIT	DR CR	BALANCE
June	6		GJ8	112 —		DR	250 —

ACCOUNT: Azziz, Victoria NO.

DATE		PARTICULARS	PR	DEBIT	CREDIT	DR CR	BALANCE
June	7		GJ9	23 —		DR	310 —

Note that all of the accounts in the accounts receivable ledger are listed in alphabetical order for easy filing and fast retrieval. When a customer asks how much he/she owes, we want to be able to look it up as fast as possible. There is no need for account numbers because accounts are arranged alphabetically in the ledger. We call this accounts receivable ledger a "subsidiary ledger" or "sub-ledger" for short. The word subsidiary means that it is an extra ledger that ties in to the general ledger.

A sub-ledger is a group of accounts that is separate from the general ledger but relates to the accounts in the general ledger. There is a sub-ledger for each customer in Accounts Receivable.

When we have a debit entry to Accounts Receivable in the general journal, we now have two postings—one to the Accounts Receivable account in the general ledger, and one to the customer's account in the accounts receivable ledger. We will post these in Section 15.5.

15.5 Posting

1. The Accounts Receivable account in the general ledger.
2. The Sales account in the general ledger.
3. The customer's account in the sub-ledger—the accounts receivable ledger.

GENERAL JOURNAL

PAGE 1

DATE		PARTICULARS	PR	DEBIT	CREDIT
Mar.	1	A/R F. Nutt	3/✓	150 —	
		Sales	40		150 —
		Sold services to F. Nutt			

GENERAL LEDGER

ACCOUNT: Accounts Receivable NO. 3

DATE		PARTICULARS	PR	DEBIT	CREDIT	DR CR	BALANCE
Mar.	1		GJ1	150 —		DR	150 —

ACCOUNT: Sales NO. 40

DATE		PARTICULARS	PR	DEBIT	CREDIT	DR CR	BALANCE
Mar.	1		GJ1		150 —	CR	150 —

ACCOUNTS RECEIVABLE LEDGER

ACCOUNT: Nutt, Fred NO.

DATE		PARTICULARS	PR	DEBIT	CREDIT	DR. CR.	BALANCE
Mar.	1		GJ1		150 —	DR	150 —

Note: Take a look at the posting reference in the general journal. We have posted 2 debits—one to the Accounts Receivable account in the general ledger and one to F. Nutt's account in the accounts receivable ledger.

When we post to F. Nutt's account, we put a tick in the P.R. column of the general journal—we do this because F. Nutt's account does not have a number and the tick reminds us that we have posted to his account.

When all of the postings are done, the balance of all of the accounts in the accounts receivable ledger must be the same as the Accounts Receivable account in the general ledger. We will see an example of this soon, but there is one more point before we leave this idea. The Accounts Receivable account in the general ledger is known as a "control account."

The control account is the account against which accounts in sub-ledgers must be checked to make sure they agree.

15.6 The Control Account

Shown below is an accounts receivable ledger that has only four accounts in it. Below that is the Accounts Receivable (control) account in the general ledger. After all of the posting is done to the accounts, we can take a trial balance of the accounts receivable ledger (the sub-ledger). The trial balance must show that the total of all the accounts in the sub-ledger equals the final balance in the Accounts Receivable account in the general ledger.

ACCOUNTS RECEIVABLE LEDGER

ACCOUNT: Adams, Keith NO.

DATE		PARTICULARS	PR	DEBIT	CREDIT	DR. CR.	BALANCE
Mar.	1		GJ1	45 —		DR	45 —

ACCOUNT: Arbuck, Sally NO.

DATE		PARTICULARS	PR	DEBIT	CREDIT	DR. CR	BALANCE
Mar.	1		GJ1	80 —		DR	80 —

ACCOUNT: Azblaster, Giff NO.

DATE		PARTICULARS	PR	DEBIT	CREDIT	DR. CR	BALANCE
Mar.	1		GJ1	112 —		DR	250 —

ACCOUNT: Azziz, Victoria NO.

DATE		PARTICULARS	PR	DEBIT	CREDIT	DR. CR	BALANCE
Mar.	1		GJ1	23 —		DR	310 —

ACCOUNT: Accounts Receivable NO.

DATE		PARTICULARS	PR	DEBIT	CREDIT	DR. CR	BALANCE
Mar.	1		GJ9			DR	685 —

Noname Business
Accounts Receivable Trial Balance
March 1, 19 ____

Keith Adams	45.00
Sally Arbuck	80.00
Giff Azblaster	250.00
Victoria Azziz	310.00
A/R Control	685.00

Keep in mind that the examples above are meant to show you the balancing steps between the general ledger and the accounts receivable sub-ledger. In a real business there would be many more accounts in an accounts receivable sub-ledger. The important point here is to understand how this whole idea about the subsidiary ledger works. When we journalize an accounts receivable entry, it gets posted into the Accounts Receivable account in the general ledger and the customer's account in the accounts receivable ledger.

15.7 Quick Recap

Take another look at the accounting cycle diagram from the start of the chapter. You have now studied how the accounts receivable ledger fits into the accounting cycle. It is not really part of the mainstream of the accounting flow but it is important in terms of dealing with our customers and keeping their balances up-to-date. The key point to remember is that the *sub-ledger must always balance with the control account in the general ledger*.

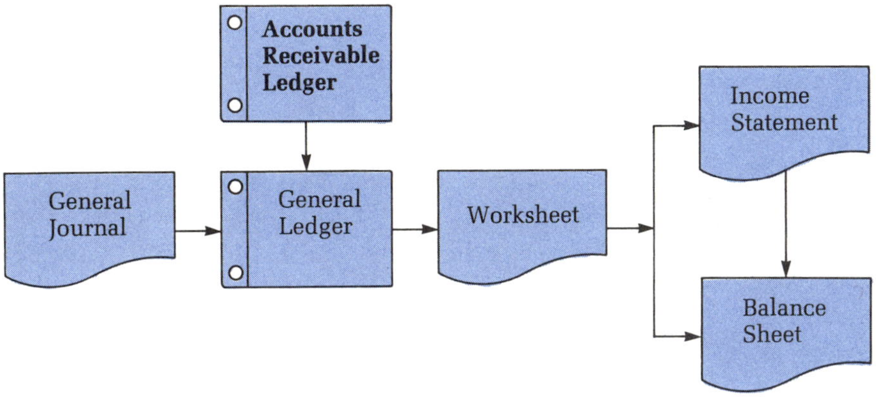

15.8 Accounts Payable

Basically, the accounts payable sub-ledger is the same as the accounts receivable sub-ledger. Here is the diagram again of the accounting cycle with the new sub-ledger for accounts payable drawn in.

The accounts payable ledger balances with its own control account in the general ledger, just like accounts receivable. So it, too, is not really part of the accounting cycle. It is, however, an important sub-ledger in terms of keeping our records straight with suppliers. Let's begin the discussion of Accounts Payable with some information about buying from suppliers.

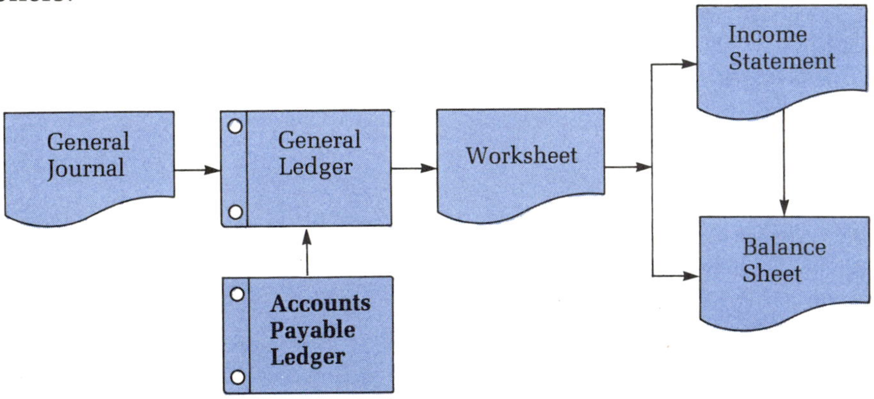

15.9 Supplier Account Balances

Assume for this section that we operate a television repair shop. In our business, we advertise that we service most makes of television sets, and many makes of VCR sets as well. Because of this we have to buy parts from many different suppliers. Shown below are two invoices from our suppliers—just to give you an idea what their bills look like.

HITACHI *1089 Eastern Avenue, Charlottetown, P.E.I. 319-8743*

SOLD TO Herman's Repair Shop
245 Main Street
Charlottetown, P.E.I.

QUANTITY	DESCRIPTION	UNIT PRICE	AMOUNT
12	Cables #75	$ 4.50	$ 54.00
6	Plugs #B-21	$ 1.20	$ 7.20
	Invoice Total		$ 61.20

INVOICE

G. PETERSON & COMPANY
Electronic Parts
2333 Oxford Street
Charlottetown P.E.I.
P2L 1G5
674-9910

ORDER NO.
DATE
INVOICE NO.
TERMS

SOLD TO Herman's Repair Shop
245 Main Street
Charlottetown, P.E.I.
P2L 1G4

QUANTITY	DESCRIPTION	UNIT PRICE	AMOUNT
24	red clips	$ .60	$ 14.40
6m	solder	$ 3.20/m	$ 19.20
			$ 33.60

INVOICE

"Imagine those crooks wanting eleven bucks to fix this!"

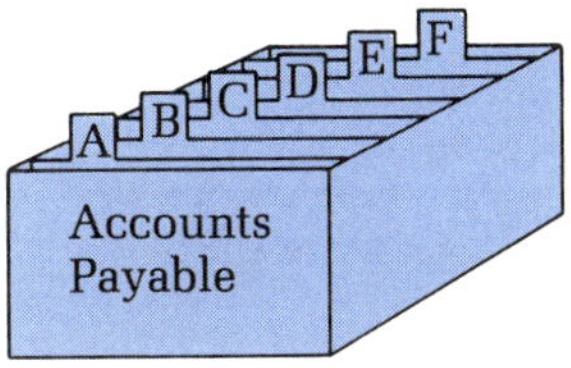

If we have many invoices and suppliers we need an orderly way to keep a record of these amounts owing, known as **accounts payable.** An informal way to do this would be to keep bills in the drawer of a filing cabinet and file bills in alphabetical order by the supplier's company name. This would be very similar to the filing tray used for accounts receivable. In the picture to the right above, accounts payable bills are filed in a drawer alphabetically.

A more formal way to keep track of supplier accounts is to have a formal ledger—an accounts payable ledger.

15.10 The Accounts Payable Ledger

During the first three days of March, our television repair business received TV parts from three different suppliers. These entries were all journalized in a general journal:

GENERAL JOURNAL

PAGE 3

DATE		PARTICULARS	PR	DEBIT	CREDIT
Mar.	1	Repair Parts Expense		75 50	
		A/P Hitachi Canada Ltd.			75 50
		Bought repair parts.			
	2	Repair Parts Expense		112 34	
		A/P Zenith Limited			112 34
		Bought repair parts.			
	3	Repair Parts Expense		44 91	
		A/P Electrohome Ltd.			44 91
		Bought repair parts.			

This time we look at the credit side of the entry as being the most important. Notice that the credit has two parts—a credit to A/P which is the Accounts Payable control account in the general ledger, and the name of the supplier who will be found in our new **accounts payable ledger.** Here is the new sub-ledger:

ACCOUNTS PAYABLE LEDGER

ACCOUNT: Electrohome Ltd. NO.

DATE		PARTICULARS	PR	DEBIT	CREDIT	DR CR	BALANCE
Mar.	3		GJ3		44 91	CR	44 91

ACCOUNT: *Hitachi Canada Ltd.* NO

DATE		PARTICULARS	PR	DEBIT	CREDIT	DR. CR	BALANCE
Mar.	1		GJ1	150—	75 50	CR	75 50

ACCOUNT: *Zenith Limited* NO

DATE		PARTICULARS	PR	DEBIT	CREDIT	DR. CR	BALANCE
Mar.	3		GJ1		112 34	CR	112 34

Note: These accounts, like those in the accounts receivable ledger, are in alphabetical order by supplier name. No account numbers are necessary.

15.11 Posting

Each of the general journal entries below has to be posted to three different accounts.

1. The Repair Parts Expense account in the general ledger.
2. The Accounts Payable account in the general ledger.
3. The supplier's account in the accounts payable ledger.

All of the journal entries have been posted. Follow them through from the general journal to the general ledger and the trial balance. It is similar to the Accounts Receivable work we did except the entries to Accounts Payable are credits instead of debits. The A/P credit gets posted to account #21 in the general ledger, and the supplier's account in the sub-ledger. (Note the tick ✓ to show this.)

GENERAL JOURNAL

PAGE 3

DATE		PARTICULARS	PR	DEBIT	CREDIT
Mar.	1	Repair Parts Expense		75 50	
		A/P Hitachi Canada Ltd.	22/✓		75 50
		Bought repair parts.			
	2	Repair Parts Expense		112 34	
		A/P Zenith Limited	22/✓		112 34
		Bought repair parts.			
	3	Repair Parts Expense		44 91	
		A/P Electrohome Ltd.	22/✓		44 91
		Bought repair parts.			

GENERAL LEDGER

ACCOUNT: *Electrohome* NO.

DATE		PARTICULARS	PR	DEBIT	CREDIT	DR. CR.	BALANCE
Mar.	3		GJ3		44 91	CR	44 91

ACCOUNT: *Hitachi Canada Ltd.* NO.

DATE		PARTICULARS	PR	DEBIT	CREDIT	DR. CR.	BALANCE
Mar.	3		GJ3		75 50	CR	75 50

ACCOUNT: *Zenith Limited* NO.

DATE		PARTICULARS	PR	DEBIT	CREDIT	DR. CR.	BALANCE
Mar.	3		GJ3		112 34	CR	112 34

ACCOUNTS PAYABLE LEDGER

ACCOUNT: *Accounts Payable* NO. *22*

DATE		PARTICULARS	PR	DEBIT	CREDIT	DR. CR.	BALANCE
Mar.	3		GJ3			CR	231 75

Noname Business
Accounts Payable Trial Balance
March 3, 19 ___

Electrohome Ltd.	44.91
Hitachi Canada Ltd.	75.50
Zenith Limited	112.34
Accounts Payable Control	231.75

Notice, again, that all of the balances in the accounts payable trial balance agree with the total shown in the accounts payable account in the general ledger.

15.12 Quick Recap

Take one final look at the accounting cycle diagram from the start of the chapter. You have now studied how the accounts payable ledger fits into the accounting cycle. It is not really part of the mainstream of the accounting flow but it is important in terms of dealing with our suppliers and keeping their balances up-to-date. The key point is that the *sub-ledger must always balance with its control account in the general ledger.*

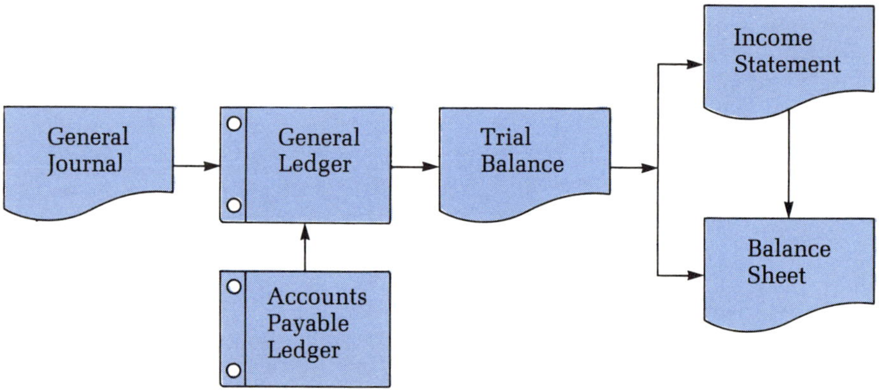

15.13 Summary

This chapter expands the accounting cycle by showing you how two sub-ledgers operate—the Accounts Receivable Ledger and the Accounts Payable Ledger.

Both of these ledgers are referred to as sub-ledgers, and both must agree with their control accounts in the general ledger. Just to make sure that they do agree to their control accounts, it is common practice to take trial balances of the accounts in the sub-ledgers. The trial balances are just a listing of all the account balances for customers and suppliers.

Time to check to see if you have met the objectives of this chapter. You should be able to

1. know what a sub-ledger is;
2. post to accounts receivable and accounts payable sub-ledgers;
3. take a trial balance of the A/R and A/P sub-ledgers; and
4. understand the need for keeping accurate records of amounts owing by customers and to suppliers.

Dictionary of Terms

Accounting Cycle The process that covers the original recording of accounting transactions, from journal entries through posting to the preparation of the financial statements.

Accounts Payable Amounts owing to suppliers.

Accounts Payable Ledger All of the supplier accounts.

Accounts Receivable Amounts owing from customers.

Accounts Receivable Ledger All of the customer accounts.

Control Account The account in the general ledger with which the sub-ledger total must agree.

Credit Limit The highest amount we are willing to let customers charge to their accounts.

Sub-Ledger A group of accounts that is separate from, but related to the general ledger.

Exercises

1. Try to fill in the missing names in this diagram of the accounting cycle without looking back at the text. If you really get stuck, put in as many names as you can remember before you go back. Mark yourself out of 7.

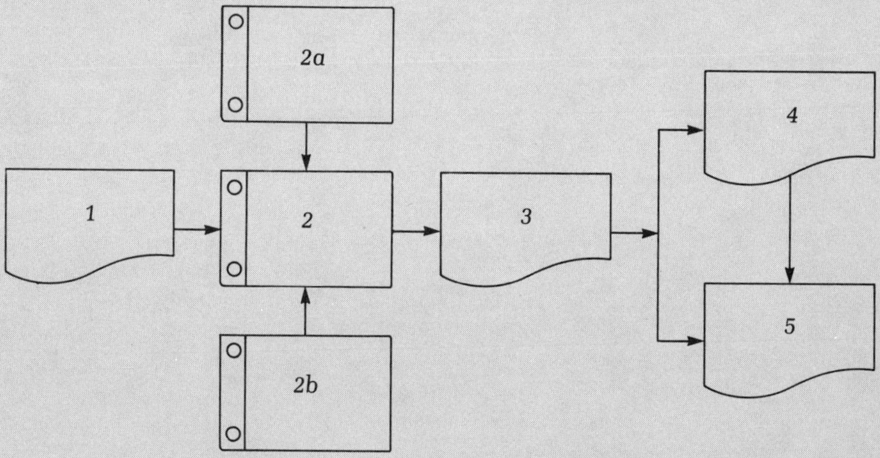

2. Look at the account below. Do you think it is from an accounts receivable ledger or an accounts payable ledger? How can you tell?

ACCOUNT: Robinson, Jeff NO.

DATE		PARTICULARS	PR	DEBIT	CREDIT	DR CR	BALANCE
Aug.	5	Invoice #65	GJ8	332.05		DR	667.32

3. Record these charge sales in a general journal, and then post the entries into the general ledger and the accounts receivable ledger.

Transactions

Oct. 1: Invoice #116, $270.00 to Anne Johnson.

5: Invoice to Karen Jurjovich, $85.00. Invoice #117.

15: Invoice #118 to Greg Wilson, in the amount of $600.00.

26: Invoice to Anne Johnson for $102.50. Invoice #119.

31: Charge sale to Greg Wilson in the amount of $49.75, invoice #120.

Once you have journalized the entries, take an informal trial balance on your calculator to make sure the sub-ledger agrees with the control account in the general ledger.

4. Record these transactions in a general journal, and then post the entries into the general ledger and the accounts payable ledger.

Transactions

Nov. 1: Bought supplies to be used for the business, $248.20, from Hobbs Wholesale Ltd. Their invoice #H-245.

4: Received the telephone bill, $102.75. Set it up as an account payable to Bell Canada.

18: Bought new furniture for the office from Wilson Stationers on account, $1 450.00. Their invoice #88-3615.

26: Received a bill from Petro Canada for gasoline for the company car, $125.00. Set it up as an account payable. Invoice #21635.

30: The Calgary Herald sent a bill for newspaper advertising, $384.50. We set this up as an amount owing. Invoice #25-261.

5. Prepare a formal trial balance for the accounts receivable ledger below. The name of the business is Anne's Typing Service.

ACCOUNTS RECEIVABLE LEDGER

ACCOUNT: Anderson, Dale NO.

DATE		PARTICULARS	PR	DEBIT	CREDIT	DR CR	BALANCE
May	31					DR	345 82

ACCOUNT: Blundell, Cathy NO.

DATE		PARTICULARS	PR	DEBIT	CREDIT	DR CR	BALANCE
May	31					DR	506 71

ACCOUNT: Devries, T.S. NO.

DATE		PARTICULARS	PR	DEBIT	CREDIT	DR CR	BALANCE
May	31					DR	1 18

ACCOUNT: Juhaszi, Monica NO.

DATE		PARTICULARS	PR	DEBIT	CREDIT	DR CR	BALANCE
May	31					DR	802 18

ACCOUNT: Lindsay, Sean NO.

DATE		PARTICULARS	PR	DEBIT	CREDIT	DR CR	BALANCE
May	31					DR	12 34

ACCOUNT: Miller, Heidi NO.

DATE		PARTICULARS	PR	DEBIT	CREDIT	DR CR	BALANCE
May	31					DR	500 31

ACCOUNT: Ringel, Heather NO.

DATE		PARTICULARS	PR	DEBIT	CREDIT	DR CR	BALANCE
May	31					DR	20 50

ACCOUNT: Taugher, David NO.

DATE		PARTICULARS	PR	DEBIT	CREDIT	DR CR	BALANCE
May	31					DR	77 88

6. Take the accounts receivable ledger below and find the missing balances for each customer. Prepare a formal trial balance of the accounts receivable ledger and see if it agrees with the control account in the general ledger, which has a $963.58 balance.

ACCOUNTS RECEIVABLE LEDGER

ACCOUNT: Carson, Chris NO.

DATE		PARTICULARS	PR	DEBIT	CREDIT	DR CR	BALANCE
Jan.	1	Invoice #245	GJ1	112 90			356 42
	3	Rec'd on account	GJ1		112 90		
	8	Invoice #260	GJ1	21 48			
	22	Invoice # 285	GJ3	75 –			

ACCOUNT: Cole, Robin NO.

DATE		PARTICULARS	PR	DEBIT	CREDIT	DR CR	BALANCE
Jan.	3	Balance Forward	GJ1				0 –
	4	Invoice #250	GJ1	11 89			
	18	Invoice #267	GJ2	108 11			
	28	Rec'd on account	GJ3		50 –		

ACCOUNT: Godden, Richard NO.

DATE		PARTICULARS	PR	DEBIT	CREDIT	DR CR	BALANCE
Nov.	5	Rec'd on account	GJ1		75 –		26 59
	10	Invoice # 215	GJ2	36 75			
	15	Rec'd on account	GJ2		75 –		
	20	Invoice # 270	GJ3	72 50			

ACCOUNT: Neave, Tara NO.

DATE		PARTICULARS	PR	DEBIT	CREDIT	DR CR	BALANCE
Jan.	1	Invoice # 246	GJ1			DR	261 80
	7	Invoice # 258	GJ1	11 29			
	13	Invoice # 265	GJ2	18 50			
	20	Invoice #271	GJ2	32 70			

ACCOUNT: Perkins, Lisa NO.

DATE		PARTICULARS	PR	DEBIT	CREDIT	DR CR	BALANCE
Jan.	2	Invoice #247	GJ1	12 95		DR	26 50
	9	Invoice #262	GJ1	13 21			
	10	Invoice #263	GJ2	44 16			
	28	Rec'd on account	GJ3		12 95		

ACCOUNT: Wilford, Jennifer

DATE		PARTICULARS	PR	DEBIT	CREDIT	DR CR	BALANCE
Jan.	15	Received on account	GJ2		100 –	DR	75 63
	16	Invoice #266	GJ2	32 47			
	18	Invoice #268	GJ2	21 90			
	29	Received on account	GJ3		32 47		

7. Given the accounts payable ledger below, find the missing balances for each supplier. Prepare a trial balance of the accounts payable ledger, and see if it agrees with the control account in the general ledger, which has a balance of $3 922.66.

ACCOUNTS PAYABLE LEDGER

ACCOUNT: Arkin Industries

DATE		PARTICULARS	PR	DEBIT	CREDIT	DR CR	BALANCE
Feb.	3	Invoice A-25	GJ4		332 10	CR	332 10
	4	Invoice A-27	GJ4		164 50		

ACCOUNT: Babcock + Wilcox

DATE		PARTICULARS	PR	DEBIT	CREDIT	DR CR	BALANCE
Feb.	1	Balance Forward				CR	568 90
	7	Invoice #1782	GJ4		302 01		

ACCOUNT: Drew Supply Ltd. NO.

DATE		PARTICULARS	PR	DEBIT	CREDIT	DR CR	BALANCE
Feb.	8	Invoice #777	GJ6		56 90	CR	281 16

ACCOUNT: Ferris Company NO.

DATE		PARTICULARS	PR	DEBIT	CREDIT	DR CR	BALANCE
Feb.	10	Invoice F31	GJ5		50 —	CR	552 83

ACCOUNT: Goober + Associates NO.

DATE		PARTICULARS	PR	DEBIT	CREDIT	DR CR	BALANCE
Feb.	15	Balance Forward				CR	0 —
	16	Invoice GA30	GJ5		302 —		
	20	Invoice GA38	GJ6		408 —		

ACCOUNT: Independent Widget Ltd. NO.

DATE		PARTICULARS	PR	DEBIT	CREDIT	DR CR	BALANCE
Feb.	5	Balance Forward				CR	650 —
	10	Paid on account	GJ5	200 —			

ACCOUNT: Harmony Outfitters NO.

DATE		PARTICULARS	PR	DEBIT	CREDIT	DR CR	BALANCE
Feb.	11	Balance Forward				CR	1 246 10
	18	Paid on account	GJ5	500 —			

ACCOUNT: *Moonlighting Manufacturing Ltd.* NO.

DATE		PARTICULARS	PR	DEBIT	CREDIT	DR. CR.	BALANCE
Feb.	13	Balance Forward				CR	392 63
	27	Paid on account	GJ6	392 63			

ACCOUNT: *Quick Fix Artists*

DATE		PARTICULARS	PR	DEBIT	CREDIT	DR. CR.	BALANCE
Feb.	2	Balance Forward				CR	471 12
	7	Paid on account	GJ4	471 12			
	9	Invoice AA82	GJ4		362 90		
	16	Invoice AA95	GJ6		486 15		
	23	Paid on account	GJ6	200 —			

Review Questions

1. How many steps are there in the accounting cycle? Name them.
2. When we prepare financial statements for a business, which statement should we prepare first?
3. When we expanded the accounting cycle, we added two new sub-ledgers to the cycle. Name them.
4. For the journal entry below, how many postings do you see?

GENERAL JOURNAL

PAGE 3

DATE		PARTICULARS	PR	DEBIT	CREDIT
Mar.	1	A/R F. Nutt	3/✓	150 —	
		Sales	40		150 —
		Sold services to F. Nutt.			

5. Why do we need sub-ledgers?
6. Explain how a young person with a paper route knows what his/her accounts receivable are.
7. How are accounts filed in an accounts receivable file?
8. Answer these questions about the ledger card.
   (a) What does the phrase "credit limit" mean?
   (b) What is Pam's month end balance?
   (c) What would you do if you owned this business and found that Pam had gone over the credit limit on her account?

9. Why are there no numbers on accounts in an accounts receivable ledger?
10. What does the term "subsidiary ledger" mean? Name two subsidiary ledgers that you know.
11. Why do you use a tick ✓ when you post into a sub-ledger?
12. What does the term "control account" mean? Explain it fully.
13. In which sub-ledger do you record entries for the suppliers of a business?
14. How do we know if the sub-ledger agrees with its control account in the general ledger?

Challenge Questions

Some of the general journal entries below have been posted incorrectly to the general ledger and/or the subsidiary ledgers. List all the posting errors you find.

GENERAL JOURNAL

PAGE 9

DATE		PARTICULARS	PR	DEBIT	CREDIT
	3	Advertising Expense		425 —	
		A/P Regina Post			425 —
		Weekly newspaper advertising.			
	3	A/R L. Lipski		107 82	
		Sales			107 82
		Sold services to L. Lipski.			
	5	Advertising Expense		75 —	
		A/P Maclean Hunter Ltd.			75 —
		Bill for advertising.			
	7	A/R C. Strange		283 45	
		Sales			283 45
		Sold services to C. Strange.			
	8	Telephone Expense		112 12	
		A/P Bell Canada			112 12
		Bill for telephone for May.			

ACCOUNTS RECEIVABLE LEDGER

ACCOUNT: Amoeba, A. NO.

DATE		PARTICULARS	PR	DEBIT	CREDIT	DR CR	BALANCE
June	2		GJ9	650 —		DR	650 —

ACCOUNT: Lipski, L. NO.

DATE		PARTICULARS	PR	DEBIT	CREDIT	DR CR	BALANCE
June	3		GJ9	108 72		DR	108 72

ACCOUNT: Strange, C. NO.

DATE		PARTICULARS	PR	DEBIT	CREDIT	DR CR	BALANCE
June	7		GJ9		283 45	DR	283 45

ACCOUNTS PAYABLE LEDGER

ACCOUNT: Bell Canada NO.

DATE		PARTICULARS	PR	DEBIT	CREDIT	DR CR	BALANCE
June	8				112 12	CR	112 12

ACCOUNT: Maclean Hunter NO.

DATE		PARTICULARS	PR	DEBIT	CREDIT	DR CR	BALANCE
June			GJ9		75 —	DR	75 —

ACCOUNT: Regina Post NO.

DATE		PARTICULARS	PR	DEBIT	CREDIT	DR CR	BALANCE
June	3		GJ9		650 —	CR	650 —

ACCOUNT: *Accounts Receivable* NO. *3*

DATE		PARTICULARS	PR	DEBIT	CREDIT	DR CR	BALANCE
June	1		GJ9	650 —		DR	650 —
	3		GJ9	107 82		DR	757 82
	7		GJ9	283 45		DR	1 141 27

ACCOUNT: *Accounts Payable* NO. *22*

DATE		PARTICULARS	PR	DEBIT	CREDIT	DR CR	BALANCE
June	3		GJ9		425 —	CR	425 —
	8		GJ9		112 12		537 12

ACCOUNT: *Sales* NO. *41*

DATE		PARTICULARS	PR	DEBIT	CREDIT	DR CR	BALANCE
June	1		GJ9		650 —	DR	650 —
	3		GJ9		107 82	CR	757 82
	7		GJ9		283 45	CR	1 041 27

ACCOUNT: *Advertising Expense* NO. *51*

DATE		PARTICULARS	PR	DEBIT	CREDIT	DR CR	BALANCE
June	3		GJ9			DR	75 —

ACCOUNT: *Telephone Expense* NO. *58*

DATE		PARTICULARS	PR	DEBIT	CREDIT	DR CR	BALANCE
June	8		GJ9	121 21		DR	121 21

Review Case

Two teenagers, Greg Shapton and Glen Millard, decide to operate a summer business cleaning windows. Since their rates are reasonable, business is booming. The name of the business is "Washbuckets."

1. Journalize these transactions into a general journal.
2. Post to the general ledger, the accounts receivable ledger, and the accounts payable ledger.
3. Take trial balances of all three ledgers.
4. Prepare formal trial balances of the sub-ledgers to make sure they agree with their control accounts in the general ledger.

Transactions

Jul. 1: Opened the business with a deposit in the bank, $2 000. (This was money loaned by the provincial government under its *Ventures* program for student entrepreneurs.)

2: Bought equipment costing $1 250.00 for the business, on account from Johnson Hardware. Invoice #J24.

2: Sold services for $45.00 to Mrs. Stone, on account. Invoice #1.

3: Sold services to Mr. Webb, on account, $38.00. Invoice #2.

4: Put an ad in the newspaper, the Kingston Whig-Standard for $35.00, on account. Invoice #1423.

4: Sold more services on account to Mrs. Stone, $42.00. Invoice #3.

5: Bought some window cleaning supplies for $76.00 on account from Harold's Discount Warehouse. Invoice #H55.

6: Sold services to Family Food Mart, $210.00, Invoice #4.

10: Sold Services to Shrubb's Shoes, on account $50.00. Invoice #5.

12: Mrs. Stone paid for invoice #1 in cash.

12: Wrote a cheque for $1 250 to pay Johnson Hardware for the equipment purchased, #1.

13: Sold services to Beckers for $110 on account.

14: Shrubbs paid their account in full, in cash.

15: Received a bill from Bell Canada for installing the business phone, $60.00. Set it up as an account payable.

15: Mr. Webb paid his account in full. The cash was deposited into the bank account.

Challenge Case

The following errors were made by a new employee hired to look after the Accounts Receivable for the Windy Drycleaners. The accountant has spotted the errors and has to make the necessary corrections in the books of account. Journalize, in general journal form, all the entries necessary to correct the books.

Error 1: A debit to Harold Smith's account was charged into H. Smyth's account in error. Amount was $45.00.

Error 2: A payment from Mrs. Gladys Burbage for $24 was recorded in the journal as $42.00.

Error 3: An invoice for $18.20 was credited instead of debited to Heather Knox's account. The entry to Sales was also reversed in error.

Take-a-Break

On Target

Listed below are twelve accounting questions, each one of which is answered by a single accounting word found in the target. When you are finished, put together any words left over to form a sentence, which will form the bull's eye of the target.

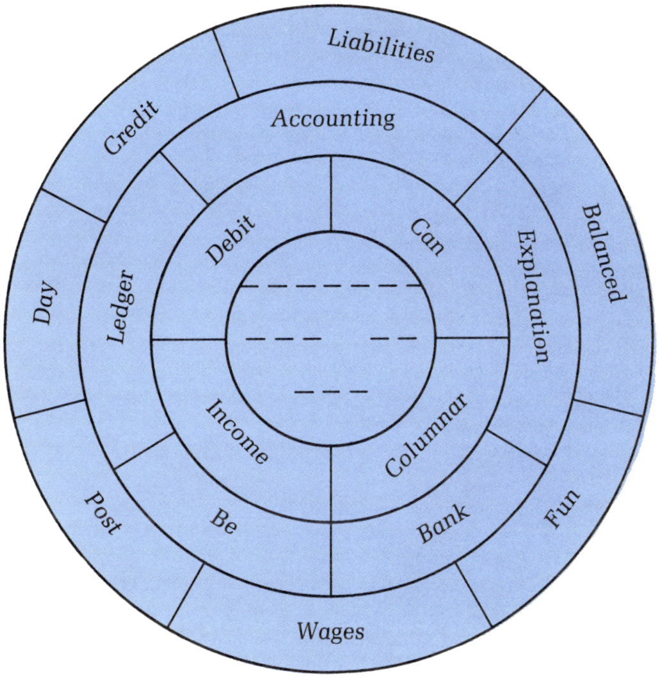

1. The letter "P" in "PR" stands for ____________.
2. Where are all 3-column accounts kept?
3. For how long is a balance sheet good?
4. Unscramble this word — BEDIT.
5. Drop one letter and rearrange to spell CRIED.
6. Goes after every entry in a general journal.
7. Your money is safe in this place.
8. Debts owing to other businesses.
9. ____________ paper is ruled.
10. Accounting is like a weigh scale, ____________.
11. Profit is old fashioned. Net ____________ is new.
12. Employees will be upset if not paid their ____________.

Accounting at Work

Office Manager

Marlene Napthen is the Office Manager of Pacific Rent-Alls, a medium-sized company that rents garden equipment, household needs, and contractor's equipment and tools.

Marlene's job as Office Manager is to supervise all of the accounting employees needed to keep this service business operating efficiently. Marlene's position in the company hierarchy is best shown in this organization chart of the firm. Marlene has a position in *junior management*.

Marlene has been working for Pacific Rent-Alls for the last five years. She joined the company out of high school when she started as a cashier.

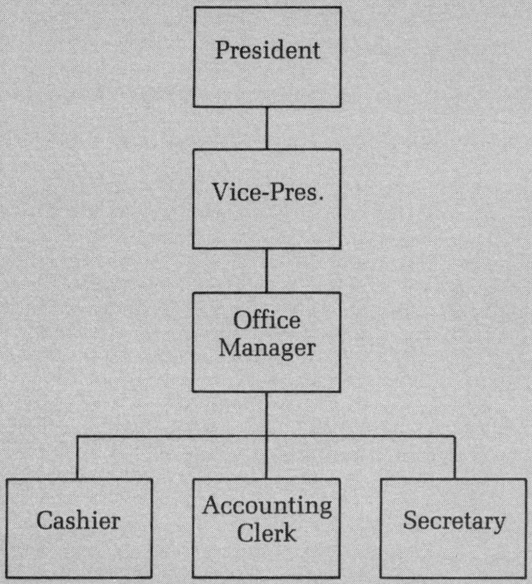

Organization Chart for Pacific Rent-Alls

Two years later she was promoted to the position of office manager. Her job is to supervise the three workers below her on the organization chart. They all report directly to Marlene. Marlene can make recommendations to her boss, the Vice-President, about hirings, raises, and firings.

In order to be better informed about all accounting aspects of the business, Marlene has been studying to become a Certified Management Accountant. She is now enrolled in her third year of the course and has been very successful so far. Her job as office manager requires her to have a good knowledge of cash, payroll, accounts receivable, accounts payable, and inventory.

Marlene's biggest challenge still lies ahead. Her boss, the Vice-President, has asked her to study microcomputers and report back to her about the feasibility of using computers at Pacific Rent-Alls. All the accounting work at the present time is done manually by the accounting clerk, the cashier, and by Marlene. Acccounting reports such as sales summaries and the monthly bank reconciliation are all done by Marlene by hand.

Questions for Discussion

1. Why do you think Marlene was promoted from cashier to be the office manager after two years? Suggest three possible reasons.
2. Is it worthwhile to try to become a C.M.A.? Why?
3. Marlene has been asked to prepare a report on computers for her boss. Where will she start to look for information?
4. From your knowledge of computers, do you see any accounting areas in Pacific Rent-Alls where computers can be used?

8

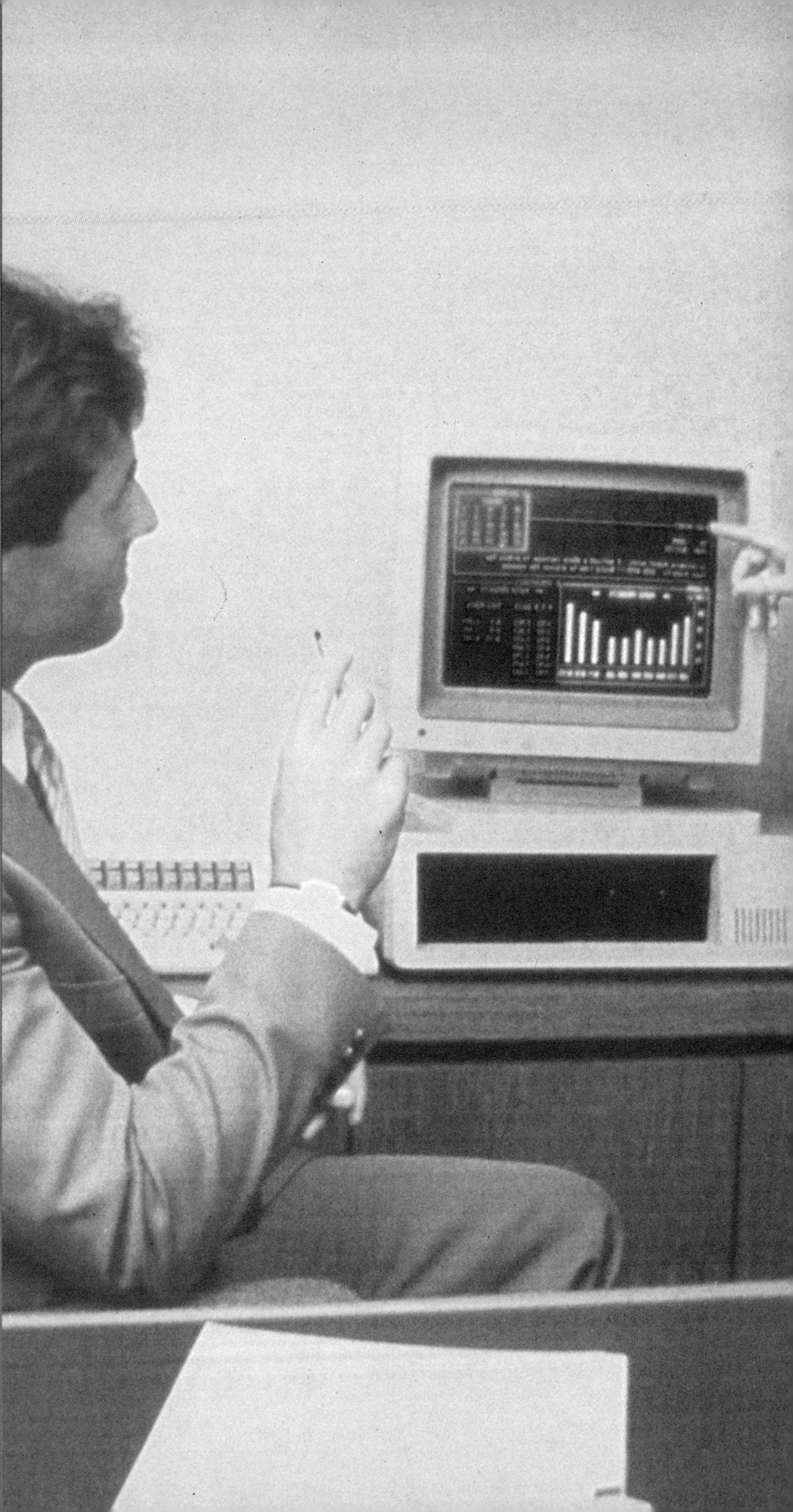

Trends in Accounting

Chapter 16
Computerized Accounting/Practice Set III

Chapter 17
Accounting Careers

Chapter 16 Computerized Accounting/ Practice Set III

Objectives

At the end of this chapter you will be able to

1. know why it is an advantage to use a computer for accounting;
2. see some similarities and differences in manual and computer accounting reports; and
3. know some useful applications of spreadsheet software to accounting topics.

16.1 Overview

It has become fairly common in many businesses today to use a computer for some or all of the accounting of that business. There are many accounting applications within the general topic of computerized accounting—general ledger applications, accounts receivable, accounts payable, and computerized payroll, one of the first applications. Because this is such an expansive topic, we can only give it a quick look in this text. Keeping this in mind, we will look at general ledger accounting and a payroll application using a spreadsheet summary.

16.2 Computers in the Accounting Cycle

In all of the accounting in this text, you will be using a manual accounting system, that is, preparing entries by hand. You record entries into journals, post to the general ledger, balance, and take off financial statements. A general ledger computer package uses the same approach as a manual accounting system. It may help if we put this in diagram form to relate it to the accounting cycle that you already know. Here is the manual cycle:

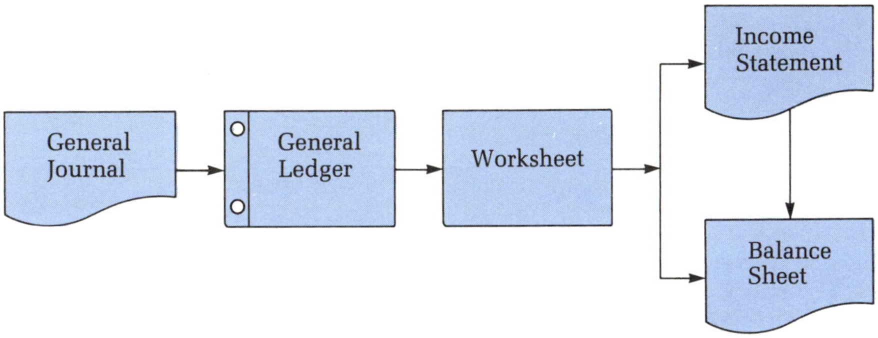

Here is a diagram for a computerized accounting system:

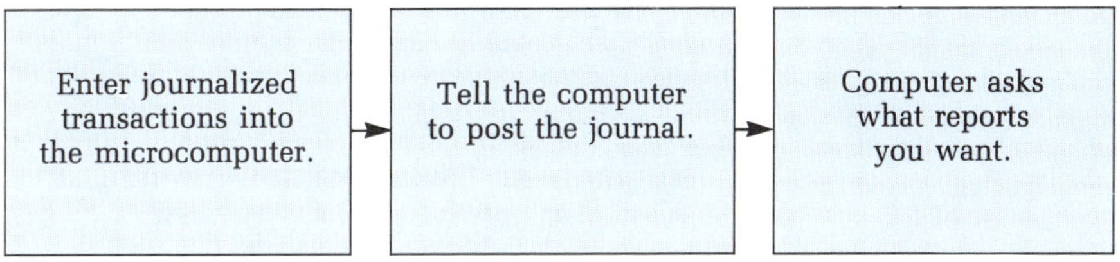

Once the user has entered the original accounting data, the computer takes over!

Figure 16-1
People who work at accounting jobs or learn accounting skills find that computers make their jobs easier.

16.3 Journalizing

Computerized accounting systems simulate the pages of a general journal so that the following will appear on the screen:

GENERAL JOURNAL

TRAN	DATE	PARTICULARS	ACC	DEBIT	CREDIT
Explanation					

Once the computer puts this journal format on the screen, the user simply tells it what account to debit and what account to credit. If, for example, you were recording the opening entry for a business, whose owner started operations with \$20 000, you know that the entry for this is to debit Cash \$20 000 and credit Capital \$20 000. To record the same entry in a computerized system, you tell the computer:

1. the date
2. the account number to debit
3. the account number to credit

This is slightly different from a manual system because you have to give account numbers instead of account names. As long as the account numbers are correct, the entry will be recorded properly by the computer. Here is the computer general journal after we have given it the date, the two account numbers, and an explanation.

GENERAL JOURNAL

TRAN	DATE	PARTICULARS	ACC	DEBIT	CREDIT
1	Jan. 1	Cash	101	20 000.00	
		Capital	301		20 000.00
Explanation: Owner invested.					

This journal entry is almost identical to a manual entry except for the column TRAN which numbers all of the accounting transactions, and the ACC column which we know as PR (Posting Reference). ACC stands for the account number.

Once the general journal entry has been keyed into the computer memory, the computer has all the information it needs to post to the ledger, automatically. You will note here that if the data is entered incorrectly, errors in the output will result. If the accounting software is well written, it will provide an error correction feature that is easy to use. One of the ways to do this is by a user prompt on the screen. Sometimes the software has small symbols on the screen to help you, and has a correction square that you can select if something goes wrong. If you make a mistake, you point to the correction square, and the software takes you through a correction routine. The tremendous advantage here is that, if you made a mistake manually, you have to change the posting, the account balance, the trial balance, and both the financial statements. If you made a mistake with an entry on the computer, it will correct all of these steps automatically. It changes the journal entry, the ledger account, the trial balance, and then produces a new set of financial statements. If you have made lots of errors so far in learning accounting, you will want to see what a time-saver this computer feature is. Once we have entered all the journal entries into the computer, it will post automatically to the accounts in the general ledger. We will see this in Section 16.4.

16.4 The General Ledger

The general ledger produced by a computerized accounting software program is reproduced on page 396. Again it is very similar to a manual account in terms of setup. You will note again that the TRAN column is present to help the computer keep track of accounting entries by number. And the balance notation column, that is, the column that tells us if the balance is debit or credit is slightly different from the 3-column accounts with which you are used to working.

Once you have the accounts on the computer screen, you can have them printed on the computer printer if you need a hard copy. Most businesses will take a hard copy of the system on a regular basis, for two reasons:

1. It is easier to read the hard copy.
2. It gives a **backup copy** in case something goes wrong with the computer.

GENERAL LEDGER

CASH 101

DATE	TRAN	DEBIT	CREDIT	BALANCE	D/C
Jan. 1	1	20 000.00		20 000.00	Dr

CAPITAL 301

DATE	TRAN	DEBIT	CREDIT	BALANCE	D/C
Jan. 1	1		20 000.00	20 000.00	Cr

One final note before we leave the computer general ledger. You will see that the account numbers used by the computer differ from the ones we have used so far in this text. This is normal. The charts of account used by different businesses will vary widely. The important point to remember is that there must be a pattern to the chart of accounts. Here is a typical numbering system for a chart of accounts in a software package:

CHART OF ACCOUNTS

100-199	Assets
200-299	Liabilities
300-301	Capital
400-499	Revenue
500-599	Purchases
600-699	Expenses

16.5 The Trial Balance

The trial balance produced by computer systems will depend on the computer and the software. The example below is almost identical to the trial balances that you have prepared so far in this text. The only difference is that the computer prepares its trial balance automatically.

T. Cervini
Trial Balance
January 1, 19 ___

Acct #	Account Name	Debit	Credit
101	Petty Cash	$ 50.00	
102	Bank	950.00	
103	Accounts Receivable	1 000.00	
150	Delivery Van	18 000.00	
201	Bank Loan		$1 000.00
202	Accounts Payable		3 000.00
301	T. Cervini, Capital		
302	T. Cevini, Drawings	1 000.00	
		$21 000.00	$21 000.00

At this point let us go into a discussion of the main feature of a computerized general ledger package, namely, the fact that the program for a good general ledger package is *menu driven*.

16.6 Menu

The main advantages of processing accounting work on the computer are of course, the speed at which the computer works, the fact that it is programmed to perform many steps like posting automatically, and finally the fact that you work from a **menu** on the screen. Here is an example. You are looking at the main menu of a general ledger accounting package.

GENERAL LEDGER

88-01-02 MAIN MENU Version 2.5

Select the action you would like to perform:

1.See Chart of Accounts
2.Journalize Transactions
3.View the Ledger
4.Correct G/L accounts
5.Prepare Closing Entries
6.View all Reports
7.Print Reports

Enter the number of the action you wish 7

The main menu is important because it has to provide all the options you will want to use with the software. And as you can see, it has to be as **user-friendly** as possible. The main menu above simply asks you to type in one number, depending on the accounting action you want to perform. Let's assume that you have done all of your accounting work and you are ready to have the computer print out the set of financial statements. If you select the number 7 you will probably get another menu on the screen. This second menu is called a sub-menu and might look like this:

```
7. PRINT BALANCE SHEET
MENU
Select the action you would like to perform:
1.Print Income Statement
2.Print Balance Sheet
Enter the number of the action you wish 2
```

This sub-menu can also result in a sub-sub-menu if you select the number 1. As we know, there are two styles of balance sheet, a report form and an account form. Therefore, the computer has been programmed to give you a choice of these two, and it appears in the form of another menu, like this:

```
2. PRINT BALANCE SHEET
MENU
Select the action you would like to perform:
1.Print Report Form Balance Sheet
2.Print Account Form Balance Sheet
Enter the number of the action you wish 1
```

Once you get to this point, you can assume that the computer is finally ready to print out a balance sheet in the format you desire.

16.7 Tree Structure

It will be easy for you to operate menu-driven software if you realize that software is often set up in the form of something called a **tree** structure. The software we have been talking about for the general ledger might be set up like this:

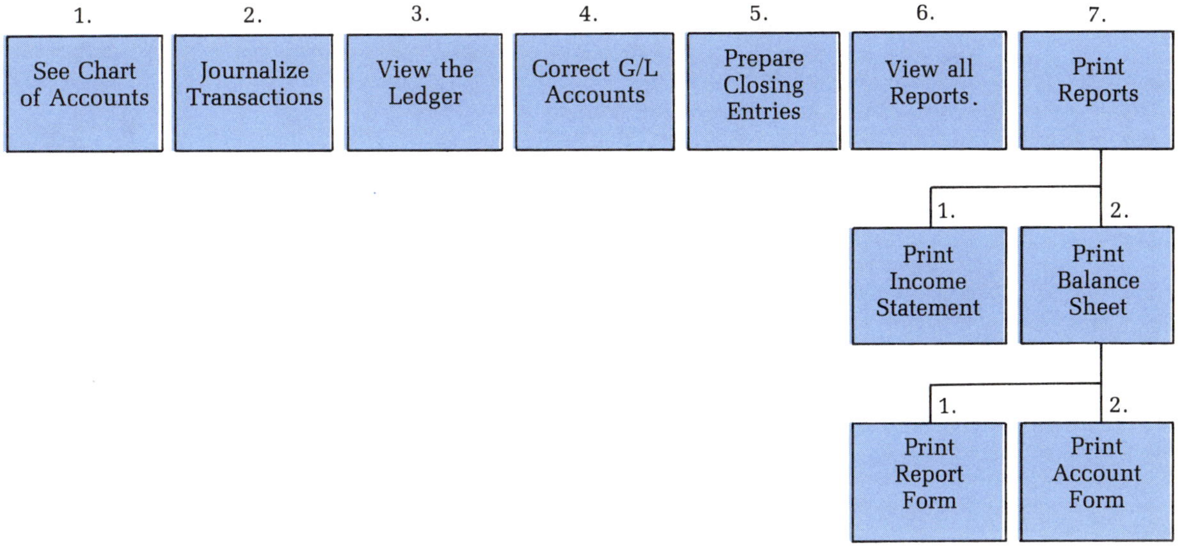

What you are doing when you use this accounting software is to work your way down through the branches of the tree to get to the function you want. Each of the branches has its own set of options as well, but the important thing is to have a visual picture of how you are climbing down the tree to the accounting operation you want. There will always be a quick way to get to the top of the tree because you do not want to have to climb back through each step that you took going down. Usually there will be a prompt that you can select to get back to the main menu quickly.

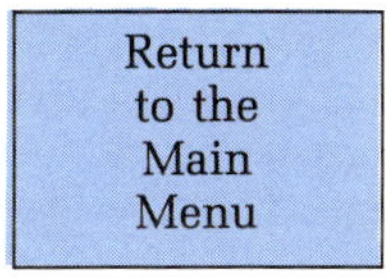

16.8 Other Accounting Software

There are many packages of computer accounting now available for business, other than the general ledger one we have studied briefly here. There are programs that handle accounts receivable and accounts payable, write cheques, prepare depreciation schedules, keep track of fixed assets, and produce mortgage schedules (Figure 16-2). It is only important for you at this point to realize the impact that computers are having in the field of accounting today, and to have an understanding of this impact. The only other thing you need to know is the use of spreadsheets in accounting. We will do this in Section 16.9.

Figure 16-2
Computers have influenced many aspects of accounting. They enable many accounting functions to be performed more quickly and easily than by conventional methods.

16.9 Spreadsheets

Spreadsheet software is fairly useful in accounting if you use it for specialized functions. First, let's explore the concept of spreadsheets and see what they are.

A **spreadsheet** is a columnar table that divides your computer screen into rows and columns. Usually when you first put the program on the screen, it will ask you how many rows and columns you want to divide the screen up into. Let's assume we responded this way:

How many rows? <u>8</u>

How many columns? <u>5</u>

The spreadsheet program will then put a matrix or grid on the screen that has 8 rows and 5 columns for data:

	0	1	2	3	4
A					
B					
C					
D					
E					
F					
G					
H					

Notice that in this example the rows are lettered and the columns are numbered. This is done so that you can refer to specific locations in the grid. Each location is usually called a **cell.** Therefore, we say cell Al, cell C3, cell H4, etc. Once the grid is set up you can put both alphabetic and numeric data into the cells. The grid below is a Sales Summary that has been set up on a spreadsheet.

	0	1	2	3	4
A					
B		DAISY FRESH CLEANERS			
C		SALES SUMMARY			
D			SALES	PERCENT	
E		WOMEN'S	30 000	60	
F		MEN'S	18 000	36	
G		CHILDREN'S	2 000	4	
H			50 000	100	

When the grid has been completed on the screen, it can be sent to the computer printer. The printout on page 402 shows you what this table looks like when printed.

Figure 16-3
A printed sales table

DAISY FRESH CLEANERS

SALES SUMMARY

	SALES	PERCENT
WOMEN'S	30 000	60
MEN'S	18 000	36
CHILDREN'S	2 000	4
	50 000	100

This summary is developed by entering all of the data onto the grid on the screen. The grid can be saved onto a computer disk and recalled again another time to be used over with new data. The real advantage of the spreadsheet is that you can *program* it to do the mathematics (or accounting) work for you. In the Sales Summary above, the spreadsheet was programmed to:

1. add the 1988 column of sales
2. find each type of cleaning as a percent of the total
3. add up the percent column

The programming of the spreadsheet is usually not very complicated. To get the Sales Summary table above we give it three sets of comands. Take a look at them and see if they make sense.

1. Add the 1988 column of sales. SUM (E2-G2)
2. Find each type of cleaning as a percent of the total. INT (E2/H2)
3. Add up the percent column. SUM (E3-G3)

Explanation

SUM (E2-G2) tells the computer to add all the cells from E2 down to G2, i.e., add E2 + F2 + G2

INT (E2/H2) says to divide the contents of cell E2 by cell H2 and print the integer (whole number)

SUM (E3-G3) adds the cells E3, F3, and G3

The best part of a spreadsheet is that once it is programmed, all you have to do is push one button on the computer and the entire spreadsheet is recalculated for you. Assume for example that WOMEN'S sales were 32 000 instead of 30 000, we could put in the new figure and the whole spreadsheet would be recalculated automatically by the computer.

	0	1	2	3	4
A					
B		DAISY FRESH CLEANERS			
C		SALES SUMMARY			
D			SALES	PERCENT	
E		WOMEN'S	32 000	60	
F		MEN'S	18 000	36	
G		CHILDREN'S	2 000	4	
H			52 000	100	

There are many applications in accounting for spreadsheets. A payroll journal could be set up on a spreadsheet format. The only data that would have to be placed on the spreadsheet is each employee's name and gross pay, as shown below. The deductions and all of the other calculations can be programmed.

	0	1	2	3	4	5
A			PAYROLL JOURNAL			
B		GROSS	DEDUCTIONS			NET
C	NAME	PAY	TAX	CPP	UI	PAY
D	ADAMS	400.00	?	?	?	?
E	BACON	350.00	?	?	?	?
F	CRISP	580.00	?	?	?	?
G		?	?	?	?	?

Once the payroll journal is set up, these amounts can be calculated automatically by the computer:

1. All the *Tax* deductions.
2. The deductions for *Canada Pension Plan*.
3. *Unemployment Insurance* deductions.
4. The *net pay* for each employee.
5. The *totals* for all columns.

After the payroll journal is set up with all of the programs put into memory, the operator or accounting clerk only has to hit one button to have this table appear on the screen:

	0	1	2	3	4	5
A			PAYROLL JOURNAL			
B		GROSS	DEDUCTIONS			NET
C	NAME	PAY	TAX	CPP	UI	PAY
D	ADAMS	400.00	80.00	6.40	5.60	308.00
E	BACON	350.00	70.00	5.60	4.90	269.50
F	CRISP	580.00	116.00	9.28	8.12	446.60
G		1 330.00	266.00	21.28	18.62	1 024.10

When the table is printed out on the computer, the payroll journal will look like this:

		PAYROLL JOURNAL			
	GROSS		DEDUCTIONS		NET
NAME	PAY	TAX	CPP	UI	PAY
ADAMS	400.00	80.00	6.40	5.60	308.00
BACON	350.00	70.00	5.60	4.90	269.50
CRISP	580.00	116.00	9.28	8.12	446.60
	1 330.00	266.00	21.28	18.62	1 024.10

16.10 Summary

Accounting has been using computers for a number of years now, and it will continue to be an important part of this type of work. Even at this early stage in the study of accounting, it is important to know that there is software, like general ledger packages, that can be used even by small businesses. In addition, software programs like spreadsheets will continue to be a useful accounting tool.

Check out the chapter objectives! You should be able to

1. know why it is an advantage to use a computer for accounting;
2. see some similarities and differences in manual and computer accounting reports; and
3. know some useful applications of spreadsheet software to accounting topics.

Dictionary of Terms

Backup Copy An extra copy of a computer file or program, usually kept on a separate disk or in the form of a printout.

Cell An area on a spreadsheet where a column and a row intersect—a storage area for a name or number.

Menu A list of choices for a user to follow on the computer screen.

Spreadsheet Software that divides the screen up into a grid-like pattern for ease of entering data and programmed instructions.

Tree Structure The form by which many menu-driven programs are stored in computer memory.

User-Friendly A term which indicates that a piece of computer software is relatively easy to use.

Review Questions

1. Name four pieces of computer software that have been developed for accounting.
2. What do the codes TRAN and ACC mean?
3. If you are entering data into a computer with accounting software and make a mistake, what would you do then? Explain fully.
4. Give two reasons why users take hard copies of reports fairly often.
5. If you were looking at some accounting software in a store and the salesperson said it was "menu driven," what does the salesperson mean?
6. Explain the term "tree structure."
7. Define the word "spreadsheet" in your own words.
8. A practical spreadsheet is shown below. Name the three parts indicated.

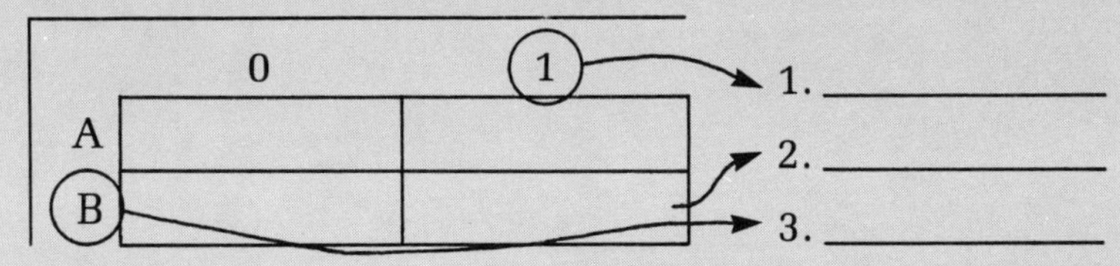

9. Look at the spreadsheet below. It's a payroll summary for a garage. What parts of the spreadsheet have probably been *programmed* for the computer to do?

	0	1	2	3
A		PAYROLL SUMMARY		
B				GROSS
C	NAME	HOURS	RATE	PAY
D	ARNOLD	40	5.00	200.00
E	BREWSTER	38	6.00	228.00
F	COOPER	40	7.00	280.00
G				708.00

10. Why is the spreadsheet a useful piece of software to use for accounting work?
11. Can a person work in accounting without knowing anything about computers? Explain.

Practice Set III

Objectives

This final practice set is to be used in conjunction with a general ledger computerized accounting system. The practice set involves the records for a summer business called *Student Landscaping*. When this practice set is completed you will be able to

1. name the various hardware components of your computer system;
2. create a computerized set of general ledger accounts for Student Landscaping;
3. journalize an opening entry and transaction entries for the business;
4. obtain a printed copy of the computer general ledger; and
5. set up a spreadsheet to record the payroll for the business.

Overview

Student Landscaping is a small business that was just started up by PJ Murray. PJ is a recent community college graduate who majored in horticulture at a small college in a city of about 35 000 people. The employees of his business are all college students with an interest in landscape design.

Step 1: Create a General Ledger Chart of Accounts

Your first objective is to set up a general ledger chart of accounts for PJ's business. Once you have started your general ledger computer package, you should see a main menu similar to the following:

GENERAL LEDGER

MAIN MENU

Select the action you would like to perform:

1.See Chart of Accounts
2.Journalize Transactions
3.View the Ledger
4.Correct G/L accounts
5.Prepare Closing Entries
6.View all Reports
7.Print Reports

Enter the number of the action you wish ___

Choose option number 1 so that you can create a chart of accounts for Student Landscaping. You will need the following accounts to complete the practice set:

Assets
Cash
Bank
Accounts Receivable
Gardening Equipment
Truck

Liabilities
Bank Loan
Accounts Payable

Owner's Equity
PJ Murray, Capital
PJ Murray, Drawings

Revenue
Landscaping Income

Expenses
Advertising Expense
Bank Charges
Bookkeeping Expense
Loan Interest Expense
Miscellaneous Expense
Supplies Expense
Telephone Expense
Truck Expense
Wages Expense

Once you have entered all of the accounts in the computer and the computer has assigned numbers to the accounts, ask for a listing of the accounts. You will probably be prompted for this by a sub-menu:

GENERAL LEDGER

CHART OF ACCOUNTS

Select the action you would like to perform:
1.Print out Chart of Accounts
2.Print out a Worksheet
3.Print out a detailed report
4.Return to Main Menu

Enter the number of the action you wish __7__

Select the appropriate choice and obtain your computer list of accounts.

Step 2: Journalizing the Transactions

At this point, we want to enter some transactions into the ledger. Go back to the main menu and select the option that lets you journalize transactions. In the model we are using, that would be option 2.

GENERAL LEDGER

MAIN MENU

Select the action you would like to perform:
1.See Chart of Accounts
2.Journalize Transactions
3.View the Ledger
4.Correct G/L accounts
5.Prepare Closing Entries
6.View all Reports
7.Print Reports

Enter the number of the action you wish __2__

The transactions for Student Landscaping that we want to journalize are all given in source document form. Look at the document and the description underneath, and select the accounts that let you journalize these into your computer general ledger. The transactions cover only one week, just enough to give you a brief idea how the computerized accounting package works.

Student Landscaping
NAME OF ACCOUNT

DEPOSITED ON THE DATE STAMPED HEREON
THE AMOUNT OF $ 25000 —

GREEN CARD BRANCH NO.

...NO. 6179

THE TORONTO-DOMINION BANK

June 1 19__

Student Landscaping
NAME

P.J. Murray
DEPOSITED BY

GREEN CARD BRANCH NO. | 4442 | ACCOUNT NO. 6179

CURRENCY		
COIN		
CHEQUES OR COUPONS (List on Reverse if Necessary)	$25000	—
TOTAL		
LESS Received in Cash		
(Please sign in presence of Teller)		
AMOUNT OF DEPOSIT $	$25000	—

NO. 1	DATE June 1, 19_
BALANCE FORWARD	$25,000.—
CHEQUE TO	Klopp Motors (Truck)
CHEQUE AMOUNT	$14,600.—
BALANCE	10 400.—
DEPOSIT	NIL
BALANCE	$10400.—

Plant Supply 3220 Winnabago Rd., Winnipeg, Manitoba L19 2K0 217-6598

ORDER NO. 3670
DATE June 1, 19
INVOICE NO. P.S. - 666
TERMS Net 30

SOLD TO Student Landscaping
100 Birch Ave.
Redwood, Manitoba
M4N 1P8

SHIP TO

DESCRIPTION	QUANTITY	UNIT PRICE	AMOUNT
Birch Trees	4		$ 160.00
Red Maple	3		$ 75.00
			$ 235.00
Term: net 30 days			

PURCHASE INVOICE

NO. 2	DATE June 2, 19__
BALANCE FORWARD	$10400. —
CHEQUE TO	Redwood Gazette
	(Advertising)
CHEQUE AMOUNT	$ 120. —
BALANCE	10280. —
DEPOSIT	NIL
BALANCE	$10280. —

NO. 3	DATE June 2, 19__
BALANCE FORWARD	$10280. —
CHEQUE TO	Bell Canada
	(Telephone)
CHEQUE AMOUNT	$ 85.00
BALANCE	10195. —
DEPOSIT	NIL
BALANCE	$10195. —

Student Landscaping

100 Birch Ave.,
Redwood, Manitoba
M4N 1P8 679-4321

To: Mrs. Rae Rose
45 Huron St. N.
Redwood, Man.

June 3, 19__

Prepare flower beds at new home - landscaping including shrubbery (as per quote)

Total: $ 145.00

Please remit full payment within 30 days.

Sales Invoice

NO. 4	DATE June 3, 19__
BALANCE FORWARD	$ 10195. —
CHEQUE TO	C. Wells
	(Bookkeeping)
CHEQUE AMOUNT	$ 200. —
BALANCE	9995. —
DEPOSIT	NIL
BALANCE	$ 9995. —

NO. 5	DATE June 4, 19__
BALANCE FORWARD	$ 9995. —
CHEQUE TO Grand+Toy (Office Supplies)	
CHEQUE AMOUNT	$ 278.50
BALANCE	9716.50
DEPOSIT	NiL
BALANCE	$ 9716.50

Student Landscaping

100 Birch Ave.,
Redwood, Manitoba
M4N 1P8 679-4321

To: Mr. Elmer Dynes
28 Main Street
Redwood, Man.

June 5, 19__

Adding pro-soil mix to existing gardens, lawn spray treatment.

Total: $ 152.00

Please remit full payment within 30 days.

Sales Invoice

DC Desert Chemical
1340 Portage Avenue, Winnipeg, Manitoba L3M 1N4 629-8754

PURCHASE INVOICE

ORDER NO. 550
DATE June 6, 19
INVOICE NO. 1126 DC
TERMS Net 30

SOLD TO

DESCRIPTION	QUANTITY	UNIT PRICE	AMOUNT
Pro-Mix	8 bags		$ 72.00
Spray-kleen	3 bags		$ 66.00
			$ 138.00

Shamrock Industries
56 Main Street, Brandon, Manitoba
M3P 2S5 752-0953

PURCHASE INVOICE

ORDER NO. 000135
DATE June 7, 19
INVOICE NO.
TERMS Net 30

SOLD TO

DESCRIPTION	QUANTITY	UNIT PRICE	AMOUNT
Speedel	12 bags	$ 19.95 ea.	$ 239.40
Total			$ 239.40
Terms: net 30 days			

NO. 6	DATE June 6, 19—
BALANCE FORWARD	$9716.50
CHEQUE TO Plant Supply	
(June 1 Invoice)	
CHEQUE AMOUNT	$ 235.—
BALANCE	9481.50
DEPOSIT	NIL
BALANCE	$9481.50

Student Landscaping
NAME OF ACCOUNT

DEPOSITED ON THE DATE STAMPED HEREON
THE AMOUNT OF $ 125 —

GREEN CARD BRANCH NO.

ACCOUNT NO. 4442 6179

THE TORONTO-DOMINION BANK

June 6 19

Student Landscaping
NAME

P.J. Murray
DEPOSITED BY

GREEN CARD BRANCH NO.

ACCOUNT NO. 4442 6179

CURRENCY		
COIN		
CHEQUES OR COUPONS (List on Reverse if Necessary)	$125	—
TOTAL		
LESS Received in Cash		
(Please sign in presence of Teller) AMOUNT OF DEPOSIT $	$ 125	—

Step 3: Print Out an Income Statement and a Balance Sheet

Once you have entered these transactions, go back to the main menu and select the option that allows you to print out reports, namely, an income statement and a balance sheet. In our sample menu, this is #7.

GENERAL LEDGER

MAIN MENU

Select the action you would like to perform:

1.See Chart of Accounts
2.Journalize Transactions
3.View the Ledger
4.Correct G/L accounts
5.Prepare Closing Entries
6.View all Reports
7.Print Reports

Enter the number of the action you wish ____

Step 4: Prepare the Weekly Payroll Journal

Since the first week of business is over for Student Landscaping, it is time to prepare the weekly payroll journal. This can be done on a spreadsheet. Load your spreadsheet program into the computer. The grid, or matrix, you get will look something like this:

	O	1	2	3	4
A					
B					
C					

Set up the following payroll journal on the spreadsheet and *program* the spreadsheet to calculate:

1. Gross Pay (Hours x Rate of Pay)
2. Income Tax at 20% of Gross Pay
3. Canada Pension Plan at 1.6% of Gross Pay
4. Unemployment Insurance at 1.4% of Gross Pay
5. Net Pay (Gross Pay – Deductions)

Payroll Journal

				Deductions			
Name	**Hrs.**	**Rate**	**Gross Pay**	**CPP**	**UI**	**Tax**	**Net Pay**
S. Allin	40	6.10	xxx.xx	x.xx	x.xx	xx.xx	xxx.xx
J. Larke	38	6.50	xxx.xx	x.xx	x.xx	xx.xx	xxx.xx
P. Ming	40	6.10	xxx.xx	x.xx	x.xx	xx.xx	xxx.xx
I. Zacks	40	6.00	xxx.xx	x.xx	x.xx	xx.xx	xxx.xx

Produce a printed copy of your journal on the computer printer.

Chapter 17 Careers

Objectives

At the end of this chapter you will be able to

1. know the names and job descriptions of the three professional accounting designations;
2. test yourself about seeking a career in accounting work;
3. see how important accounting is to Business courses at the community college level; and
4. have an idea about the kinds of jobs available in accounting for high school and college graduates.

17.1 Introduction

There are many careers in bookkeeping and accounting that a high school student can aspire to. This chapter will talk about some of these careers. It will also discuss the educational requirements of some of these jobs and the places where students can look for more information about careers in accounting.

Figure 17-1
There is a wide range of careers for people who have accounting skills and qualifications.

17.2 What Do Accountants Do?

Accountants have a variety of job prospects. Here is a list of some of their roles:

- Plan and administer accounting systems for government and business.
- Assist in preparing budgets and cash flow analysis statements.
- Advise on financial problems for all sizes of business.
- Specialize in working in certain accounting areas such as:

Accounts Receivable	Accounts Payable
Cash Receipts	Payroll
Cash Disbursements	Fixed Assets

- Prepare or review tax returns; advise on tax matters.
- Arrange credit for customers; credit collections and reportings.
- Analyze and interpret financial statements.

17.3 Educational Requirements

There are three professional degrees that students can aspire to in accounting:

Chartered Accountant C.A.

Students wishing to become a C.A. will have to graduate from a secondary school at a level that will prepare them for university. Each student must then take 3–4 years of a university degree program, plus a program of 3–5 years with the *Institute of Chartered Accountants of Ontario.*

All applicants must work with a C.A. firm for a minimum of 2 years as they study with the Institute.

Certified General Accountant C.G.A.

Obtaining a career as a C.G.A. requires graduation from a secondary school plus completion of a 5-year program with the *Certified General Accountants Association of Ontario*. Students must be employed in an accounting job for at least 2 years while studying for the C.G.A.

These courses may be taken either by lecture or by correspondence courses.

Certified Management Accountant C.M.A.

Students wishing to become a C.M.A. will have to graduate from secondary school and finish a 5-8 year program with the *Society of Management Accountants of Ontario.* Students must be employed for 4 years in an accounting job while studying for this degree.

These courses may be taken either by lecture or by correspondence courses.

17.4 Chartered Accountants

In Canada we have large national accounting firms such as Clarkson Gordon, Price Waterhouse, and Touche Ross & Co.

We also have many smaller accounting firms, some of which are province-wide, some regional, and some with only one office.

A quick look at the yellow pages of your phone book under the heading ''Accountants-Public'' will show you how many firms are in your area. It should be noted that a C.A., or Chartered Accountant, refers only to those people who have passed the exams of an Institute of Chartered Accountants. A **C.A.** is a professional accountant, someone with special expertise. Some people work in jobs where they do accounting work and

Figure 17-2
A Chartered Accountant's firm

call themselves accountants. In the strictest sense they are not professional accountants if they have not earned a professional designation such as a C.A., a C.M.A., or a C.G.A. degree.

The photo shows a C.A. firm in a small city. This particular firm happens to have many offices across Canada. The person who runs one of these offices is usually a "partner" in the firm. Professional accounting firms are usually business partnerships. A large firm might have 50 or 60 partners. The organization chart for a C.A. office might look something like this:

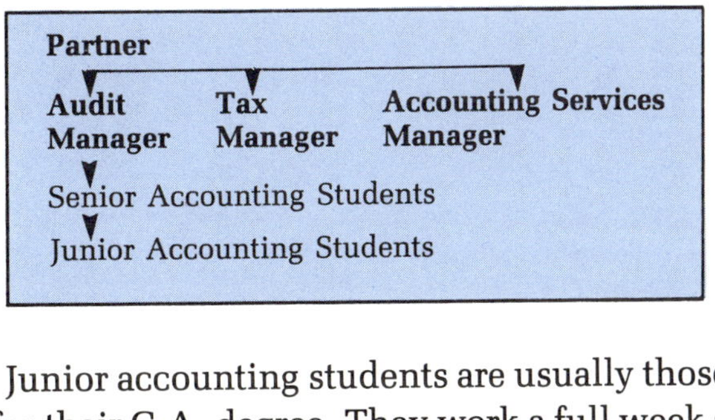

Junior accounting students are usually those people who are studying for their C.A. degree. They work a full week at a C.A. firm and study at night working toward their C.A. exams. Once they have obtained their C.A. degree, they will aspire to work their way up the C.A. firm, eventually to become a partner in the firm.

The following questions and answers are taken from a recent pamphlet published by the Institute of Chartered Accountants. They will give you a better idea of the roles of a Chartered Accountant.

Q: What is a Chartered Accountant?

A: Basically a C.A. is an individual known for her/his knowledge of such areas as financial accounting, auditing, taxation, management accounting, and finance. Through education and experience, the C.A. has developed objectivity, independence, technical competence, and high ethical standards.

Q: What are the opportunities for women in the C.A. profession?

A: Traditionally, most members of the C.A. profession have been men. Although women constitute less than 10% of the current membership, they make up more than 25% of the student body. The results of the Uniform Final Examination show that women are doing very well.

Q: Could you discuss some of the personal benefits of becoming a C.A.?

A: There can be impressive monetary benefits, of course, but, right from the start, you benefit as an individual. The experience you gain from working with people and situations in diverse industries teaches you organization and timing. It also develops your professional judgement. You will find that this decision-making ability will make you a valuable member of your community. All types of organizations — sports, charitable, cultural — will be looking for your knowledge and your assistance.

Figure 17-3
Women play an important role in the accounting profession.

Q: Can you discuss some fields of concentration?

A: You might want to develop in a number of areas such as data processing, bankruptcy, management consulting, or tax. You could be involved in some accounting services, auditing of company books, a fraud investigation, or preparation of special reports.

17.5 Certified General Accountant

The second professional designation for accountants that we should study is a **C.G.A.,** or Certified General Accountant. A C.G.A. is a person who has a job in accounting and gains working experience as he/she studies for a professional degree. A C.G.A. is an accountant who, for the most part, finds a job in business or government. The work will likely involve a lot of in-house accounting, and a C.G.A. will work for a specific company during most of his/her accounting career. Certified General Accountants could start in a junior accounting position and then work their way up through the management ranks to be a company Controller, Treasurer, Vice-President of Finance, or even the President. There is a whole range of accounting jobs in industry for people with an accounting background.

A Chartered Accountant working for a public C.A. firm will spend a lot of time travelling from one business to the next doing *auditing* work — checking books for fairness and accuracy. A C.G.A. will probably spend a career with one company or with one of the levels of government. In addition, a person who earns a C.A., C.G.A., or C.M.A. will have mobility if he/she decides to try to change jobs, or to change from one company to another.

17.6 Certified Management Accountant

The third professional designation for accountants is a **C.M.A.** or Certified Management Accountant. Until 1986 a C.M.A. was referred to as an R.I.A. or Registered Industrial Accountant. The designation was changed because the role of the C.M.A. was changing from an accountant who used to be involved mostly in cost accounting, to an accountant with expanding roles. C.M.A.s are still doing cost accounting but they have moved into a whole new sphere of management accounting including costing, taxation, financial analysis, financial reporting, etc. Like C.G.A.s, C.M.A.s are usually employed out of high school in an accounting position. They work during the day and study at night. Courses are taken by attending lectures at different centres across Canada, or by correspondence if students do not live close to a lecture centre.

Once a student has achieved a professional designation, such as the C.M.A., many doors to other careers will open up. One final note before we leave the area of professional accounting — the exams to become a professional accountant are not easy. Failure rates are high and the workload is very demanding. Section 17.8 will look at accounting and community colleges.

17.7 Test Yourself

Here's a little quiz to test if you have what it takes to choose a career in accounting. Read each of the questions in the quiz to the left, and give yourself 3, 2, or 1 point(s) using the scoring guideline to the right.

1) Do I like to work with numbers?
2) Can I do simple arithmetic?
3) Can I add a column of figures in my head?
4) Do I enjoy working by myself without others around?
5) Can I speak and write English fairly well?
6) Do I know how to add, subract, multiply, and divide using a calculator?
7) Do I mind using the phone?
8) Have I enjoyed the accounting course I'm taking this year in school?
9) Is my work fairly neat, and are my figures easy to read?
10) Can I stick with a problem in accounting until it's balanced?

"3" If you read the question and say "YES, THAT IS REALLY ME," score 3.

"2" If you read the question and say, "THAT'S ME," score only 2 points.

"1" If your reply is "THAT'S SORT OF ME," score 1.

Add up your score, and check the box below:

Accountant's Scorecard

25-30

Go for it — you love working with numbers.

15-24

Well, maybe — give it some thought.

0-14

Time to discuss career options with others.

17.8 Accounting & Community Colleges

The following report from Employment and Immigration Canada may provide some interesting reading for you. The table below shows the results of a survey of graduates of Business courses at Community Colleges, two years after the students graduated. Note that *clerical occupations* has the highest percentage of employed graduates at 19.3%. Ten percent of graduates are working as bookkeepers and accounting clerks. These are high figures.

Table 17-1: ***Occupation of Community College Graduates in Business, Management, and Commerce***

Occupation of Graduate Two Years After Graduation	Per Cent Distribution
Career Program	
Clerical and related occupations	
Bookkeepers and accounting clerks	10.0
Secretaries and stenographers	3.6
Tellers and cashiers	2.9
Electronic data-processing equipment operators	1.4
Stock clerks and related occupations	1.4
General office clerks	1.4
Managerial, administrative and related occupations	
Sales and advertising management occupations	5.7
Accountants, auditors and other financial officers	5.7
Financial management occupations	1.4

If you scan down the list, you will see that there are other careers where accounting training would be very useful, if not necessary, for example, *tellers and cashiers, general office clerks* and finally *financial management occupations, accountants, auditors, and other financial officers*. If we add up all of the figures, then 33.5% of Business graduates from community colleges have found employment in accounting-related fields. This is encouraging news!

We should look at one more table from Employment and Immigration Canada to see if we can project accounting needs into the next decade. The same report provides the data below. In summary, it indicates that there will be job openings in accounting in the foreseeable future, about 42 000 jobs from 1985–1992. These will occur because of people who retire or leave accounting jobs, and due to increased needs in the field of accounting. Some knowledge of computers will probably be essential.

Table 17-2: ***Employment Trends in Accounting***

Average salaries, full-time employed two years after graduation (1984)			
Community college: $18,000	University: $24,700		
Employment trends (000s)			
1985:149.6	1992:170.2		Change: 20.6
Estimated attrition due to labour force withdrawals (000s)			1985-92: 21.7
	Total requirements (000s)		42.3
Sex composition (1981)	**All occ.**	**Age composition (1981)**	**All occ.**
Females: 31%	40%	Under 25 years: 6%	25%
Males: 69%	60%	Over 54 years: 9%	12%

17.9 Community College Courses

Students taking an introductory accounting course, such as this one, may proceed to a community college. As an additional incentive students who take accounting in high school, and do well, are sometimes given credit off college courses during the first or second semester. If you are thinking of a career in some aspect of accounting, it would be wise to think about college before entering the job market.

Figure 17-4
Want to pursue an accounting career? Further study after high school may be the best way to fulfill your plans.

The following information is taken from the calendar at a community college and is typical of community college courses. It shows important pieces of information that are useful to know if you have any thoughts at all about going further in the study of accounting.

High School	**College Year 1**	**College Year 2**	
Secondary School Diploma →	First Year is common to most Management Management Studies Programs →	Accounting →	College Diploma
or		or Data Analysis →	
Mature Student →		or Data Processing →	
		or Finance →	
		or Purchasing →	

Usually, students are expected to have graduated from high school before they are accepted at community college. The phrase "mature student" refers to someone who has been out of school for a period of time. Such people are given special consideration in being admitted to college. It is something you may want to consider if you decide to work after high school and then later decide to go to college. It can be done!

Figure 17-5
Community colleges offer courses that help students prepare for a career in the business world.

In year one at college, most courses are shared with students from other fields of study. Here is an example of first year courses offered at one community college:

Table 17-3: ***Typical Program of Study at Community College in Accounting***

Semester 1 courses	Hrs/Week
Three hours English elective	3.0
Principles of Accounting	4.0
Business Data Processing	4.0
Economics	3.0
Finance	3.0
Introduction to Marketing	3.0
Total =	20.0

Many community college courses in accounting are two years long, and are designed to prepare students for work in an accounting environment. Students of such courses will be able to handle routine accounting functions upon graduation, and will be able to fill supervisory roles in this field fairly quickly. They will be able to find employment in a variety of accounting positions in business and industry, public accounting, and government departments. Graduates from college may also go on to enrol in C.G.A. or C.M.A. programs. Graduates who do this will usually receive credits for some of their college courses, thus cutting down the time required to earn a professional designation.

It is important to note that accounting is a basic part of most Business programs at the college level. Look at the programs on page 427 to see that there is an accounting component in each one.

The point of all of this information is that if anyone is going to pursue a career in Business, it is advisable to have a basic understanding of accounting. Even though you will not be working directly on accounting, you may be analyzing or making decisions using accounting data and you will want to understand it as much as possible.

17.10 Accounting Jobs

There are many accounting jobs which exist in business and industry. Take a look at the help wanted ads in your local newspaper, and try to decide which jobs can be handled with high school training in accounting, which require community college graduation, and which require a professional designation, such as C.A., C.G.A., or C.M.A. As you check

Table 17-4: **Accounting Components in Community College Courses**

	Semester			
Program	**1**	**2**	**3**	**4**
Marketing	accounting applications	accounting applications		
Finance	principles of accounting	principles of accounting	management accounting	
Purchasing	principles of accounting	principles of accounting		
Tourism				basic accounting
Data Processing	principles of accounting	principles of accounting		
Medical Secretary			accounting secretarial	accounting medical

through the ads, look for key phrases that recur, such as ''communication and organizational skills necessary,'' ''computer an asset,'' and ''applicant must be a hard worker.''

17.11 Summary

This chapter has been designed to show you that there are several ways a student interested in accounting can pursue a career in accounting. You can aspire to be a Chartered Accountant only if you have a university degree. But you may become a Certified Management Accountant or a Certified General Accountant with further studies after high school. The job market seems to indicate that there are still jobs for high school grads in bookkeeping and in special accounting areas such as accounts receivable, accounts payable, payroll, credit and collections, and in computerized accounting. Students who take a beginning course in accounting can aspire to solid careers in accounting with a little direction, and as usual, some hard work.

If you have met the chapter objectives, you should be able to

1. know the names and job descriptions of the three professional accounting designations;
2. test yourself about a career in accounting work;
3. see how important accounting is to Business courses at the community college level; and
4. have an idea about the kinds of jobs available in accounting for high school and college graduates.

Dictionary of Terms

C.A. Chartered Accountant

C.G.A. Certified General Accountant

C.M.A. Certified Management Accountant

Review Questions

1. For what do the initials C.A., C.G.A. and C.M.A. mean?
2. Name six areas of accounting that a person can specialize in as a career.
3. Of the three professional accounting designations, which one requires that you go to university?
4. There are two forms of study that can be used to earn a C.G.A. or C.M.A. degree. What are the two forms?
5. Indicate if these statements about chartered accounting firms are **True** or **False**.
   (a) Anyone who works in accounting may use the initials C.A. after his/her name.
   (b) C.A. firms are controlled by a group of "partners."
   (c) The number of women who are chartered accountants in Canada is increasing.
6. Accountants sometimes specialize in certain fields of accounting. Name five different fields.
7. How does a C.G.A. differ from a C.A.?
8. (a) What was the old name for a C.M.A.?
   (b) In what type of work did C.M.A.s used to specialize?
   (c) What types of accounting roles do C.M.A.s have now?
9. In the 1985 report from Employment and Immigration Canada, what percent of people working are employed in clerical occupations? In this category, what are the top three "clerical occupations"? What percent of college graduates are employed in accounting-related fields?
10. Look at the second table from Employment and Immigration Canada in Section 17.8. List the things this report tells you about jobs in accounting, using these guidelines for your answer:
    (a) the number of job openings
    (b) the impact of computers
    (c) the number of males versus females employed in accounting
    (d) the age of people working in accounting jobs

11. Can a student who is not a graduate from high school go to community college? Explain.
12. Is accounting very important in Business courses at the community college level? Explain.
13. Scan the want ads on page 14 in Chapter 1. Make a list of all the different characteristics about people that you see in the ads:

    e.g. ''must have excellent typing''

    ''must be independent''

    Hint: You can find at least ten points mentioned.

Special Projects

Project 1

Look at the Help Wanted ads of a newspaper in your area. Try to find ten jobs that are related to accounting.

(a) Categorize the ten jobs according to the accounting cycle, using the diagram of the full accounting cycle on page 204.

(b) Summarize what kind of people the jobs require in a one-page report.

Project 2

Go to the Guidance area in your school. Ask to see the *calendar*, or outline of courses, for either the C.G.A. program or the C.M.A. program, at a local college. Set up an information table and find out what the booklet says about these points:

(a) Admission

(b) Academic requirements

(c) Practical work experience

(d) Professional examinations

(e) Methods of instruction

Project 3

Pretend you are writing an *Accounting at Work* profile for this book, and visit one of the businesses or industries in your area that has an accountant. Interview that person about the job he/she is doing.

Ask these kinds of questions:

(a) What level of education do you have?

(b) What exactly does your job entail?

(c) What do you like best in your job?

(d) Is any part of your work routine?

(e) What are the chances of promotion for people with your training?

Project 4

In groups, ask a professional accountant from your area (perhaps one who was interviewed in Project 3) to visit your school and speak to the class about his/her job.

(a) First, write a letter inviting the accountant chosen to visit your school, outlining the sort of information you would like the accountant to present to the class.

(b) Prepare for the time of the presentation some questions you would like to ask the accountant.

(c) After the accountant's visit, write a thank-you note.

Project 5

Check your local newspaper, use the phone, or write to get information about types of software that are sold for business and home computers. Write a report to summarize your findings.

Project 6

Using the information you have gained in this textbook, particularly from this chapter and from the *Accounting at Work* sections of the book, plot a future career for yourself. Include this information:

(a) The job I would like as a career

(b) Jobs I can do to help myself get there

(c) Educational requirements of (a) through college education

(d) Educational requirements of (a) and (b) through high school education.

Accounting at Work

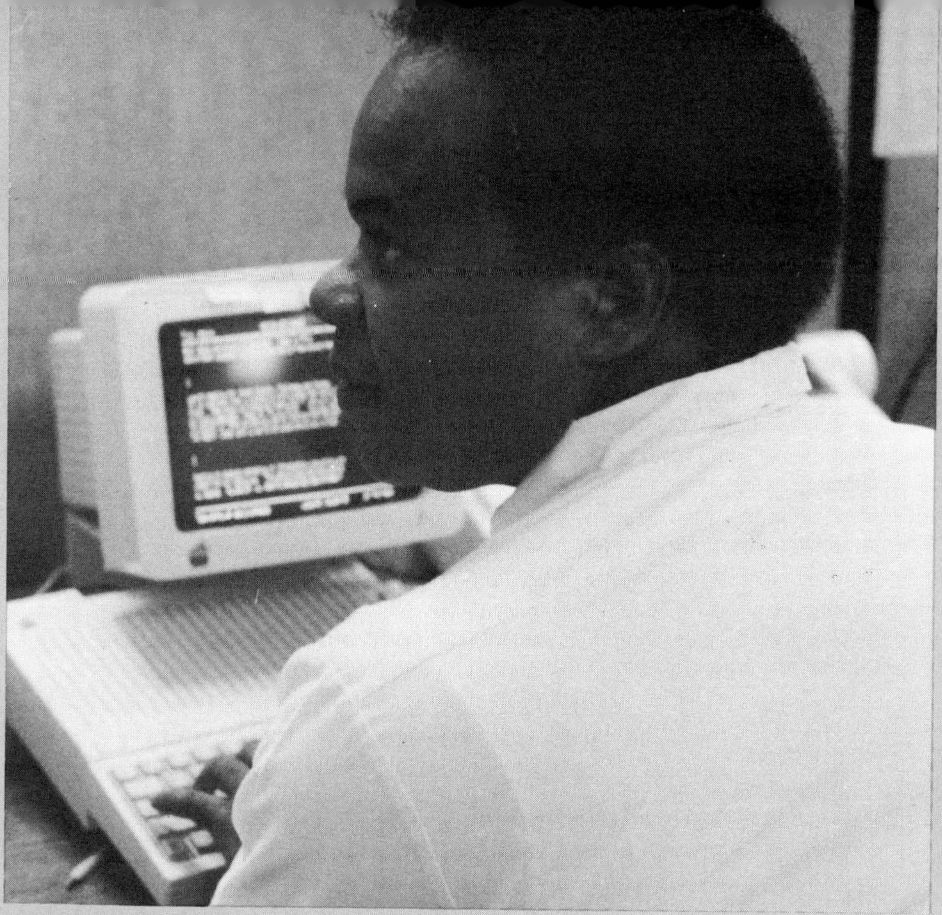

Data-Entry Clerk

Gus Richardson is employed by the Tordon Dental Clinic as a data-entry clerk. The clinic has four dentists that serve the public in a large shopping mall. The accounting records are computerized, and all the entries to the computer are made by Gus. The computer system is set up so that when Gus ''logs on'' first thing in the morning, he sees a menu that lets him choose what accounting function he wants.

The screen menu that Gus sees is shown below.

TORDON DENTAL CLINIC

MAIN MENU

1. General Ledger
2. Billing Program
3. Appointment Schedule

Which selection? ______

Gus chooses the accounting function that he wants to start with, and then follows as the computer prompts him through the accounting process. Let's assume that a customer has phoned in and wants to make an appointment for her daughter. Gus selects #3 on the main computer menu and this takes him to the sub-menu that handles appointment scheduling. The computer screen he sees looks like this:

```
TORDON DENTAL CLINIC
APPOINTMENT SCHEDULING

1. New appointment
2. Cancel appointment
3. Change appointment

Which selection? _____
```

Notice that there are three choices in the sub-menu. Gus will select number 1 since he wants a new appointment date for the customer's daughter. Once he selects this number, the computer will ask a couple of other questions, such as a preference for a certain time, or a preference for a certain day of the week. Gus should have the new appointment for the customer in a matter of seconds. The computer system is user-friendly but Gus has found that his accounting knowledge enables him to handle some of the accounting packages, for example, the General Ledger program. This background is particularly helpful when he has to make correcting entries.

Gus enjoys his work because he has always been interested in computers and this gives him a chance to use his knowledge and earn a good salary. Gus took courses in both computers and accounting in high school and therefore he is very familiar with the software package that is being used by the Tordon Clinic. In fact, Gus knows the computer system and the accounting package so well that he is able to recommend some changes to it that will improve the efficiency of the system for the dentists.

Questions for Discussion

1. When a computer is ''user-friendly,'' does this mean that the person who operates it does not have to know anything about the computer? Discuss.
2. Did Gus find his background in accounting and computers helpful?
3. Are there any problems that you think Gus will experience from sitting in front of a computer screen for most of the day?
4. If Gus wants to ''get ahead,'' where do you think his present job will lead him?

Glossary

A

account A place to record the effects of business transactions.

account balance The amount obtained by subtracting one side of an account from the other.

account form A type of balance sheet where the assets are on the left side and the liabilities and owner's equity are on the right side.

accounting cycle The process that covers the original recording of accounting transactions, from journal entries through posting to the preparation of the financial statements.

accounts payable Amounts owing to other people or businesses for the purchase of goods and services.

accounts payable ledger Record of all accounts owed by the business to suppliers for the purchase of goods and services.

accounts receivable Amounts owing to a business by its customers for the sale of goods and services.

accounts receivable ledger Record of all customer accounts.

adjusting entries Accounting entries made on a worksheet to adjust accounts at year end.

administrative expenses Expenses which are incurred for the office and general operations of a business, and not sales.

assets Anything that a person or business owns.

audit tape The tape showing daily cash transactions produced by a cash register, used to prepare the daily balance form.

B

backup An extra copy of a computer file or program, usually kept on a separate disk or in the form of a printout.

balance A procedure which ensures that debits equal credits.

balance sheet A statement showing the financial condition of a business or person on a specific date.

bank reconciliation A calculation which determines the true balance of a bank account.

book of original entry A place where accounting transactions are first recorded.

C

CA Chartered Accountant.

cash payments journal A journal used to record all transactions that decrease (credit) the bank account.

cash receipts journal A journal used to record all transactions that increase (debit) the bank account.

cell An area on a computer program spreadsheet where a column and a row intersect; a storage area for a name or number.

C.G.A. Certified General Accountant.

chart of accounts A list of all the accounts and their numbers used by a business.

classifying Breaking accounts down into groups.

closed out To make an account balance zero.

closing entries Accounting entries that close out drawings, sales, and expense accounts to zero at the end of a fiscal year.

C.M.A. Certified Management Accountant.

combination journal A multicolumn journal used for recording accounting transactions, sometimes called a synoptic journal.

control account The account in the general ledger with which the sub-ledger total must agree.

cost of goods sold The purchase price of inventory that has been sold.

credit An amount of money which a business has at its disposal to purchase goods or services on account; the right side of an account.

credit limit A service that classifies a business or person and rates their ability to purchase goods or services on account; usually determined by credit history.

credit memo A memo from the bank putting funds into a customer's account.

creditor A firm or person to whom we owe money.

current account A chequing account that businesses use to make regular daily deposits and write cheques.

current assets Assets which are in the form of cash, may be converted to cash, or used up within a year.

current liabilities Debts which will be paid in less than a year.

D

daily balance form A form used by a business to balance its cash on hand with transactions at the end of a business day.

debit The left side of an account.

debit memo A memo from the bank withdrawing funds from a customer's account.

debtor A customer who owes money to a business.

depreciation A process of allocating the cost of an asset over its useful life.

drawings An amount withdrawn by an owner from a business for personal use.

E

employee earnings record card A payroll document in which the employer keeps track of an employee's earnings for the whole year.

expenses Costs incurred by a business for daily operations.

explanation The description of an accounting transaction that appears after the debit and credit entries in the general journal.

extended Amounts are transferred from the Trial Balance columns on a worksheet to either the Income Statement or the Balance Sheet columns.

F

financial statements The income statement and the balance sheet.

fiscal year The time period over which a business keeps track of its operations.

fixed assets Assets which will last longer than one year.

freight-in An account used to record the cost of shipping goods from the manufacturer to the place of business.

fundamental accounting system Assets = liabilities + owner's equity + revenue − expenses.

G

general journal A place where accounting transactions are formally recorded.

general ledger The main ledger with accounts used to prepare the financial statements of a business.

gross pay An employee's wages before deductions, statutory and voluntary, have been taken from it.

gross profit Sales minus cost of goods sold.

H

heading The main title on a balance sheet showing the name of the person or business, the title, and the date.

I

income statement A financial statement showing the results of the operations of a business over a specific time period.

indented Leaving two or three spaces away from the left margin of the journal to record an accounting entry.

inventory The stock or supplies on hand that the business has available to sell or use.

J

journalizing Recording transactions in a journal.

L

ledger A record of the accounts of a business.

liabilities Any debts owing to other people or businesses.

liquidation The order in which debts are paid.

liquidity The ability of a business to convert its assets into cash quickly and easily.

long-term debt Any liabilities which are not expected to be paid back in less than a year.

M

menu A list of choices for a user to follow on the computer screen.

multiple entry An accounting transaction which has more than one debit, and/or more than one credit.

multipurpose journal A multicolumn journal used for recording the transactions of a small business; sometimes called a combination journal or a synoptic journal.

N

net income The profit made by a business from operations during its fiscal period.

net loss The loss incurred by a business from operations during its fiscal period.

net pay An employee's wages after deductions, both statutory and voluntary, have been taken from it.

NSF cheque Non-sufficient funds — there is not enough money in an account to cover the amount of the cheque.

O

on account A term which refers to an amount owing on goods or services which are not paid for immediately.

opening entry The accounting entry made when a business first starts operation.

owner's equity The difference between assets and labilities.

P

partnership A business owned by two or more people.

personal chequing account An account that people use to write cheques to pay household and personal bills.

personal exemptions The amounts an employee is allowed to deduct from income before paying income tax.

post-closing trial balance A trial balance of the general ledger taken after the closing journal entries are posted.

posting Transferring an entry from a journal to a ledger.

posting reference Initials and a page number which indicate to where an accounting entry has been posted or from where it has come.

prepaid expenses Expenses which will benefit more than one time period.

profit A term meaning the same thing as net income.

proprietorship A business operation owned by one person.

purchases Goods that a merchandise business buys from suppliers and resells for a profit.

purchases journal A journal used to record all transactions which result in an increase (credit) to the accounts payable accounts.

R

report form A type of balance sheet where accounts are listed down the page.

revenue A heading referring to all the sales or income accounts of a business.

Revenue Canada The government department in Canada that handles the revenues of the country.

S

sales A revenue account of a business.

sales journal A journal used to record all charge sales.

sales tax payable A current liability account which must be paid to the provincial government, usually monthly.

savings account An account that individuals put money in to earn interest.

selling expenses Expenses incurred as a direct result of trying to sell goods or services.

service business A business where the personal skills of the owner or other staff are sold to the customer.

signature card The card completed by a customer when a bank account is opened to show a specimen signature.

special journals A term that refers to journals handling only certain accounting transactions.

spreadsheet Computer software program that divides the screen up into a grid-like pattern for ease of entering data and programmed instructions.

statement of earnings A payroll form which accompanies each pay (whether cash or cheque), explaining how the employee's take-home pay was calculated.

statutory deductions Deductions that employers are required by law to calculate and deduct — Canada Pension Plan, Unemployment Insurance, and Income Tax.

sub-ledger A group of accounts that is separate from, but related to, the general ledger.

synoptic journal A multicolumn journal used for recording accounting transactions, sometimes called a combination journal.

T

T4 slip A statement of earnings and deductions given to each employee to complete a tax return.

T-account An account in the shape of a ''T'' used to record financial changes.

taxable income Income on which income tax is calculated and deducted.

totals The amounts arrived at when the columns on a worksheet are totalled.

transaction A business event that affects two or more accounts in the ledger.

transposition error An accounting error where digits are reversed (e.g., 48 written as 84).

tree structure The form by which many menu-driven programs are stored in computer memory.

trial balance A listing of all account balances in a ledger to see if the accounting books are balanced (total debits equal total credits).

U

user-friendly A term which indicates that a piece of computer software is relatively easy to use.

V

voluntary deductions Payroll deductions that the employee allows to be deducted from a paycheque (e.g., Blue Cross, Canada Savings Bonds).

W

working capital Current assets minus current liabilities.

working capital ratio Current assets divided by current liabilities.

worksheet An accountant's working paper used to prepare the financial statements for a business.

Y

year end The last day of a business fiscal period.

Index

Credits

For permission to reprint copyrighted and trademarked material grateful acknowledgement is made to the following: Bank of Montreal, Figures 5-1(b), 11-4, 11-5, 11-6, unit openers 2, 3, 4, 6, 7, 8; The Bank of Nova Scotia, Figure 11-8; Canada Trust, Figure 1-1; Employment and Immigration Canada, *Job Futures: An Occupational Outlook to 1992*, 1986, 17-3; Fredericton Visitors and Convention Bureau, Figure 14-1; Imperial Oil, Figures 1-F, 1-3(a), 10-1(b), 11-2(b), 16-1(c), 17(a), 17(b); Institute of Chartered Accountants, Figure 17(a); Junior Achievement of Metro Toronto, Figures 15-1(a), 16-1(a), 17-4, 17-5; Ontario Hydro, Figures 1-3(b), 2-1, 2-3, 2-4, 3-1, 4-1, 4-2, 6-2, 7-1, 8-1, 9-1, 10-1(a), 10-1(c), 13-1, 16-1(b); Sharp Electronics of Canada, Figure 11-2(a); Revenue Canada, reproduced with the permission of the Minister of Supply and Services Canada, Figures 10-D, 10-E, 10-F, 10-G, 10-H; Royal Bank of Canada, Figures 10-3(c), 1-3(d), 2-2, 3-2, 9-2, 10-1(d), 11-3; Tele-Direct, Figure 4-A; Tim Horton Donuts, Figure 11-1; Toronto Academy of karate, Figure 3-3; Universal Press Syndicate NY, Figures 1-G, 4-B, 4-G, 5-I, 8-A, 8-C, 10-B, 10-I, 11-D, 15-I.